Praise for *Global Leadership:*

"*Global Leadership: The Next Generation* successfully blends insightful new knowledge about high-potential leaders with hands-on, practical steps that all of us can take to lead more effectively in the global economy of today and tomorrow."

JOHN ALEXANDER
President, Center for Creative Leadership

"An indispensable manual for any professional who's committed to growing themselves and their awareness of the world we're going to be living in. This takes what could easily be a murky subject (global leadership) and gives it a reality you can touch and feel. Goldsmith et al. have done all the legwork to paint for us an objective and thorough landscape of the best practices at the top, with a wealth of triggers to stimulate productive thinking and concrete action. Bravo!"

DAVID ALLEN
President, The David Allen Company
Author of *Getting Things Done:
The Art of Stress-Free Productivity*

"*Global Leadership* is a research-based break-through book. As today's employees are increasingly educated, expert, confident and independent, the nature of effective leadership has changed. Marshall Goldsmith and his colleagues convince us that the effective leaders of the global future will command respect and inspire followers because they have intellectual openness, deep professional knowledge, effective interpersonal skills and a leadership style that reflects profound self-awareness, personal authenticity and grounded confidence. Optimism as well as pragmatism pervades this excellent book as the authors believe that leadership is a learned skill and they provide the tools for all of us to achieve it."

JUDITH M. BARDWICK
Author of *Danger in the Comfort Zone*
and *Seeking the Calm in the Storm*

"WOW! What a treasure! This is an invaluable resource book for coaching, personal development and organizational leader development. The profile of the Global Leader of the Future is clear and compelling. The research that generated the profile is innovative and sound. But, even more important than the authors' clear presentation of the profile, they include a ton of helpful, practical, immediately usable suggestions on how to develop that specific behavior. Their extensive suggestions included in the 'What To Do,' 'How To Do It,' 'How To Use This Skill Further,' 'Results You Can Expect,' and 'Further Readings' sections are the real gems of this work. I urge readers to whip out their pens and pencils and get ready to mark up, underline and make multiple margin notes as they devour this valuable guide book. Be prepared to explore this book several times, each time finding new insights. This book is a 'must-read' for anyone who coaches others, wishes to develop herself/himself or is responsible for leader development in any organization."

JIM BELASCO
Co-Executive Director Knowledge Dialogue
(formerly Financial Times Knowledge Dialogue)

"Clear thinking and practical ideas shine through in this useful and complete guide-book to global leadership in the 21st century. The concepts discussed in this book will help anyone build leadership competence."

KEN BLANCHARD
Coauthor, *The One Minute Manager®* and *Whale Done!™*

"Recognizing that an information-age global economy poses unprecedented chal-lenges to the next generation of CEOs, the authors of this lucidly written, research-based book address the question of what new qualities, traits, and skills will be required of those who will be running the organizations of the future. Their answers are both pro-found and persuasive. One of the best business books I have ever read."

NATHANIEL BRANDEN, PH.D,
Author of *The Six Pillars of Self-Esteem* and *Self-Esteem at Work*

"In turbulent times, leadership is critical. A company must have a leader, it must be effective. *Global Leadership* tells us what qualities and attributes an effective leader of the next generation must possess. I commend Goldsmith and his coauthors for this extraordinarily valuable book."

SUBIR CHOWDHURY
Chairman and CEO, ASI Consulting Group
Author of *The Power of Six Sigma*

"Leonardo da Vinci once said, 'Practice should always be based upon a sound knowledge of theory.' This book is an outstanding example of this statement. In an el-egant, but very pragmatic way, the reader is 'coached' through the often bewildering labyrinth of the literature on leadership. By taking this journey, the reader will get a handle on what it means to become an effective global leader."

MANFRED KETS DE VRIES
Raoul de Vitry d'Avaucourt
Clinical Professor in Leadership Development
Director of the Centre of Leadership Research and Development
INSEAD, France & Singapore

"*Global Leadership: The Next Generation* is an extraordinary resource for estab-lished and up and coming leaders. It gives practical ideas and a step-by-step guide on how to manage the critical challenges that leaders face today."

VIJAY GOVINDARAJAN
Professor, Tuck School of Business at Dartmouth

"Leaders in the years ahead will need to act as global citizens. *Global Leadership* not only demonstrates why, but lays out precisely how this can be done. Remarkable and essential."

SALLY HELGESEN
Author of *The Female Advantage: Women's Ways of Leadership* and
Thriving in 24/7: Six Strategies for Taming the New World of Work

"Buy two copies!—One for you, and one for the leader of tomorrow that you are developing. You have before you a paper docent, a guide and thought-provoking teacher to defining your role in *Global Leadership*. The content will inspire you, the activities will make you a major player."

PAUL HERSEY
Chairman, Center for Leadership Studies

"At last, a handbook that illuminates the challenges of leadership in a global and tenuous future. Never was this perspective on global leadership needed more than now. We are grateful."

FRANCES HESSELBEIN
Chairman, Leader to Leader Institute

"Goldsmith and his colleagues have succeeded in a most ambitious challenge: to bring clarity, insight and practical how-to-do-it wisdom to the complex issues of global leadership. The book is a most useful compendium of what global leaders must master in the future."

JON KATZENBACH
Senior Partner of Katzenbach Partners LLC
Author of *Peak Performance* and *Why Pride Matters More Than Money*

"It is hard to imagine a more complete handbook on how to lead in the 21st century than this one. The combination of theory, action, real examples and skill building recommendations makes it a perfect resource for anyone designing a leadership development program or anyone who simply wants to be a better leader of their current team."

BEVERLY KAYE
CEO, Career Systems International
Co Author of *Love 'Em or Lose 'Em: Getting Good People to Stay*

"The authors start with the conviction that leadership can be learned, then help every reader to make of herself or himself a next generation leader. This is a practical, excellent guide to global leadership and should be read by all."

D. QUINN MILLS
Harvard Business School
Author of *Wheel, Deal, and Steal*

"This book could be the I-Ching of leadership—open it anywhere for good advice you can apply to the challenge of the moment."

GIFFORD PINCHOT
Author of the best-selling *Intrapraneuring: Why You Don't Have to leave the Corporation to Become an Entrepreneur*

"What a terrific resource! This book is truly invaluable to anyone leading in the 21st century world. All business is global business today and the next generation of managers will need to learn the 'what' and 'how' of becoming a global leader. The best place to start is this book. Hats off to the authors for producing a terrific well-researched and practical book."

BOB ROSEN
CEO, Healthy Companies International
Author of *Global Literacies and Leading People*

"As the world shrinks into a global community, *Global Leadership: The Next Generation* likely will become a valuable companion for executives and managers, especially as they strive to address the diversity and complexity that comes with globalism. The authors not only foster an understanding of the frameworks and competencies needed for success as a global leader, but also an awareness of how to develop the necessary capabilities. At once, they are appropriately broad in their scope, while offering depth in the 'how-to' details required for practical application. In both global and domestic arenas, managers will find this book helpful."

R. R. THOMAS, JR.
President, The American Institute for Managing Diversity

"This is an essential book for anyone involved in international business. I have addressed large and small audiences of executives in 24 countries over the last two years, and this book contains the best thinking of some of the best thinkers of the future."

BRIAN TRACY
Author of *Turbo Strategy*

"Marshall Goldsmith and his team have done it again! *Global Leadership: The Next Generation* uncovers new possibilities and identifies new leadership competencies that are emerging in our global age. This book is full of practical tips that help implement the solid conceptual ideas offered."

FONS TROMPENAARS
Founder and managing director
Trompenaars Hampden-Turner Intercultural Management Consulting
Author of *Riding the Waves of Culture*

"Leadership matters. No one disputes this. With *Global Leadership*, we now know what matters most and how to do it! This is a wonderful compendium of ideas, tools, and actions that any leader anywhere can use to be successful. I will keep and use this book as a reference guide for developing leaders."

DAVE ULRICH
Professor, University of Michigan School of Business
co-author of *The HR Scorecard*

"What the future requires of organizational leaders is not what the past has needed, and *Global Leadership* provides an indispensable step-by-step guide for developing what is demanded. Grounded in the experience of 200 future leaders worldwide, the authors furnish the essential 'what-to-dos' and 'how-to-do-its' for 15 key capabilities ranging from mastering technology to thinking globally."

MICHAEL USEEM
Director of the Wharton School Center for Leadership
Author of *The Leadership Moment* and *Leading Up*

GLOBAL LEADERSHIP
THE NEXT GENERATION

FT Prentice Hall

FINANCIAL TIMES

In an increasingly competitive world, it is quality of thinking that gives an edge—an idea that opens new doors, a technique that solves a problem, or an insight that simply helps make sense of it all.

We work with leading authors in the various arenas of business and finance to bring cutting-edge thinking and best learning practice to a global market.

It is our goal to create world-class print publications and electronic products that give readers knowledge and understanding which can then be applied, whether studying or at work.

To find out more about our business products, you can visit us at www.ft-ph.com

Pearson
Education

Marshall Goldsmith | Cathy L. Greenberg | Alastair Robertson | Maya Hu-Chan

GLOBAL LEADERSHIP

THE NEXT GENERATION

FT Prentice Hall
FINANCIAL TIMES

An Imprint of PEARSON EDUCATION
Upper Saddle River, NJ • New York • London • San Francisco • Toronto • Sydney
Tokyo • Singapore • Hong Kong • Cape Town • Madrid
Paris • Milan • Munich • Amsterdam

www.ft-ph.com

Library of Congress Cataloging-in-Publication Data

Global leadership: the next generation/
    Marshall Goldsmith...[et al.].
        p. cm.—(Financial Times Prentice Hall books)
    Includes bibliographical references and index.
    ISBN 0-13-140243-9
    1. Leadership. 2. Executive ability. 3. Technological innovations—Management.
4. Globalization. I. Goldsmith, Marshall. II. Series

HD57.7.G653 2003
658.4'092—dc21

Editorial/production supervision: *Kerry Reardon*
Development editor: *Russ Hall*
Cover design director: *Jerry Votta*
Cover design: *Anthony Gemmellaro*
Art director: *Gail Cocker-Bogusz*
Interior design: *Meg Van Arsdale*
Manufacturing manager: *Alexis Heydt-Long*
Manufacturing buyer: *Maura Zaldivar*
VP, executive editor: *Tim Moore*
Editorial assistant: *Richard Winkler*
Marketing manager: *John Pierce*
Full-service production manager: *Anne R. Garcia*

© 2003 by Pearson Education, Inc.
Publishing as Financial Times Prentice Hall
Upper Saddle River, NJ 07458

Financial Times Prentice Hall books are widely used by corporations
and government agencies for training, marketing, and resale.

For information regarding corporate and government bulk discounts please contact:
Corporate and Government Sales (800) 382-3419 or
corpsales@pearsontechgroup.com

Printed in the United States of America

1st Printing

ISBN 0-13-140243-9

Pearson Education LTD.
Pearson Education Australia PTY, Limited
Pearson Education Singapore, Pte. Ltd.
Pearson Education North Asia Ltd.
Pearson Education Canada, Ltd.
Pearson Educación de Mexico, S.A. de C.V.
Pearson Education–Japan
Pearson Education Malaysia, Pte. Ltd.

FINANCIAL TIMES PRENTICE HALL BOOKS

For more information, please go to www.ft-ph.com

Business and Technology

Sarv Devaraj and Rajiv Kohli
The IT Payoff: Measuring the Business Value of Information Technology Investments

Nicholas D. Evans
Business Agility: Strategies for Gaining Competitive Advantage through Mobile Business Solutions

Nicholas D. Evans
Business Innovation and Disruptive Technology: Harnessing the Power of Breakthrough Technology...for Competitive Advantage

Nicholas D. Evans
Consumer Gadgets: 50 Ways to Have Fun and Simplify Your Life with Today's Technology...and Tomorrow's

Faisal Hoque
The Alignment Effect: How to Get Real Business Value Out of Technology

Thomas Kern, Mary Cecelia Lacity, and Leslie P. Willcocks
Netsourcing: Renting Business Applications and Services Over a Network

Ecommerce

Dale Neef
E-procurement: From Strategy to Implementation

Economics

David Dranove
What's Your Life Worth? Health Care Rationing...Who Lives? Who Dies? Who Decides?

David R. Henderson
The Joy of Freedom: An Economist's Odyssey

Jonathan Wight
Saving Adam Smith: A Tale of Wealth, Transformation, and Virtue

Entrepreneurship

Oren Fuerst and Uri Geiger
From Concept to Wall Street: A Complete Guide to Entrepreneurship and Venture Capital

David Gladstone and Laura Gladstone
Venture Capital Handbook: An Entrepreneur's Guide to Raising Venture Capital, Revised and Updated

Erica Orloff and Kathy Levinson, Ph.D.
The 60-Second Commute: A Guide to Your 24/7 Home Office Life

Jeff Saperstein and Daniel Rouach
Creating Regional Wealth in the Innovation Economy: Models, Perspectives, and Best Practices

Finance

Aswath Damodaran
  The Dark Side of Valuation: Valuing Old Tech, New Tech, and New Economy Companies

Kenneth R. Ferris and Barbara S. Pécherot Petitt
  Valuation: Avoiding the Winner's Curse

International Business

Fernando Robles, Françoise Simon, and Jerry Haar
  Winning Strategies for the New Latin Markets

Investments

Harry Domash
  Fire Your Stock Analyst! Analyzing Stocks on Your Own

Philip Jenks and Stephen Eckett, Editors
  The Global-Investor Book of Investing Rules: Invaluable Advice from 150 Master Investors

Charles P. Jones
  Mutual Funds: Your Money, Your Choice. Take Control Now and Build Wealth Wisely

D. Quinn Mills
  Buy, Lie, and Sell High: How Investors Lost Out on Enron and the Internet Bubble

D. Quinn Mills
  Wheel, Deal, and Steal: Deceptive Accounting, Deceitful CEOs, and Ineffective Reforms

John Nofsinger and Kenneth Kim
  Infectious Greed: Restoring Confidence in America's Companies

John R. Nofsinger
  Investment Blunders (of the Rich and Famous)…And What You Can Learn from Them

John R. Nofsinger
  Investment Madness: How Psychology Affects Your Investing…And What to Do About It

Leadership

Jim Despain and Jane Bodman Converse
  And Dignity for All: Unlocking Greatness through Values-Based Leadership

Marshall Goldsmith, Vijay Govindarajan, Beverly Kaye, and Albert A. Vicere
  The Many Facets of Leadership

Marshall Goldsmith, Cathy Greenberg, Alastair Robertson, and Maya Hu-Chan
  Global Leadership: The Next Generation

Frederick C. Militello, Jr., and Michael D. Schwalberg
  Leverage Competencies: What Financial Executives Need to Lead

Eric G. Stephan and Wayne R. Pace
  Powerful Leadership: How to Unleash the Potential in Others and Simplify Your Own Life

Management

Rob Austin and Lee Devin
Artful Making: What Managers Need to Know About How Artists Work

Dr. Judith M. Bardwick
Seeking the Calm in the Storm: Managing Chaos in Your Business Life

J. Stewart Black and Hal B. Gregersen
Leading Strategic Change: Breaking Through the Brain Barrier

William C. Byham, Audrey B. Smith, and Matthew J. Paese
Grow Your Own Leaders: How to Identify, Develop, and Retain Leadership Talent

David M. Carter and Darren Rovell
On the Ball: What You Can Learn About Business from Sports Leaders

Subir Chowdhury
Organization 21C: Someday All Organizations Will Lead this Way

Subir Chowdhury
The Talent Era: Achieving a High Return on Talent

James W. Cortada
Making the Information Society: Experience, Consequences, and Possibilities

Ross Dawson
*Living Networks: Leading Your Company, Customers, and Partners
in the Hyper-connected Economy*

Robert B. Handfield, Ph.d, and Ernest L. Nichols
Supply Chain Redesign: Transforming Supply Chains into Integrated Value Systems

Harvey A. Hornstein
*The Haves and the Have Nots: The Abuse of Power and Privilege in the Workplace...
and How to Control It*

Kevin Kennedy and Mary Moore
Going the Distance: Why Some Companies Dominate and Others Fail

Robin Miller
The Online Rules of Successful Companies: The Fool-Proof Guide to Building Profits

Fergus O'Connell
The Competitive Advantage of Common Sense: Using the Power You Already Have

Richard W. Paul and Linda Elder
Critical Thinking: Tools for Taking Charge of Your Professional and Personal Life

Matthew Serbin Pittinsky, Editor
The Wired Tower: Perspectives on the Impact of the Internet on Higher Education

W. Alan Randolph and Barry Z. Posner
*Checkered Flag Projects: 10 Rules for Creating and Managing Projects that Win,
Second Edition*

Stephen P. Robbins
The Truth About Managing People...And Nothing but the Truth

Ronald Snee and Roger Hoerl
*Leading Six Sigma: A Step-by-Step Guide Based on Experience with GE and Other
Six Sigma Companies*

Jerry Weissman
Presenting to Win: The Art of Telling Your Story

Marketing

Michael Basch
CustomerCulture: How FedEx and Other Great Companies Put the Customer First Every Day

Deirdre Breakenridge
Cyberbranding: Brand Building in the Digital Economy

Jonathan Cagan and Craig M. Vogel
Creating Breakthrough Products: Innovation from Product Planning to Program Approval

James W. Cortada
21st Century Business: Managing and Working in the New Digital Economy

Al Lieberman, with Patricia Esgate
The Entertainment Marketing Revolution: Bringing the Moguls, the Media, and the Magic to the World

Tom Osenton
Customer Share Marketing: How the World's Great Marketers Unlock Profits from Customer Loyalty

Yoram J. Wind and Vijay Mahajan, with Robert Gunther
Convergence Marketing: Strategies for Reaching the New Hybrid Consumer

Public Relations

Gerald R. Baron
Now Is Too Late: Survival in an Era of Instant News

Deirdre Breakenridge and Thomas J. DeLoughry
The New PR Toolkit: Strategies for Successful Media Relations

Strategy

Thomas L. Barton, William G. Shenkir, and Paul L. Walker
Making Enterprise Risk Management Pay Off: How Leading Companies Implement Risk Management

Henry A. Davis and William W. Sihler
Financial Turnarounds: Preserving Enterprise Value

CONTENTS

Chapter 12   DEMONSTRATING INTEGRITY   217

Chapter 13   LEADING CHANGE   231

Chapter 14   ANTICIPATING OPPORTUNITIES   251

FOREWORD

E*motional awareness*—becoming aware of who you are and how you respond to those around you, the situations that arise, and the plans that are pending—is a hot topic. With groundbreaking books like *Primal Leadership* by Daniel Goleman, Richard Boyatzis, and Annie McKee and *The Heart of the Soul* by Gary Zukav and Linda Francis, it appears the human condition is being redefined. Professional and personal emotional acumen are melding, which is not a surprise for those of us who have been teaching the successful character traits of the "authentic leader" for some time. We have been reprogramming, reinventing, and evolving our roles as leaders in a challenging environment for decades. It is this movement towards wholeness that will allow us to maximize our "humanity" both in the business world as "global leaders" as well as in our personal world. Living an integrated personal and professional life has never been more important.

This book is a piece of the ever-growing puzzle in the development of the human condition to serve as global leaders. It is a missing element from most books of its genre in that it promotes a personal awareness of leadership through self-analysis and then provides a means to begin the journey with a step-by-step guide of actions to take to achieve wholeness as a leader. In any development effort, it is critical to consider all the elements of self-development on the journey to emotional awareness or emotional intelligence. In our pursuit of authentic leadership, focusing on the right blend of "self-help" and "self-awareness" is significant to our continued growth and to our sense of personal mastery.

Most fields of development are, ironically, the least developed and the least evolved. Perhaps economic development is one of the best examples. We don't understand even the basics of how a centralized and corrupt regime can peacefully mutate toward a freer, more market-based economy. Political development is even farther behind. Who knows how we move a dictatorship toward democracy? And finally, perhaps the most thwarted, is human development, the evolution toward wholeness, toward integration, toward authenticity, and the restoration of self, which brings us to recognize the magnitude of what we are trying to do through this book. We are convinced that even a small step toward evolution will require a new set of competencies.

Our research since 1997 indicates that global leadership requires a new set of competencies blended with a wholeness of emotional experiences. These include technological savvy, anticipating opportunity, personal mastery, constructive conflict, thinking globally, appreciating diversity, building partnerships, sharing leadership, creating a shared vision, demonstrating integrity, empowering people, leading change, developing people, ensuring customer satisfaction, and maintaining a competitive advantage.

To achieve these competencies requires dedication, practice, and most importantly, a place to begin. This book offers you the opportunity to do just that. It opens the door to starting a self-motivated, self-paced, in-depth view of your domains of leadership based upon a multiyear research study of existing as well as up-and-coming young leaders from around the world.

Learning to experience emotional awareness and building upon our own personal mastery for global leadership is likely to be one of the most difficult and challenging personal commitments any one of us will ever make. Without this talent, our ability to work in a boundaryless, worldwide community will be virtually impossible. True global leadership can come only with the alignment of our own capabilities, our evolutionary brains, our motivations, and our hearts.

Some people can easily combine the application of practice and experience with self-awareness; others need a road map to stay on the journey. This book is one such road map. It supports the path to global leadership in both a national as well as an international environment. It integrates the domains of leadership from our global, multiyear study with the ongoing evolution of the development of emotional awareness required for the success of the human spirit in the environment we knew (or thought we knew) as business today.

—Warren Bennis
July 2002

PREFACE

This book is good. It has lots of solid mind protein for leaders who are preparing themselves and others for tomorrow's challenges. The lead writer, Marshall Goldsmith, is known for his happy salutation, "Life is good." So it is with this optimistic yet tough-minded book. It is good in several ways: The research was done by a very good team of top practitioners, scholars, and consultants (I am quite biased because I was privileged to be a member of the team), headed by two Accenture partners. Cathy Greenberg was a tireless leader of our various journeys and always the first to encourage us to let our thoughts leap out of the box. Alastair Robertson (now head of the worldwide leadership development practice for Stackhouse Garber & Associates) gave us a great leadership combination: wisdom and droll British humor, a lifesaving combination. The leaders interviewed as part of our research were very good indeed. They were forthcoming about their own deficits and thoughtful about the future. The resource sections at the end of each chapter, written by Maya Hu-Chan, add a practical, step-by-step, how-to-guide to becoming a global leader.

In my 35 years of leadership studies, often as a struggling practitioner, I saw the same problem again and again: good managers failing to grow into their leadership shoes and good leaders going stale. I wrote *The Paradox of Success* about this problem ten years ago, and alas it seems that the problem has gotten worse, not better (I can only hope my words didn't contribute to the deteriorating situation). One very definite cause of failure is would-be leaders focusing early on the wrong topics. They become specialists and then stop growing in their general wisdom.

How does this book set itself apart from other leadership books? First, it tackles the big problem of leadership entropy that can be solved only by vigorous, fresh learning. Most leaders do not have good mentors or coaches to point out or help with learning deficiencies. This book can help make up for that loss, although I cannot resist offering a plug for the good coaches and mentors. Soon you will know them by whether or not they embrace this research.

Second, the book offers clear data on where learning deficiencies exist for many leaders. The wise and time-restrained leader knows the value of such databased evidence and will benefit by examining and choosing from the wide range of topics the research respondents were willing to address. The subjects ranged from technical to highly personal and from the global to the close-to-home. It might be especially valuable for human resource and training professionals to see how their work and the programs they design can benefit from this book's research.

Finally, the research team never lost sight of the need to be practical, crosscultural, and organizationally diverse. The gift to the reader is that the book can be used in many ways. Some may engage in a typical, linear read. Others may jump from section to section. It is well organized for that purpose. Many readers, especially those charged with management development, will use this book as a reference. The good readers will be those most open to learning ventures. For them this book is catnip.

Enjoy the book, and remember that for those who keep learning, "life is truly good."

—John O'Neil

ACKNOWLEDGMENTS

The key thoughts behind *Global Leadership: The Next Generation* were those of the more than 200 high-potential leaders from 120 companies around the world who donated their time to this effort. Their ideas made this book possible. We would like to thank them for their generous donation of care and time.

The major resource person who helped put this project together was Sarah McArthur. Without her, *Global Leadership: The Next Generation* would have never been completed. Sarah is a gifted editor whose patience with this complex process has been amazing to us!

Jeremy Solomons conducted many of the interviews and did an outstanding job summarizing key learnings. Rosalyn Weisman did a fantastic job of data analysis. John Wheaton was an invaluable researcher behind the resource guide.

We would like to thank the following friends, clients, and colleagues for their invaluable time, dedication, and special insights to contribute to this project: Kathy Affeldt, Chris Butler, Fred DiBona, Joe Diapolito, Marjorie Dorr and the Anthem Leadership Team, Joe Frick, Vijay Govindarajan, Rick Greene, Donna Moore, Brian Underhill, and Paul Wieand.

We would also like to thank Tim Moore and the team at Prentice Hall for their persistence and dedication to this project.

Special thanks go to the family members of the authors—for Cathy, especially her parents Barbara and Bernard Greenberg, her daughter Elisabeth, and her Life Partner Gary. Liz Kuh and Michelle Vetsikas were a major source of inspiration throughout the project.

FORUM®
where learning means business™

The Forum Corporation is a global leader in workplace learning. For more than three decades, Forum has pioneered new ways to help its clients achieve business results by addressing their most important business challenges with learning solutions. Whether the issue is driving growth and profitability, reducing costs, minimizing employee turnover, developing leadership talent, or improving customer loyalty and retention, Forum aligns people with corporate strategies to deliver tangible business results.

As recognized experts in Leadership Development, Forum helps its clients turn their leaders into a competitive advantage by:

- Implementing Strategic Change

  Forum helps clients accelerate the achievement of business results by equipping leaders with the necessary knowledge, skills and tools to connect the work of their business unit with the company's vision and strategic objectives, engage the support of their people, and drive business success.

- Creating High Performing Culture

  Forum helps clients translate corporate values into leadership actions. Across geographies and diverse business units, or following a merger or acquisition, this common culture can spell the difference between high performance and lackluster results.

- Developing and Retaining Leadership Talent

  Forum partners with clients to build and retain the talent that is key to competitive performance. We design comprehensive leadership development systems that link to strategy and provide research-based content and the implementation resources to ensure consistency, quality, and lasting change in leadership behavior.

Across all capabilities, Forum consultants work with clients to define the opportunity, create the solution, and quantify the business impact. Forum's research-based learning content in management, leadership, teams, sales, and service builds the skills and knowledge needed to motivate and sustain employee performance. Our global resources implement and support clients' learning strategies on a worldwide basis.

Forum's offices are located throughout North America, Europe, and Asia. For more information, please visit www.forum.com or contact one of the following headquarters:

North America	Europe	Asia
1.800.FORUM.11	+44. (0)20.7850.7500	852 2810 7071
Boston, MA	London, England	Hong Kong

Forum is where learning means business.

ABOUT THE AUTHORS

MARSHALL GOLDSMITH

Marshall Goldsmith is a world authority in helping successful leaders achieve a positive, measurable change in behavior: for themselves, their people, and their teams. In 2002 Marshall was featured in both a *New Yorker* profile and a *Harvard Business Review* interview. He has been listed in *Forbes* as one of five top executive coaches and in *The Wall Street Journal* as one of the "top 10" executive educators. Marshall is one of the select few consultants who has been asked to work with over 60 major CEOs. His leadership development processes have impacted over one million people. His work has been positively recognized by many of the leading organizations in his field, including the American Management Association, the American Society for Training and Development, the Center for Creative Leadership, the Conference Board, the Human Resource Planning Society, and the Institute for Management Studies.

Dr. Goldsmith has a Ph.D. from UCLA and is on the faculty of executive education programs for Dartmouth, Oxford, and Michigan universities. He is co-author or co-editor of 15 books, including *The Leader of the Future* (a *Business Week* "Top 15" bestseller), *The Organization of the Future* (a Library Journal "best business book"), *The Leadership Investment* (Choice award winner as an "academic business book of the year"), *Coaching for Leadership,* and *The Many Facets of Leadership*. Five of his books have been ranked as number one in their field by Amazon.com.

CATHY L. GREENBERG

Cathy L. Greenberg, is an internationally recognized authority on leadership and human behavior. A sociobiologist and managing partner in two of the world's largest consulting firms, Accenture and CSC (Computer Sciences Corporation), she holds a doctorate in the behavioral sciences.

With two decades of expertise, Dr. Greenberg focuses on the successful management and integration of business strategy and human performance. Cathy maximizes the outcomes of transformational business change, through executive coaching, cultural and organizational assessment and journey management during start-ups, enterprisewide change, and mergers and alliances. Working with executives and CEOs in the global Fortune 500, she has spanned all industries including the US Army War College Special Forces. Cathy, a keynote speaker at the World Economic Forum, has appeared in *The London Times*, *The Financial Times*, Australia's *The Boss*, Stanford Executive videos, and a host of international media, radio, and talk shows.

Cathy, an executive in her own right, was a founding partner in charge of CSC's Global Organizational Change Practice and the cofounder of the Executive Leadership Theme Team at the Accenture Institute for Strategic Change. She and a team of worldwide experts completed the most comprehensive work to date on developing the *Executive of the Future* and is featured in the Drucker Foundation series *Leading Beyond Walls*, Coaching for Leadership, and *The Future of Leadership*. Cathy is a host at the global Women.Future.com event and founder of the Alliance for Women in Leadership (A4WL), an organization targeting the special needs of women leaders. For more information, contact CLGreenberg@goamerica.net.

She has one daughter, Elizabeth, and resides in Philadelphia most of the year.

ALASTAIR ROBERTSON

Alastair Robertson is a world-renowned leadership expert, speaker and author with 28 years experience both as an executive in the consumer products industry and in consulting/coaching. He has worked extensively with clients on the development of leadership behaviors specifically linked to the building of enhanced performance, tailored to the context of an organization's business strategy. He is a specialist in individual, team, and organization leadership assessment and behavior development, building on personal motivational strengths, and is an advisor/coach to many European and USA based executives. His clients include many Fortune 500 companies, across all industry sectors.

Alastair is also a frequent public speaker, and has been a keynote speaker for many organizations, including Forbes, the Economic Times of India, the South African CEO Forum, the Accenture Leadership Dialog Series, and many major corporations. He is often a TV and radio guest, and has also been featured in major national and international newspapers and business magazines. His home is in Boston and he can be reached by email at alastairrobertson@sgainteractive.com.

MAYA HU-CHAN

Maya is an international management consultant, executive coach, leadership development educator and a founding partner of Alliance for Strategic Leadership Coaching & Consulting (A4SL C&C). She specializes in global leadership, executive coaching, 360 leadership feedback, cross-cultural communication, and diversity.

She has coached thousands of leaders in Global 100 companies to improve their leadership competency.She has worked with major corporations throughout North America, Asia, Europe, South America, and Australia.

Maya is the contributing author of the following books: *Coaching for Leadership: How the World's Greatest Coaches Help Leaders Learn* (2002); *Partnering: The New Face of Leadership* (2000); and *A Study in Excellence: Management in the Nonprofit Human Services* (1989).

In addition, she is the author of numerous leadership resource guides for clients such as AT&T, Budget Rent-a-Car, Calpers, Eastman Kodak, Johnson & Johnson, Northern Telecom, Siemens, and Sun Microsystems.

Born and raised in Taipei, Taiwan, Maya received her B.A. in Journalism from National Chengchi University in Taiwan, and Master's degree in Communications from Annenberg School of Communications at the University of Pennsylvania.

INTRODUCTION

*The leadership models of the past provide little
guidance for the business context of the future.*

Global Leadership: The Next Generation is a summary of two years of knowledge acquisition, research, and interviews sponsored by Accenture and concluded in
partnership with Marshall Goldsmith and his colleagues in the Alliance for Strategic
Leadership. This book also builds upon valuable contributions by Warren Bennis and
John O'Neil.

This book is unique. Instead of interviewing *current* CEOs and executives (who will
not be running the organizations of the future), we interviewed *future* CEOs and executives who *will* be running the organizations of the future. What lies within these
pages is written from the point of view of the next generation of global leaders. Accenture
sponsored thought leader panels and focus and dialogue groups with high-potential
leaders from around the world. In addition to these groups, more than 200 specially selected high-potential leaders from 120 international companies were interviewed in
great depth. Since each company could nominate no more than two future leaders,
these were some of the *highest* potential leaders in the world! Over three-fifths of these
future leaders were under the age of 40, and more than a third were in their 20s. It is
from research that the Global Leader of the Future Inventory, the basis for the chapters and sections of this book, was developed.

LEADERSHIP CAN BE LEARNED

There has been an unprecedented surge of interest in business leadership in recent
years, particularly in the qualities that the effective leader should possess now and in
the future. With the shape of companies and the style of operation changing so fast, there
is a natural concern that current leadership standards and styles are not keeping pace
and will be still further behind in years to come. In markets of all sorts, leadership is
getting tougher, particularly at the top: Corporations grow in size and complexity; competition becomes ever sharper and stakeholders, more demanding.

Perhaps in consequence, leaders are staying in the top jobs for shorter and shorter periods. In some sectors, average tenures have halved over the past decade, perhaps due to stress, challenges, politics, health, or other reasons.

In the business context, the interaction between leader and led makes each combination unique. A simplistic, one-size-fits-all prescription can sometimes be valueless. But leadership can be learned, so we decided to conduct wide-ranging research to identify the many competencies, values, and characteristics that leaders and potential leaders must develop to meet not just present challenges, but the rather larger ones posed by the far-reaching changes expected in future corporate structures. Development lead times imply that companies must start the process right now if they are to be successful in developing the next generation of global leaders.

Many factors are transforming the context of leadership today: Globalization and technological change lead to heightened competition, which in turn leads to new organizational models. Boundary integration, the result of alliances and mergers, technology, and globalization, as well as the emergence of a knowledge-based workforce so varied and different from its predecessors, place a relentless emphasis on innovation, adaptability, and collaboration. Information technology offers new working practices, but demands new strategies. These chaotic changes are leading to an ever-more complex business environment, full of leadership challenges.

Because no individual is likely to embody all of the needed and critical capabilities, and because the very nature of business organization—merged, allianced, outsourced, and virtual—is beginning to dictate it, shared leadership is expected to gain preeminence as the operating model of the future. In the future, there will be fewer "all-knowing" CEOs; instead, leadership will be widely shared in executive teams. New demands for collective responsibility and accountability for results will emerge, as will new competencies for sharing leadership. The sheer number of alliances and networks means that more than one person will lead these structures.

Effective leadership will be key to sustained business success. Current leaders are rightly concerned by their challenge in recruiting, training, and developing the leaders who will be needed in the future. The future leaders in our study see the value of these new competencies and are willing to have their performance measured by them. If future leaders have the wisdom to learn from the experience of present leaders, and if present leaders have the wisdom to learn new competencies from future leaders, both can share leadership in a way that ultimately benefits their organization.

USING THIS BOOK

THE CHAPTERS

Each chapter of this book offers a description of one of the 15 dimensions of the effective global leader, as well as a resource section that includes action steps, additional resources, and suggested reading materials. The chapter text offers the authors' insights into the dimensions of leadership, as well as supportive quotes from our interviews, conducted by Maya Hu-Chan and Jeremy Solomons, with more than 200 high-potential leaders from 120 companies and organizations around the world. To protect the interviewees' anonymity, we have not used any names; however, we have included each respondent's industry, age, and country of employment and origin. (Please see Appendix B for a list of the interview questions.)

The resource section at the end of each chapter (signified by a gray bar at the side of the page) is designed to help *you* improve as a leader. To use the resource sections, follow the steps outlined below:

1. Identify several items to improve upon from the Global Leader of the Future Inventory.

2. Find these areas and specific items in the Table of Contents.

3. Turn to the page(s) you identified in the Table of Contents and review the information for suggested actions, additional resources, and readings.

4. Reflect on who in your environment may have the qualities and characteristics you have selected as items to improve upon from your list. Keep track of who these people are for future networking.

Focus only on those areas that you choose to improve upon. This will result in the most effective use of this resource section. Use the information to help you develop an action plan for improved performance.

The information for each leadership dimension item is organized into six sections:

1. What to do: This section includes a list of actions you can take to improve the way you demonstrate and convey the desired global leadership qualities. If you like an action but have a hard time picturing how you would implement it, see the next section.

2. How to do it: This section includes suggestions that specifically describe the behaviors, attitudes, and actions that better demonstrate global values of leadership. You are encouraged to read the entire list. After reading the entire list, if you do not find an action that suits you, then research the cross-reference items.

3. How to use this skill further: This section includes suggestions for actions you can take to augment your efforts to improve your behavior or to capitalize on the strengths you already have in this particular skill. Suggestions from this section are not limited to the workplace. You can apply these suggestions to your life outside the office to enhance a particular skill.

4. Results you can expect: This section provides suggested specific results that may occur upon improving your performance.

5. Readings: The reading lists include classic masterpieces, top-weighted management resources, cutting-edge resource books that illustrate the most up-to-date leadership issues, and other helpful management tools to improve your skills. We chose materials and resources that have excellent professional and reader reviews, and we attempted to get multiple perspectives on each topic.

6. Related items: This section lists related items within the book that you can cross-reference with the current item number to gain the greatest benefit.

7. Networking: Refer to your list of potential leadership partners to continue your own efforts to capitalize on the strength of shared leadership models.

THE GLOBAL LEADER OF THE FUTURE INVENTORY AND INTERVIEW QUESTIONS

The Global Leader of the Future Inventory, included as an assessment tool, has been developed based on the further involvement of A4SL (Alliance for Strategic Leadership), Marshall Goldsmith, and Kim Jackson. The inventory as well as the interview questions used in our research phase to initiate discussions of leadership and to measure perceptions of the criticality and importance of selected global leadership dimensions for the past, present, and future have been revamped for use as assessment tools by the readers of this book. You will find the interview questions and inventory in Appendixes B and C respectively. Use these tools to determine areas in which you might improve, or use them in a group or team to assess areas for development. Use the chapters for their in-depth description of leadership qualities and characteristics and how to achieve effective leadership. If you are interested in using this survey on its own or as part of a larger leadership development program, visit the Forum Corporation Web site *(http://www.Forum.com)* or contact one of the following Forum offices for assistance:[1]

- In the United States, Canada, and South America: 1-800-FORUM11 (367-8611)
- In Europe and the Middle East: +44-0-20-7010-2600
- In Asia and the Far East: 852-2810-7071

SUMMARY

Our research findings show that the 15 dimensions of leadership will be key for the effective global leader of the future. No one leader can be expected to excel in every dimension. This leads us to the conclusion that shared leadership across a team of leaders may be the standard mode of operation in which excellent global companies do business in the future. This theme will be consistently repeated and reinforced in many of the chapters of this book.

---

[1] The Forum Corporation is a pioneer in the use of 360-degree feedback. Forum, with 700 professionals worldwide, is a global leader in workplace learning. As the corporate learning arm of Pearson plc, Forum partners with the world's leading companies to help them implement strategy, solve problems, and perform better. Forum consultants are recognized experts in leadership development, branding the customer experience, building world-class sales teams, and creating blended learning solutions.

1 EMERGING TRENDS FOR GLOBAL LEADERS[1]

T raditional business patterns are changing as globalism spreads. Convergence is everywhere: Competitors are also suppliers, customers, and partners; industry boundaries are disappearing and global enterprises are rapidly emerging. Convergence within industries, marked by the mergers of the 1980s and 1990s, has been compounded by convergence between industries. Alliances, partnerships, and strategic outsourcing create new global models, never experienced before, which give access to the full range of skills, resources, and market offerings that success now demands.

Executive leadership models of the past provide little guidance for creating the models of the future. How will new leaders be able to guide their organizations through uncharted and often unanticipated global shifts, to bring value to their investors, employees, partners, and customers? In a complex global business environment, no specific, single model will fit the broad range of situations that leaders will encounter.

FIVE EMERGING CHARACTERISTICS OF GLOBAL LEADERS

The degree of change in leadership profiles from past or present to the future has interesting implications for leadership development, with both consistent themes and emerging trends. Many qualities of effective leadership—characteristics such as communicating a shared vision, demonstrating integrity, focusing on results, and ensuring customer satisfaction—will never change. however, five factors, discussed in the following sections, have emerged as clearly more important in the future:[2]

1. Thinking globally
2. Appreciating cultural diversity
3. Developing technological savvy
4. Building partnerships and alliances
5. Sharing leadership

THINKING GLOBALLY

The trend toward globally connected markets will become stronger. Leaders will need to understand the economic, cultural, legal, and political ramifications. Leaders will need to see themselves as citizens of the world with an expanded field of vision and values. Two factors making global thinking a key variable for the future are the dramatic projected increases in global trade and integrated global technology, such as e-commerce.

Future leaders will have to learn how to manage global production, marketing, and sales teams to achieve competitive advantage. To do so, the global leader must be capable of understanding and leading across global regions. There are few differences across regions in the basic leadership profile, lending support to the "global village" view of the world. A home-centric view will not be tolerated. Most likely, global leaders will have lived in, or at least spent substantial time in, different regions of the world.

New technology is another factor that makes global thinking a requirement for future leaders. New technology will make it feasible to export white-collar workers around the world. Computer programmers in India will communicate with designers in Italy to help develop products that are manufactured in Indonesia and sold in Brazil. Technology can help break down barriers to global business. Leaders who can make globalization work in their favor will have a huge competitive advantage.

APPRECIATING CULTURAL DIVERSITY

Future leaders will also need to appreciate cultural diversity, defined as diversity of leadership style, industry style, individual behaviors and values, race, and sex. They will need to understand not only the economic and legal differences, but also the social and motivational differences that are part of working around the world and across nations, states, and regions of diverse peoples and cultures. Understanding other cultures is not just good business practice; it is a key to competing successfully in the future.

An appreciation of cultural diversity will need to include both the big and the small things that form a unique culture. Religion is one of the most important variables affecting behavior in a region. Smaller issues, such as the meaning of gifts, personal greetings, or timeliness, will also need to be better understood.

The ability to motivate people in different cultures will become increasingly important. Motivational strategies that are effective in one culture may be offensive in another culture. The same recognition that could be a source of pride to one could be a source of embarrassment to another. Leaders who can understand, appreciate, and motivate colleagues in multiple cultures will become an increasingly valued resource.

DEVELOPING TECHNOLOGICAL SAVVY

As organizational change couples with technological innovation in products, planning, managing, communicating, producing, and delivering effectively, the global organization becomes a virtual network operating through technology. Information and communication systems are becoming the backbone of the global enterprise. Most executives are not responsible for their information technology systems, but they are required to understand the strategic application of technology and to lead the company in using it. If they are planning to engage in electronic commerce, technological leadership is especially important.

Many future leaders who have been raised with technology view it as an integrated part of their lives. Many present leaders still view technological savvy as important for staff people and operations, but not for them. We need not all become gifted technicians or computer scientists, but we need to

- Understand how the intelligent use of new technology can help us.
- Recruit, develop, and maintain a network of technically competent people.
- Know how to make and manage investments in new technology.
- Be positive role models in leading the use of new technology.

Organizations with technologically savvy leaders will have a competitive advantage. Without technological savvy, the future of integrated global partnerships and networks would be impossible.

BUILDING PARTNERSHIPS AND ALLIANCES

More organizations are forming alliances today. This trend will be even more dramatic in the future. Reengineering, restructuring, and downsizing are leading to a world in which outsourcing of all but core, brand-related activities may become the norm. The ability to negotiate complex alliances and manage complex networks of relationships is becoming increasingly important. Joint leadership of new business models is vital to a successful global venture.

Developing and operating efficiently under new, complex, and shifting social architectures means that tomorrow's leaders will function inside of alliances, partnerships, and ventures like never before. A bias toward the status quo is an unaffordable luxury. Tomorrow's leaders will need to be less controlling; more emotionally astute; culturally attuned; and most importantly, willing to share authority and decision making. Leadership in the future will require teams of collaborative leaders, each possessing many of those skills required for effective global leadership.

The changing role of customers, suppliers, and partners has implications for leaders. In the past it was clear who your friends (customers and collaborators) and enemies (competitors) were. In the future, these roles will become more blurred. Building positive, long-term, win-win relationships will become critical.

Sharing Leadership

Sharing leadership may be a requirement, not an option. In an alliance structure, telling partners what to do and how to do it may quickly lead to having no partners.

Chief executive officers are no longer the sole decision makers; they have to create an environment in which other leaders, who subscribe to the common vision and purpose, collaborate to make effective decisions. Unlike individualist leaders today, successful leaders in the future will strive for integration, not control. The singular role will give way to internal networks of influence that alter the very foundations of the organization.

Leaders must also learn to develop a social architecture that encourages bright, confident people to work together successfully and to exercise their own creativity. They will need the capacity for personal leadership, stemming from a deep self-awareness that develops from the inside out rather than the outside in.

In dealing with these knowledge workers—people who know more about what they are doing than their managers know—old models of leadership will not work. Future leaders will operate in a mode of asking for input and sharing information. Knowledge workers may well be difficult to keep. They will likely have little organizational loyalty and view themselves as professional free agents who will work for the leader who provides the most developmental challenge and opportunity. Skills in hiring and retaining key talent will be valuable for the leader of the future.

Because no one individual is likely to embody all of these critical capabilities, and because the very nature of business organization—merged, allianced, outsourced, and virtual—is beginning to dictate it, shared leadership is expected to gain preeminence as the operating model of the future. In the future, there will be fewer single CEOs; instead, leadership will be widely shared in executive teams. New demands for collective responsibility and accountability for results will emerge, as will new competencies for sharing leadership. The sheer number of alliances and networks mean that more than one person will lead these structures.

Effective leadership is the key to sustained business success. Chief executives are rightly concerned to recruit, train, and develop the leaders who will be needed in the future. Most high-potential future leaders see the value of these new competencies and are willing to have their performance measured by them. If future leaders have the wisdom to learn from the experience of present leaders, and if present leaders have the wisdom to learn new competencies from future leaders, they can share leadership in a way that benefits the organization.

SUMMARY

No one leader can be good at everything, which leads us to the conclusion that shared leadership across a team of leaders will be the way in which excellent global companies do business in the future. Not many companies today have developed either the talent management processes or the organizational constructs to support this leadership approach. Fortunately, however, support for shared and/or team-based leadership is growing and evolving to meet the increased demand. Future leaders must know their particular strengths and how to draw upon the complementary strengths of others—sharing leadership roles as needed.

ENDNOTES

1. Goldsmith, M. and Walt, C. "New Competencies for Tomorrow's Global Leader." *Leading Beyond the Walls,* eds. Hesselbein, F., Goldsmith, M., and Sommerville, I. The Drucker Foundation/Jossey-Bass: New York. 1999.

2. The original research upon which the Global Leader of the Future Inventory is based was conducted by Cathy Greenberg, formerly Cathy Greenberg-Walt, and Alastair Robertson with support by the Accenture Institute for Strategic Change and with alliance partners Marshall Goldsmith, Warren Bennis, and John O'Neil. The research methodology and findings are presented in Appendix I.

2

THINKING GLOBALLY

*We stand on a precipice, stepping into a new era, a time of
enormous change and uncertainty characterized by the
emergence of the first truly borderless, interconnected global
economy. It's the world's youngest economy, fueled by the
spread of free markets and democracy around the world.*[1]

In the past, the ability of an executive leader to think, understand, and work
within the global environment was not nearly as important as it is today. This need for
a relatively new set of characteristics has been brought to the forefront by the dramatic increases in global trade and integrated global technology, such as e-commerce.
This is not confined to leaders who work within the global environment. Domestic,
"networked" leaders, those executives who run organizations with multiregional locations across same nation states, will be impacted by the same issues as a "global" leader,
yet on a scale that emphasizes state regulations and intrastate laws.

Globalization and the boom in information technology have brought new players,
products, and services into business. As long as competition remained largely domestic, standards of quality, price, and service were governed by domestic norms. But global competition imposes such higher global standards of customer service, creativity,
and innovation that even companies with no global ambitions are forced to meet to
protect their market shares.

In addition to competition, the business environment is characterized by alliances
between governments, industries, and companies. The European Union, the North
American Free Trade Agreement, and the Association of Southeast Asian Nations are
just some of the groupings within which barriers are being dismantled. Companies have
formed cross-industry alliances, such as utilities and telecommunications firms, software and hardware, banks and insurance; they are forming ever-larger and more complex groups by merger and acquisition.

Where acquisitions are out of the question, some companies are choosing to form alliances, even with competitors, to offer the customer a special product or service. Translated into the global marketplace, such convergence assumes even greater significance. Links are growing fast, whether among airlines, pharmaceutical firms, automotive companies, or consumer credit groups. The labels of competitors, partner, supplier, and customer are becoming interchangeable. Figure 2.1 illustrates the different levels of convergence.

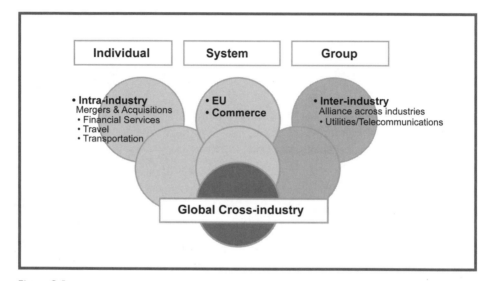

Figure 2.1
Global convergence.
(Model developed by Cathy Greenberg, 1999.)

The goal of global integration—to take advantage of the economies of scale and worldwide learning while still responding to local needs—is becoming more realistic. As globally connected markets become stronger, all leaders, domestic and global, will need to understand the economic, cultural, legal, and political ramifications of globalization, and they will need to *act as global citizens*[2] with an expanded field of vision and values.

THE IMPACT OF GLOBALIZATION

As the interdependence between companies from around the world grows, domestic and international politics and the rules of trade are being reformed. For example, recently General Electric was blocked in its attempt to make an acquisition because of antitrust concerns in Europe (even though it had received approval in the United States). Leaders who understand and recognize this fundamental impact of globalization will forge the way to the future. Globalization is inescapable. The Information Age, with its relatively recent and ongoing changes in technology and knowledge distribution, is dissolving the borders and boundaries of countries around the world. For instance, today a designer in Milan may coordinate efforts with producers in China and an ad agency in London on a product that will be sold in Chicago. As a result of these dissolving borders, leaders of domestic organizations find themselves confronting issues comparable to those of leaders of global companies. The national environment, with its diversity of people, cultures, business methods, and leadership styles, has components similar to those of the global environment, such as rapidly developing technology; mergers and acquisitions; competition, partnerships, and alliances; boundary integration; and free trade agreements. To achieve competitive advantage within the expanding business environment, leaders must be capable of understanding and competing across many regions and cultures. Leaders *will need to understand what globalization* [boundary integration] *really means: (1) marketing products in different countries* [as well as regions, cities, and states] *in many different ways, and (2) changing pricing if necessary.*[3] The obvious case study here is the European Union. With the advent of the Euro as a common currency, price differences for the same products in different countries have become transparent.

In the future, businesses will be set up either as a network of partnering entities under the umbrella of the company's main headquarters or as a system of alliances between companies across many cultures. Either way, companies will be involved in the local communities of different countries and/or national regions, states, and cities with a range of economic situations, political environments, and cultural and business norms. *Culture and habits can create a big barrier or be a great advantage.*[4] As such, the successful leader must have a global business understanding, including

1. A financial understanding of the world economy.

2. An understanding of different cultures—for example, the American way or the Japanese way doesn't work in all cultures. It can be very harmful to try to enforce one culture on others.

3. An understanding of the *[global/regional]* markets, so that they understand how markets play off each other—for example, the leader must understand what kind of effect the price of oil, plastic, iron ore, power, et cetera has on different scales.[5]

Globalization impacts every area of a company from its customer base, vendors and distributors, and marketing strategy to its alliance networks, partnerships, and competitors. For instance, the price of power in Alabama will impact the competitive status of the customers of the power company. These *customers* may have to compete with other global suppliers. If the costs to the power company's customers become too high and the customers become noncompetitive, the power company will ultimately lose business (even though they may not *directly* compete with other global power companies).

Global leaders must be aware of country, national, and intrastate laws and business regulations; social and political events; and government involvement in business. Even time zones have an impact, such that *we will be coordinating global strategies on a broader scope.*[6] Cultures and societies have put limitations on what leaders can do: Basic ethics, policies, and regulations preclude certain behaviors within each country. In a global environment those behaviors become hazy because they are guided by different laws, policies, and mechanisms. This complicates matters to a great extent. For example, when the Rolling Stones go on a world tour, they take four immigration attorneys with them, because their rights are different in each country they visit. This fuzziness will help future leaders be more effective if they learn to use it to their advantage: Future leaders must learn how each system fits into the global business network and how to work within and across those systems.

Another factor that makes global thinking a requirement for future leaders is technology. As businesses create global systems, technology is created to support the growth of those systems, and people around the world can communicate easier and cheaper than ever before.

A World of Approaches

In the last 20 years, globalization has radically changed the environment in which business is conducted. Because *different countries have different ways of doing business,*[7] a key skill of the global leader of the future is flexibility and the ability to refrain from labeling other perspectives as "right" or "wrong."

Within this growing business environment, there will be many different solutions and approaches to each situation. Each culture, company, and individual will bring a unique communication style and work ethic. Decision making and leadership styles will vary from person to person, from organization to organization, and from culture to culture.

It will be important to first agree on common objectives, then allow the organizations to get the job done in a manner that is necessary for their culture and environment. To make other organizations in different countries conform to one way would not allow a comfortable working environment. Everything cannot be standardized.[8]

It is hard enough for people of the same culture to communicate and work well together. People from different backgrounds who want to work together have to understand not only personalities, but also their own and others' backgrounds and what shapes their value systems. For instance, until recently, many Westerners who worked in the Middle East had virtually no knowledge of the Koran, even though the Koran is the most important book impacting the culture of the region.

When working with businesses that are physically spread around the world or within different regions of a country, the global leader must understand the different companies' individual needs. Because a diverse range of factors drives companies in different areas, the leader should understand the motivation driving each organization. A company in Brazil may be profit-driven, and a company in China may be employee-driven. Similarly, an organization in eastern Spain, such as in the city of Andalusia, will have a greatly different customer base than the same company in the city of Madrid.

> They need to see the interaction between globally different people, business units, et cetera, and see how the input of their decisions impacts the company. They must step out of their country [region] and look at the world to get a better global role and perspective. They should not force their culture's needs and values onto other cultures.[9]

The global leader will strive to understand the perceptions and motivations and social aspects of the countries within which the business is or would like to be involved. Through research, study, and experience the leader will understand the frame of reference of different cultures and thus be capable of leading across a global divide. He or she must understand the other culture's frame of reference and then influence that culture from its perspective rather than impose his or her own.

GAINING EXPERIENCE

> The global leader of the future will need to have a global perspective with experience. [He or she] should have lived in a different culture and country—and possess language skills. This company has prepared me by shipping me around the world a lot. I attend conferences focusing on our industry on a global basis. I participated last winter in a global, political, economic, symposium put on by Oxford in England. And we have an informal network in the company and I travel to different parts of the organization and basically "keep in touch." This is kind of a continuing development for personal and organizational development.[10]

Global leaders can gain knowledge and experience through a mixture of long-term foreign postings, short-term assignments in other locations, frequent overseas visits, participation in multicultural projects, and general exposure to people and ideas from different cultural backgrounds through reading, academic courses, professional and personal associations, films, and so on.

A deep awareness of the cultural differences between countries and within regions is necessary for global business success, as is a moderate ability to speak the language;

knowledge of the financial system, laws, and regulations; and an understanding of the business practices and cultural norms of the countries within which the company is involved.

[The global leader] *should partake in international immersion.*[11] Such experiences benefit the leader not only in the business sense, but also in the sense that they provide the opportunity for him or her to view life from another perspective.

The most gratifying time of my career was when I spent three years in the UK and Hong Kong, because I learned to suspend judgment. I learned that there are no right or wrong answers, just different [answers]. It's what we saw when we made an acquisition this year—there are no right or wrong answers, just different. Leaders need to build on the best of both sides.[12]

From a business standpoint, there are many reasons that the global leader will *need to understand that country and its culture.*[13] For one, understanding is the foundation upon which successful business relationships are built. Without a working knowledge of the ways in which business is conducted in different regions of the world, it is difficult, if not impossible, to break into, much less succeed in, the global market. Humorous examples abound of companies whose slogans designed to be positive and uplifting in one language are actually offensive and insulting in a new language. For another reason, because the average customer varies from place to place, effective marketing and sales depend on knowing and providing for the needs of the customer in each region. The global leader with experience in different cultures will have a great advantage in working with diverse peoples, in knowing which products and services will sell in which regions, and in determining how to successfully market those products and services.

Marketing in different countries can be quite challenging. Add that to the fact that there are sometimes many different dialects within one region of a country and it is often a recipe for disastrous misunderstandings. For instance, when Coca Cola was first marketed in China, it was sold as "Ke-kou-ke-la." After printing thousands of signs, it was discovered that, depending on dialect, the phrase means either "bite the wax tadpole" or "female horse stuffed with wax." The Pepsi slogan, "Come alive with the Pepsi Generation," translated into Taiwanese, means "Pepsi will bring your ancestors back from the dead." The Kentucky Fried Chicken slogan, "Finger-lickin' good," is "Eat your fingers off" in Chinese.[14] Rather than experience these cultural debacles, the leader should strive to understand the global marketplace and the countries and regions within which he or she does business.

THINK GLOBALLY, ACT LOCALLY

Through the global marketplace, the countries of the world are linked today more than ever before. As such, *global leaders need to have a global view and understand benefits on a global level.*[15] It is no longer sufficient for leaders to view business solely from a national or local point of view. The global leaders of the future will have a *worldwide perspective when making decisions,*[16] and they *will need in-depth strategic thinking, such as being a global trends observer.*[17]

> The leaders of tomorrow must have the ability to suspend, for the moment, their cultural background and assume the culture of the people with whom they are dealing in order to understand and pinpoint new opportunities. Then the leaders must be able to take this information from the microscopic investigation to the more macroscopic global perspective in order to guide decisions that are consistent with a global vision.[18]

For example, before Accenture went public in July 2001, it was a group of 34 legally separate entities spread throughout the world. The total partnership was a matrix of those entities. To go public, all of the partnerships had to be on the same page, doing the same thing at the same time, for the right reasons. Prior to the IPO, CEO Joe Forehand spent over six months visiting each partnership to understand its frame of reference. He went with colleagues who could take those different points of view and understand what they would mean to an IPO situation. In turn, each partner committed to the IPO. The parnters voted to do this not only for reasons suiting their own business needs, but also because the six-month dialogues allowed all parties to develop a common vision of the future that the partners believed was critical to remain a market leader. In this positive example of thinking globally, Forehand, his colleagues, and the partnerships started from different points of view and then worked together towards a global outcome.

On the other hand, *95 percent of U.S. companies that go to China fail because they don't understand the views and biases in other countries. They have the wrong game plan. They are doing their business for self-interest that does not work because foreign companies don't have the same mission and motivation. Most American companies are not making money in Asia. They are doing business there for strategic reasons. They are taking a hit now for what they perceive as strategic long-term advantage.*[19] In our (the authors') own work in establishing a global coaching network, we realized that our first ventures in China were going to be unprofitable from a short-term revenue perspective, yet very valuable from a long-term learning and growth perspective.

A GLOBAL VILLAGE

An organization's international success is dependent upon a globally literate team. To this end, the global leader of the future will help to educate people and prepare them to do business with different cultures. Each member of the team will be prepared to do business with people from around the world. *You can't be an independent global leader— you need an organization behind you.*[20] Many global customers want "one-stop shopping." They will no longer accept the complexity of having to deal with different suppliers and billing systems that are providing the same product in different locations.

Part of this preparation includes overcoming stereotypes and ignorance. There are people who think that a two-week vacation in Russia or a relative's experience in China gives them the knowledge they need to make judgments about an entire culture. This will not bode well when conducting business. Neither will the commonsense approach, because what may be common sense to one culture may be offensive to another.

To initiate a general understanding of the cultures and countries within which a company does business, the global leader might ask company employees questions such as What do they need to know to do business internationally? How do they see other cultures? How do they see their own culture? And then compare and contrast different value systems. Whether the answers are right or wrong is not important at this point; what is important is to begin to *expand people's global knowledge.*[21]

Next, the global leader must acquire a culture-specific education. Each person should have a thorough understanding of the culture in which he or she will be doing business *before* getting on the plane. The understanding should be more than demographic. It should include cultural values, beliefs, how the country operates, and what is (and is not) appropriate.

The leader might hire an expert to teach the team or may ask a colleague who has worked abroad to share his or her experiences, especially with particular clients or partners with whom they have been working. If such steps are not taken to help others understand the different impacts of globalization, it may be very difficult for individuals from different cultures to understand each other; actions from people of other cultures can easily be misinterpreted, and misunderstandings are more likely to happen.

> There are fewer boundaries in global business, due to changes in the market, and leaders need to be adaptable and flexible to take advantage of opportunities that are created. Education needs to come from different sources; they will need a network of trusted advisors and confidants in the different regions where they are doing business. There will need to be much more diversity on their management team, different viewpoints and perspectives, and [they must] have the insight to take global strategies and localize them. Learning from each other is part of the education process.[22]

Another crosscultural challenge for the global leader is working in one country and reporting to another. In this case, the global leader is leading from the middle as the go-between or interpreter between the local people, (i.e., the government, suppliers, customers, workers, colleagues) and the company headquarters. The global leader becomes an interpreter of sorts, communicating headquarters' goals to the local business people and explaining the reality of the situation in the foreign country to those at headquarters.

CONCLUSION

International business success is dependent upon the leader's understanding of the global landscape and the ability to rapidly adapt to the changes that impact the businesses environment. Leaders of domestic organizations as well as those of global companies must handle issues of globalization such as competition, mergers and acquisitions, dissolving borders, and cultural diversity. Therefore, the great challenge for the new generation of leaders will be to gain direct knowledge and real experience in a wide variety of geographical areas and to build and articulate a clear vision, even as both the workforce and clientele become increasingly diverse.

The importance of thinking globally to the next generation of global leaders is illustrated in our research. We developed a list of the 100 success factors, in order of importance, for leaders past, present, and future. According to those leaders surveyed, the three most important success factors for a leader in the past were (1) demonstrating self-confidence as a leader; (2) striving to achieve personal excellence in whatever he or she does; and (3) demonstrating honest, ethical behavior in all interactions. Looking at the present day, the picture changes a little bit: (1) demonstrating self-confidence as a leader remains number 1; (2) creating and communicating a clear vision for her or his organization moved from number 8 for past leaders to number 2 for present; (3) consistently treating people with respect and dignity gained importance, moving from seventh to third position For the future, (1) consistently treating people with respect moved to first position; (2) understanding the impact of globalization on her or his business took a startling leap forward from the 71st (present) and 77th (past) positions to number 2; and (3) creating and communicating a clear vision for her or his organization remained in the top three, though it took a step back for understanding globalization.

Not only did understanding the impact of globalization move into the top three, it rocketed there from near the bottom of the pack in both the past and present surveys. The high-potential leaders in our study are sending a clear message. While thinking globally may have been an *option* for the leader of the past, it will be a *requirement* for the leader of the future.

Rosemarie Greco is principal of GRECOventures and a director of five corporations: Exelon Corporation, Pennsylvania Real Estate Investment Trust, Radian Group, SEI Investment Management, and Sunoco. Rosemarie is former chief executive and president of CoreStates Bank, N.A., and president of CoreStates Financial Corporation, its parent company.

Bringing It Together: Eliciting Different Views and Opinions

Rosemarie considers herself a "web thinker"; she engages others in a particular outcome by thinking out loud with them but not giving them her impressions (in other words, leading by teaching). Her style of leadership is quite probably a direct result of the formative years of her career as a first-grade schoolteacher in the arch diocese.

Early in her teaching career, Rosemarie would teach an entire week's lesson in one day. She soon found that although she was prepared and put forth the lessons, the students weren't learning. The key, she found, was "to check for understanding, to listen, and then to start over again." She learned what she feels is the greatest leadership quality: to acquire knowledge, to test for knowledge, and then to grow knowledge.

The Winning Combination: Adaptable, Inspirational, and Honest

When Rosemarie's job search widened, she went into banking. While she was in the middle of the bank branch manager program, banks began hiring Vietnam veterans, and she trained these managers for their jobs.

Rosemarie had no interest in "running the transition." Her interests were to solve problems by helping others lead the effort. She vested in others' potential and found a natural advocacy in those she enabled. Not locked into the "boundaries" of the business, she outlined the vision and affected change by identifying and creating an outcome around it. While she did not have the "technical" knowledge, she used the "belief" in the outcome to rally people to the cause. The key to inspiring others, she says, is that you must "prove yourself to be totally honest and embrace discomfort in the unknown."

Thinking Globally

Thinking globally not only entails thinking about the different countries and cultures "out there," it also means considering the diversity of cultures, opinions, and viewpoints inside the company: Knowing the process across the entity helps to elucidate the problems and issues and to solve them globally (at different operations, branches, or departments).

Rosemarie took a unique approach to align CoreStates. With the support of her advocates in the system and after taking time to understand CoreStates' business, issues, and potential solutions, Rosemarie introduced "cultural" exchange programs across its operations. In this way, employees shared their perspectives and created a common outlook across the organization. Each person gained an understanding of how the business worked, and it helped undo barriers to solving problems. Rosemarie then concurrently promoted and gave different roles to people to show them that they could do different jobs. This approach was quite a success. During her tenure as CEO, the $45 billion institution was ranked as one of the most profitable and efficient banks within its peer group, and Rosemarie was often referred to as the highest-ranking woman banker in the country.

THINKING GLOBALLY

ITEM 1: Recognizes the Impact of Globalization on Our Business

WHAT TO DO

- Determine if your company is a global organization, and if so, to what extent.
- Understand how the global economy affects your business and the industry within which it operates.
- Understand industry and organizational trends and how these trends relate to the global landscape.
- Determine the countries within which your company currently does business or within which the company would like to explore doing business.
- Determine the technology and resources needed to further the company's global business efforts.
- Determine which country your information technology supplier is from. If this is likely to change, explore the countries that new IT suppliers might be from.

HOW TO DO IT

- Define the areas of the company, such as marketing, sales, and manufacturing, that have, or should have, a global focus.
- Define the percentage of your organization, workforce, and managers who are either located in foreign countries, citizens of other countries, or working outside their native country.
- Analyze the percentage of customers, suppliers, manufacturers, competitors, and investors located in foreign countries now and in the future.
- Figure the percentage of revenues and profits that come from foreign markets. Are the markets within which you expect your company to grow foreign or domestic?
- Forecast industry and global business trends and activities, inside and outside the organization, to be prepared for changes and to take advantage of opportunities. Explore the effects of these trends and activities on the business.
- Explore and develop global business opportunities.
- Decide which products, if any, your company currently produces will be marketable in those countries with which your company would like to do business.

- Ask IT staff to gather information about global technology improvements and advances, and to present a global communications improvement plan.

HOW TO USE THIS SKILL FURTHER

- Develop international contacts. Discuss the market, demographics, and cultural and business norms in different countries.
- Take a university course in global economics that provides a macro view of world economic systems and how they interact. Study how economic events in one country affect other countries.
- Join a discussion group whose focus is world events and the impact of those events on countries, people, governments, and businesses.

RESULTS YOU CAN EXPECT

- You may have a better understanding of the global economy and its effect on your company and its industry.
- Others may come to you for insight into the possibilities and challenges of global expansion.
- You may become a highly valued member of your company.

READINGS

- *Boston to Beijing: Managing in the Global Marketplace.* Nancy J. Adler, Rob Bloom, & John Szilagyi. 2001. South-Western, London, ISBN 324074751.
- *Eight Giant Steps to Global Domination: A Personal Guide to Finding Your Niche, Conquering Your Market, and Taking Your Company to the Top.* Kenn Viselman. 2000. McGraw-Hill, New York, ISBN 007136241X.
- *Global Literacies: The New Language for Business Leaders.* Robert Rosen with Carl Phillips, Marshall Singer, & Patricia Digh. 2000. Simon & Schuster, New York. ISBN 0684859025.
- *Global Marketing.* Warren J. Keegan & Mark C. Green. 1999. Prentice Hall, Upper Saddle River, NJ, ISBN 0130842680.
- *Growth Warriors: Creating Sustainable Global Advantage for America's Technology Industries.* Ronald Mascitelli. 1999. Technology Perspectives, Northridge, CA, ISBN 0966269705.
- *The Lexus and the Olive Tree: Understanding Globalization.* Thomas L. Friedman. 2000. Anchor Books, New York, ISBN 385499345.
- *Regions and the World Economy: The Coming Shape of Global Production, Competition, and Political Order.* Allen J. Scott. 2000. Oxford University Press, Oxford, England, ISBN 0198296584.
- *The Global Entrepreneur: Taking Your Business International.* James F. Foley. 1999. Dearborn Trade, Chicago, ISBN 1574101242.

- *The World in 2020: Power, Culture and Prosperity.* Hamish McRae. 1996. Harvard Business School Press, ISBN 875847382.

ITEM 2: Demonstrates the Adaptability Required to Succeed in a Global Environment

WHAT TO DO

- Understand how the global economy affects your business and the industry within which it operates.
- Understand industry and organizational trends, and how these trends relate to the global landscape.
- Broaden your view and knowledge about the cultural and business norms of other countries.
- Be willing to adapt your management style when necessary.
- Strive to be flexible and less conservative under different circumstances.
- Try to understand why sometimes you may resist change. Identify the root cause and overcome it.
- Develop a positive attitude when facing difficult situations.
- Keep an open mind in all situations.

HOW TO DO IT

- Forecast industry and global business trends and activities, inside and outside the organization, to be prepared for changes and to take advantage of opportunities. Explore the effects of these trends and activities on the business.
- Explore and develop global business opportunities.
- Develop and maintain international contacts. Discuss the market, demographics, and cultural and business norms in different countries.
- Develop relationships with people in your company from other cultures and countries. Discuss globalization, business practices, and cultural norms with them. Discuss the similarities and differences in the ways in which they would understand, handle, and interpret different situations.
- Look at global events from the perspective of others before making judgments.
- Observe your opinions and beliefs about international events and other countries' cultures.
- Learn specific business practices of other countries. Analyze how these styles have been successful or unsuccessful in the global market.
- When considering adapting a different management style, ask yourself *Why not?* instead of *Why?*

- Ask people with whom you work for specific feedback on how you are doing in adapting your management style to the global environment.
- Remain open to alternatives and new ideas.

HOW TO USE THIS SKILL FURTHER

- Participate in crosscultural training and encourage your staff to do the same. Share your learning with each other.
- Volunteer to lead projects involving adaptation, innovation, and globalization.
- Identify one or two people in your organization who excel in this area. Discuss techniques, business practices, and cultural norms with these colleagues.
- Journal all of your experiences in other countries.

RESULTS YOU CAN EXPECT

- You may be seen by others as progressive and cooperative.
- There may be less confusion and frustration when dealing with complex global issues.
- You may be asked to communicate the organization's global goals to others.

READINGS

- *Culture's Consequences: Comparing Values, Behaviors, Institutions, and Organizations Across Nations.* Geert Hofstede. 2001. Sage, Thousand Oaks, CA, ISBN 0803973233.
- *Global Literacies: Lessons on Business Leadership and National Cultures.* Robert H. Rosen, Patricia Digh, Marshall Singer, & Carl Phillips. 2000. Simon & Schuster, London, ISBN 684859025.
- *Strategic Flexibility: Managing in a Turbulent Environment.* Gary Hamel & Don O'Neal. 1999. John Wiley & Sons, New York, ISBN 0471984736.
- *Successful Manager's Handbook.* Susan Gebelein, Lisa A. Stevens, Carol J. Skube, & David G. Lee. 2000. Personnel Decisions International, Minneapolis, MN, ISBN 093852920X.
- *The New Global Leaders: Richard Branson, Percy Barnevik, and David Simon.* Manfred F. R. Kets De Vries & Elizabeth Florent-Treacy. 1999. Jossey-Bass, San Francisco, ISBN 787946575.
- *The Quest for Global Dominance: Transforming Global Presence into Global Competitive Advantage.* Vijay Govindarajan & Anil K. Gupta. 2001. Jossey-Bass, San Francisco, ISBN 787957216.
- *The Reengineering Revolution.* Michael Hammer & Steven Stanton. 1995. HarperCollins, New York, ISBN 0887307361.

ITEM 3: Strives to Gain the Variety of Experiences Needed to Conduct Global Business

WHAT TO DO

- Determine the countries within which your company currently does business or within which the company would like to explore doing business.
- Explore and develop global business opportunities.
- Realize that the knowledge and understanding of other countries, cultures, and business practices is critical to conducting successful global business.
- Learn about the cultural norms and business practices in other countries where you want to conduct business.
- Learn the related foreign languages and encourage your coworkers to do the same.
- Recognize that success in your career requires continued development of skills and knowledge, including those in the global arena.
- Identify specific individuals, within and outside of your organization, who have global experiences as resources.

HOW TO DO IT

- Participate in crosscultural training and encourage your staff to do the same. Share your learning with each other.
- Forecast industry and global business trends and activities, inside and outside the organization, to be prepared for changes and to take advantage of opportunities. Explore the effects of these trends and activities on the business.
- Develop international contacts. Discuss the market, demographics, and cultural and business norms in different countries.
- Develop relationships with people in your company from other cultures and countries.
- Discuss globalization, business practices, and cultural norms with (1) people from other cultures and countries and (2) those who have had experiences doing business globally. Discuss the similarities and differences in the ways in which they would understand, handle, and interpret different situations.
- Ask people who are familiar with the countries with which you would like to do business for insights about the similarities and differences between your culture and business practices and theirs. Identify the differences that could be problematic in conducting business.
- Spend time with natives of other countries. Compare different perspectives due to different backgrounds. Find out the similarities too.
- Learn the language of the country before you conduct business there. Make language proficiency a hiring requirement for particular positions.

- Create opportunities to travel abroad to expand your knowledge and global perspective.

HOW TO USE THIS SKILL FURTHER

- Participate in crosscultural communication workshops or training to get a deeper understanding of other cultures.
- Ask for more opportunities to go abroad to work with people from other cultures.
- Build friendships with people from different cultures.

RESULTS YOU CAN EXPECT

- You may become more competent in dealing with intercultural business relationships.
- You may gain more opportunities to be promoted.
- You may be seen as having potential for higher levels of responsibility.

READINGS

- *Culture Clash: Managing in a Multicultural World.* H. Ned Seelye & Alan Seelye-James. 1995. NTC Business Books, Lincolnwood, IL, ISBN #0844233048.
- *International Success: Selecting, Developing, and Supporting Expatriate Managers.* Meena S. Wilson & Maxine A. Dalton. 1998. Center for Creative Leadership, Greensboro, NC, ISBN 1882197453.
- *Successful Manager's Handbook.* Susan Gebelein, Lisa A. Stevens, Carol J. Skube, & David G. Lee. 2000. Personnel Decisions International, Minneapolis, MN, ISBN 093852920X.
- *Up Is Not the Only Way: A Guide to Developing Workforce Talent.* Beverly L. Kaye. 1997. Consulting Psychologists Press, Palo Alto, CA, ISBN 891060995.
- *The Lexus and the Olive Tree: Understanding Globalization.* Thomas L. Friedman. 2000. Anchor Books, New York, ISBN 385499345.
- *The World in 2020.* Hamish McRea. 1995. Harvard Business School Press, Boston, ISBN 0256115842.

ITEM 4: Makes Decisions that Incorporate Global Considerations

WHAT TO DO

- Determine if your company is a global organization, and if so, to what extent.
- Learn the business practices of other countries and cultures.

- Compare the business practices of successful multinational companies with those of your company. Identify similarities and differences between practices.
- Develop an understanding of how current, past, and possible future world events will affect the organization.
- Move beyond a domestic business focus by expanding your international mindset.

HOW TO DO IT

- Analyze how the global economy affects your business and the industry within which it operates.
- Decide which products, if any, your company currently produces will be marketable in those countries with which your company would like to do business.
- Analyze how industry and organizational trends relate to the global landscape.
- Study the competition: How does it sell products internationally?
- Study the business practices of successful multinational companies.
- Talk with people in your network, especially those from other countries, to learn the business and social etiquette of other cultures.
- Analyze global economic patterns and the effect of large organizational shifts on global industries.
- Analyze the impact of world events on your industry and organization. Ask for the opinions of people from different countries and cultures, and consider your own as well.
- Identify the potential barriers in conducting business with other countries.
- Spend time with natives of other countries. Compare different perspectives due to different backgrounds. Find out the similarities too.

HOW TO USE THIS SKILL FURTHER

- Read books, newspapers, and other literature that focus on world events, global business, and your industry.
- Develop international contacts. Discuss the market, demographics, and cultural/business norms in different countries.
- Join a discussion group whose focus is world events and the impact of those events on countries, people, governments, and businesses.

RESULTS YOU CAN EXPECT

- You may have a better understanding of the global economy and its effect on your company and its industry.
- Others may come to you for insight into the possibilities and challenges of global expansion.
- You may become a highly valued member of your company.

READINGS

- *Cultures and Organizations: Software of the Mind, Intercultural Cooperation and Its Importance for Survival.* Geert Hofstede. 1996. McGraw-Hill, New York, ISBN 0070293074.
- *Designing the Global Corporation.* Jay Galbraith. 2000. Jossey-Bass, San Francisco, ISBN 787952753.
- *Riding The Waves of Culture: Understanding Diversity in Global Business.* Alfons Trompenaars & Charles Hampden-Turner. 1997. McGraw-Hill, New York, ISBN 0786311258.
- *Special Blend: Fusion Management from Asia and the West.* Lynette Lithgow. 2000. John Wiley & Sons, New York, ISBN 0471845507.
- *Successful Manager's Handbook.* Susan Gebelein, Lisa A. Stevens, Carol J. Skube, & David G. Lee. 2000. Personnel Decisions International, Minneapolis, MN, ISBN 093852920X.
- *The Differentiated Network: Organizing Multinational Corporations for Value Creation.* Nitin Nohria, Sumantra Ghoshal, & Cedric Crocker, 1997, Jossey-Bass, San Francisco, ISBN 787903310.
- *The Multinational Mission: Balancing Local Demands and Global Vision,* C. K. Prahalad & Yves L. Doz. 1999. Simon & Schuster, London, ISBN 684871327.
- *The Organization of the Future.* Frances Hesselbein, Marshall Goldsmith, & Richard F. Beckhard. 2000. Jossey-Bass, San Francisco, ISBN 787952036.

ITEM 5: Helps Others Understand the Impact of Globalization

WHAT TO DO

- Realize that a multinational organization is not likely to be successful unless its employees understand the organization's global vision and have access to the information they need to achieve the vision.
- Ensure that you and your employees have a clear understanding of the company's global vision and strategies.
- Check your information for accuracy before sharing it with others or drawing any conclusions.
- Blend key ideas into a concept that is meaningful to and easily understood by all concerned.
- Encourage others to ask questions if they do not have sufficient information to make a decision.
- Develop a global vision based on facts that can be supported.
- Keep the global vision statement short and simple.

- Encourage your employees to keep each other informed and share the global vision and strategies freely.

HOW TO DO IT

- Review the information to make sure it does not generalize, exaggerate, leave out important facts, or understate matters.
- Write the name of your source(s), thereby establishing proof for your views.
- Consider what would happen if you fail to synthesize the information to attain a global vision and communicate it to others.
- When needed, interpret and elaborate on the global vision statement; define terms, clear up confusion, and add alternatives and suggestions.
- When presenting the global vision, be as specific as possible and avoid "fuzziness" or hinting.
- Discuss techniques with managers who excel at this area.
- Regularly ask employees what you can do to help them achieve the vision.
- Help employees analyze the information in a complex situation and develop a clear global vision.
- Share specific global strategies and procedures in your organization that align with the vision.
- Conduct staff meetings and/or round table discussions regularly to share information about recent global development of the organization.
- Plan your information-giving session to avoid interruptions and assure attentiveness.
- Communicate company information to your employees in an open and positive way.

HOW TO USE THIS SKILL FURTHER

- Ask for honest feedback on how you are doing in this area.
- Volunteer to help a multinational philanthropic organization develop its global vision.

RESULTS YOU CAN EXPECT

- There may be less confusion and frustration when dealing with complex issues.
- There may be fewer crises and less stress.
- You may be asked to communicate organizational goals and values to others.

READINGS

- *Common Knowledge: How Companies Thrive by Sharing What They Know.* Nancy M. Dixon. 2000. Harvard Business School, Boston, ISBN 0875849040.
- *Communicating in Groups and Teams: Sharing Leadership.* Gay Lumsden & Donald Lumsden. 1999. Wadsworth Publishing, Florence, KY, ISBN 0534562329.

- *From Third World to World Class: The Future of Emerging Markets in the Global Economy.* Peter Marber. 1999. Perseus, Reading, MA, ISBN 0738201324.
- *International Success: Selecting, Developing, and Supporting Expatriate Managers,* Meena S. Wilson & Maxine A. Dalton. 1998. Center for Creative Leadership, Greensboro, NC, ISBN 1882197453.
- *The New Business of Business: Sharing Responsibility for a Positive Global Future,* Willis Harman & Maya Porter. 1997. Berrett-Koehler, San Francisco, ISBN 1576750183.

ENDNOTES

1. Reprinted with the permission of Simon & Schuster Adult Publishing Group from *Global Literacies: The New Language for Business Leaders,* Robert H. Rosen, Ph.D., with Carl Phillips, Marshall Singer, and Patricia Digh. Copyright © 2000 by RHR Enterprises.

2. Technology, Canada, 56. Throughout this book we will use quotes taken directly from our interviews with next-generation leaders. These quotes are set in italics or boxed. Each leader is identified only by industry, country, and age.

3. Health care, France, 44.

4. Products and services, United States, 44.

5. Products and services, United States, 33.

6. Technology, Sweden, 32.

7. Technology, United States, 36.

8. Transportation, United States, 40.

9. Products and services, United States, 35.

10. Products and services, United States/England/Norway, 49

11. Technology, Canada, 48.

12. Products and services, United States, 42.

13. Transportation, Canada, 47.

14. http://www.lovedpet.com/jokes/mishaps.html

15. Technology, United States, 28.

16. Technology, South Korea, 46.

17. Products and services, Mexico, 34.

18. Technology, United States, 26.

19. Technology, United States, 36.

20. Government, Switzerland/United States, 45

21. Technology, United States, 37.

22. Technology, Japan, 41.

23. Information and quotes from interview with Rosemarie Greco conducted by Cathy Greenberg, April 2002.

3 APPRECIATING DIVERSITY

T he rich diversity of culture and thought around the world is one of our great-est resources. Global leaders of the future will use differences of ideas, methods, and motivations throughout the workforce and around the globe to build organizational and individual competency. Yet, this great resource is a double-edged sword, as cross-cultural exchanges present us with unlimited possibilities for misunderstandings and cultural blunders.

As so many companies grow and expand around the world, the trend toward more diversity in the workplace increases. Successful global companies will identify, recruit, and train a diverse blend of professionals with different backgrounds, cultures, styles, and motivations into positions of increasing power and responsibility.

In the midst of individual contributors with such diverse cultural, religious, sexu-al, and personal backgrounds, success will call for leaders who are comfortable with *di-versity tension*—the stress and strain that accompanies mixtures of differences and similarities. The task of global leaders is not to minimize this tension but rather to use it as a creative force for change and, of course, to make quality decisions in the midst of identity differences, similarities, and pressures.

Finally, leaders will prepare and empower their associates to understand without judging, to be requirements-driven, and to be comfortable with diversity tension if they wish to be productive and successful. It is not enough for the leaders to possess these capabilities; they must also develop these capabilities throughout the organization.

THE VALUE OF DIVERSITY

As people relocate from country to country, region to region, city to city, and as corporations continue to expand across national and international borders, the business arena is becoming a melting pot for people of different cultures, races, ages, and socioeconomic and religious backgrounds. Leaders can no longer presume that they share a similar cultural base or outlook with those with whom they work and do business. Thus, leaders will be required to understand the dynamics of diversity (through historical, political, and economic references) and how it affects the workplace, and to look upon differences in worldviews, life and communication styles, and ethics and etiquette positively.

> The leader of the future must be flexible enough to adapt to a diverse workforce. For example, the Italians are [generally] vocal and passionate, while the Japanese tend to be more quiet and subtle, and not [to engage] in public forums. This is not any reflection on a person's capabilities, but more of a cultural orientation.[1]

Appreciating diversity will mean understanding both the "big things" and the "small things" that help form a unique culture, including leadership and work styles (formal vs. informal); decision-making styles (intuitive vs. analytical); information-sharing methods (written, oral, face-to-face); and motivations (power, achievement, affiliation). The global leader of the future won't need to sit in everyone's chair, but he or she will need to accept and understand that there are many different methods, positions, and styles with which people can accomplish goals and succeed in today's business environment. In other words, *the global leader needs to understand where people are coming from, but not go native.*[2]

For example, few Europeans or Americans who work in the Middle East have taken the time to read (much less understand) the Koran, even though it is clear that religion is one of the most important variables that impacts behavior in the region. Smaller issues, such as the meaning of gifts or the importance of timeliness, will also need to be understood crossculturally. Motivational strategies that are effective in one region may actually be offensive in another region. The same public recognition that could be a source of pride to a "prominence"-motivated salesperson from the United States could be a source of embarrassment to an "achievement"-motivated scientist from Japan. Leaders who can effectively understand, appreciate, and motivate colleagues from multiple cultures, eras, generations, regions, and countries will become an increasingly valued resource in the future.

DIVERSITY TRAINING AND DEVELOPMENT

Strengthening diversity is an ongoing business challenge without easy answers. Yet, when channeled and guided effectively, diversity in the workforce and customer base challenges ideas and helps businesses produce and thrive, leading to measurable and lasting results at all levels of business. For example, 40 of the 50 companies on *Fortune* magazine's (2002) reported list of 50 diversity leaders are Fortune 500 companies. This list includes the successful company Fannie Mae, which ranks 20th on the Fortune 500, 52nd on the Global 500, and first as Best Company for Minorities.[3]

However, due to a lack of training and education on generational differences among other issues, leaders in many companies frequently run into conflicts and misunderstandings around core values, especially diversity. This has contributed to discrimination lawsuits, including those against Texaco in 1996 and the current discrimination suit against the USDA.

The discrimination suit against Texaco brought diversity to the limelight of corporate America. After top Texaco executives were caught on tape using racial slurs against African Americans, the company paid $176.1 million to settle the suit. Had cultural diversity training been an integral part of Texaco's leadership development process, it's highly possible that the organization would have avoided the suit altogether. Another more current example of the challenges of diversity is the $20 billion class action lawsuit against the U.S. Department of Agriculture, in which approximately 20,000 Hispanic farmers nationwide claim that the USDA has systematically and discriminatorily denied them loans and failed to investigate complaints as required by law.[4]

As evidenced by these examples, increasing workplace diversity and the laws protecting individuals require people to have greater workforce sensitivity and to be aware of individuals' perspectives and rights in the countries within which the companies operate. Thus, diversity training and multigenerational leadership development are an integral part of the global leader development process.

For purposes of discussion, "multigenerational leadership" isn't just leading people of different ages. What we mean by multigenerational is leading individuals with different frames of reference or ideological differences. The history, politics, and economic environment in which an individual is raised will strongly impact his or her skills, abilities, and perspectives in all situations. For instance, in the United States, those born in the baby boomer generation grew up with the Vietnam War and Watergate. As a result, there is a lack of trust in government. On the other hand, the generation before them grew up in a time of war heroes and a post-Depression economic environment. These environmental differences will impact generational views of a business.

Executives must be *better rounded culturally. They will have had more eye-opening experiences that have helped them to be more comfortable with people with diverse backgrounds and opinions, and they will have been exposed to diverse environments and have been given the opportunity to see different aspects of business.*[5]

Many companies have incorporated diversity training into their corporate cultures with great results. One such organization is SBC Communications. SBC has established a workforce diversity team that works with human resources and department leaders to ensure that its policies, practices, and processes are inclusive and nondiscriminatory. Currently, the company ranks fourth on *Fortune's* Best Companies for Minorities, 69th on the Global 500, and 27th on the Fortune 500. It also holds the honors of the National Association for Female Executives' (NAFE) Top Companies for Executive Women and Employer of the Year by the National Business and Disability Council.[6]

Successful global leaders will take advantage of these programs. They will be curious about *the way others view products, service, approach, and process,*[7] and they will actively gather as much information and experience as possible. The global leader's preparation will include formal training and informal coaching in diversity, global leadership development, crosscultural and language instruction, and more intangible skills, such as emotional literacy, that is, the degree to which we can identify, appreciate, and manage our emotions, especially when working with others whose cultures, backgrounds, and viewpoints are quite different from our own.

> [Global leaders] must be aware of cultural differences. There are significant differences in culture [beyond] language. For instance, more countries will be using English as a second language. People may understand the words, but they may not understand the [underlying] message. There may be misinterpretation. Example: Many Japanese people can speak and literally understand English. However, when they say yes, it doesn't mean "I agree"; it means "I understand." We need to understand the language and the cultural interpretation. For example, Germans are...precise and highly disciplined, like engineers. However, Italians are more evolutionary and creative, like artists. When dealing with people, it's important to understand what they mean.[8]

Although organizations have restructured and reorganized, many still find it difficult to prosper in today's global marketplace. Many firms are finding that their conventional structures, traditional corporate cultures, and lack of leveraging diverse talents and perspectives prevents their meeting global market demands. Flexible leaders who are capable of managing diverse groups of people throughout the world are the competitive edge these companies need to succeed.

EMBRACING IDEAS AND PERSPECTIVES

The G8 Summit brings together the leaders of Canada, France, Germany, Italy, Japan, Russia, the United Kingdom, and the United States. In addition, the European Union participates and is represented by the president of the European Council and the President of the European Commission. At the G8 Summit in Okinawa (2000), leaders recognized that information technology has created a global, multinational environment in which people must frequently interact and relate crossculturally. Summit leaders endorsed cultural diversity as a source of "social and economic dynamism with the potential to enrich human life in the 21st century."[9]

To make the most of this potential, effective global leaders will work to create a flexible, general framework within which different ideas and perspectives are embraced and incorporated.[10] Within this framework there will be diversity tension, or social dynamism. This tension, or dynamism, that results from diversity in the workplace is not synonymous with conflict. In fact, it is quite possible for tension to exist between parties indefinitely without evolving into conflict.

In dealing with diverse situations, whether of race, religion, creed, or diversity of style or thought process, it is important for executives to understand the difference between cooperating and complying with others as opposed to collaborating with others. Teams that collaborate fully understand the difference between a collaborative process, which encourages conflict and harnesses diversity, as opposed to a compliance or cooperative context, which seeks to have people "get along" with others as opposed to working through serious issues. *Collaboration,* as a process, is the team management embodiment of harnessing creative tension. Collaborative teams do not seek to avoid conflict. (In fact, conflict is an essential part of the creative and decision-making processes.) Instead, collaboration gives people a process by which their differences can be used and made productive, utilized instead of suspected, valued instead of denied. Collaboration is the vehicle whereby conflict, whether generational, national, or stylistic, is used productively to create a positive outcome.

For example, Juan Camargo, human resources coordinator for Venezuela's state-owned oil enterprise, Petróleos de Venezuela (PDVSA), states that HR processes run smoothly because his company's policy on its joint ventures in the United States, Sweden, Germany, and the Caribbean is to respect local policies and practices. He maintains that the biggest challenge of PDVSA's international alliances stems from the cultural tensions and people issues that are the result of working relationships between Latinos, Europeans, and Americans. The friction between PDVSA's workers can be caused by such simple things as time-keeping as well as by more complex issues such as personal values. Rather than enforcing a values-based corporate culture on its worldwide workforce, PDVSA leaders attempt to understand and utilize cultural complexities to their advantage; thus, the company requires leaders who have been exposed to and are open to different cultures, countries, and work styles.[11]

Regarding diversity tension, the issue for leaders becomes that of maintaining a sufficient comfort level with the tension that will help produce creative solutions and high performance in the workplace. Thus, open-minded leaders who seek and exploit diversity tension by accepting and appreciating many dimensions of thought, style, and cultural difference within the workplace as well as by identifying and utilizing commonalties across multiple generations, regions, and countries around the world will be a key ingredient of organizational success.

Effective executives listen to all points of view. They are curious and intrigued by different perspectives, not threatened by them.[12]

This open-mindedness is not only beneficial in embracing innovative ideas or new technology, but it is also essential when recruiting, managing, and leading a global multigenerational, multicultural workforce. It is the responsibility of the global leader to be open to all kinds of people and to recognize the opportunities and different perspectives that diversity brings to an organization.

Realizing that success is dependent on teamwork, the global leader of the future will welcome and include all individuals by empowering and trusting people to do their best work; inviting team members to participate in meetings and task forces; and encouraging contributions in the form of opinions, skills, and abilities.

These executives look at every thing, every person, and every point of view as if it could be a really cool thing. They have an open-mindedness to listen and draw in all types of people and all types of views. They acknowledge the better parts of different perspectives. They have a great appreciation of differences and they have the confidence to listen openly. These leaders follow up on the unconventional and they encourage others to do the same.[13]

MOTIVATING PEOPLE

To motivate people in the workplace means to help them deliver their best possible performances, to be more productive, and to feel satisfied with their positions and growth within the organization. As both the workforce and clientele become increasingly diverse with widely differing perspectives, needs, expectations, and contributions, this seemingly simple agenda becomes a far greater challenge for leaders who *must adapt to a different way of leading in order to inspire and effectively lead.*[14]

A large part of this adaptation will include the leaders' ability to define individual and team roles and to delegate authority and responsibility. Making the most of the increasingly diverse workforce will require leaders to encourage and guide employees to work in their areas of strength and then to build strong internal teams of diverse individuals with complementary motivations and skills.

For instance, a leader might build a team that includes three people: one who is highly adept at sales, one who fosters a team environment, and one who understands the culture of the country within which the company sells its product. The result of such a combination would be a department that works well together selling the company's product to the targeted country.

These leaders foster the talents of the individual workers. They motivate their employees to do the best jobs and they leverage the diversity.[15]

The effective leaders of the future will build partnerships with employees to gain an understanding of each person's strengths, needs, and desired career path. By forging such relationships, leaders excite individuals about their jobs and motivate them to remain with the company. These relationships also provide significant knowledge and insight about employees that helps leaders to build working teams of diverse yet complementary employees, thereby strengthening the organization.

For example, regardless of the generation to which he or she belongs, the effective leader must be able to guide multiple generations with widely different needs and motivations. Age gap differences include younger workers who may be less inclined to make sacrifices for their company because they have seen organizations lay off their parents during periods of downsizing and restructuring.

The models of compensation, reward, recognition, and training need to change with the needs and priorities of individuals. It is the leader's job to figure out how to meet their needs, train and develop them, and get the job done. For instance, the younger workforce has seen their parents working 70- to 80-hour weeks only to get laid off when the company downsizes. They see this and ask themselves, "Why be loyal to a company that may lay me off when I turn 50?"[16]

In the following quote, an "older" executive expresses how he is challenged to understand the logic and knowledge of younger workers:

I grew up without computers, but my kids have grown up with a PC for games. One of them started using the computer at four years of age. Therefore, they are three-dimensional—the Nintendo generation. They use their intellectual capacity in a totally different way than myself. For example, I would read a book and try to make conclusions from what I read. My brain was working in a very hierarchical and logical way to solve problems. But when my kids use the computer to solve problems, they are using a three-dimensional way of thinking.

Therefore, my younger coworkers have a totally different way of thinking than mine. The challenge for me is to understand the difference.

Also, the Internet is changing everything. My kids spend five hours a day on the Internet. The younger people are more prepared to work for global organizations.

The challenge is to understand how these young people think and to give them challenges in their work. We underestimate how smart, international, and global these young workers are. Even English is very natural for them.[17]

According to human resources expert Beverly Kaye (author of international bestseller on retaining talent, *Love 'Em or Lose 'Em: Getting Good People to Stay*), every organization, whatever its industry, location, or size, will likely include members of the silent generation (born 1933 to 1945), baby boomers (born 1946 to 1964), generation Xers (born 1965 to 1976), and millenials—or generation Ys—(born 1977 to 1998). Each generation will most likely have a different motivational as well as value set, which the leader will need to recognize. For instance, silent generation individuals are likely to be team oriented, focusing on hard work and paying dues; baby boomers, who are the leaders of industry today, tend to be positive achievers; Xers are independent knowledge workers; and millenials are comparable to the silent generation in that they are team oriented, have been brought up with the computer, and are likely to be technologically savvy.[18]

The older leaders came from an era when there was a strong set of work ethics and company loyalty. They had traditional values and believed that if they worked hard, everything would work out. The Xers value quality of life as much as they value fast-paced corporate advancement or material goods. They are more fluid as a workforce. They have the confidence to move on if their current company doesn't meet their needs. They are more willing to manage their careers themselves instead of expecting the company to do it. Younger people are less inclined to stay late at the office or work weekends. They want to be able to work at home and have more flexibility. Instead of the "9 to 5 in the office" mentality, they may prefer to do their work elsewhere on a more flexible daily schedule.[19]

Generational conflict often results from the misunderstanding of the style and motivational differences of each age group. For instance, a traditional CEO, who was very excited about hiring a certain 30-year-old MBA, spent a great amount of time interviewing him and convincing the executive team that he was the right person for the job. However, after the young executive was hired, irreconcilable issues arose. The young executive not only believed that he had free rein to make whatever changes he felt the company needed, but he also believed it was acceptable to use the organization as a stepping stone into the industry. The CEO, who had thought that he was hiring a loyal supporter of the organization and the industry that it served, ended up firing the executive whose professional viewpoints were so different from his own and that of the rest of the executive team.[20]

TABLE 3.1 Generational Differences in the Workplace

	XER	BOOMER
Approach	Innovation	Process
Environment	Virtual	Physical
Role of Technology	Strategic	Supportive
Enterprise	Free Agent	Conglomerate
Competency	Technology	Business Acumen
Management Style	Energy to Influence	Monitor to Control
Leadership Style	Make Your Mark	Fit the Mold

However, once understood and harnessed, these differences can complement each other for the organization's benefit. Table 3.1 summarizes some of the most critical generational differences.

Across all geographic regions, it will be important for both older and younger generations to understand one another's distinct values and to harness these differences for success. Although generation Xers and millenials have succeeded in casting off the label of slackers, they are now viewed by baby boomers as a workforce of educated, driven self-starters who also exhibit impatient, disloyal, and self-centered behaviors. The difficulty in leading a multigenerational workforce is not purely an older generation misunderstanding a younger one's values. The skills and ideals of the baby boomer generation are not being recognized by younger employees. The challenge for organizations of the future will be to capitalize on the entrepreneurial spirit of its young leaders and the insights of its experienced executives, thus successfully integrating the positive characteristics of each group.

For instance, senior executives of the silent and boomer generations who have a vast array of business experience may or may not have experience opening and closing companies; counter this with many generation X executives who may have opened or closed five or six organizations during the dotcom era.

The following are ways that organizations can reduce uncertainty and conflict within the workforce:

GUIDELINES FOR LEADING A MULTIGENERATIONAL CORPORATION

- Develop a culture and environment that permits multiple work styles to flourish.
  - Promote the understanding of needs and motivations of all employees.
  - Utilize the unique skill sets of each generation.
  - Display value for experience and creativity.
  - Develop a common set of values based on relationships and history.
  - Provide recognition for accomplishments.

    While conflict between the values of the boomer generation and those of the Xers may seem natural, it is the synergy of these two work groups that will provide the most successful leadership in the near future. To develop this synergy, corporations need to develop an understanding and open culture that supports individuality and provides guidance to employees. The resultant strong corporate culture will develop from the bottom up, not from the top down.

- Create a multigenerational leadership team.
  - Provide a voice for all generations in the executive suite.
  - Foster innovation through constructive conflict and dialogue."
  - Mediate philosophical differences between the generations.
  - Facilitate the communication of corporate issues across generations.
  - Develop shared vision through analysis of past experiences and future trends.
  - Remove unnecessary bureaucracy and allow both generations to lead.

    The support of a group of diverse people is best achieved by providing them with representation in the decision-making process. A multigenerational leadership team provides a voice for the concerns of both the boomers and Xers, who can then be more effective in developing a vision for the company that is shared by all. By bringing together both boomers and Xers in the leadership roles, companies can expand the competency set of the executive suite. Differing values and experiences can often lead to conflict, of course, but the "constructive abrasion" of the diverse styles also is likely to lead to new forms of value creation.

- Develop a strong team mentoring program between generations.
  - Develop a process of understanding history, politics, economics, and life balance between the generations.
  - Develop trust between boomers and Xers.
  - Transfer knowledge and skills between generations.
  - Provide personal and professional direction.
  - Provide leadership training through observation.
  - Buffer Xers from corporate bureaucracy.
  - Develop emotional maturity in younger executives.

    Leaders are recognized at younger ages. While most 20-something professionals have the technical skills and creativity to drive the organization into the future, many do not have the business skills and experience necessary to provide direction and guidance to others. Mentors not only transfer basic business skills and knowledge, but also guide young employees in developing their individual leadership characteristics. For instance, suppose an older person who is just learning to use her company's new software product presents an idea for promoting its sale, but her idea is impatiently discounted by a young leader. A mentor might challenge this young leader to explore team building and diversity in the workplace. Open-mindedness to ideas is not something that can be effectively taught in the classroom; it is best developed through experience, observation, mentoring, and feedback.

    It is obvious how mentoring benefits Xers, but boomers also gain from this experience. For instance, younger employees can transfer technical knowledge and act as a sounding board for new ideas. The greatest benefit of interaction between the two groups is the development of crossgenerational relationships built on trust and respect so important to success.

- Foster employee loyalty to smaller communities within the organization.
  - Promote an entrepreneurial spirit at community level.
  - Provide a level of consistency for workers in an era of constant change.
  - Improve retention of younger "knowledge workers."
  - Provide corporate direction while permitting a sense of autonomy.

- Recognize employees for creativity and experience on a team basis.

- Companies gain when they develop an environment in which employees feel that their contributions are rewarded and their concerns are noticed. This can be accomplished by promoting the formation of smaller communities within the organization. Communities can be formed around project teams, common interests, and skills.

For instance, although some companies instituted e-commerce teams on an ad hoc basis, IBC was the first to create an "e-commerce organization," which required a new infrastructure, an organizational model, and a budget. Under the direction of the CIO SVP of marketing and the SVP of human resources and strategy, IBC's e-commerce community was created in an effort to drive the strategy of the organization. Groups of individuals from across marketing, provider services, communications, IT, and HR collaborated on the creation of a new organizational and leadership model to implement the e-commerce vision and strategy. This type of community started with the CEO, Fred DiBona, who was able to execute the strategy and successfully implement the infrastructure required to support it with the help of hundreds of IBC professionals under the direction of Yvette Bright. A crossdiscipline and crossgenerational work team was responsible for this widely publicized and successful program in the healthcare industry, the first phase of which was developed and implemented in less than a year.

Smaller groups can provide their members with performance feedback and direction much more accurately than a larger corporation is able to do. The smaller group setting makes it easier for employees to maintain their individuality.

Rewarding communities for their results allows employees' entrepreneurial spirits to thrive. In addition, they will more readily take ownership in a work group in which they can see the results of their actions. A community structure helps employees develop personal pride in their work and loyalty to the organization.

In the late 1990s the executive team of a large Australian financial services firm decided to demutualize the company in nine months. It was crucial that the team of 100 full-time core members and 200 part-time contractors and specialists complete the extensive transformation effort on time and within budget. The executive team set up compensation schemes and performance objectives, as well as rewards for particular programs (or project team tasks), as incentive to implement the tremendous amount of change in a very short period of time. The transformation was completed according to plan, and in an unheard of gesture of recognition, the CEO authorized a reimbursement scheme, cutting a check to every member of the team, including core members as well as contractors.

TEACHING THE VALUE OF DIVERSITY

> Not only will the global leaders of the future have tolerance for other approaches, these leaders will be good teachers who will help others acquire appreciation for those who are different.[21]

A well-rounded, diverse team will produce valuable brainstorming sessions, imaginative problem solving and decision making, unique perspectives on strategic planning, and inventive product development ideas. Recognizing that discrimination prohibits the expression of ideas, the leader will be a role model for appreciating diversity. He or she will model acceptable behaviors to influence those around him or her as to what is acceptable and what is not. This person will discourage sexist, racist, and ethnic comments, jokes, and slurs that negatively stereotype different groups. In this way, the leader will not only promote a healthy, cooperative, and diversified working environment, but will also help the organization to avoid lawsuits like that filed against Foster Farms Dairy. Foster Farms was sued in March 2002 by six African American men alleging racial discrimination, retaliation, harassment, and failure of the company to prevent discrimination in the workplace. Another instance is the $21 million sexual harassment suit against Daimler-Chrysler. (The company's appeal is still pending over what stands as one of the largest individual verdicts for harassment.)

Future leaders will openly discuss the topic of diversity with their teams, and they will help teach employees how to become more sensitive to differences. They will help *people to respect each others' differences,*[22] and they will have the *ability to communicate, to resolve conflict, and to negotiate differences between employees.*[23] For instance, *the fact-based person may have a natural intolerance for the feeling-based person. Therefore, the effective leaders will be the ones who can get to the core issues despite how different employees' styles are.*[24]

Vitro, a Mexican glass company established in 1900, which became a conglomerate over the years, is returning to its roots as a glass company. However, as opposed to being Mexican-centric, the company is focused on being a global organization. As part of this globalization process, the company is investing in its leaders to educate them about what working globally means and about the diversity they will encounter in the global environment. The proactive company has sent most of its top executives to the one-year Harvard Executive Program, which educates leaders about global business insights, thinking, leadership, and strategies. In addition, when considering partnerships, acquisitions, and mergers with companies in other countries, senior executives participate in a cultural immersion or alignment process, which highlights the differences between doing business in the Mexican culture and doing business in cultures around the world. During this immersion process, leaders learn to better understand different cultures and how to consider their own reactions not only from a business negotiation standpoint but also from both a social and interpersonal standpoint.

With such a diverse workforce, conflicts between individuals with unique perspectives will inevitably arise. Part of the leader's role will be to facilitate debates and to teach the value of conflict as an opportunity to gain knowledge. Rather than viewing these differences in viewpoints as negative, he or she will turn them into opportunities in which individuals can learn about themselves and each other.

CONCLUSION

As city, state, and country boundaries rapidly dissolve, the need for leaders to appreciate diversity in thought, style, and motivation increases. Leaders have to understand not only the economic and legal differences but also the social and behavioral differences that are part of working in different regions around the world. Developing an understanding of the many cultures that make up individual regions and countries around the world is not just a good business practice—it is a key to being able to compete successfully in the future.

As traditional values and roles are challenged by an increasingly diverse workforce, the effect of conflict is being felt in the organization. To be successful in addressing the concerns and motivations of this workforce, companies must foster an open culture built on personal relationships, small group loyalty, strong mentoring, and diverse leadership teams. This will ultimately lead to a better understanding and appreciation of differences, increased tolerance of ideas, and the broader sharing of knowledge.

APPRECIATING DIVERSITY

ITEM 6: Embraces the Value of Diversity in People

WHAT TO DO

- Realize that differences in race, culture, and background are advantages, not deficits, for effective teamwork and problem solving.
- Recognize the value of having a diverse workforce by utilizing the full potential of all employees and building on complementary skills, backgrounds, and cultural knowledge.
- Create an inclusive work environment.
- Assess the different learning styles and strengths in people.
- Explore ways to use different styles and talents advantageously.
- Recognize and reward successes that result from valuing diversity.

HOW TO DO IT

- Involve people from a variety of backgrounds in your decision-making and problem-solving processes.
- Make people feel welcomed in your work group.
- Make people feel valued for bringing their opinions and skills to the organization.
- Encourage people to come up with different ideas and perspectives to solve problems and spot opportunities.
- Involve a wide variety of people in your professional and personal life. Take the time to get to know them.
- Confront people who stereotype others or display prejudiced behavior.
- Refuse to accept behaviors that attack the self-respect of others.
- Set clear goals for your organization, and manage performance, not personalities.
- Ask your manager, associates, and employees to give you feedback on how you are doing in this area.
- Encourage your employees and coworkers to be more appreciative of the differences in people.

HOW TO USE THIS SKILL FURTHER

- Learn to appreciate people from diverse backgrounds through travel, books, and films, and by attending local cultural events.
- Participate in diversity training.
- Become friends with individuals whose backgrounds and experiences are different from your own.

RESULTS YOU CAN EXPECT

- Work groups may be more open to ideas from all members.
- Diversity issues may be more openly handled in ongoing team activities.
- Work attitudes and productivity may improve due to the inclusion and full utilization of people's talents.

READINGS

- *Bridging Differences: Effective Intergroup Communication*. William B. Gudykunst. 1998. Sage: Thousand Oaks, CA, ISBN 0803933304.
- *Building a House for Diversity: A Fable About a Giraffe and an Elephant Offers New Strategies for Today's Workforce*. Marjorie I. Woodruff & R. Roosevelt Thomas, Jr. 1999. AMACOM: New York, ISBN 814404634.
- *Difficult Conversations: How to Discuss What Matters Most*. Douglas Stone, Bruce Patton, Sheila Heen, & Roger Fisher. 2001. Penguin USA: New York, ISBN 014028852X.
- *Geeks and Geezers*. Warren G. Bennis & Robert J. Thomas. Harvard Business School Press: Boston. 2002. ISBN 1578515823.
- *Redefining Diversity*. R. Roosevelt Thomas. 1996. AMACOM: New York, ISBN 814402283.
- *Social Inclusion: Possibilities and Tensions*. Peter Askonas & Angus Stewart. 2000. Palgrave: Hampshire, England, ISBN 0312231660.
- *The Leader of the Future: New Visions, Strategies, and Practices for the Next Era*. Frances Hesselbein, Marshall Goldsmith, & Richard Beckhard. 1996. Jossey-Bass: San Francisco, ISBN 0787901806.
- *The Web of Inclusion*. Sally Helgesen. 1995. Currency/Doubleday: New York, ISBN 0385423640.

ITEM 7: Effectively Motivates People from Different Cultures or Backgrounds

WHAT TO DO

- Acknowledge that cultural and social differences exist.
- Realize that differences in race, culture, and background are advantages, not deficits, for effective teamwork and problem solving.
- Recognize the value of having a diverse workforce by utilizing the full potential of all employees and building on complementary skills, backgrounds, and cultural knowledge.
- Assess the different styles and strengths in people.
- Explore ways to effectively motivate people who have different styles and talents.
- Recognize that traditional American values often conflict with values of other cultures.
- Treat others with respect and dignity.
- Recognize the importance of maintaining fair standards. This means treating people equally regardless of their gender, race, age, or background.
- Help your work group recognize that discrimination can be a barrier to teamwork and can interfere with the achievement of productivity and quality goals.
- Involve diverse groups in solving problems and developing opportunities.
- Recognize and reward successes that result from valuing diversity.

HOW TO DO IT

- Encourage people to come up with different ideas and perspectives to solve problems and spot opportunities.
- Strive to understand what motivates each of your employees through observation and dialogues. Don't make any assumptions.
- Know the key motivators of each employee and use them effectively.
- Refuse to accept behaviors that attack the self-respect of others.
- Set clear goals for your employees, and manage performance, not personalities.
- Equally encourage the development of all employees in your organization by making them aware of development opportunities.
- Follow through, and recognize both individual and team contributions in ways that are sensitive to individual needs.
- Ask your manager, associates, and employees to give you feedback on how you are doing in this area.
- Encourage your employees and coworkers to be more appreciative of the differences in people.

HOW TO USE THIS SKILL FURTHER

- Learn to appreciate people from diverse backgrounds through travel, books, and films, and by attending local cultural events.
- Participate in diversity training.
- Become friends with individuals whose backgrounds and experiences are different from your own.

RESULTS YOU CAN EXPECT

- Your employees may be more satisfied with their work.
- Diversity issues may be more openly handled in ongoing team activities.
- Work attitudes may improve, as may success in achieving performance goals.

READINGS

- *Boston to Beijing: Managing in the Global Marketplace.* Nancy J. Adler, John Szilagyi, & Rob Bloom. 2001. South-Western: London, ISBN 0324074751.
- *Bridging Differences: Effective Intergroup Communication.* William B. Gudykunst. 1998. Sage: Thousand Oaks, CA, ISBN 0803933304.
- *Geeks and Geezers.* Warren G. Bennis & Robert J. Thomas. 2002. Harvard Business School Press: Boston, ISBN 1578515823.
- *Communicating with Strangers: An Approach to Intercultural Communication.* William B. Gudykunst & Young Yun Kim. 1996. Addison-Wesley: Boston, ISBN 0201113740.
- *Global Literacies: Lessons on Business Leadership and National Cultures.* Robert H. Rosen, Patricia Digh, Marshall Singer, & Carl Phillips. 2000. Simon & Schuster: London, ISBN 684859025.
- *Mentoring and Diversity.* Belle Rose Ragins, David Clutterbuck, & Lisa Matthewman. 2001. Butterworth-Heinemann: Woburn, MA, ISBN 750648368.
- *Redefining Diversity.* R. Roosevelt Thomas. 1996. AMACOM: New York, ISBN 814402283.
- *Riding the Waves of Culture: Understanding Diversity in Global Business.* Alfons Trompenaars & Charles Hampden-Turner. 1997. McGraw-Hill: New York, ISBN 786311258.
- *Workforce 2020: Work and Workers in the 21st Century.* Richard Judy & Carol D'Amico. 1997. Hudson Institute: Santa Barbara, CA, ISBN 1558130616.

ITEM 8: Recognizes the Value of Diverse Views and Opinions

WHAT TO DO

- Realize that differences in race, culture, and background are advantages, not deficits, for effective teamwork and problem solving.
- Value your diverse workforce by utilizing the full potential of all employees and building on complementary skills, backgrounds, and cultural knowledge.
- Show interest in gathering and developing new ideas of others.
- Realize that understanding other's thinking may enhance your own ideas and make you appear less stubborn.
- Expect others to have good ideas.
- Express an interest in what is being said.
- Suspend judgment while you concentrate on understanding an idea.
- Check your understanding and let others know you have heard them accurately.
- Establish an objective, consistent way of evaluating nontraditional ideas.
- Let others know they can question and disagree openly.
- Put yourself in the other person's shoes. Look at the situation from the other person's point of view before defending your own.
- Assess the different styles and strengths in people.
- Explore ways to use different styles and talents advantageously.
- Recognize and reward successes that result from valuing diversity.

HOW TO DO IT

- Involve people from a variety of backgrounds in your decision-making and problem-solving processes. Gather associates together for brainstorming sessions.
- Encourage people to come up with different ideas and perspectives to solve problems and spot opportunities.
- Involve a wide variety of people in your professional and personal life. Take the time to get to know them.
- Gather ideas from people who normally don't deal with the problem to gain a new perspective.
- Have more one-on-one meetings to establish rapport and to learn others' viewpoints.
- Put aside any negative feelings about past experiences.
- When you are questioned, respond in a nondefensive manner; this gives people permission to question and creates a more open and honest mode of communication.
- Don't argue about why you are right. Simply state your point of view.
- Ask others for their opinion before you state yours. When stating your opinions, preface your statements with words such as, "In my opinion..." or "I think...."
- Ask questions that require more than a yes or no response.

- Get support from customers, suppliers, peers, and subordinates for nontraditional ways of doing work by discussing ideas with them and getting their input about changes.
- Investigate and practice various techniques, such as brainstorming, for generating ideas.
- Schedule time in staff meetings for sharing innovative solutions, ideas, and perspectives.
- Ask your manager, associates, and employees to give you feedback on how you are doing in this area.
- Encourage your employees and coworkers to be more appreciative of the differences in people.

HOW TO USE THIS SKILL FURTHER

- Form a task force that meets regularly to discuss new ideas, information, and other perspectives that concern the company.
- Learn to appreciate people from diverse backgrounds through travel, books, and films, and by attending local cultural events.
- Assume a facilitator role in group discussions.
- Become friends with individuals whose backgrounds and experiences are different from your own.

RESULTS YOU CAN EXPECT

- You may have better rapport with associates.
- Work groups may be more open to ideas from all members.
- Diversity issues may be more openly handled in ongoing team activities.
- Work attitudes may improve, as will success in achieving performance goals.

READINGS

- *75 Cage-Rattling Questions to Change the Way You Work: Shake-Em-Up Questions to Open Meetings, Ignite Discussion, and Spark Creativity.* Dick Whitney & Melissa Giovagnoli. 2000. McGraw-Hill: New York, ISBN 0070700192.
- *Collaborative Creativity: Unleashing the Power of Shared Thinking.* Jack Ricchiuto. 1996. Oak Hill Press: Winchester, VA, ISBN 1886939128.
- *Communicating with Strangers: An Approach to Intercultural Communication.* William B. Gudykunst & Young Yun Kim. 1996. Addison-Wesley: Boston, ISBN 0201113740.
- *Geeks and Geezers.* Warren G. Bennis & Robert J. Thomas. 2002. Harvard Business School Press: Boston, ISBN 1578515823.
- *Mastering the Infinite Game: How East Asian Values are Transforming Business Practices.* Charles Hampden-Turner & Fons Trompenaars. 2001. Capstone: Mankato, MN, ISBN 1900961083.

- *The Differentiated Network: Organizing Multinational Corporations for Value Creation.* Nitin Nohria, Sumantra Ghoshal, & Cedric Crocker. 1997. Jossey-Bass: San Francisco, ISBN 787903310.
- *Workforce 2020: Work and Workers in the 21st Century.* Richard Judy & Carol D'Amico. 1997. Hudson Institute: Santa Barbara, CA, ISBN 1558130616.

ITEM 9: Helps Others Appreciate the Value of Diversity

WHAT TO DO

- Understand your own values.
- Examine and confront your own prejudices.
- Question and challenge your own assumptions before making decisions.
- Recognize that traditional American values often conflict with values of other cultures.
- Treat others with respect and dignity.
- Recognize the importance of maintaining fair standards. This means treating people equally regardless of their gender, race, age, or background.
- Avoid and discourage any tendencies to joke about differences.
- Help your work group recognize that discrimination can be a barrier to teamwork and interfere with the achievement of productivity and quality goals.
- Involve diverse groups in solving problems and developing opportunities.
- Help your group learn to value diversity and manage differences.
- Model inclusive behaviors.
- Recognize and reward successes that result from valuing diversity.

HOW TO DO IT

- Talk with people individually to understand their values to help avoid stereotyping that interferes with sound decision making.
- Involve a wide variety of people in your professional and personal life. Take the time to get to know them.
- Confront people who stereotype others or display prejudiced behavior.
- Refuse to accept behaviors that attack the self-respect of others.
- Set clear goals for your organization, and manage performance, not personalities.
- If someone makes discriminating but subtle comments, ask the person for the evidence or rationale for his or her belief. Then discuss the impact of the comment on other people in the organization.
- If someone makes comments that are an obvious put-down, simply say, "That's not appropriate." Be firm and assertive.

- Follow through and recognize both individual and team contributions in ways that are sensitive to diversities.

HOW TO USE THIS SKILL FURTHER

- Learn to appreciate people from diverse backgrounds through travel, books, and films, and by attending local cultural events.
- Participate in diversity training.
- Become friends with individuals whose backgrounds and experiences are different from your own.

RESULTS YOU CAN EXPECT

- Work groups may be more open to ideas from all members.
- Diversity issues may be more openly handled in ongoing team activities.
- Work attitudes may improve, as will success in achieving performance goals.

READINGS

- *Bridging Differences: Effective Intergroup Communication.* William B. Gudykunst. 1998. Sage: Thousand Oaks, CA, ISBN 0803933304.
- *Communicating with Strangers: An Approach to Intercultural Communication.* William B. Gudykunst & Young Yun Kim. 1996. Addison-Wesley: Boston, ISBN 0201113740.
- *Cultures and Organizations: Software of the Mind—Intercultural Cooperation and Its Importance for Survival.* Geert H. Hofstede. 1996. McGraw-Hill: New York, ISBN 0070293074.
- *Mentoring and Diversity.* Belle Rose Ragins, David Clutterbuck, & Lisa Matthewman. 2001. Butterworth-Heinemann: Woburn, MA, ISBN 750648368.
- *The Differentiated Network: Organizing Multinational Corporations for Value Creation.* Nitin Nohria, Sumantra Ghoshal, & Cedric Crocker. 1997. Jossey-Bass: San Francisco, ISBN 787903310.
- *Workforce 2020: Work and Workers in the 21st Century.* Richard Judy & Carol D'Amico. 1997. Hudson Institute: Santa Barbara, CA, ISBN 1558130616.

ITEM 10: Actively Expands Her or His Knowledge of Other Cultures

WHAT TO DO

- Realize that the knowledge and understanding of other cultures is critical to conducting successful global business.

- Learn about the cultural norms and customs in other countries in which you want to conduct business.
- Find various ways to obtain the knowledge of other cultures through interactions, language study, travel, and so on.
- Show respect for people from other cultures.
- Show interest in and respect for other cultural practices.
- Learn the related foreign languages and encourage your coworkers to do the same.
- Recognize that both similarities and differences exist between different cultures.

HOW TO DO IT

- Identify people from other cultures in your organization or networks. Ask them for insights about the similarities and differences between your culture and theirs.
- Identify cultural difference that could be problematic in conducting business.
- Participate in crosscultural communication workshops or training to get a deeper understanding of other cultures.
- Learn the language of the country before you conduct business there. Make language proficiency a hiring requirement for particular positions.
- Rotate staff whenever possible so that people get exposed to other cultures.
- Talk with and spend time with people from other cultures.
- Spend time with natives of other countries. Compare different perspectives that result from different backgrounds. Find out the similarities too.
- When you are in another country, record your observations in a journal. Reflect on them by asking yourself, "What surprises me?" and "What is similar?"
- Do not assume that a person of one culture represents the opinions of his or her entire culture.
- Do not become a cultural bully yourself.

HOW TO USE THIS SKILL FURTHER

- Ask for more opportunities to go abroad to work with people from other cultures.
- Build friendships with people from different cultures.

RESULTS YOU CAN EXPECT

- You may become more competent in dealing with intercultural relationships.
- You may gain more opportunities to be promoted.

READINGS

- *Culture Clash: Managing in a Multicultural World.* H. Ned Seelye & Alan Seelye-James. 1995. NTC Business Books: Lincolnwood, IL, ISBN 0844233048.

- *Culture, Ethnicity, and Personal Relationship Processes.* Stanley O. Gaines. 1997. Routledge: Philadelphia, ISBN 0415916534.
- *The Cultures of Globalization.* Fredric Jameson & Masao Miyoshi. 1998. Duke University Press: Durham, NC, ISBN 0822321696.
- *The Executive Guide to Asia-Pacific Communications: Doing Business Across the Pacific.* Davis James. 1995. Kodansha: New York, ISBN 1568360401,
- *Managing Across Cultures: A Learning Framework.* Meena S. Wilson, Michael H. Hoppe, & Leonard R. Sayles. 1996. Center for Creative Leadership: Greensboro, NC, ISBN 1882197259.
- *Nationalism and Modernism: A Critical Survey of Recent Theories of Nations and Nationalism.* Anthony D. Smith. 1998. Routledge: Philadelphia, ISBN 415063418.
- *The World in 2020: Power, Culture, and Prosperity.* Hamish McRea. 1995. Harvard Business School Press: Boston, ISBN 0256115842.

ENDNOTES

1. Technology, Japan, 41.

2. Research and development, United States, 46.

3. *http://www.fortune.com/indexw.jhtml?co_id=498&channel=list.jhtml&list_frag= survey_results.jhtml&list=28&_DARGS=%2Ffragments%2Ffrg_f500snap_list_company_ranking.jhtml_A&_DAV=list.jhtml*

4. *http://success.yellowbrix.com/pages/success/Story.nsp?story_id=32481552&ID= success*

5. Telecommunications, United States, 37.

6. *http://www.sbc.com/corporate_citizenship/diversity_in_action/in_the_workplace/ 0,5931,61,00.html*

7. Pharmaceutical, United States, 41.

8. Products and services, Switzerland, 45.

9. *http://www.jmission-eu.be/interest/g8comm.html*

10. We will pick up on the use of "constructive conflict" throughout this book. Suffice it to say here that when we create new frameworks, we will likely create some constructive conflict as well.

11. *http://www.shrmglobal.org/publications/hrworld/leaders.htm#50*

12. Healthcare, United States, 33.

13. Pharmaceutical, United States, 41.

14. Technology, Japan, 41.

15. Technology, United States, 36.

16. Products and services, United States, 36.

17. Technology, Finland, 41.

18. B. Kaye, D. Scheef, & D. Thielfoldt. "Engaging the Generations" in *Human Resources in the 21st Century.* Eds. M. Effron, R. Gandossy, & M. Goldsmith. John Wiley & Sons: New York. 200⸱

19. Telecommunications, United States, 34.

20. W.G. Bennis & R. J. Thomas. Geeks and Geezers. Harvard Business School Press. Boston. 2002

21. Technology, United States, 45.

22. Technology, United States, 35.

23. Technology, United States, 36.

24. Technology, United States, 45.

4 DEVELOPING TECHNOLOGICAL SAVVY

Leaders from around the world consistently express the view that technological savvy will be a key competency for the global leader of the future. One trend on this issue is clear: The *younger* the participant, the greater the emphasis on the importance of technological savvy. Most young future leaders cannot recall a time in their lives when there were no computers or host of digital gadgets. Many present leaders, on the other hand, still view technological savvy as something that is important for staff people but not for the line officers who run the "real" business.

Technological savvy doesn't mean that future leaders will need computer programming or Web design skills to lead their companies to success. It does mean that leaders should understand how technology, used appropriately, can benefit their organizations and that they should put in place systems to build and retain a network of technically competent people. The technologically savvy leader will increase productivity through the effective management and use of technology.[1]

Unfortunately, in many long-established organizations there is an inverse correlation between an executive's rank in the organizational hierarchy and his or her technological savvy. Developing technologically savvy executives may be one of the great challenges faced by the organization of the future.

In order to develop an executive team that is technologically savvy, organizations will have to go well beyond sending the executives to a training program. Technology must become part of the executive's day-to-day life, not just a one-day program or event. As such, organizations will have to commit an ongoing investment of time and resources in order to maintain a competitive advantage.

SUCCEEDING IN TOMORROW'S WORLD

Organizational change is coupled with technological innovation, not just in products, but also in planning, managing, communicating, producing, and delivering effectively. Information and communication systems have become the backbone of the global enterprise. Although most executives are not responsible for their information technology system, they are required to understand the strategic application of technology and to lead the company in using it. If they are planning to engage in electronic commerce, technological leadership is especially important. Imagine, for instance, a manager of a company with alternating shifts in San Francisco and New Delhi (as many companies do to maximize 24/7 productivity) not knowing the working of the communications network that allows the exchange of product information. Or, picture anyone in international finance not knowing, in a thorough way, how exchange rates are handled in real time by computers.

> There's a whole new level of literacy—not just in languages, but also technological literacy.[2]

In addition, leaders will need to understand enough about technological infrastructures to determine their potential for adding value to the company. For instance, there are great new ways to communicate, and there are software packages that make it possible, but if the infrastructures are not set up properly or are not compatible with the software, if security measures are too tight or not tight enough, it's not possible to take advantage of the potential for adding value. Leaders must have enough knowledge to evaluate the information put forth by their teams on these issues so that they can make decisions that will benefit the company.

Accenture, for example, recently implemented an enrollment system for a large health services organization. Focusing on adding value to the company, Accenture attempted to increase the potential for the return on investment by lowering the cost of the implementation. Accenture proposed using offshore resources in India, which would save the company hundreds of thousands of dollars. Although the technology created value-added cost reduction, communicating was difficult due to the different time zones. An instant messaging system was set up so that the teams could talk to each other in real time. However, the client's technology infrastructure was laden with security and firewalls that made the instant messaging system ineffective. Even though they had the technology, the teams were competent, and they wanted to share information, the time delay caused by the client's security system became a huge burden, and the added value that had been anticipated by having an offshore team at a reduced price was virtually eliminated.

Organizations are more networked. Technology such as email allows instant communication. This creates both opportunities and challenges for executives. Executives can communicate instantly with all members of the organization or contact any one in particular without having to go through a formal procedure. The ease of communication and the low cost of corresponding with people around the world allow companies to operate around the clock. Information, such as the details of projects and support services, can be exchanged immediately between groups and individuals who are involved in business development. Technology makes it easier for an executive to influence the organization through personal communiqués in a variety of media. For instance, during the attacks in the United States of September 11, 2001, many senior executives used voice mail and email to distribute multiple messages daily. The national emergency broadcasting system was not used; news networks and community and business leaders supplied people with the information they needed via the Internet and electronic communications.

However, there is a downside to so much communication technology. Take, for example, the stressed young CEO who travels with her laptop, Blackberry, cell phone, and Palm Pilot. While she can do her work any time and anywhere, without thoughtfully managing this slew of communication devices, she becomes an on-call executive whose work is likely to envelope her 24 hours a day, seven days a week.

Another benefit of technology is that the hoarding of information for political or defensive reasons becomes more difficult, since more people are included in the communication network. This can have great benefits, as illustrated in the following example. Recently, a large company implemented a SAP (systems, applications, and products) in data processing to replace its manual procurement system. The electronic system added value to the company and reduced costs for the different departments by automating all ordering, tracking all inventories, and curtailing vendor use. When the company implemented the SAP, department heads put their manual purchasing files into the SAP system. One individual had been embezzling money from the company by writing checks for services to artificial companies that he had set up under false names with bank accounts that he had opened. As long as the system was manual, this was possible; however, when the SAP system was implemented, it became apparent that there were some vendors not in the system but still receiving checks. After an investigation, it was found that these vendors didn't exist. This is just one instance in which it is apparent that any kind of system that requires individuals to communicate over a network will uncover information. To be effective, companies and leaders need to share information and data, yet openness can be vulnerable, so firewalls and other security measures must be used. Knowledge of these technologies is required to strike a happy balance so safety doesn't impede effectiveness.

Technology is driving change. Now, we communicate person-to-person much of the time. In the future we will work with people we seldom see. Therefore, we will need to be effective with the new technology so that we can connect with people in different geographic areas. For example, we will use email, faxes, cell phones, et cetera to help employees feel close to the headquarters even when they are located far away and we see each other face-to-face only once a year. Future leaders must adapt themselves to the changing technology.[3]

The global leader will use technology systems as communications tools, but not in the traditional, simple sense of sending and receiving messages and directives. More so than in the past, leaders will take advantage of these communications systems as natural checks and balance measures. Unlike a hard copy, interoffice memo, these systems allow for more two-way communication in which each individual receiving the communication has the opportunity to rebut, add to, and question what the leader has said via the same technology. This supports a natural environment of growth and creativity, and allows team members to build trusting, supportive relationships that benefit the company.

Future leaders will use these systems to extend their presence throughout the organization—that is, they will replace the traditional "management by walking around" approach with valuable "anytime, anyplace" communication, enabled by multiple technologies ranging from the Internet to videoconferencing and digital wireless networks.

For instance, as businesses expand across the globe, the advent of videoconferencing brings people who work in different countries "face to face." It gives leaders the opportunity to see the people with whom they are doing business, their mannerisms and facial expressions, things that they would otherwise never see. This lends an element of trust to a crossglobal relationship that might not be possible sight unseen.

Another growing technological advancement is the evolving and improving Blackberry advanced wireless handheld communication system, which allows for virtual conversations through the use of multiple technologies. Leaders will take advantage of these new and existing technologies because they are not going to be in as many face-to-face situations. They will have to be able to communicate any place, any time, and they will have to know which communication mechanism to use to do so. The better a leader is at understanding how to communicate with people and understanding what information they need, the better he or she will be at using the technical components of communication mechanisms.

With so many communication tools currently at our disposal, to be effective, the global leader must know not only how to use the tools, but also which tool to use at what time, which medium requires what tone of voice, who to send the information to, and what type of information is required. For instance, if financial information is needed, a voice mail probably wouldn't work, but an email would.

One ongoing communication challenge that leaders face is being available to answer questions and discuss ongoing projects and progress with employees. Many executives set aside blocks of time each day for phone calls and meetings to discuss ongoing projects with team members; however, the imbalanced ratio of one leader to many employees often results in missed or hurried appointments that do not benefit either party. The effective use of today's technology tools, such as email and the Internet, has the potential to increase communication between leaders and their teams by making it possible to conduct business from a variety of places any time of day. In addition, it is possible to post progress updates, give assignments, and deliver information about departmental and business-wide policies and initiatives to people around the world.

Another challenge for many current executives is that they feel intimidated by new technology. They are embarrassed to admit that their children, or even their grandchildren, often know more than they do! How many of you have ever burned a CD off the Internet?

There are reasons for this: Global leaders have generally achieved a great deal of success in life and often do not want to play a game they feel they cannot win. These leaders must understand that technological savvy does not require winning a competition or being an expert, and must learn how to understand the impact of technology and to recruit and communicate with technical experts.

Global leaders may be averse to technology because they have seen what happens when private emails between executives and their team members get dragged through the courts; because emails and attachments don't always transfer properly and calendaring systems sometimes don't set up an important appointment; or because cell phones are capable of losing a connection at the most important point in a negotiation with a key client. These leaders must realize that technological savvy involves discretion, patience, a developed understanding of the impact of technology, and the ability to recruit and communicate with technical experts. In other words, global leaders do not need to become technical experts, but they should be adept enough to hire people who are.

> The marketplace is much different now than it was a decade ago. There is more of a demand for talented and educated people with a technical background. The global leaders need to attract new talents and keep existing talents. They must create an environment where young people are constantly learning new things and where they have a clear and visible career path.[4]

This can even be true in "high-tech" organizations. Most people believe that Lou Gerstner, former CEO of IBM, did a fine job of leading the corporation. He has often noted that he is not a technical expert, but he has clearly demonstrated the technological savvy needed to lead IBM. Scott McNealy, CEO of Sun Microsystems, did not have the technical vision that led to the creation of the Java programming language. He did have the technological savvy needed to work with technical visionaries and ultimately see the business value of their efforts. Leaders who understand the difference between technological savvy and technical expertise are much more willing to begin acquiring the new skills needed for the future success of their organizations.

RECRUITING EXPERTS

A main function of the global leader of the future will be to effectively hire advisers who not only understand new technology, but also can explain how it can help businesses to gain a competitive advantage.

> Collaborative leadership failings occur when we don't take the time to involve the right technical expertise and when we don't build the team spirit; when we don't have a common objective or understanding; and when we don't have good communication.[5]

Hugh McColl, former CEO of NationsBank, has noted that in the past he could develop a vision for the bank and communicate his vision to employees. He focused on collaboration by soliciting the input of valued technical advisers before communicating the vision. He has been successful by applying both internal and external expert advisers on business plans and technological strategies.

They must be able to effectively use a team of technical experts. We need to be able to access the expertise of others and use them for decision making. [6]

Individuals with the proper support, training, and education can maximize the use of technological savvy to achieve goals otherwise unattainable. For instance, the technological savvy of a team of 12 United States Special Forces was critical to the collaboration between the Northern Alliance and the US military in Afghanistan. The Special Forces team members, armed with just their technological knowledge, knowledge of the region's history, religion, and culture, and limited combat experience, were able to leverage the impact of strategically placed bombs with great accuracy and thus help defeat the Taliban and Al-Quaeda forces in Afghanistan. [7]

Finding people who have technical talent, business knowledge, and effective communications skills is extremely difficult—and expensive. For example, the going rate for beginning salaries in Silicon Valley can be 30 percent to 50 percent higher than in the rest of the United States, and the same sort of disparity exists, to a degree, in the other technological centers of the world. Even for companies that are not technology companies themselves, the skilled labor comes higher simply because the demand for such talent remains high. Future leaders will have little choice but to make the investment, because for some, technical skills will be more important than language skills.[8]

Global leaders of the next generation should focus on the technological capacities and competencies that are coming with the next generation of the workforce. Many companies, while they have created and installed the necessary technological infrastructures, have not had a workforce that was motivated or capable of using the tools. The incoming workforce has been brought up with technology. These young people have the competence and the capability to use the technological infrastructures in which companies have been investing.

INCREASING PRODUCTIVITY

Almost all the high-potential leaders surveyed believe that the global leader of the future will need a far deeper knowledge of the benefits—and limitations—of technology.

Much as automobile companies have invested in improvements in the combustion engine since Etienne Lenoir patented the first practical gas engine in 1860, leaders must assess and invest in information and technological infrastructures as the distribution of knowledge becomes an increasing component of organizational success.

It's not necessary that they understand all the technological details, but they will need to be able to make informed decisions as to whether or not proposed investments in technology will lead to beneficial changes in performance, activity, and procedures. For instance, does a technology investment result in added revenue, reduced expense, or better customer service?

Such understanding will need to be integrated into the core of the business to help the organization maintain a competitive advantage. Developing this knowledge will include an exploration into the specific applications that will have the most impact on each part of the business. For example, *the future leaders will need to use the entire range of communication modes and skills as they guide their organization through dramatic change. They must select which communication tool will be the most effective for each situation, whether it be email, telephone, teleconferencing, face to face, et cetera.*[9]

It is important to learn what different technologies can make a difference to the organization. For example, if a leader is constantly traveling, desktop videoconferencing may eliminate the need for many face-to-face meetings and save huge amounts of time and money. If a leader manages people who work in different time zones (or on different shifts), then asynchronous data conferencing—essentially, electronic bulletin boards—may be effective.

The key is to be selective: Understand which technologies can offer clear benefits and focus on those in the short term. *The pressures and expectations will be to leverage the technological changes. For example, it's actually cheaper to send people overseas. It's better using the Internet.*[10]

Developing a technologically savvy executive team will require an investment—in time, in money, and in commitment. As with any investment, the organization will need to conduct a cost-benefit analysis to determine priorities. As new technology becomes more and more a part of the core process of the organization, the benefit of this investment increases, as does the cost of not making the investment.

> With the highly decentralized way of doing business today, in which people are scattered all over the world, there is a challenge. At BellSouth, they use technology to communicate to the local offices instead of having someone travel all over the place. They use television broadcasting to carry the message forward to even the remote places.[11]

Successful organizations of the future will do whatever is needed to equip their leaders with the skills needed to effectively increase productivity in the information age. However, the psychological commitment to developing a technologically savvy leadership team has often lagged behind the financial commitment. Many organizations today are investing billions of dollars in new technology and investing almost nothing in developing the technological savvy of the leaders who are ultimately responsible for making the resource allocation decisions. This can lead to grave problems when it comes time to incorporate the software into the workplace. Take, for instance, the company that invests thousands of dollars in a new customer accounting system, only to find that the software is not compatible with the old system. Not only has the company paid for the new software, it must pay to train employees to use it, and it must pay the many hours of overtime that it will take to manually input the old data into the new system.

CONCLUSION

A future global leader who is not able to use global electronic mail and conference systems, laptop computers, and modems will be a rarity. These leaders need to be fully conversant with technological tools and advances, and able to use them. There is a great need for global leaders who are technologically capable, both individually and organizationally.

The development of technological savvy will require much more than the half-hearted efforts that many organizations have made in the past. Even many nontechnical organizations are finding that the wise use of new technology is becoming a critical key to their survival. As the impact of new technology increases in importance to the business, the strategy of hiring a few technically gifted people and expecting them to "carry" the rest of the organization will no longer work. In the future, technical knowledge will have to be successfully integrated into the core of the business in order to help the organization achieve a competitive advantage. Leaders at all levels, especially executives at the top. will need to understand this integration.Organizations that invest the necessary time, money, and commitment into the development of executives who are committed and competent in the management of new technology will have a huge competitive advantage in tomorrow's new world.

DEVELOPING TECHNOLOGICAL SAVVY

ITEM 11: Strives to Acquire the Technological Knowledge Needed to Succeed in Tomorrow's World

WHAT TO DO

- Determine what technological skills and knowledge you must develop to reach your full potential within the company.
- Recognize that success in your career requires continued development of technological skills and knowledge.
- Involve your supervisor or coach in deciding your technical training and development needs.
- Devise a plan to increase your skills.
- Request assignments that will help increase your technological knowledge and skills.
- Take on technologically challenging assignments and responsibilities.
- Stay current on the technological advancements in your business.
- Build your self-confidence.
- Be willing to ask others for help and guidance.

HOW TO DO IT

- Take the responsibility to explore new areas of interest, and seek adequate training to develop yourself for new responsibilities.
- Examine your past and current assignments and review them with your supervisor. Discuss with him or her the following questions:
- Have I tried new things that develop or enhance my technological skills lately?
- Do I have the potential and ability to handle more challenging tasks?
- Am I willing and ready to take new responsibilities?
- Are there technological skills or knowledge that I am lacking that may hinder my progress?

- Ask others for developmental feedback on how you apply the new skills on the job.
- Read the latest industry trend journals, magazines, and newsletters to keep current on new technological developments, your competition's advancement, and technological changes in the industry.
- Join and become involved with industry associations. Network to stay current on the technological advances in the industry.

HOW TO USE THIS SKILL FURTHER

- Identify someone who is highly successful or competent in the area in which you are interested. Ask for his or her help and guidance.
- Regularly communicate any new information you may have acquired with your work group.
- Push yourself to spend the time and effort to acquire a new technological skill or talent. Spend an hour a day a few times a week, and challenge yourself to learn a skill that has always intimidated you.

RESULTS YOU CAN EXPECT

- People may compliment you on how you have improved and developed your potential.
- Your performance may improve because you have greater confidence and motivation.
- You may discover other talents in yourself to further increase the productivity of your work unit.
- People may comment on or express appreciation for the way you have inspired them to expand their capabilities.

READINGS

- *Creating You & Co: Learn to Think Like the CEO of Your Own Career*. William Bridges. 1998. Perseus: Reading, MA, ISBN 738200328.
- *Cyberschools*. Glenn R. Jones, Alvin Toffler, & Heidi Toffler. 2000. Cyber Publishing Group: Englewood, NJ, ISBN 1885400764.
- *Good to Great: Why Some Companies Make the Leap...and Others Don't*. James C. Collins. 2001. HarperCollins: New York, ISBN 0066620996.
- *Listening: The Forgotten Skill*. Madelyn Burley-Allen. 1995. John Wiley & Sons: New York, ISBN 0471015873.
- *Profit Patterns: 30 Ways to Anticipate and Profit from Strategic Forces Reshaping Your Business*. Adrian J. Slywotzky, David J. Morrison, Ted Moser, Kevin A. Mundt, & James A. Quella. 1999. Random House: New York, ISBN 0812931181.
- *Successful Manager's Handbook*. Susan Gebelein, Lisa A. Stevens, Carol J. Skube, & David G. Lee. 2000. Personnel Decisions International: Minneapolis, ISBN 093852920X.

- *Thriving in 24/7: Six Strategies for Taming the New World of Work*. Sally Helgesen. 2001. Free Press: London, ISBN 684873036.

ITEM 12: Successfully Recruits People with Needed Technological Expertise

WHAT TO DO

- Identify and prepare high-potential, technologically adept employees at every level of your organization.
- Keep in mind that you can only be as good as your people.
- Create a good reputation for your organization to attract top-notch talent in the technological field.
- Specify roles and responsibilities for each position in your organization.
- Involve others in the recruitment process.
- See recruiting the "right" people as your responsibility.
- Improve your interviewing skill and process.
- Search for talent inside your organization and among people in other departments.
- Effectively outreach for external candidates.
- Match the individuals to appropriate jobs.

HOW TO DO IT

- Develop and periodically update job descriptions specifying the experiences, knowledge, skills, and abilities required for each position in your organization.
- Identify specific skills and work styles that will fit in your future plan and current team structure, and recruit accordingly.
- Even at entry-level recruitment, identify those who have technological skills and talents. Track their progress, and give them every opportunity to excel.
- When grooming candidates at mid-level, understand that they should already have developed technological expertise, and not just raw talent. Study their history with the organization and identify not only their assets and deficiencies, but also their future career plans. Give them tasks that will extend their skills.
- After some time, identifying those people who would excel in the technological arena can be relatively clear cut. Find those who have proven a high level of skills for the specific position to be filled.
- Have other members of your team help develop job descriptions and conduct interviews. Ask them to rate each candidate independently, and synthesize all ratings, discuss discrepancies, and make the best decisions.

- Ask candidates to describe what they have done in the past in areas relevant to the job under consideration.
- Check references thoroughly.

HOW TO USE THIS SKILL FURTHER

- Identify who is especially good at recruiting, and get his or her advice.
- Participate in professional organizations so that you will have more opportunities to meet talented individuals. Keep in touch with them even if you have no current opening.
- Discuss techniques with managers who excel at recruiting the "right" people. Sit in on their interview meetings to observe and learn.

RESULTS YOU CAN EXPECT

- The productivity and teamwork of your organization may improve.
- People may seek your advice for recruiting the "right" people for their organization.
- People may compliment you on how your team or department has improved.

READINGS

- *Competing for Talent: Key Recruitment and Retention Strategies for Becoming an Employer of Choice,*. Nancy S. Ahlrichs. 2000. Davies-Black Publishing: Palo Alto, CA, ISBN 0891061487.
- *Love 'Em or Lose 'Em: Getting Good People to Stay*. Beverly L. Kaye & Sharon Jordan-Evans. 1999. Berrett-Koehler: ISBN 1576750736.
- *Successful Manager's Handbook*. Susan Gebelein, Lisa A. Stevens, Carol J. Skube, & David G. Lee. 2000. Personnel Decisions International: Minneapolis, ISBN 093852920X.
- *Strategic Interviewing: How to Hire Good People*. Richard R. Camp, Mary E. Vielhaber, & Jack L. Simonetti. 2001. Jossey-Bass: San Francisco, ISBN 0787953946.
- *The Boss's Survival Guide*. Bob Rosner, Allan Halcrow, & Alan S. Levins. 2001. McGraw-Hill: New York, ISBN 71362738.
- *What Color Is Your Parachute?* Richard Nelson Bolles. 2002. Ten Speed Press: Berkeley, CA.: ISBN 1580082424.
- *Winning the Talent Wars*. Bruce Tulgan. 2001. W.W. Norton: New York, ISBN 0393019586.

ITEM 13: Effectively Manages the Use of Technology to Increase Productivity

WHAT TO DO

- Determine the technological needs of your company, department, or team.
- Understand how technology functions as a tool to build and maintain relationships between your group and other departments.
- Determine how different automation processes might improve productivity in the company.
- Lay out a development plan that clearly specifies the technology (communication, software, hardware, etc.) that will help you obtain results.
- Analyze the benefits of different technological options, advancements, and programs to your company.
- Understand the budgeting process so that you can contribute realistic ideas for advanced technology that improve productivity and profitability.
- Ensure that each of your employees understands how to use the company's technology.

HOW TO DO IT

- Take the responsibility to manage your company's technological resources.
- Look for new technology that can simplify business processes and increase the pace to obtain end results.
- Determine the part technology plays in each step that must occur from the time a task enters your department until it leaves your department. Eliminate unnecessary steps.
- Identify interrelationships between divisions, departments, and throughout the company. Analyze the role technology currently plays or could play in improving the productivity of these relationships.
- Research each technology option thoroughly: Contact vendors, set up demonstrations, ask to view prototypes.
- Talk with an expert in the IT department about establishing and managing a budget and updating hardware, software, and other technology in your department.
- Assess the internal resources of other departments in your organization to see how their work processes are set up and what resources are available to you.
- Develop or ask for a written job description of responsibilities; identify what technical and functional knowledge is needed for each responsibility.
- Clearly communicate to your employees the steps and procedures of each automated task that you currently use in accomplishing projects and producing results.

HOW TO USE THIS SKILL FURTHER

- Seek input from those in your organization known for improving productivity through the use of technology.
- Ask peers about the computer technology they use and how it benefits them and their department.
- Meet with someone in the IT department. Ask him or her to give you some guidance about the technological options available to you.

RESULTS YOU CAN EXPECT

- The productivity of your department may increase.
- The revenue of your organization may increase.
- You may discover other talents in yourself to further increase the productivity of your work unit or organization.

READINGS

- *22 Management Secrets to Achieve More With Less.* John H. Zenger. 1997. McGraw-Hill: New York, ISBN 0070727171.
- *Improving Staff Productivity: Great Ideas to Increase Profits.* Benjamin Harrison Carter. 1999. PSI Research–Oasis Press: Central Point, OR, ISBN 1555714560.
- *Managing Human Resources: Productivity, Quality of Work Life, Profits.* Wayne F. Cascio. 1997. McGraw-Hill: New York, ISBN 0070119449.
- *Organizing Your Work Space: A Guide to Personal Productivity.* Odette Pollar, Debbie Woodbury, & Ralph Mapson. 1999. Crisp Publications: Menlo Park, CA, ISBN 1560525223.
- *Skill Wars, Winning the Battle for Productivity and Profit.* Edward E. Gordon. 1999. Butterworth-Heinemann: Woburn, MA, ISBN 0750672072.
- *Successful Manager's Handbook.* Susan Gebelein, Lisa A. Stevens, Carol J. Skube, & David G. Lee. 2000. Personnel Decisions International: Minneapolis, ISBN 093852920X.
- *The 80/20 Principle: The Secret to Success by Achieving More With Less.* Richard Koch. 1999. Doubleday: New York, ISBN 0385491743.
- *The Service Profit Chain: How Leading Companies Link Profit and Growth to Loyalty, Satisfaction, and Value.* James L. Heskett, W. Earl Sasser, & Leonard A. Schlesinger. 1997. Free Press: London, ISBN 0684832569.
- *Zapp!: The Lightning of Empowerment: How to Improve Quality, Productivity, and Employee Satisfaction.* Jeff Cox (Contributor), William C. Byham (Preface). 1998. Fawcett Books: New York, ISBN 0449002829.

ENDNOTES

1. M. Goldsmith & C. Walt. "Developing Technological Savvy." In *Leader to Leader.* Jossey-Bass and the Drucker Foundation: San Francisco, Winter, 1999.

2. Technology, United States, 35.

3. Products and services, Mexico, 46.

4. Products and services, United States, 24.

5. Products and services, United States/England/Norway 49.

6. Pharmaceutical, United States, 41.

7. Information from interview with MG CMDT USAWC Robert R, Ivany conducted by Cathy Greenberg. December 2002. This information does not represent the opinions of the United States Army.

8. Government, United States, 27.

9. Investments, United States, 27.

10. Telecommunications, United States, 36.

11. Telecommunications, United States, 34.

5 BUILDING PARTNERSHIPS[1]

The hierarchical model of leadership, once so prevalent in organizations around the world, is being replaced with a new kind of leadership that relies on partnerships[2] and persuasion through the power and value of ideas. Global leaders will use influence rather than command and control management as their operating style. They will let go of the hierarchy while not abdicating leadership, and they will extend their spheres of influence outside the organization to other companies, industries, and countries that are predicated on financial models that underscore the accountability of the partnership.

Business boundaries are becoming looser, and communities are converging across organizations, regions, and industries. Electronic commerce transcends time, geography, and culture. As alliances, partnerships, mergers, and acquisitions continue to increase and industries restructure, new communities of business will be formed. Worldbid.com, which facilitates 24-hour access to local, national, and international markets, is an example of a growing community of business networks that serve to link trade sectors around the globe.

Within this increasingly interconnected global environment, the ideal leader of the future will be a person skilled at building partnerships inside and outside the organization. There is probably no better illustration of what it means to build a global partnership than that of the relationship between Presidents Ronald Reagan and Mikhail Gorbachev, which, in the 1980s, after four decades of discourse, ended the Cold War between the United States and Russia. In the 40 years that this war was waged, these two great blocks of power formed two extensive military operations: the North Atlantic

Treaty Organization (NATO) created by western powers in 1949 and the Soviet-dominated Warsaw Pact established in 1955. After a series of summit talks between the two super-power leaders, which began in 1985, the two leaders agreed to eliminate much of their countries' nuclear missiles, and by 1987, the arms race to accumulate advanced military weapons was ended.

CREATING TRUST

To begin building partnerships, global leaders must first establish trust with coworkers and employees. To do so, the leader should treat coworkers as partners, not competitors, by sharing knowledge openly and honestly, and establishing an enduring relationship of trust. Without trust, relationships are based on competition, which eliminates the possibilities for collaboration of ideas and resources between people. With trust, leaders can work together toward a common purpose.

Trust takes time to build. Yet in today's turbulent business environment, time is a luxury. Global leaders are forced to gain and give trust quickly, or they will lose opportunities. For instance, prior to this past decade many leaders functioned in departmental silos within their organization. Often to the detriment of the company, leaders hoarded their most talented employees, and as a result, these individuals weren't promoted and the company's growth was compromised. Especially in less siloed organizations, leaders are beginning to understand that sharing resources leads to the maximum benefit for all.

It helps to set up forums that allow for a natural sharing of knowledge, ideas, and talents. Recently, at a Leadership Dialogue Series held by the co-authors, one CEO revealed how his organization is promoting the crosspollination of knowledge. Each quarter, the senior executive team convenes and lists the top ten talents that they have in each of their functional areas. They look across the organization to see where else the talent might be leveraged. Through these forums, the team has built the trust and confidence in each other that makes them capable of sharing and helping in other areas in the company. This is not something that leaders do naturally. The inclination is to hoard talent, because leaders don't trust that talent will be leveraged properly in other areas of the organization. In this CEO's organization, they share talent, because the forum has been set up to allow the sharing to happen naturally.

To build trust, these leaders respect the confidences of others. They share their own intentions, and they act quickly, yet they are cautious, choosing wisely what information to share and with whom. In most interactions, they will lean toward trust and open communication, because they know that people who are informed can contribute more to the organization. For instance, prior to the merger of two large pharmaceutical companies, senior executives participated in a Leadership Dialogue Series process in which each executive listed the top ten talents of each of their functional areas and then decided where the talent should be shared during the merger. The results were very positive. Not only was the merger more effective, but more people participated in the merger. The talent sharing enabled the crosspollination between the three participating eastern states, smoothing out the transition across the organization.

KEEPING IT POSITIVE

Successful global leaders create an atmosphere that encourages innovation and open communication. They welcome constructive feedback and dialogue. Although it's easy to become cynical about one's company and coworkers, effective global leaders realize that destructive comments about other people and groups undermine trust in partnerships, and thus they discourage destructive comments.

> They have good conflict resolution. They stay cool. They help people manage conflict. They don't take sides. They get people to communicate and work toward a constructive end. They can referee.[3]

The global leaders of the future are role models for avoiding unnecessary, negative comments about their coworkers, the organization within which they work, and other organizations. These leaders realize that bashing others is a bad habit that gives people a poor impression of them and the company, and that it creates an atmosphere of cynicism and apathy that undermines any possibility of change. Effective global leaders provide recognition and support for people who have the courage to tell the hard truth before issues become disasters.

> One success story has to do with our collaboration with another company on the marketing of a drug. In order to take this drug and make it better, each of our companies had to respect and understand the level of control each party wanted. We needed to know the expertise that each organization could contribute. Also, we had to know what each party wanted and we had to have mutual respect and communication. We had to see the big picture.
>
> An example of a failure is the three aborted attempts to merge two large pharmaceutical companies. These collaborations failed because of interpersonal disputes on the senior level. There were personality differences with the leaders. These leaders could not get along with each other due to history, ego, ambition, et cetera. They could not see the greater, common good—the "big picture."[4]

FORGING PARTNERSHIPS AND ALLIANCES ACROSS THE COMPANY

Building partnerships and alliances is more important not only in relationships within departments of the organization; it has become more important for relationships *across* the organization. As the work environment has become more complex, it has become necessary to coordinate activities with crossfunctional teams and not just rely on the traditional hierarchy.

> ...We had a start-up company with the job of purchasing pieces of jets. They started with five people and have grown to over 400 with a total turnover of approximately 450 million dollars. Many departments, such as sales, marketing, and production, pitched in to get this complicated business to work successfully. An example of a failure is what is happening at another center.... The main reason why these operations failed is because we were not collaborative.[5]

PARTNERING WITH DIRECT REPORTS

The traditional assumptions that have "bonded" employees with organizations are changing rapidly. For instance, layoffs, downsizing, and restructuring have created an environment in which employees no longer expect that their organizations will provide them with lifetime job security. As a result of this diminishing expectation, workers' "blind" loyalty to the companies that employ them has decreased.

Today, almost all high-potential leaders see themselves as "free agents," not as "employees" (in the traditional sense).[6] They see the leader of the future as a person who can build "win-win" relationships and who is sensitive to their needs for personal growth and development. In return, they feel not only a desire but also a responsibility to deliver value back to the leader and to the organization. In simple terms, they see the leader of the future as their *partner*, not their *boss*!

As Peter Drucker has expressed, one of the great challenges for leadership in the future will be the management of knowledge workers. Knowledge workers are people who know more about what they are doing than their manager knows.[7] The managers of knowledge workers of the future will have to be good partners. *They won't have a choice!* If they are not great partners, they won't have great people.

PARTNERING WITH COWORKERS

One of the great challenges for the leader of the future is breaking down traditional boundaries that limit mobility, ideas, and growth, such as longstanding, ingrained hierarchical perimeters that prevent employees and executives from communicating openly and honestly, and the borders that competition has instilled that keep company departments from collaborating.

The successful leader of the future will share people, capital, and ideas across the organization. People need to be shared so that they can develop the expertise and breadth needed to manage the entire organization. Capital needs to be shared so that mature businesses can transfer funds to high-growth businesses. Ideas need to be shared so that everyone in the organization can learn from both successes and mistakes in the most efficient way possible. As the world becomes more complex, this type of integration becomes more important and has great benefits for the CEO and the organization.[8] The CEO is rewarded by the success of the entire organization, not just the success of any one unit.

While these advantages are easy to see from the vantage point of the CEO, they can be more difficult to execute from the position of the lower-level manager. At Anthem East, President Marjorie Dorr recognized this challenge and initiated a campaign in which associates could present ideas focused on high-growth business opportunities to the Anthem East Leadership Team (the senior executive team). In this way, Marjorie was helping the organization capture business-external opportunities. If the idea won its budget from the executive team, it was implemented by a team of associates. If the idea did not win its budget, it was still a great learning experience for the associate, who would learn from the process of putting together the idea and the budget, and by presenting the plan to the leadership team. It also put younger executives and high-potentials in front of the leadership team. Thus it was a win-win for the individual, regardless of whether or not the idea was integrated into the organization.

Leaders at all levels have to *learn* to share people, capital, and ideas. In some cases they must choose to experience a short-term loss so that the organization can achieve a long-term gain. In the past, many leaders were taught to compete with colleagues for people, resources, and ideas. They have been rewarded for "winning" this competition. In the future, leaders must learn to collaborate with colleagues across the organization. The success of the larger organization will depend upon the leaders' abilities to become great partners with their coworkers. In many cases the participants in our research believed that developing partnerships with coworkers was an even bigger challenge for leaders than developing partnerships with direct reports.

Partnering with Managers

Other than the CEO, every leader in the organization has a manager. The changing role of leadership will mean that the relationship between managers and direct reports will have to change in *both* directions. Not only will managers need to change, direct reports (who also may be leaders) will need to change. Many leaders of the future will be operating more like the managing director of an office in a consulting firm than the operator of an independent small business. This is true not only in the business sector, but also in the human services sector. The new leader of the United Way, Brian Gallagher, recently described the ideal future leaders of this organization as partners *leading in a network, not managers leading in a hierarchy.*[9]

A consulting firm that could be a benchmark in partnering between junior and senior people is McKinsey and Company. At McKinsey, a director may often have less detailed knowledge about a client than does a more junior principal. Leaders at all levels are trained to do what is in the best interest of their clients. If they are given a directive that they believe is not in the best interest of their clients, they are taught that they are *obligated* to challenge it. This philosophy at McKinsey teaches leaders at all levels to have very adult and responsible relationships with their managers.

While partnering with management can be a lot more complex than "taking orders," it is becoming a requirement, not an option. When direct reports know more than their managers, they have to learn how to influence "up" as well as "down" and "across."

BUILDING TEAMS

Companies that seek a competitive advantage through their people must develop relationships between leaders, managers, and employees that encourage a feeling of partnership. At a leadership program for generating teamwork, one leader creatively initiated these relationships and defined team roles by giving out symbolic salt and pepper shakers and tiny flashlights at the meeting. The salt and pepper shakers symbolized each individual's need to spice up and add flavor to the team; the flashlights symbolized that each leader would be the guiding light for his or her team. Holding the teamwork program and accentuating it by giving out these gadgets showed team members that while the president was serious about what the teams needed to do to crosspollinate with each other and work with the leaders, she wanted it to be a fun learning experience. The result was great: The president had the highest rating of employee satisfaction the company had seen in years.

Skilled people want to have a say in how their jobs are structured, how the company is doing, and what it is planning for the future. They often respond well to team-based and influence-based leadership. However, the hierarchical and bureaucratic structures of many companies can make this quite difficult on site. Predicated on a merger, the president of Anthem East, Marjorie Dorr, took her entire leadership team on a leadership journey to the swamplands in Florida to move her team to the next level of leadership. For three days, the team spent their days canoeing through the swamps. They had meager food, no place to sleep, no bathrooms, and just the clothes on their backs. At night when they pulled into camp, they built their shelter. Marjorie's goal for this adventure was to make the team understand that they need each other to survive. Although some of the team had not wanted to make the trip, they pulled together. They came back reinvigorated, and they now knew they could rely on each other even in the direst of circumstances. After the trip, the operational bottom line improved significantly, and each leader responded well to team-based and influence-based leadership. It wasn't just titles that were important to them anymore. Participating in the outing changed how the individuals respected each other and how they behaved with each other.

As companies look for more innovative ways to grow, they are going to be entering into more unique relationships with their colleagues and other companies through alliances and partnerships. Therefore, the idea of team building is still going to be around for a while. Leaders need to be able to get the most out of groups of people in order to get things done as well as be able to make sure that each individual person feels valued. This is true teamwork.[10]

Effective global leaders encourage two-way flows of information and feedback, leading to wider ownership of projects and ideas, more participatory management, and more consensual decision making. In most traditional, hierarchical organizations, this type of system is not set up. For instance, before the Leadership Dialogue Series, executives at Anthem didn't share resources, nor did leaders participate in management from a crossfunctional perspective. During the series, leaders gathered for one evening a month to talk about the challenges and decisions they faced that needed the participation of other managers in the room. The participants arrived with their challenges prioritized, all issues were then put on a flip chart and prioritized by impact on the ROI. After a discussion, each manager voted on the issues. In this way, decisions were made more quickly by the entire team. Because the company had been set up for individual problem solving, this was an entirely new process—and it worked well. The leadership meetings are now a natural part of the leadership team's decision-making practice.

Often, to kick-start a participative, crossfunctional meeting structure, leaders must put into place an artificial infrastructure, such as a leadership team or titular head that meets on a regular basis. With time, the new practice becomes a natural part of the company's infrastructure. For instance, at a large healthcare organization, a leadership team effort across the functional groups for enrollment, marketing, e-commerce, IT, and strategy was put in place. The heads of each group met weekly to plan the budget for the coming fiscal year. Over time and with great success, this crossfunctional status meeting has become a regular part of the ongoing planning process for the company.

In addition to planning the budget, the leaders from the different areas of this large healthcare organization have put together a dependency matrix of projects, roles, and responsibilities for each leader. This matrix is the basis upon which they delegate authority and responsibility to strong internal teams with complementary skills and upon which is based an impact chart of individuals, teams, and functional groups that, although not participating, are impacted by projects and/or changes in the leader's area. The leaders create a liaison relationship with these impacted groups, who become project participants either by completing the impact matrix survey or by attending future meetings in which the issue is discussed. These groups are responsible for participating, which negates finger pointing and blaming on the basis of not being informed and not being part of the decision process.

In my previous job, I was the general manager for four years. At first, the department heads were very competitive with each other. But over the four years, we began to collaborate more and work together with a team approach.

We shared accountability and set the example of working as a team—not individual initiative. The results of this teamwork were more profitability, customer satisfaction, employee retention, and quality service.[11]

CREATING NETWORKS OUTSIDE THE ORGANIZATION

Building partnerships and alliances of all kinds will be far more important in the future than it was in the past. Many organizations that seldom formed alliances in the past are regularly forming alliances today.

The airline industry is an example of a networking success. Major competitors had to collaborate in designing software and hardware. They needed to form a joint venture.[12]

This trend of forging long-lasting external alliances and partnerships based on mutual trust, respect, and interests will be even more dramatic in the future.

The changing role of customers, suppliers, and partners has dramatic implications for future global leaders. In the past it was clear who "friends" (customers and partners) and who "enemies" (competitors) were. In the future these roles will become more blurred.

I believe the business stream will exist less of one huge company with a few affiliates, and there will be more companies with many affiliates. Affiliations will be less formal, and the organizations will be flatter with a tremendous amount of structural flexibility. These affiliated organizations will have to work together to anticipate and proactively implement changes as assumptions are reevaluated.[13]

In fields as diverse as energy, telecommunications, and pharmaceuticals, the same organization may be a customer, supplier, partner, or competitor. Informal strategy includes building a network of unplanned and unstructured communication between leaders in different parts of the world.

In this "new world" the ability to build positive, long-term, win-win relationships with many organizations becomes a critical and key talent. Defeating an "enemy" who may turn out to be a potential customer can prove to be a short-term victory.

Global leaders must be relationship driven...[They must] build networks to deliver results and work with others, including competitors, customers, employees.... They must have the ability to understand that someone who is their customer one day may be their competitor the next day and vice versa. This is the whole key to the network.[14]

PARTNERING WITH CUSTOMERS

As companies have become larger and more global, there has been a shift from buying standalone products to buying integrated solutions.[15] One reason for this shift is economy of scale. Huge retail corporations, like Home Depot and Wal-Mart, do not want to deal with thousands of vendors. They prefer to work with fewer vendors who can deliver not only products but systems for delivery that are customized to meet their needs. A second reason is the convergence of technology. Many customers now want "network solutions," not just hardware and software.

As relationships with their customers continue to change, leaders from supply organizations will need to become more like partners and less like salespeople. The trend is a shift toward building long-term customer relationships, not just achieving short-term sales. For example, a large healthcare provider recently went through a process of vendor partnering in which each vendor was asked to partner with the customer by adhering to specific quality standards and price ranges for their products. In return, the vendor would be put at a priority position on the customer's vendor list. Companies that were interested in moving from a transaction relationship to a partnership agreed to the long-term relationship with the client. Those that didn't were cut off the vendor list. The relationship benefited the vendors because they became priority suppliers to the customer; it benefited the customer, whose supplier list went from 400-plus vendors to about 150. The sustainable, high-level partnership thus maximized opportunities for both customer and supplier.

This trend towards partnerships means that suppliers need to develop a much deeper understanding of the customer's total business. They must be willing to look at the big picture in terms of delivery and reliability. They must make many small sacrifices to achieve a large gain. In short, they will need to act like partners.

At Accenture, the leadership has built in the practice of sharing risk and responsibility with the client. Depending on its needs, Accenture partners with its customers by establishing teams comprised of individuals from both Accenture and the client organization. These teams are responsible for the project, and the relationships go on for the life of the project, usually one to five years. Thus Accenture uses a team-building method to partner with its customers.

PARTNERING WITH SUPPLIERS

As the shift toward integrated solutions advances, leaders will have to change their relationship with suppliers. A great example is IBM. "A growing percentage of IBM's business now involves customized solutions incorporating non-IBM products and services. While the idea of IBM selling non-IBM products was almost unheard of in the past, it is now becoming commonplace—to the benefit of customers and, in the long run, to IBM itself."[16] The same trend is occurring in the pharmaceutical and telecommunications world.

In a world in which a company sold standalone products, partnering with suppliers was not only seen as unnecessary, it may have been viewed as unethical! The company's job was to "get the supplier down" to the lowest possible price in order to increase margins and profitability. Leaders who partnered with suppliers may well have been viewed as "helping the enemy" or having a "conflict of interest." Today, many leaders realize that their success is directly related to their supplier's success. In fact, Northrop Grumman, one of America's leading defense contractors, actually includes commitment to suppliers as one of its core values.

Today, suppliers are often seen as key partners. Leaders of the future will be able to transcend differences and focus on a common good—serving the ultimate end user of the product or service. For instance, in order to bring the client whole solutions, Accenture has created partnerships and working alliances with manufacturers of hardware and software. In these instances Accenture leaders might bring representatives from their vendor companies as part of the Accenture team. These representatives participate in the discussion of the client's strategy and suggest the possible technological solutions that would be provided by the suppliers. In this way, the client sees an integrated organization that works in partnership with its vendors.

Another way in which Accenture creates value for the client and provides customers to its suppliers is through second-party alliances with its vendors. For instance, Accenture might be asked to implement an e-commerce system. It would then create the Web interface, implement the technology infrastructure, and help the client acquire hardware and software to support the client's strategic set of initiatives. Because Accenture has a second-party alliance with IBM or Microsoft, for instance, it can help the client procure hardware and software at discounted prices. The benefits to the client are threefold: It does not have to deal separately with many suppliers, Accenture can provide better discounts on hardware and software, and it also has the opportunity to work with proven Accenture vendors.

Critical to working with suppliers, especially suppliers who were at one time competitors, is recognizing that when the company is at risk or is experiencing a failure, finger-pointing, scapegoating, and blaming are not productive options. However, these tactics are used, as was the case in the 1990s when Firestone and Ford blamed each other for the malfunctioning Explorer. To combat such challenges, one car manufacturer has offered to teach process skills and quality skills to its suppliers. This offer was revolutionary, because the car industry is historically competitive. Now that there are fewer vendors, suppliers, and car companies, because they've merged and integrated, the common good is paramount. In such instances, looking at suppliers as key partners is critical behavior change for companies.

PARTNERING WITH COMPETITORS

The most radical change in the role of leader as partner has come in the area of partnering with competitors. This has moved from the unthinkable to the commonplace. For instance, Digital Equipment Corporation and Hewlett-Packard were staunch competitors.

After Digital Equipment Corporation integrated with Compaq in the late 1990s, Compaq merged with Hewlett-Packard. In these merger situations, competitive companies merge because they have market opportunities or market share to gain by the alliance.

Mergers between competitors start contentiously, but usually within two to three years into the merger process, the relationship changes and the collaboration creates something very valuable to the market.

Another style of collaboration between possible competitors is co-branding. The impetus for the idea of co-branding often starts out as a competitive challenge. How will the company market its product? Does it emphasize the product or what is in the product? For instance, many products now put the Equal (artificial sweetener) co-brand on their package. Equal takes a back seat as the secondary brand on the product, yet the collaboration benefits Equal as well as the product that carries its brand.

A unique collaborative effort to boost the building economy in San Diego, California, was instigated in the 1990s by the San Diego Builder's Association. The Association started a house-raising competition in which teams of up to 700 people were to build a house in four hours. Vendors participated by donating materials, and unions worked together on the same sites. The competition created a media hype for the housing market, because they were able to build the houses cheaply. The vendors, builders, and unions participated together in the competition because the survival of the building community was at risk. The result was increased unity, new and improved methods of construction, and a positive impact on the construction economy in San Diego.

Most of the high-potential leaders that we interviewed saw competitors as potential customers, suppliers, and partners. Few had clear lines of demarcation. While there are still some noted exceptions to this trend (e.g., Coca-Cola and Pepsi), the direction of the curve is very clear. Most organizations that rely on knowledge workers have varied and complex relationships with competitors.

When today's competitors may become tomorrow's customers, the definition of "winning" changes. People have memories. Unfairly "bashing" competitors or striving to ruin their business could have harsh long-term consequences.

Competitor bashing is common practice among large hardware and software vendors versus large consulting vendors. Many companies offer consulting and strategy services, while other companies offer hardware and software services and free consulting. The company that offers the free consulting may tell the customer that the expense of a consulting service is greater than necessary. The consulting company may claim that "you get what you pay for with free services." Both of these methods lead to confusion for the client. In this case it is the responsibility of the leader in the customer organization to determine what will lead to quantitative value for his or her organization. These leaders must understand all the quantification elements of each competitor in order to equate one against the other and to distinguish between the products and services offered. One method of accomplishing this is to list ten necessary characteristics and base the decision on whether or not the competitors offer these as part of their products and services. However, in any case, the negative comments lead to increased animosity between the competitors and leave little room for future collaborations.

While competitors should not expect collusion or unfair practices, they should expect integrity, respectful treatment, and fair dealing.

The effective global leader of the future will create a network of relationships to achieve organizational goals and objectives. They will get input and buy-in from all levels, including clients and suppliers, before global goals and objectives are fully adopted and incorporated into short-term and medium-term projects and long-term strategies.

These leaders will build and reinforce new matrices of real and virtual teams and projects. Employees will report to many different leaders, who will focus on people, relationships, and processes, not just ideas, data, and products.

Effective global leaders will seek and build tactical and strategic alliances, joint ventures, and partnerships with external counterparts around the world. They will outsource nonproprietary work to specialized, third-party providers.

A key characteristic for global leaders of the future is the ability to manage outsourced corporate resources, which are expected to account for a far higher percentage of overall available resources than they are today.[17]

As reengineering, restructuring, and downsizing lead to a world in which outsourcing of all but core activities becomes the norm, the ability to negotiate complex alliances and manage networks of relationships will become a critical skill for many leaders of the future.

CONCLUSION

Building partnerships is a difficult task. It involves negotiations and open communication about each party's roles and responsibilities, and it also entails taking risks and believing that each party involved in the relationship will meet its obligations. Three necessary components to all partnerships are

1. Belief—in the partner's capabilities, skills, and promises.
2. Trust—that the partner will follow through on commitments.
3. Accountability—that the partner will be responsible for any shortcomings.

In addition, there must be a foundation in place by which to measure each partner's success, and no party should be held totally responsible for any outcomes, whether they be positive or negative. To this end, it is critical to establish the necessary characteristics, responsibilities, and roles at the front end of the relationship. One solution is to have each partner create a matrix of activities to be achieved; the skills, talents, and competencies needed; and, if possible, the names of individuals who will fill each role. To lessen the risk, each partner should fill in the matrix before the financial model is agreed upon. For instance, one partner may take 70 percent of responsibility for the project, while the other partner takes 30 percent. The financial model must underscore this relationship, or the partnership will be unlikely to work.

The trends toward more partnering are reinforcing each other. For example, as employees feel less job security, they begin to see suppliers, customers, and competitors as potential employers. The fact that leaders need to learn more about these other organizations, build long-term relationships, and develop win-win partnerships means that the other organizations are even more likely to hire the leaders. In many cases this is seen as a positive, not a negative, by both organizations. As the trend toward outsourcing increases, it becomes more difficult to determine who is a customer, supplier, direct report, manager, or partner.

Most high-potential leaders believe that the leader of the future will need to be far more skilled than the leader of the past at building relationships. In many ways the "old world" was simpler. Telling workers (who know less than we do) what to do is a lot simpler than developing relationships with partners (who know more than we do). Being able to work in a "silo"—a position in which the employee doesn't believe he or she needs to know what's going on in the rest of the corporation, like a low-level accountant—is a lot simpler than having to build partnerships with peers across the organization. "Taking orders" from managers is a lot simpler than having to challenge ideas that are not going to meet customer needs. Selling a product to customers is a lot simpler than providing an integrated solution. Getting the lowest price from suppliers is a lot simpler than understanding their complex business needs. Vying with competitors is a lot simpler than having to develop complex customer-supplier-competitor relationships.

As organizations expand across the globe, global leaders preside over workers located anywhere in the world, and in an alliance or partnership, they may have to generate results from staff in other companies, with different corporate cultures, styles, and reporting relationships. As such, global leaders must build teams and create networks to accomplish organizational goals. By exploring and building partnerships and relationships with companies and individuals within and outside their organizations, global leaders add incredible value to and continue the success of the company.

BUILDING PARTNERSHIPS AND ALLIANCES: HOW DIBONA DOES IT[18]

In April 1990, G. Fred DiBona, Jr., was named president and CEO of Independence Blue Cross (IBC). As president, Fred has spearheaded innovations in customer service, fiscal management, provider relations, and product development that have positioned IBC as a national leader in the health insurance industry. Fred's devotion to trust, partnerships and alliances, and community have helped make IBC the region's largest health insurer with more than 3 million members and over 7,000 employees.[19]

A Team Built on Trust

Over the years, Fred has put together a strong team of people. Many of his staff people have been with him for nearly 20 years. Because Fred has hired people whom he believes understand that they will succeed by making the team succeed, he trusts that his people have the best interests of the company at heart. Fred is not in a position of micro-management. He lets his people operate, and his door is open at those critical points when they need to come back and touch base. Most importantly, Fred's people understand and are comfortable with the delineation between a "Fred issue" and an individual issue, which allows Fred time for developing new concepts and strategies.

Cultivating Relationships

As a leader, Fred develops and cultivates internal staff relationships that are critical to the success of IBC's strategy. Fred stays close to the issues within IBC so that he can successfully implement strategies across the organization and the industry. For instance, in 2001 Fred worked with the IBC Leadership Team and the executive steering committee to develop and lead the vision process of an extremely aggressive e-commerce strategy. The resulting rollout took less than 90 days!

Fred takes a leadership role across the IBC family of businesses, including Amerihealth, Keystone, and IBC. He has developed relationships with all stakeholders so that he can understand and respond to issues through the extensive internal and external networks he shares in government, the community, and with customers, staff, and providers. He leverages his business savvy and skills in problem resolution to resolve challenging issues.

Community Involvement

Much of Fred's responsibility at IBC includes building partnerships and alliances outside the company. In April 2001 his contributions to the civic life of the region were recognized when he received the William Penn Award from the Greater Philadelphia Chamber of Commerce, the highest award given by the business community. In 1996, serving as chairman of the annual fund raising campaign of the United Way of Southeastern Pennsylvania, he was credited with reversing a six-year downward financial slide, raising nearly $50 million. In tribute to the success of this campaign, he was named United Way CEO of the Year for 1996.

BUILDING PARTNERSHIPS

ITEM 14: Treats Coworkers as Partners, Not Competitors

WHAT TO DO

- Recognize that cooperating and collaborating with others will enable you to achieve more than you could alone.
- Understand the functions of other departments and the roles of your coworkers in achieving company goals.
- Make explicit how others' goals are compatible with your goals and how their success benefits you.
- Increase effective communication and collaboration with people in your company.
- Commit to improve interdepartmental relationship and idea exchanging.
- Avoid labeling and stereotyping others.
- Recognize the value of a win-win orientation toward others.
- Create a relationship of trust between you and your coworkers.
- Recognize and encourage ongoing interactions among employees across the organization.
- Involve stakeholders in the development of your goals and plans.
- Invite ongoing feedback from your coworkers.

HOW TO DO IT

- Review the company goals, organizational structure, and departmental objectives.
- Explain to members of your organization how other groups' objectives relate to them.
- Identify others who are affected by the work of your group. Invite them to participate in or react to the development of your goals and plans.
- Hold joint meetings with other groups so that everyone can share their specific role, needs, and perspective.
- Look for ideas or suggestions of others that you agree with or can support.
- Try to balance offering your viewpoints with accepting others' ideas to build a sense of shared commitment to team decisions.

- Create opportunities for people to meet informally across levels and across departments to learn more about each other.
- Share credit with others.
- Encourage the free flow of business and technical information between organizations.
- If you offer resources or information to others, keep your word. Do what you say you are going to do.
- Show your trust in others by being open about your own mistakes or problems.
- Encourage your team to ask their counterparts for assistance in solving problems.
- Recognize others' assistance.
- Ask for feedback from others. When appropriate, use it. If you can't use it, explain to them why not.

HOW TO USE THIS SKILL FURTHER

- Encourage members of your work group to volunteer for crossfunctional teams so that they can meet their counterparts from other departments.
- Recognize, anticipate, and meet others' needs.
- Model the principle of supportive relations. Don't participate in putting down others; make each interaction one of support and respect.

RESULTS YOU CAN EXPECT

- You and others may work in a nondefensive manner to find solutions to problems. You may all be open and honest about your needs.
- You may get more done with less aggravation.
- Others may spontaneously offer you the resources or the information you need.

READINGS

- *Boards that Make a Difference: A New Design for Leadership in Nonprofit and Public Organizations*. John Carver. 1997. Jossey-Bass: San Francisco, ISBN 0787908118.
- *Corporate Cultures: The Rites and Rituals of Corporate Life*. Terrence E. Deal & Allan A. Kennedy. 2000. Perseus: Reading, MA, ISBN 0738203300.
- *Encouraging the Heart: A Leader's Guide to Rewarding and Recognizing Others*. James M. Kouzes & Barry Z. Posner. 1999. Jossey-Bass: San Francisco, ISBN 787941840.
- *Gung Ho! Turn On the People in Any Organization*. Kenneth H. Blanchard & Sheldon Bowles. 1997. William Morrow: New York, ISBN 068815428X.
- *Hidden Value: How Great Companies Achieve Extraordinary Results with Ordinary People*. Charles A. O'Reilly & Jeffrey Pfeffer. 2000. Harvard Business School Press: Boston, ISBN 875848982.

- *Thank God It's Monday!: 14 Values We Need to Humanize the Way We Work*. Ken Cloke, Joan Goldsmith, & Warren G. Bennis. 1996. McGraw-Hill: New York, ISBN 786310960.
- *The Essential Drucker*. Peter Ferdinand Drucker. 2001. HarperBusiness: New York, ISBN 66210879.
- *The Leadership Challenge: How to Keep Getting Extraordinary Things Done in Organizations*. James M. Kouzes, Barry Z. Posner, & Tom Peters. 1996. Jossey-Bass: San Francisco, ISBN 0787902691.

ITEM 15: Unites His or Her Organization into an Effective Team

WHAT TO DO

- Show and explain to individuals on your team how their jobs or tasks and responsibilities are interdependent.
- Help the group take ownership for their work as a team.
- Share the benefits that comes from teaming with individuals and the group.
- Demonstrate or express your belief that the group can work effectively as a team; create the expectation that individuals will work together.
- Develop a team made up of people with complementary strengths.
- Do not overlook individual needs. Attend to individual needs prior to or during the team process.
- When appropriate, keep feedback focused on the group's working relationships.
- Make sure your team members understand their responsibilities and their role within the organization.
- Get a sense from other team members of how they see their roles in contrast with other team members.
- Encourage individuals to look for and build on points of agreement.
- Explain and model team behaviors to the group.
- Recognize and reward those individuals who work well on a team.
- Have fun with your team.

HOW TO DO IT

- Get the team members to generate and agree to a set of ground rules for working together as a team.
- Encourage the group to agree on ways to handle team issues or conflicts among themselves.

- Explain (and model) that team members listen with interest to each other, do not interrupt, do not make team decisions without listening to everyone first, and act in a manner that values the diversity of people and ideas.
- Encourage individuals to look at each other as resources for the project or task they are working on, or for meeting the department objectives.
- Reward and recognize teams by celebrating successes or providing tangible rewards.
- Assess your ability to be a good team player; be a role model or work to improve your skills.
- Express positive comments about the team's ability to work together. Cite previous successes they have had in working together.
- Observe those managers who manage teams well, and ask them for advice.
- Ask the team members what they need from you to work better together.
- Ask to sit in on a meeting of a team known for working well together; take notes of what you observe and make suggestions to your team based on what you have seen.

HOW TO USE THIS SKILL FURTHER

- Take a management course in team building. Offer the group ideas on team building after you complete the course.
- Practice team building techniques with a group outside of work.
- Conduct a team building session with your team.

RESULTS YOU CAN EXPECT

- People may ask to be on your team.
- Employees may express their enthusiasm for being on your team.
- Quality and productivity of your team may improve.

READINGS

- *Leading Self-Directed Work Teams: A Guide to Developing New Team Leadership Skills*. Kimball Fisher. 1999. McGraw-Hill: New York, ISBN 0071349243.
- *Pioneering Organizations: The Convergence of Individualism, Teamwork, and Leadership*. Larry N. Davis & Chip R. Bell. 2000. Executive Excellence: Provo, UT, ISBN 1890009849.
- *Teaming Up*. Darrel Ray & Howard Bronstein. 1995. McGraw-Hill: New York, ISBN 0070516464.
- *Teams At the Top*. Jon R. Katzenbach. 1998. Harvard Business School Press: Boston, ISBN 0875847897.
- *The 17 Indisputable Laws of Teamwork: Embrace Them and Empower Your Team*. John C. Maxwell. 2001. Thomas Nelson: Nashville, TN, ISBN 0785274340.

- *The New Why Teams Don't Work: What Goes Wrong and How to Make It Right*. Harvey A. Robbins & Michael Finley. 2000. Berrett-Koehler: San Francisco, ISBN 1576751104.
- *The Performance Culture: Maximizing the Power of Teams*: Darrel Ray & Howard Bronstein. 2001. IPC Press: London, ISBN 0970950500.
- *Tips for Teams*: Kimball Fisher, Steven Rayner, & William Belgard. 1995. McGraw-Hill: New York, ISBN 0070212244.

ITEM 16: Builds Effective Partnerships Across the Company

WHAT TO DO

- Understand the functions of other departments and their roles in achieving company goals.
- Be clear about the importance of every individual and team to your organization's success.
- Make explicit how others' goals are compatible with your goals and how their success benefits you.
- Build teamwork among different groups across the organization through formal committees.
- Create a climate of trust between your department and other departments.
- Practice ethical and sensible organizational politics.
- Make each interaction with other departments one of support and respect.
- Recognize and encourage ongoing interactions among employees across disciplines.
- Foster an environment that utilizes constant communication, clarity of ideas, and performance plans that will encourage open communication between departments.
- Have strong communication pathways that keep everyone informed. Secretive behavior might be seen as politically motivated or self-motivated.
- When communicating with others, carefully select your words, anticipating the effect they will have.
- Involve stakeholders in the development of your goals and plans.
- Invite feedback from others.

HOW TO DO IT

Encourage the free flow of business and technical information between departments.
- Review the company goals, organizational structure, and departmental objectives.
- Explain to members of your organization how other groups' objectives relate to them.
- Increase your interaction with employees and colleagues in other departments.

- Hold joint meetings with other groups for all to share their specific roles and perspectives.
- Evaluate your staff on their willingness and ability to work as part of a team in the organization.
- Encourage your employees to develop relationships with people across the organization.
- If you offer resources or information to others, keep your word. Do what you say you are going to do.
- Show your trust in others by being open about your own mistakes or problems.
- Encourage your team to ask their counterparts for assistance in solving problems.
- Recognize and praise others' assistance.
- Identify individuals or groups who are affected by the work of your team, and invite them to participate in or react to the development of your goals and plans.
- Ask for feedback from others. When appropriate, use it. If you can't use it, explain to them why not.
- Communicate your support for your organization's mission outward and upward as well as in your own organization.

HOW TO USE THIS SKILL FURTHER

- Seek ways to further support others. Anticipate and meet their needs.
- Encourage members of your work group to volunteer for crossfunctional teams so that they can meet their counterparts from other departments.
- Volunteer to serve as a counselor in a community organization.
- Practice open communication with your spouse, family, and friends.

RESULTS YOU CAN EXPECT

- You may be asked to serve on planning teams and as an advisor outside your own organization.
- You may expect new assignments and opportunities that broaden your career in the company.
- Communications across departmental boundaries may increase.
- Departments may work more closely and efficiently, and thus become a unified company team.

READINGS

- *40 Tools for Cross-Functional Teams: Building Synergy for Breakthrough Creativity*. Walter J. Michalski & Dana G. King. 1998. Productivity Press: Portland, OR, ISBN 1563271982.
- *A Simpler Way*. Margaret J. Wheatley & Myron Kellner-Rogers. 1996. Berrett-Koehler: San Francisco, ISBN 1881052958.

- *Collaborative Creativity: Unleashing the Power of Shared Thinking*. Jack Ricchiuto. 1996. Oak Hill Press: Winchester, VA, ISBN 1886939128.
- *Dance Lessons: Six Steps to Great Partnerships in Business & Life*. Chip R. Bell & Heather Shea. 1998. Berrett-Koehler: San Francisco, ISBN 1576750434.
- *Diagnosing and Changing Organizational Culture: Based on the Competing Values Framework*. Kim S. Cameron & Robert E. Quinn. 1998. Addison-Wesley: Boston, ISBN 0201338718.
- *Journey to the Emerald City: Achieve a Competitive Edge by Creating a Culture of Accountability*. Roger Connors & Tom Smith. 1999. Prentice Hall: Upper Saddle River, NJ, ISBN 0735200521.
- *The Boundaryless Organization: Breaking the Chains of Organizational Structure*. Ron Ashkenas, Dave Ulrich, C. K. Prahalad, & Todd Jick. 1998. Jossey-Bass: San Francisco, ISBN 078790113X.

ITEM 17: Discourages Destructive Comments about Other People or Groups

WHAT TO DO

- Refrain from making destructive comments.
- Set a standard in your organization and sphere of influence of not allowing destructive comments.
- Explain how this standard aligns with your company's values; stress the importance of all employees behaving in alignment with these values.
- Manage in a way that recognizes and values diversity.
- Help people stay focused on performance or issues; stop them when they attack people or nonspecific "theys."
- Be clear about what is constructive appraisal and what is destructive criticism.

HOW TO DO IT

- Ask employees and colleagues to alert you when you make destructive comments.
- Discuss the standard at staff meetings, and hold employees accountable when negative comments are made.
- Give yourself an incentive to discourage destructive comments by considering what will happen if you withhold your leadership and allow the comments to continue.
- Encourage and reward people who speak to the point without being influenced by negative emotions or resorting to destructive comments.
- Ask peers, coworkers, and employees to be responsible for reminding each other to stick to the standard.

- Hold one-on-one meetings with people in your organization who persist in making negative comments; remind them of your expectations and that you need to see an immediate change in their behavior.
- When destructive comments are made, politely but firmly interrupt; stop people from using negative labeling or jargon about other people or organizations.
- Ask people to come up with ideas for expressing themselves in a positive way; reward their efforts with recognition and praise.
- Give constructive feedback in a positive way so that you are an example of how to give criticism without being destructive.
- Take the time to explain (in private as needed) why comments are destructive as opposed to critical; some people do not know the difference.
- Encourage people to consider the short-term and long-term consequences of their destructive comments before they make them.
- Discuss this company value at staff meetings (yours and those you attend); listen to the dialogue and address issues as they arise.
- Write a positive statement about this topic and keep it where you can see it daily.

HOW TO USE THIS SKILL FURTHER

- Be aware of your own behavior; observe when and about whom you make destructive comments.
- Make each interaction with your colleagues, employees, and other departments in the company one of support and respect.
- Make it a rule at your house not to allow your family to make destructive comments; apply the rule.

RESULTS YOU CAN EXPECT

- You may gain a reputation for being even-handed and positive.
- People may ask to work with you because of your positive influence.

READINGS

- *High Five! The Magic of Working Together*. Ken Blanchard, Sheldon M. Bowles, Don Carew, & E. Parisi-Carew. 2000. William Morrow: New York, ISBN 688170366.
- *How to Win Friends & Influence People*. Dale Carnegie, Dorothy Carnegie, & Arthur R. Pell. 1998. Pocket Books: New York, ISBN 0671027034.
- *People Skills*. Robert Bolton. 1986. Simon & Schuster: London, ISBN 067162248X.
- *Redefining Diversity*. R. Roosevelt Thomas. 1996. AMACOM: New York, ISBN 814402283.
- *The Consensus Building Handbook: A Comprehensive Guide to Reaching Agreement*. Lawrence Susskind, Sarah McKearnan, & Jennifer Thomas-Larmer. 1999. Corwin Press: Thousand Oaks, CA, ISBN 0761908447.

- *The Diversity Advantage: A Guide to Making Diversity Work*. Lenora Billings-Harris & Roger E. Herman. 1998. Oakhill Press: Winchester, VA, ISBN 188693925X.
- *The Magic of Dialogue: Transforming Conflict into Cooperation*. Daniel Yankelovich. 2001. Touchstone Books: Carmichael, CA, ISBN 0684865661.

ITEM 18: Builds Effective Alliances with Other Organizations

WHAT TO DO

- Recognize the advantages that come from teaming with individuals from other industries and countries.
- Seek ways to build mutually beneficial and long-term relationships with other internal and external organizations.
- Create a climate of trust between your company and other organizations, anticipating any work that may be done with them in the future.
- Recognize that it takes more effort to build a trusting business relationship when you are working with people from another business.
- Make each interaction with another company one of support and respect.
- Understand that every organization is a "human" organization. Get to know the key people who always seem to make a difference, and establish a rapport with them.
- Consider third parties as potential collaborators that would be mutually beneficial in terms of quality and/or competitiveness.
- Meet with colleagues from different companies and make explicit how their goals are compatible with your goals and how you can work together to eliminate redundancies and be more efficient.
- Network with people from other geographical areas. They may be more willing to share information if they don't see you as a direct competitor.
- Build teamwork among different groups inside and outside the organization through formal committees.
- Encourage employees to join professional associations where they can get to know people with whom they can share information about the market trend.
- Recognize and encourage ongoing interactions among employees across disciplines.

HOW TO DO IT

- Communicate your support for your company's mission outward and upward.
- Review the company goals, organizational structure, and departmental objectives.
- Explain to members of your organization how other company's objectives relate to them.
- Hold joint meetings with other companies for all to share their specific roles and perspectives.

- Identify organizations that are affected by the work of your company and invite them to participate in or react to your company's goals.
- If you offer resources or information to others, keep your word. Do what you say you are going to do.
- Ask for feedback from others. When appropriate, use it. If you can't use it, explain to them why not.
- Show your trust in others by being open about your own mistakes or problems.
- Explain to members of your organization how other groups' objectives relate to them and how they can work together.
- Encourage your employees to develop relationships with people from different organizations to help them achieve company goals and results.
- Seek ways to further support others. Anticipate their needs and meet them.
- Encourage people from your company to get to know people from other companies.

HOW TO USE THIS SKILL FURTHER

- Attend alliance-building and leadership workshops. Practice your skills with a group outside of work.
- Participate in friendship-building activities, such as sporting events, in order to develop long-term relationship with other organizations.
- Volunteer to join networking groups.

RESULTS YOU CAN EXPECT

- The productivity of your organization may increase.
- You may be asked to serve on planning teams and as an advisor outside your own organization.
- You may expect new assignments and opportunities that broaden your career in the company.

READINGS

- *Fast Alliances: Power Your E-Business*. Larraine D. Segil. 2000. John Wiley & Sons, New York, ISBN 471396834.
- *Free Market Fusion*. Glenn R. Jones. 1999. Cyber Publishing Group: Englewood, CO, ISBN 1885400683.
- *Instant Teamwork: Motivate and Energize Your Team Now!* Brian Clegg & Paul Birch. 1999. Kogan Page: London, ISBN 074942804X.
- *Intelligent Business Alliances: How to Profit Using Today's Most Important Strategic Tool*. Larraine D. Segil. 1996. Times Books: New York, ISBN 812924665.
- *International Management: Text and Case*. Paul W. Beamish, Allen Morrison, & Philip M. Rosenzweig. 1997. Richard D. Irwin: Burr Ridge, IL, ISBN 0256193495.

- *Teaming Up*. Darrel Ray & Howard Bronstein. 1995. McGraw-Hill: New York, ISBN 0070516464.
- *The Collaboration Challenge*. James E. Austin. 2000. Jossey-Bass: San Francisco, ISBN 0787952206.
- *The Leadership Challenge: How to Get Extraordinary Things Done in Organizations*. James M. Kouzes & Barry Z. Posner. 1996. Jossey-Bass: San Francisco, ISBN 0787902691.

ITEM 19: Creates a Network of Relationships that Help to Get Things Done

WHAT TO DO

- Be clear about the importance of every individual and team to your organization's success.
- Understand the functions of other departments and their roles in achieving company goals. Obtain this information through fellow colleagues.
- Meet with colleagues from different departments. Explain how their goals are compatible with your goals and how you can work together to eliminate redundancies and be more efficient.
- Build teamwork among different groups across the organization. Establish formal committees to achieve better results.
- Create a climate of trust between your department and other departments. Anticipate any work that may be done with them in the future.
- Recognize and encourage ongoing communication among employees across disciplines.
- Make each interaction with other departments one of support and respect.

HOW TO DO IT

- Review the company's goals, organizational structure, and departmental objectives with colleagues from other areas of the enterprise.
- Encourage the free flow of business and technical information between departments.
- Explain to members of your organization how other groups' objectives relate to theirs and how they can work together to help eliminate redundancies of work.
- Hold joint meetings with other groups for all to share their specific roles and responsibilities.
- Evaluate your staff on their willingness and ability to work as part of a team in the organization.
- Encourage your employees to develop relationships with people across the organization to help them achieve company goals and results.

- Identify others who are affected by the work of your group, and invite them to participate in or react to the development of your goals and plans.
- Communicate your support for your company's mission outward and upward as well as in your own organization.
- Encourage people around the company to get to know each other. Encourage your work group to volunteer for crossfunctional teams and to ask others for assistance in solving problems.
- Seek ways to further support others. Anticipate and meet their needs.

HOW TO USE THIS SKILL FURTHER

- Practice networking skills with people outside of work.
- Make each interaction you have one of support and respect.
- Participate in friendship-building activities, like sporting events and company celebrations, to develop long-term relationships with your coworkers, employees, and people in other organizations.

RESULTS YOU CAN EXPECT

- The productivity of your organization may increase.
- You may be asked to serve on planning teams and as an advisor outside your own organization.
- You may expect new assignments and opportunities that broaden your career in the company.

READINGS

- *21 Irrefutable Laws Of Leadership*. John C. Maxwell. 1998. Thomas Nelson: Nashville, TN, ISBN 785274316.
- *Beep! Beep!: Competing in the Age of the Road Runner*. R. Chip Bell & Oren Harari. 2001. Warner Books: New York, ISBN 446676543.
- *Danger in the Comfort Zone: From Boardroom to Mailroom--How to Break the Entitlement Habit That's Killing American Business*. Judith M. Bardwick. 1995. AMACOM: New York, ISBN 814478867.
- *The Magic of Dialogue: Transforming Conflict into Cooperation*. Daniel Yankelovich. 2001. Touchstone Books: Carmichael, CA, ISBN 0684865661.
- *The ROI of Human Capital: Measuring the Economic Value of Employee Performance*. Jac Fitz-Enz. 2000. AMACOM: New York, ISBN 814405746.
- *Teaming Up*. Darrel Ray & Howard Bronstein. 1995. McGraw-Hill: New York, ISBN 0070516464.
- *Trust in the Balance: Building Successful Organizations on Results, Integrity, and Concern*. Robert Bruce Shaw. 1997. Jossey-Bass: San Francisco, ISBN 0787902861.

ENDNOTES

1. Portions of this chapter were originally published in *Partnering: The New Face of Leadership*. Copyright © 2003 Larraine Segil, Marshall Goldsmith, James Belasco, AMACOM Books division of American Management Association, New York, NY. Reprinted by permission of the publisher. All rights reserved. *http://www.amacombooks.org*.

2. In this chapter, we use the term *partnership* to mean a short- or long-term business relationship for the purpose of achieving a goal—not necessarily to mean a legal entity.

3. Telecommunications, United States, 32.

4. Healthcare, France, 44.

5. Transportation, Canada, 47.

6. See "Coaching Free Agents." Goldsmith, Sommerville, & Greenberg-Walt. In *Coaching for Leadership*. Eds. Marshall Goldsmith, Laurence Lyons, and Alyssa Freas. 2000. Jossey-Bass. San Francisco.

7. Drucker, Peter. *The Essential Drucker*. HarperBusiness: New York, 2001, p. 78.

8. Ashkenas, Ron, Dave Ulrich, Todd Jick, & Steve Kerr. *The Boundaryless Organization*. Jossey-Bass: San Francisco, 1995.

9. Brian Gallagher, personal interview with Marshall Goldsmith, January 24, 2002.

10. Healthcare, United States, 33.

11. Pharmaceutical, United States, 41.

12. Technology, Poland, 39.

13. Technology, United States, 26.

14. Products and Services, United States/England/Norway, 49.

15. Goldsmith, Marshall. "On a Consumer Watershed." *Leader to Leader*, no. 5, Summer 1997. Drucker Foundation, Jossey-Bass: San Francisco.

16. Goldsmith, Marshall. "On a Consumer Watershed." *Leader to Leader*, no. 5, Summer 1997. Drucker Foundation, Jossey-Bass: San Francisco.

17. Investments, Taiwan, 32.

18. Information and quotes taken from interview with G. Fred DiBona, Jr., conducted by Cathy Greenberg, December 2001.

19. Information taken from G. Fred DiBona, Jr., Esq. Curriculum vitae, American Specialty Health press releases *(http://www.ashplans.com/NewsPress/content/Articles/2000/p_sep072000c.asp)* and Atlas Venture News and Events, *http://www.atlasventure.com/news_content.asp?ne_id=367*; *pr@navimedix.com*.

6

SHARING
LEADERSHIP

S hared leadership is rapidly emerging in the corporate world. With global expansion, intra-industry and inter-industry restructuring, and increasing numbers of mergers and flattening organizations, the need for dynamic flexibility and a broad base of knowledge and expertise is greater than ever. Shared leadership, by virtue of its use of the combined best of leaders' abilities, is being tested as one possible solution for meeting these challenging business needs.

PARTNERSHIPS AND MERGERS

As two or more companies unite, their executive management teams must integrate, and boards of directors must determine who will lead the new company. Many companies are electing to share this leadership between two (or more) people.

Global leaders of the future must have the ability to manage organizations in a non-hierarchical and multidimensional way. Future leaders will need special skills and much credibility in order to manage companies in this way, because it will be very unclear "who is the boss of whom."[1]

The executive team model is the most successful form of shared leadership to date. As merged companies grow exponentially in size and focus, so too does their need for a broader base of senior management expertise and experience. As part of mergers and acquisitions, companies incorporate a "leadership team strategy" into their plans and practices.

> One example of success was our 1997 marketing program. During that year, our marketing program changed a great deal. There was a collaborative effort between several departments. The sales and marketing, planning and analysis, and customer service departments worked together to develop strategies. Leaders from each of these groups shared their views, which helped to make it a financially successful year.
>
> The reason that some other collaborative leadership efforts fail could be due to the wrong mix of people. If the decision-making team is composed of some leaders with strong personalities who dominate the other leaders, there may be one-sided judgments made.[2]

When companies merge, either the separate leadership teams must work together effectively to determine a cohesive way of structuring their business practices or a new leadership team with equal representation is created.

For example, Intergraph Corporation and Bechtel share leadership in a partnership in which Intergraph supplies software, hardware, and technical assistance to support Bechtel's global engineering and construction projects. Kenan Communications joins with Accenture in delivering state-of-the-art billing and customer care solutions to communications providers worldwide. Both firms dedicate personnel who work together on client projects; Accenture personnel are trained in the Kenan suite of solutions. Another example is the partnership between Independence Blue Cross (IBC) and Highmark. These two companies share transaction processing to maximize strengths across their Blue Cross and Blue Shield network, thus serving both eastern and western Pennsylvania as separate companies within the National Blue Cross and Blue Shield Association. Other examples of shared alliance and partnership leadership can be found in the many strategic supplier relationships that formed in the past two decades.

MAXIMIZING TALENT

Shared leadership involves maximizing all of the human resources in an organization by empowering individuals and giving them an opportunity to take leadership positions in their areas of expertise.

Because things are so complex these days, we have to have successful collaborative leadership. We have to allow for different competencies in different areas. Each person participates with his/her skill, knowledge, and cultural background.... For example, I work with someone from India. He can explain how the Indians are thinking, and I can explain and show how the Swedes are working and thinking. He can take what he's learning about our culture and work habits back to his country and I can work more effectively with India.[3]

With more complex markets increasing the demands on leadership, the job in many cases is simply too large for one individual. It is hard to imagine that a single individual can excel at all of the competencies required for global leadership of the future. So, in order to be successful, leaders *need to identify the kinds of skills needed to run a company and have them at the top level. Also, leaders must know their limitations and be willing to listen to the experts.*[4]

For instance, at Electronic Ink, a company in Philadelphia that creates user interfaces for Web design, the role of CEO was too extensive for one leader. As a result, it was split into two positions with equal status and complementary skills sets and responsibilities. CEO Harold Hambrose is responsible for the technical side of the business and Chief Operating Officer (COO) Johanna Hambrose heads up marketing and communications. After splitting the role of CEO, the leaders built on the new team, hiring experts to head up research and development, architecture and design, and sales. Using the shared leadership model gave these leaders the opportunity to focus on the areas in which they are most talented, to hire team leaders, and thus develop a successful, well-rounded company.

Additionally, as many companies experience a transition from the old "top-down approach" of management to a flatter, more decentralized work environment, this style of leadership is becoming more common. In flattened organizations responsibility and accountability are shared at all levels of the company.

For example, Electronic Ink uses a flattened operating model to design digital solutions for its clients that will help increase their productivity. When the technical team meets with a client to discuss system goals and requirements, they meet in a room with a one-way mirror. On the other side of the mirror are the other teams that will be working on the project, usually the designers and sales executives. Although the technical people have the job of making the system work for the client, they are not capable of asking all the questions and getting all the nuances that are needed to make sure that the system meets every one of the client's needs. Thus, the teams responsible for the ergonomics, the interface, and the capacity of the system are behind the mirror passing questions, in real time via interactive media, to the technical team. In this way, everyone participates without overwhelming the client. The result is a flatter organization in which the client is not burdened by redundant meetings with several layers of the company.

Flattening also means that power, authority, and decision making are more widely and deeply dispersed, both laterally and vertically, giving each individual an opportunity to show his or her prowess in certain areas of the company. The global leaders who recognize, develop, and make use of the expertise of each individual will further the company's success.

THE VALUE OF COLLABORATION

In a world in which leading across a fluid network may become more important than leading from above a fixed hierarchy, being able to effectively share leadership is a requirement, not an option. Telling partners what to do and how to do it in an alliance structure may quickly lead to having no partners. All parties will have to be able to work together to achieve the common good.

As the number of partners in partnerships and alliances increases, demands for shared leadership increase exponentially. Many alliances can include 20 or more partners, complicating demands on leaders and reinforcing the need for collaborative leadership. *When there is failure in collaborative leadership, it is because there is no trust between the different parties. They are on different agendas. They are not driven by the same vision and there is no alignment.*[5]

The growing number of partnerships and alliances allows organizations with common objectives to work jointly on specific projects or engagements. Basic to the success of each partnership and alliance is an ability to work together; the leaders must be able to constructively collaborate. Often, new leadership teams are created, with representation from each of the partners in the alliance, requiring several leaders to work together effectively in a broad coalition.

For example, many companies have a board of directors, which is comprised of 10 to 20 people who have different alliance relationships to the company of which they are board members. These boards are put together by the company to incorporate different perspectives and expertise into the creation of a company strategy or vision. Before Drexel University merged with MCP Hahnemann University in July 2002, its boards of directors were separate entities. The members of the MCP Hahnemann board were from the medical field, hospital systems, and local businesses that supported the hospitals. The Drexel board was a board of companies that supported the community that Drexel served. Its board was comprised mainly of business people and attorneys from local legal firms. To ensure the merger, the two boards had to work together in an alliance; however, there was not yet a trusting, working relationship established between them, and there was great concern as to how to create an alliance of the two boards that would support the merger. The solution was to hold a series of combined meetings in which the Drexel and MCP boards met collectively. The chairs collaborated on the agenda prior to the meetings. In so doing, they created an alliance and organizational structure that helped execute the merger. This merger placed complicated demands on the leadership that were met with a strategy of cooperation.

With the rapid shifts occurring in the business marketplace, different skills from different partners will need to be leveraged at different times in order to create competitive advantage in short time frames. There will be no "one right way" of working; there will instead be the need for rapidly finding the "best way at this time," a process which only a truly collaborative environment can facilitate.

FOSTERING A TEAM ENVIRONMENT

It is not realistic to expect any one individual to possess all the various iterations of strengths and skills necessary to lead a company through a decade or more of roller coaster markets, global expansion, and economic changes. Therefore, successful global leaders will *allow employees and associates to bring a lot more to the workplace*.[6]

Knowing that the company's success depends on the knowledge sharing and collaboration of its people, the global leader of the future will strive to create an environment in which people focus on the larger good of the team and company rather than on short-term personal gains.

> An example of a failure would be when our company tried to implement telecommunication globally. It failed because people didn't want to share resources. They wanted to own the resources.[7]

In developing the company's brand of leadership, the global leader of the future should concentrate on building a team of leaders who (1) feel a sense of ownership for the success of the business, and (2) can rely upon on each other's strengths during the different challenges the company will face.

> The successful examples that I have seen have involved organizations that require a leadership team that are not just order-takers. The global leaders need to surround themselves with a management team that they trust and empower, and the management teams need to share the responsibility for ownership of that company and feel the personal commitment to make it work. Successful collaboration means forming the right management team of people, people who will speak the truth even if it means disagreeing at times. However, they will have total commitment and support if the leader has to make decisions different from what they wanted.[8]

For instance, challenges might include a few years of a surge of technological innovation; then, the market may fall and there may be a period of cost-cutting; subsequently, there may be a takeover or an acquisition of another company that takes precedence.

Recently, a large healthcare provider invested in an insurance company whose customers were in different regions around the United States. The company didn't realize that healthcare markets in various parts of the country would respond differently to its product and marketing. In the marketplace where the provider was based, it had been particularly successful with an individual choice brand of insurance for families. However, this brand wasn't popular in the newly acquired regions, and the company acquired significant losses. Consequently, it went through a period of cost-cutting in an effort to divest itself of these regions. The company set up a division, headed by the COO, specifically to accomplish this. The work that the COO was doing in operations to maintain effective technical systems and operations had to be transferred to another person in the company. When the COO came back to the company's headquarters, the company was going through a period of technological investing. The COO did not have enough experience in this area, and so the company hired someone with expertise in the field to head this endeavor. Then a potential merger opportunity came up and the company hired another executive to lead it.

Over a period of just a few years, multiple things will hit a company. No one will be an expert on all of these situations, nor will one individual have the time to simultaneously handle the myriad of challenges that hit a company in any given year. For this reason, leaders in most companies will have the knowledge to be a generalist, but will expect, for periods of time, to be specialists who help the company work through certain situations. When leaders are asked to be specialists, they should surround themselves with a team of experts who under their guidance will give the advice and provide the talent that will get the job done. This team of experts will provide the knowledge necessary to survive and thrive throughout these challenges. *The most important element is being able to surround yourself with diverse people and creating an environment in which they can excel.*[9]

By publicizing themselves as part of a team and willingly sharing the limelight both inside and outside of the company, the global leader creates an environment in which people avoid "turfism." Thus, the company takes on a team quality rather than a star quality, and the perception by the outside world is that there is a competent, diverse group at the top who can leverage different strengths depending on what's happening in the business world.

SEI Investments promotes teamwork and eliminates turfism through the physical environment of the company, in which everybody at the company sits in an open space. There are no offices; not even CEO Al West has an office. He sits in the center of the office, surrounded by members of his team.

Another great example comes from the sports model of basketball star Michael Jordan, whose many championship titles attest to his philosophy. In every sport, there are great players who never win titles because they aren't part of the team. Michael believes that it's those great players who are willing to sacrifice small, personal victories for the greater good of the team who become champions. If a great player works with the team and doesn't take over the court, not only is a win more likely, but the credit goes to the team, not the individual, and the environment becomes one of collaboration rather than competition, of teamwork rather than turfism.

I had a business operation and I worked with a guy who ran a technology group. Together we worked to put in a huge new application. Our common goal was to get this in and get it to work. We shared resources, dealt with obstacles together, and we both owned it. There was an equal stake and we addressed it as such. We were both going to win or we were both going to lose.[10]

CONCLUSION

The topic of shared leadership is currently being vigorously debated. Questions have been raised regarding the usability and effectiveness of a collaborative leadership model, yet few answers have been provided. The global markets have provided vivid examples of success and failure, and a few whose fate has yet to be determined. Although shared leadership is presently being challenged, research findings have signaled that this will be the leadership model of the future. The most successful and well-known leadership partnership is that of Goldman Sachs' co-presidents John A. Thain and John L. Thorton. Since 1999, these two leaders have successfully accomplished what many leaders have been unable to do—shared leadership.

It is predicted that the sheer number and importance of alliances and networks will ensure that leadership will be widely shared in executive teams. Because all 15 dimensions of the global leader of the future are unlikely to reside in one super leader, competencies will have to be pooled among a leadership team, thereby creating the need for a new competence—sharing leadership.

In addition, as new pressures emerge for collective responsibility and results accountability, chief executive officers will have to create an environment in which other leaders, who subscribe to the common vision and purpose, collaborate to make effective decisions. Unlike individualist leaders of the past, successful leaders in the future will strive for integration, not control. The singular role will give way to internal networks of influence that alter the very foundations of the organization.

THE ULTIMATE TEAM AT ELECTRONIC INK, INC.

In 1990, Harold Hambrose, CEO of Electronic Ink, Inc., founded the Philadelphia-based, high-tech company to not only enhance the competitiveness and productiveness of companies in different industries, but also to be a source of personal and social motivation to himself and his employees.

Initially, Harold hired individuals who were quite similar to himself: they were "misfits" with a vision around technological savvy coupled with social responsibility. In addition, Electronic Ink marketed to customers with similar principles and values, which limited the company's potential clients.

In 1995, Johanna Hambrose joined Electronic Ink. An alter ego for Harold, she was very unlike the other people in the organization. Although she had the same vision regarding service, tech savvy, and social responsibility, her different vantage point and strengths helped to balance the company and thus diversify its marketability.

The combination of Harold and Johanna has proved to be a powerful one. As the CEO and COO, respectively, they share leadership of the company. Harold leads teams in his areas of expertise: the creation of technology driven information displays, products, and services. Johanna leads teams in her areas of expertise: sales, marketing, and people.

In addition to the strength of shared leadership, Johanna and Harold attribute the success of the company to the manner in which they handle clients. Again, this involves an innovative style of shared leadership, in this case designed to make the client, and their customers, comfortable. The client and one or two design specialists, a tech person, or another person with whom the client is comfortable, meet in a small room with a one-way mirror to discuss the client's needs, projects, and goals. On the other side of the one-way mirror is a large room with Electronic Ink professionals and the client's customer. Electronic Ink's client and the rest of the project team pass questions electronically to the person meeting with the customer. In this way, the customer is not overwhelmed with questions by many different people, the client's customer works with the person with whom he or she is most comfortable, and the team knows what his or her needs are and can ask questions that will provide valuable insight into the customer's needs, desires, and goals. In this way, everyone is involved from the beginning of the project, rather than Electronic Ink's client telling the rest of the team what to do and what the customer wants, and thus hierarchical leadership is averted. The entire team shares responsibility for and leadership of the project.

Harold and Johanna believe that the company is so successful not only because they have a great team that is focused on the development and deployment of digital solutions that are both usable and useful, but also because the entire company is passionate about finding new and imaginative ways to share leadership and thus achieve more for their clients in every situation.

SHARING LEADERSHIP

ITEM 20: Willingly Shares Leadership with Business Partners

WHAT TO DO

- Understand how your position in the company and the jobs or tasks and responsibilities of your business partners are interdependent.
- Develop a team made up of people with complementary strengths.
- Give power away to the most qualified individuals to strengthen their capabilities.
- Value other's expertise and opinions.
- Be a role model. Demonstrate and express your belief that you and your business partners will share leadership, take ownership for your work, and collaborate with each other as a team.
- Ensure that business partners fully understand their roles and responsibilities.
- When appropriate, empower business partners to take the lead in making decisions.
- Effectively delegate responsibility to business partners, and provide support when needed.
- Do not overlook individual needs. Attend to individual needs prior to or during the team process.
- Keep feedback focused on the group's working relationships and how they share responsibilities and support each other.

HOW TO DO IT

- Get your business partners to agree on their roles and responsibilities.
- Encourage and empower qualified business partners to make decisions and solve their own problems rather than coming to you.
- Give assignments describing the outcome desired (clear performance goals), but let business partners use the means they think best to achieve the outcome.
- Don't second guess the decisions of those you have empowered to make them.
- When discussing the responsibility to be delegated, work with the business partners to determine decision-making parameters and how to overcome other issues or concerns.
- Consider yourself a resource rather than the manager.

- Set appropriate follow-up meetings to review progress, and take corrective action if necessary.
- Discuss with your teams ways to give them greater freedom to do their jobs or achieve their goals.
- Listen respectfully to the business partner's decision and how the partner came to it (give full attention, good eye contact, no interruptions, ask for more information, paraphrase, and summarize what the person has said).
- Take time to think of areas where more power might be shared. List the pros and cons of giving people greater work freedom.
- Ask to sit in on a team meeting of a leader who is known for effectively sharing leadership; take notes of what you observe and apply the techniques you've learned.
- Request feedback from your manager and business partners on how you are doing in sharing leadership.

HOW TO USE THIS SKILL FURTHER

- Practice sharing leadership with a group outside of work.
- Remind yourself how you learned by doing as well as by being directed.

RESULTS YOU CAN EXPECT

- People may ask to be on teams in your organization.
- Business partners may express their enthusiasm for being on your team.
- Quality and productivity of your organization may improve.

READINGS

- *Breakthrough Business Meetings: Shared Leadership in Action*. Robert E. Levasseur. 2000. iUniverse.com: Silicon Valley, CA, ISBN 0595092632.
- *Dance Lessons: Six Steps to Great Partnerships in Business & Life*. Chip R. Bell & Heather Shea. 1998. Berrett-Koehler: San Francisco, ISBN 1576750434.
- *Managing With Power: Politics and Influence in Organizations*. Jeffrey Pfeffer. 1996. Harvard Business School Press: Boston, ISBN 875844405.
- *Power Up: Transforming Organizations Through Shared Leadership*. David L. Bradford & Allan R. Cohen. 1998. John Wiley & Sons: New York, ISBN 0471121223.
- *Organizing Genius: The Secrets of Creative Collaboration*. Patricia Ward Biederman & Warren G. Bennis. 1998. Perseus: Reading, MA, ISBN 201339897.
- *Teaming Up*. Darrel Ray & Howard Bronstein. 1995. McGraw-Hill: New York, ISBN 0070516464.
- *Tips for Teams*. Kimball Fisher, Steven Rayner, & William Belgard. 1995. McGraw-Hill: New York, ISBN 0070212244.

ITEM 21: Defers to Others When They Have More Expertise

WHAT TO DO

- Give power away to the most qualified individuals to strengthen their capabilities.
- Define the limits of decision-making power.
- Cultivate a climate in which people feel free to take initiative on assignments.
- Give qualified people discretion and autonomy over their tasks and resources.
- Encourage and reward problem-solvers and decision makers.
- Reward teams and individuals who demonstrate initiative and engage in additional decision-making responsibilities.
- Involve people who have gained adequate experience in their departments and jobs in more problem solving and decision making.
- Promote a feeling of employee ownership with their projects.

HOW TO DO IT

- Encourage and empower qualified associates to make decisions and solve their own problems rather than coming to you.
- Give assignments describing the desired outcome (clear performance goals), but let the employee use the means he or she thinks best.
- Don't second guess the decisions of those you have empowered to make them.
- When discussing the responsibility to be delegated, work with the associate to determine decision-making parameters and how to overcome other issues or concerns.
- Consider yourself a resource rather than the manager.
- Set appropriate follow-up meetings to review progress, and take corrective action if necessary.
- Discuss with your teams ways to give them greater freedom to do their jobs or achieve their goals.
- Listen respectfully to the individual's or team's decision and how they came to it (give full attention, good eye contact, no interruptions, ask for more information, paraphrase, and summarize what the person has said).
- Ask employees who are close to the customers to provide input before decisions are made.
- Take time to think of areas where more power might be shared. List the pros and cons of giving people greater work freedom.
- Make sure that the decision-making process involves the appropriate people, especially the people on the front lines.
- Discuss techniques with managers who excel at empowering and delegating.

- Lead a task force that requires a lot of delegating, and request a member or an observer to give you feedback on how well you are doing.

HOW TO USE THIS SKILL FURTHER

- Delegate more to people who are close to the customers.
- Take on challenging responsibilities and delegate them to qualified employees.
- Remind yourself how you learned by doing as well as by being directed.

RESULTS YOU CAN EXPECT

- You may spend less time directing other's projects.
- You may develop a sense of accomplishment from the achievements of your people rather than from your own direct efforts.
- Your employees may feel they are more like partners.
- Your associates and employees may be more empowered.
- You may have more time to do management and strategic planning.

READINGS

- *Essential Drucker: In One Volume the Best of Sixty Years of Peter Drucker's Essential Writings on Management*. Peter Ferdinand Drucker. 2001, HarperBusiness: New York, ISBN 66210879.
- *Intrapreneuring in Action: A Handbook for Business Innovation*. Gifford Pinchot & Ron Pellman. 1999. Berrett-Koehler: San Francisco, ISBN 1576750612.
- *Leadership and Self-Deception: Getting Out of the Box*. The Arbinger Institute. 2000. Berrett-Koehler: San Francisco, ISBN 1576750949.
- *Management 21C: Someday We'll All Manage This Way*. Subir Chowdhury. 1999. Financial Times/Prentice Hall: Upper Saddle River, NJ, ISBN 273639633.
- *Management by Vice: A Humorous Satire on R&D Life in a Fictitious Company*: C. B. Don & M. E. Cohen. 1999. Sterling Ter Libra: Yorba Linda, CA, ISBN 0967008441.
- *Pioneering Organizations: The Convergence of Individualism, Teamwork, and Leadership*. Larry N. Davis & Chip R. Bell. 2000. Executive Excellence: Provo, UT, ISBN 1890009849.
- *The Knowing-Doing Gap: How Smart Companies Turn Knowledge into Action*. Jeffrey Pfeffer & Robert I. Sutton. 2000. Harvard Business School Press: Boston, ISBN 1578511240.

ITEM 22: Strives to Arrive at an Outcome with Others (As Opposed to for Others)

WHAT TO DO

- Recognize that successful negotiation engages people in seeking a solution satisfactory to all parties.
- Build agreements between parties.
- Be willing to compromise (give and take) in tough conflicts.
- Strive to create win-win solutions.
- Reward teams and individuals who demonstrate initiative and engage in additional decision-making responsibilities.
- Involve people who have gained adequate experience in their departments and jobs in more problem solving and decision making.
- Promote a feeling of employee ownership with their projects.
- Set a climate in which people are encouraged to air their opinions and make decisions.
- Be receptive to questions and concerns.
- Listen and stay open-minded when others disagree.
- Don't discourage others when this type of discussion occurs.
- Clarify your understanding of important points.
- Encourage people to tell you their ideas.

HOW TO DO IT

- Look for situations that you can accept and certain outcomes that the other side wants. Try to "meet in the middle."
- Take the time to listen and respond to people's concerns.
- Be open and friendly. Let people know they can question and disagree.
- When you feel frustrated, don't get emotional or angry. Talk about it.
- When you are questioned, respond in a nondefensive manner; this gives people permission to question.
- Remain nondefensive; actively listen to their reasons.
- Indicate approval by saying such things as, "I can see how this type of thing could cause a problem...."
- Restate the point the speaker presented.
- Ask open-ended questions to make sure you get all the information, both facts and feelings.
- Seek feedback from associates about your effectiveness in handling conflict situations and reaching consensus.

- Discuss techniques with managers who excel at encouraging and enrolling others in ideas.

HOW TO USE THIS SKILL FURTHER

- Increase your interaction with employees.
- Volunteer to serve as a counselor in a community organization.
- Practice with your spouse and children.

RESULTS YOU CAN EXPECT

- You may have a better understanding of how others around you think and feel.
- You may build people's confidence and experience fewer people problems.
- People may ask you to be a mediator to solve their conflicts.
- There are no hard feelings between parties after the negotiation.

READINGS

- *12 Steps to Robust Decisions: Building Consensus in Product Development and Business*. David Ullman. 2001. Trafford Publishing: Victoria, CA, ISBN 1552125769.
- *Dealing With Anger*. Sandy Livingstone. 1997. SL Discovery Consulting Services: St. Albert, Alberta, ISBN 0968179312.
- *Essentials of Negotiation*. Roy J. Lewicki, David M. Saunders, & John W. Minton. 2000. McGraw-Hill: New York, ISBN 0072312858.
- *Powerskills: Building Top-Level Relationships for Bottom-Line Results*. James P. Masciarelli. 2000. Nimbus Press: Gloucester, MA, ISBN 0967711118.
- *The Keys to Conflict Resolution: Proven Methods of Settling Disputes Voluntarily*. Theodore W. Kheel & William L. Lurie. 1999. Four Walls Eight Windows: New York, ISBN 1568581343.

ITEM 23: Creates an Environment Where People Focus on the Larger Good (Avoids Suboptimization or Turfism)

WHAT TO DO

- Reward individuals when they assist others and build on team relationships.
- Encourage team members to cooperate with each other rather than compete among themselves.
- Develop informal and formal recognition processes for effective team performance.

- Demonstrate and express your belief that the group can work effectively as a team, and reward them when their individual efforts help to get the job done.
- Help people see how their job or tasks and responsibilities are interdependent.
- Encourage individuals to look at each other as resources for the project or task they are teamed on.
- Give timely recognition when your team meets its objectives.

HOW TO DO IT

- Make sure responsibility and accountability are clearly assigned and communicated to minimize misunderstanding and confusion.
- Review progress with teams or individuals on a regular basis to keep the team focused. Don't forget to recognize and reward individual and team efforts along the way to keep enthusiasm high.
- Get suggestions or discuss techniques with managers who excel at team-building skills as well as at rewarding and recognizing the efforts of individuals and teams.
- Express positive comments about the team's ability to work together, and cite previous successes they have had in working together.
- Assess your own ability to help others in the team; be a role model or work to improve.
- Evaluate individuals on their willingness and ability to help others in the organization.
- Give employees regular feedback specifically related to the action or behavior on teamwork.
- Be cheerful and enthusiastic about the success of your team.
- Use one-on-one communication, staff meetings, performance appraisals, and merit increase recommendations as tools to recognize achievement of quality and productivity goals.
- Praise and promote high performers who exemplify the essence of teamwork, collaboration, trust, and respect.

HOW TO USE THIS SKILL FURTHER

- Seek ways to further support others. Anticipate their needs and meet them.
- Make each interaction with other departments one of support and respect.

RESULTS YOU CAN EXPECT

- People may be more willing to help each other.
- Your team may be more cohesive, cooperative, and productive.
- Your people may perform well and feel satisfied with their work.

- Your people may have more fun at work. You may notice more energy, productivity gains, and higher quality performance in your organization.

READINGS

- *40 Tools for Cross-Functional Teams: Building Synergy for Breakthrough Creativity.* Walter J. Michalski & Dana G. King. 1998. Productivity Press: Portland, OR, ISBN 1563271982.
- *Breakthrough Technology Project Management.* Bennet P. Lientz & Kathryn P. Rea. 2001. Academic Press: San Diego, ISBN 0124499686.
- *Geeks and Geezers: How Era, Values, and Defining Moments Shape Leaders.* Warren Bennis & Robert Thomas. 2002. Harvard Business School Press: Boston, ISBN 1578515823.
- *Hot Groups: Seeding Them, Feeding Them, and Using Them to Ignite Your Organization.* Jean Lipman-Blumen & Harold J. Leavitt. 2001. Oxford University Press: Oxford, ISBN 0195144058.
- *Mastering Virtual Teams: Strategies, Tools, and Techniques That Succeed.* Deborah L. Duarte & Nancy Tennant Snyder. 2000. Jossey-Bass: San Francisco, ISBN 0787955892.
- *Mining Group Gold: How to Cash In on the Collaborative Brain Power of a Group.* Thomas A. Kayser. 1995. McGraw-Hill: New York, ISBN 0786304294.
- *The One Minute Manager Builds High Performing Teams.* Ken Blanchard, Donald Carew, & Eunice Parisi-Carew. 2000. William Morrow: New York, ISBN 0688172156.
- *Tips for Teams*, Kimball Fisher, Steven Rayner, & William Belgard. 1995. McGraw-Hill/HarperBusiness: New York, ISBN 0070212244.

ENDNOTES

1. Technology, Spain, 44.
2. Products and Services, United States, 29.
3. Technology, Sweden, 35.
4. Telecommunications, United States, 32.
5. Technology, United States, 33.
6. Investments, United States, 36.
7. Technology, Finland, 41.
8. Technology, Japan, 41.
9. Products and services, United States, 36.
10. Investments, United States, 48.

7

CREATING
A SHARED VISION

*...Leaders unleash the power of collective intelli-
gence. They assemble extraordinary people, focus
them on meaningful work, connect their wisdom,
and motivate them to do great things.* [1]

Formal hierarchy will always have an important role in organizations, but effective global executives of the future will need the skill to navigate outside the traditional lines of authority. They will have to work across geographic borders and across
the functional boundaries and strata of the organization; they must encourage open
exchange and capitalize on the ideas of everyone; and they must be able to influence
peers and subordinates through the power of ideas and information as much as by
position.

Influence requires much more than just good ideas and knowledge. It requires the
ability to convey ideas compellingly to others. A leader must understand the goals of
others, inside and outside the organization, and tailor ideas to meet mutual needs if his
or her vision is to be accepted. Finally, the effective global leader should develop an effective overall strategy that clearly defines departmental priorities, which will aim the
entire company in the same direction.

CREATING A VISION

With great capacity for communicating, future leaders will create clear and compelling visions that inspire and stretch people beyond expectations.

Future executives must have a strong belief and conviction about their vision for the company. They must communicate this vision to all facets of the workforce, from the highest paid to the lowest. The message should be simple, clear, and restated often.[2]

These leaders must see things differently, from a different perspective than others. They may gather and organize the same information, but they must have the ability to transform it into a new conception, a new vision. A great challenge for global leaders is to uncover the overarching outcome of where they and the company are headed. Then, through clearly stated objectives, leaders must communicate this vision to potential followers, so that each person understands his or her role in achieving it, as well as to potential customers, so that they know what to expect from the company and its products and services. Global leaders use every opportunity to communicate their message, becoming much like a politician who states and restates the mission.

For example, since the creation of the Dell Computer Corporation in 1984, Michael Dell (founder and CEO) has continuously restated his vision to sell customized computer systems directly to customers. More recently, the company has hit on an advertising campaign that relays this mission yet again. The commercials feature a young man who helps people, especially young people, get the computers they want. One advertisement tells the story of two kids who are participating in an internship program at Dell. The supervisor shows them the customer service center and explains that this is where orders are taken for Dell Computers. The kids tell the supervisor that they have an idea: What if people visit the Dell Web site before coming into the service center to indicate what they will use their computer for and what their interests are—for instance, burning CDs, accessing the Internet, or downloading pictures and graphics? The supervisor tells the kids that Dell already does this. The purpose of the advertisement is to again get across to the public that the mission of Dell is to give customers every opportunity to get the exact computers they need. Through this campaign, Michael Dell has overcome a great challenge in the marketplace, which is to get across, especially to young people, the vast array of services that Dell offers in terms of customization of equipment.

Because such a large part of the global leader's role is to articulate the company vision to great numbers of people simultaneously—and to individuals located all over the world—he or she must be capable of and comfortable in communicating through many different mediums. Realizing that it takes multiple venues to get a message across, these leaders are at ease speaking in front of large groups and the media, as well as communicating by email, video conferencing, and the Internet. With so many communication mediums at our disposal, global leaders must learn to direct information through the right medium—be it email, voicemail, the Internet, a Web site, or professional media, such as radio or television commercials—when communicating a message, or the message will be lost. For instance, when there is a message of utmost importance to the company, leaders may choose to leave an all-company voicemail that gives an overview of the situation. If more details are necessary, the voicemail may point teams to an email or Web site that gives additional information. However, individuals are alerted through the voicemail system, because often so much information comes across email, it is nearly impossible to prioritize the importance of it.

> This leader must be comfortable getting in front of people to communicate changes clearly and concisely. Informality is very important. Nothing can replace face-to-face interaction.[3]

Even with the rapid expansion of communication technology, no one leader can reach everyone. Effective global leaders will recruit those individuals whose goals and objectives are consistent with the company vision to help spread the message.

GETTING INPUT FROM OTHERS

Influence is not just top-down. In next-generation companies, ideas come from all sources, all directions—anyone's input can be influential in the organization. The forces driving this change are a combination of fundamental marketplace shifts and demands, new technologies, newly shaped organizations, and new kinds of workers.

Recently, at an Accenture leadership program, high-potential recruits raised an important issue about influencing others. The recruits revealed that they felt powerless to persuade leaders who are already very much evolved in terms of their business acumen and networks. Program leaders countered this concern. They explained that everyone has a unique perspective that is useful to the company. Younger individuals are often especially versed on technical subjects and can offer fresh perspectives as a result of recently exiting the educational environment. Influencing has less to do with age, tenure, or company knowledge, and more to do with a combination of understanding marketplace shifts and demands, new technology, the organizational shape, and how these things complement and affect each other.

Before CoreStates merged with First Union (which then became City Union), human resources executive Yvette Hyater Adams started a unique mentoring program. Participants in the program were paired with other individuals who had extraordinarily different educational or cultural backgrounds from themselves. For instance, Yvette, a black female, partnered herself with a white male in a senior executive position. This unique, high-impact program—part diversity program and part influence and learning—gave participants the opportunity to influence each other's thinking from a very different perspective.

> Every key person should be involved in helping to define the company's values and mission.[4]

Effective global leaders of the future know that each individual in the company has a unique set of skills and knowledge that, if tapped into, can benefit the company as a whole. For instance, younger workers often have more knowledge about personal computers and the Internet than do more seasoned colleagues. Analyzing and incorporating these different viewpoints adds dimension to the company vision; it gives leaders a better overall picture of where the company is and where it should be headed; and it can help forecast potential disasters, avoid duplication of efforts, and clarify goals and strategies.

Many global leaders are beginning to recognize that leveraging diversity, such as differences of race, gender, and ethnicity, is crucial to creating, sharing, and executing the company vision. Especially when targeting specific markets, such as the Hispanic market, it is essential to include individuals who understand the community. For instance, Andrew Reeder, journalist and radio host, has engaged in promoting a vision of leadership in the Hispanic community through Hispanic Business Radio (HBR). Experts and successful leaders from the Hispanic business community, and entertainers such as former ambassador to Mexico John Gavin, are involved in creating throughout North America the vision of HBR, which is to develop community identity, to illustrate real-life examples of leadership success in the Hispanic community, to create brand identity, and to promote Hispanic leaders and their successors.

Much like Andrew Reeder has asked successful Hispanic executives and leaders to share their ideas on promoting Hispanic business, global leaders of the future will use the backgrounds and expertise of each individual in the company to create a shared vision. People with different viewpoints will invariably see the company and how it relates to customers and communities in varying lights. Incorporating these different perspectives into the company vision will not only make the individuals more effective ambassadors for the organization, because they believe in the vision, it will help to brand products and services and to grow the organization throughout the communities it serves.

As Edgar Schein, who is considered one of the founders of the field of organizational psychology, notes that leaders will need to effectively involve others and elicit participation "because the tasks will be too complex and the information too widely distributed for leaders to solve problems on their own."

When we got our new president, he decided that we needed to clarify our vision. So he put together teams of leaders in all of the different units to work together. Our goals have been based on this vision. This is our third year working this way, and it has been very productive. This is an example of the collaboration of different leaders from different departments working together to establish a vision for the entire organization.[5]

Traditionally, leaders have not engaged in the widespread involvement of others as they construct key business decisions, often preferring to stay close to a small band of confidantes as the decision process unfolds. However, this heavily top-down approach, in which one person makes a decision with limited and only very senior executive input for others to then carry out, is no longer effective.

For instance, prior to initiating the campaign in which associates presented their ideas to the Anthem East Leadership Team (the senior executive team), problems and challenges were addressed with a top-down approach. The leaders found that people were far more willing to participate and to take on more accountability and responsibility when they were involved as participants in business strategies and decisions. When they understood the consequences and rewards of participating, as well as how the process would work, what the ROI was, and how it would be achieved, more people wanted to be involved in programs even if they were of a higher risk nature. As such, they were much more effective in creating the vision.

The leadership team devised a system to give everyone access to the status of different areas of the organization. At the entrance to the Anthem East building, they put a large poster with a pie chart, colored by area. The chart, which was updated regularly, showed how much each area had improved, or not, during each quarter. Although different people were responsible for the different areas of the pie chart, anybody could participate in helping to achieve the goals.

This type of system isn't possible in a top-down approach, because not everyone understands how the different areas of the company are measured. If only the people at the top know how things are measured, then they are the only ones who can make improvements, because they are the only ones who understand how to measure the improvements. If everybody in the company knows how to measure the improvement, then anyone can improve an area and then demonstrate to others how it works.

Global leaders must have buy-in from the peers, teams, and staff if their global vision of the company is to be successful; in other words, they must have the support of the individuals involved if complications and disagreements at the implementation stage are to be avoided. Successful leaders know that people are more likely to be supportive of a vision if they have been included in its creation. These leaders also know that people who are involved in the direction of a project from its inception will be more committed, because they feel responsible for the success of the project.

CREATING MOMENTUM AND INSPIRING OTHERS

Positional power may still matter, and "because I said so" can still compel action from employees lower in the pyramid, but when ideas and directives support a vision that people—peers, partners, even those over whom the leader has no direct authority—believe in, they will be inspired rather than compelled. Under a command-and-control style, workers frequently avoid decisions for which they have not received a specific directive. By contrast, imparting a meaningful vision gives people a reason to follow a leader's direction and provides a guide for all decisions.

An effective global leader will excite people about the company's future and inspire pride for the company's products and services. The leader's role is to define the company vision, to put it in the right context, and to communicate it in such a way that individuals are proud to be a part of the organization.

In 2001, after Fred DiBona, president and CEO of Independence Blue Cross (IBC), led the creation of an e-commerce strategy as part of the company's mission, he turned over the implementation and execution of that strategy to a handful of senior leaders in the organization to oversee its success. The inspired team, led by Joe Frick and Chris Butler, was then extended to include Yvette Bright (nicknamed eVette for her leading role in the e-commerce venture), John Janney, Kathy Lister, and a consulting company to execute the strategy. These leaders in turn incorporated the support of countless others in IT, marketing, provider services, communications, and many other parts of the IBC family of companies. What began with an inspired vision has turned into what is now one of the most successful e-commerce implementations in the history of health services.

Charisma is one characteristic that will always be vital to successful leadership. Executives may have all of the necessary technical and industry knowledge, but they will not be effective if they cannot motivate and empower those who are subordinate to them.

Constantine Papadakis, president of Drexel University, is a charismatic leader who not only leads, but who allows others to lead when necessary. For example, during the merger with MCP Hahnemann University School of Medicine and Drexel, now the Drexel University College of Medicine, Dr. Papadakis often handed the baton to his subordinates to lead various aspects of the merger meetings, such as finances, organization design, transitions, project teams, and negotiations with various functional departments. For example, if the meeting was about the budget, he would hand it over to the finance leader; if the meeting was about how the hospitals would be impacted by the relationship with the medical school, he would hand it over to the dean of the medical school. Often these leaders came from MCP Hahnemann as well as from the Drexel Board. Although he was capable of chairing these meetings himself, he chose to let others lead. Thus, by introducing his leadership team at every opportunity and giving them the limelight to demonstrate their technical and industry knowledge, he became a more charismatic leader in the eyes of the board.

A leader must be charismatic so that others will follow without feeling that they are being "bossed around." Charisma is a key component of gaining the respect of employees and leading the workforce through influence rather than through formal authority. As the command-and-control model of power loses the respect and loyalty of the younger workforce, the need for dynamic leaders who inspire all parties involved to share the common vision and create the common good is increasing.

Another key component in gaining the respect of employees is trust. Trust gives leaders an advantage, because it leads to loyalty and stability in an otherwise turbulent world. Many things affect trust in leadership, including major changes in the company and ineffective communication about the company. Without trust, a company will suffer from skepticism, low morale, and low confidence in leadership.

During periods of major change, the most effective communication will be simple and focused. Too much communication will get lost in the confusion of the times. During such times, an effective global leader will amplify a few simple, common points repeatedly, which will reduce anxiety and increase commitment to the leader and the mission.

During his short tenure as CEO of Anthem, and prior to the initial public offering (IPO), Larry Glasscock quickly gained the respect and trust of the healthcare communities across the U.S. markets that Anthem serves. Anthem's IPO was cited on Wall Street as one of the most successful in the history of healthcare, and it was in large part due to the respect the employees and communities had for Larry and the trust he had garnered in a very short period of time as the company's chief executive. Larry gained this respect primarily because of his ability to increase the value of Anthem's services to the public, his ability to manage relationships with providers, and his ability to retain a first-class leadership team through multiple mergers in all four corridors of the United States (east, south, Midwest, west). His ability to demonstrate shared leadership and the use of associate-led teams to spearhead common issues across the firm has been a trademark of his leadership. Larry is a humble leader who is recognized by his industry and his associates for sharing and communicating key performance metrics throughout the organization, which drives its overall shareholder value through empowered teams and leaders.

On the other hand, a CEO in a similar situation in Australia did not fair as well when he attempted to lead a merger with the company's London-based organization, because he did not understand the cultural implications of dealing with crosscultural sentiment in a highly political environment during a demutualization.

Within global organizations, trust must be developed across international borders. This can be especially difficult, given the distance, cultural, and language barriers, but it is absolutely necessary if the company is to forge its way into the global marketplace.

In Asian companies, and in Japanese companies in particular, it is believed that rotation is important to the development of individuals and essential for CEOs. Near the end of their tenure, CEOs are sent on a "sunset cruise." At this time, executives are allowed to choose whichever country or part of the organization they would like to spend time in before they retire.

In the 1990s, the CEO of a large computer manufacturing company, headquartered in Tokyo, decided to spend his remaining tenure at the California distribution center. There was mistrust between the senior executive team, three members of which came from the United States and three of which came from Japan. Upon arrival, the Japanese executives began inspecting the U.S. center, which angered the U.S. executives. In addition, the Japanese insisted on keeping their own records, separate and apart from those of the U.S. center, and during meetings the Japanese spoke Japanese to each other and English to the U.S. team, who did not understand Japanese. This kept the U.S. team in the dark about how the Japanese felt about certain issues. The U.S. CEO hired a consultant to help facilitate trust building and confidence among these six executives. Initially, there was resistance from the Japanese, because they were required to speak English with the consultant, the consultant was a woman, and she had hired an interpreter who was a Japanese-American. As a matter of fact, many people who had been assigned to the U.S. company were Americans who spoke Japanese. Many Japanese executives were displeased with this, because they felt it took away from their culture and their language to have Americans speaking Japanese. However, in order to continue operating the U.S.

distribution center, the Japanese executives were required to change, opening up themselves and their culture to the Americans in order to begin trust building.

Ultimately, through the U.S. and Japanese executive teams working together, it was found that the U.S. team was indeed inflating their sales, only to cancel delivery orders a month before delivery. The bonus system in the United States was subsequently changed to reward based on delivery rather than on sales, and in doing so, over-ordering was eliminated.

Supporting the Vision with Strategy

Leaders who can spark our imaginations with a compelling vision of a worthwhile end that stretches us beyond what is known today and who can show us a clear path to our objectives are the ones we follow. In the future, the leadership role will focus more on the development of an effective strategy, the creation of the vision, and an understanding of their impact, and will empower others to carry out the implementation of the plan.

The hectic pace of today's world makes it challenging for global leaders to spend much time developing effective strategies for their businesses. Yet, however compelling a vision or however inspiring a communicator, no mission will be successful without a well thought out strategy in which people understand their roles and contributions. The future global leader's role therefore must include developing a strategy that ties together the mission of the company with the needs of customers and other stakeholders.

In a turbulent global business environment, such as at the time of this writing, companies may be involved in cycles of mergers, acquisitions, and sales. In such times, the process of developing and maintaining a "magnetic north" is crucial to the survival of the company. At a Latin American family business, leaders do not value the process of shared leadership, which is exemplified by the fact that each leader is busily focused on his or her own target. Leaders have put defining a common vision for the company and developing a strategy to attain it on the back burner, and they are making business decisions based on increasing the short-term revenue of their departments rather than making decisions that are in the long-term best interest of the company. As a result of this lack of shared leadership and strategy, leaders waste time and energy steering their departments at a tangent to where the company wants to be in the future; it causes activities to be driven by silo politics as opposed to crosscompany commitment; and it fails to address the issues of how crossfunctional, cross–business unit, and cross–silo leadership is essential to move the company to the future.

Defining Roles and Priorities

The effective global leader will clearly define priorities and expectations for each member of the organization, and everyone, including the leader, will be evaluated against those expectations. These leaders will make the objectives clear and interesting to motivate and challenge their staff.

The challenge is to give people a well-defined task, clear vision, and a clear target. Leaders need to provide them with guidance and motivate them to complete the mission.[6]

One of the pressures of the changing leadership role is to do more—faster and with less. To avoid overwhelming individuals with too much work, the effective leader will set a short list of priorities for his or her team, aiming everyone at the same target. Defining roles and setting objectives will ensure that each person's energy is devoted to what is most important to the company.

Take, for example, the actions of Peter McCausland, chairman and CEO of Airgas, a $2 billion industrial gas distribution company of about 8,000 people, which was built from approximately 300 acquisitions over the last two decades.

In early 2002, Peter recognized that to focus the energy of these integrated businesses and to then grow market share in a highly fragmented market, there was a need to turn significant management attention to not only what Airgas should be as a business, but also to the operating model they needed to have and how executives should seek to behave as leaders in taking an already highly successful company to the next level.

Peter and his team spent considerable time, over approximately a six-month period, critically examining not only the "what," but also the "how" of the Airgas business they wanted, and they recrafted the key elements of what was important to the company when building the operating model and leadership vision for Airgas. They worked tirelessly on this as a top team, were unwavering in their self-examination as leaders, and produced not only a compelling, practical vision of working, but also one that was able to be fully connected with their employees throughout the business. These actions are noteworthy for two reasons: First, they were undertaken by an already highly successful company, Airgas, as part of refocusing the energy of its people to become even better, and second, the passion of the leader was singularly important in ensuring that the vision of working was connected with not just the top executive group, but also with everyone in the business, thereby translating vision into personal commitment and operational benefit. Leaders must keep stakeholders informed of any changes in priorities to avoid wasting time and energy.

CONCLUSION

Creating a shared vision is integral to any company's success, because it aligns the company's stakeholders, operations, and structure with its mission and vision. In the future, the strongest companies will be those with a common vision, an effective strategy, and a workforce that shares in the commitment to accomplishing the vision. Much of the future global leader's role will be to invite others to participate in the development of the mission, to communicate it in such a way as to inspire support and enthusiasm, and to develop a strategy and define priorities that will focus the entire company on achieving the vision.

BECOMING A GLOBAL LEADER[7]

Paul Curlander is chairman and chief executive officer of Lexmark International, a leading developer, manufacturer, and supplier of printing solutions for offices and homes in more than 150 countries. Paul has been at Lexmark, a spin-off of IBM, in different capacities since it was founded in 1991.

Learning to Create a Vision

Paul works hard at being a leader in a tough business with few boundaries. "I am not a natural leader.... I have to work hard at it," he says. Paul attributes much of his success to following the philosophies of two of his mentors: his father, who taught him to view issues from a long-term perspective and to strive for excellence; and his college professor, who convinced him to seek out a topic of interest and to learn from the best to be the best.

Creating a Shared Vision of Lexmark's Future

Early in the development of the Lexmark culture, Paul, in the tradition of his mentors, used a strong, future-oriented focus to pull people together and capture their imaginations, hearts, and long-term loyalty to the new business. At first the senior team was not aligned. Each person acted individually, not as a member of a team, so people with different capabilities were integrated into the team. Yet, although there was strong improvement, the team members were still not focused on the same goals.

Paul continued to involve people in the development of the strategy for Lexmark through his practice of strong leadership, communication, and teamwork. He made clear the problems at Lexmark and what was needed to fix them. The team focused on common goals, and today it consists of seven strong executive leaders (three who came from outside the company) who share leadership and are achieving a goal together. Everyone is pointed in the same direction and focused on the same future.

Says Paul of focusing his team on Lexmark's success, "If we keep focused on the future, we can overcome being unhappy with the current situation. You have to see the long-term picture. How we build towards that future success, even if we do not like the current situation, is important." It appears that this philosophy is working. In 2001, Lexmark reported more than $4.1 billion in revenue.

CREATING A SHARED VISION

ITEM 24: Creates and Communicates a Clear Vision for His or Her Organization

WHAT TO DO

- Recognize that an effective organization is based on a shared vision that is understood and accepted by everyone.
- Involve employees in developing a clear vision for your organization.
- Solicit input from employees for their vision of their job, the team, and the organization.
- Align team objectives with the overall vision of the organization.
- Let your employees know how their contribution can help achieve the vision.
- Encourage the full participation of everyone concerned in creating and communicating the vision.
- Work with your staff or management team to update the vision periodically.
- Encourage people to anticipate future opportunities for both the organization and themselves.

HOW TO DO IT

- Communicate new ideas with confidence and enthusiasm, and convey a can-do attitude.
- When presenting a new idea, provide as much background information as possible to your work group.
- Schedule regular meetings with your entire team to review and update the vision and mission, evaluate team performances, and set new objectives based on the vision.
- Before the meeting, analyze internal and external factors that influence the organization's effectiveness, and discuss these variables at the beginning of the meeting.
- Ask each team member to write down his or her vision and present it to the group.
- Work with your group to reach consensus on the team's vision, mission, and strategies. Check the consistency with your company's vision.

- Set specific goals for the whole group rather than just for individual performers.
- Discuss the vision with your manager and get his or her suggestions.
- Align specific organizational policies, procedures, and operations with the overall vision.
- Ask people for suggestions and ideas on how to achieve the vision.
- Read daily newspapers, trade magazines, and the company's annual reports.
- Discuss techniques with managers who excel at creating and communicating a clear vision for their organization.

HOW TO USE THIS SKILL FURTHER

- Volunteer to serve on a crossfunctional committee.
- Volunteer to lead a team or group activity where creating and communicating the vision is essential.
- Practice open communication with your spouse and children.

RESULTS YOU CAN EXPECT

- Your reputation as a visionary leader may grow.
- You may be asked to serve on planning teams or as an advisor outside your own organization.
- You may expect to get new assignments and opportunities to broaden your career in the company.

READINGS

- *Becoming a Person of Influence: How to Positively Impact the Lives of Others*. John C. Maxwell & Jim Dornan. 1997. Thomas Nelson: Nashville, TN, ISBN 0785271007.
- *Built to Last*. James C. Collins & Jerry I. Porras. 1997. HarperBusiness: New York, ISBN 887307396.
- *Working Knowledge*. Thomas H. Davenport & Laurence Prusak. 2000. Harvard Business School Press: Boston, ISBN 1578513014.
- *Managing for Excellence: The Guide to Developing High Performance in Contemporary Organizations*. D. L. Bradford & A. R. Cohen. 1997. John Wiley & Sons: New York, ISBN 0471127248.
- *Seize Tomorrow, Start Today: Renew Your Vision, Revitalize Your Organization, and Stay Ahead of the Future*. James A. Belasco & Jerre L. Stead. 2000. Warner Books: New York, ISBN 446676047.
- *The Leader of the Future: New Visions, Strategies, and Practices for the Next Era*. Frances Hesselbein, Marshall Goldsmith, & Richard Beckhard. 1996. Jossey-Bass: San Francisco, ISBN 0787901806.
- *Together We Can: Celebrating the Power of a Team and a Dream*. Dan Zadra. 2001. Compendium: Lynwood, WA, ISBN 1888387424.

ITEM 25: Effectively Involves People in Decision Making

WHAT TO DO

- Let your employees know how their contribution can help achieve the vision. They *can* make a difference.
- Realize that a company is not likely to be successful unless its employees feel responsible for the company's success and failures
- Demonstrate or express your belief that employees can work effectively as a team; create the expectation that individuals will make decisions together.
- Solicit input from employees for their vision of where they see their job, the team, and the organization going, and ask for suggestions on how to achieve the company objectives.
- Involve people, especially those who have gained experience in their departments and jobs, in more problem solving and decision making for the team and the organization.
- Provide others with sufficient information to permit them to develop creative yet workable ideas.
- Be clear about boundaries. Let people know what is and what is not open to negotiation.

HOW TO DO IT

- Hold regular meetings with others (managers, peers, workers) to share and gather information and data, and identify possible areas for improvement.
- Before the meetings, analyze internal and external factors that influence the organization's effectiveness, and discuss these variables at the beginning of the meeting. Ask each team member to write down his or her vision and present it to the group.
- Encourage all team members to express their opinions.
- Maintain objectivity when reviewing new ideas.
- Supply the resources and information others need to make decisions.
- Involve your staff and/or management team in creating and updating the work plan and strategies.
- Work to reach consensus on the team's vision, mission, and strategies.
- Observe managers who are good at involving people in decision making, and ask them for tips.

HOW TO USE THIS SKILL FURTHER

- Volunteer to lead a team or group activity in which team involvement and consensus building is essential.

- Ask for feedback on how well you involve people in reaching group decisions.
- Ask your work unit for feedback on how well you listen to them.

RESULTS YOU CAN EXPECT

- Your reputation as a leader may grow.
- Your manager and peers may give you positive feedback about your interaction with teams.
- Others may ask you for advice on helping teams reach consensus and achieve their goals.
- Morale, commitment, and productivity may noticeably improve.

READINGS

- *Essential Drucker: Best of Sixty Years of Peter Drucker's Essential Writings on Management*, Peter Ferdinand Drucker. 2001. HarperBusiness: New York, ISBN 66210879.
- *The Art of Empowerment: The Profit and Pain of Employee Involvement*. Ron Johnson & David Redmond. 1998. Financial Times Management: London, ISBN 0273630938.
- *The American Workplace: Skills, Compensation, and Employee Involvement*. Casey Ichniowski, David I. Levine, Craig Olson, and George Strauss (Eds.). 2000. Cambridge University Press: Cambridge, ISBN 0521650283.
- *The Improvement Engine: Creativity & Innovation Through Employee Involvement: The Kaizen Teian System*. Japan Human Relations Association Staff. 1995. Productivity, Inc.: Portland, OR, ISBN 1563270102.
- *The Leader of the Future: New Visions, Strategies, and Practices for the Next Era*. Frances Hesselbein, Marshall Goldsmith, & Richard Beckhard. 1996. Jossey-Bass: San Francisco, ISBN 0787901806.
- *The New Unionism: Employee Involvement in the Changing Corporation*. Charles C. Heckscher. 1996. Ilr Press: Ithaca, NY, ISBN 0801483573.

ITEM 26: Inspires People to Commit to Achieving the Vision

WHAT TO DO

- Recognize that an effective organization is based on a shared vision and mission that is understood and accepted by everyone.
- Support an exciting vision of the future by clearly stating goals and standards you and your work group have agreed upon.
- Let your employees know how their contribution can help achieve the vision.

- Encourage and expect high energy and performance from people in your organization.
- Solicit input from employees for their vision of where they see their job, the team, and the organization going. Ask for suggestions on how to achieve the vision.
- Know what aspects of the job excite your employees, and then provide them with opportunities to pursue these activities.
- Help others align their personal and career goals with the vision of the organization.

HOW TO DO IT

- Enthusiastically discuss and communicate the company's future and your employees' roles in it.
- Clearly communicate the vision of the company to employees, and link it directly to individual goals whenever possible.
- Communicate your passion and support outward and upward as well as in your own organization.
- Provide clear performance standards, feedback and coaching, technical training, development opportunities, recognition, and rewards to achieve high performance in your work group.
- Constantly recognize and reward people who are making improvements or efforts on improving.
- Work with your staff or management team to create and update the vision, mission, and strategies.
- Celebrate success as a team.
- Observe managers who are good at inspiring and motivating people, and ask them for tips.

HOW TO USE THIS SKILL FURTHER

- Think about the teams that you have been a member of. Ask yourself, "Do I fully understand the purpose of the group and its directions?" and "What contributed to my feeling responsible or not feeling responsible for the success of those groups?"
- Develop interdepartmental sports teams outside of work and have quarterly games that involve high spirits and energy (as well as a little friendly competition among employees).

RESULTS YOU CAN EXPECT

- Employees may develop a deeper sense of commitment toward achieving company goals.
- Your manager may give you positive feedback about how you inspire people to achieve the vision.
- Others may ask you for your ideas on how to motivate teams to achieve their goals.

- Morale of your group may noticeably improve.
- Productivity of your team may increase.

READINGS

- *The Brand You 50: Or Fifty Ways to Transform Yourself from an 'Employee' into a Brand That Shouts Distinction, Commitment, and Passion!* Tom Peters. 1999. Knopf: New York, ISBN 0375407723.
- *Complete Idiot's Guide to Project Management.* Sunny Baker & Kim Baker. 2000. Alpha Books: Madison, WI, ISBN 0028639200.
- *Emotional Intelligence at Work: The Untapped Edge for Success.* Hendrie Weisinger. 1997. Jossey-Bass: San Francisco, ISBN 0787909521.
- *How to Be a Star at Work: 9 Breakthrough Strategies You Need to Succeed*: Robert E. Kelley. 1999. Times Books: New York, ISBN 0812931696.
- *The Leader of the Future: New Visions, Strategies, and Practices for the Next Era.* Frances Hesselbein, Marshall Goldsmith, & Richard Beckhard. 1996. Jossey-Bass: San Francisco, ISBN 0787901806.
- *The Professional Service Firm 50: Or, Fifty Ways to Transform Your 'Department' into a Professional Service Firm Whose Trademarks Are Passion and Innovation.* Tom Peters. 1999. Knopf: New York, ISBN 0375407715.
- *The Project 50: Fifty Ways to Transform Every Task into a Project That Matters!* Tom Peters. 1999. Knopf: New York, ISBN 0375407731.
- *Zapp!: The Lightning of Empowerment: How to Improve Quality, Productivity, and Employee Satisfaction.* Jeff Cox & William C. Byham. 1998. Fawcett: New York, ISBN 0449002829.

ITEM 27: Develops an Effective Strategy to Achieve the Vision

WHAT TO DO

- Realize that a company is not likely to be successful unless its employees feel responsible for the company's success and failures.
- Ensure that you and your employees have a clear understanding of the company's vision.
- Keep informed about your company's objectives, actions, and agenda.
- Communicate your support of company vision outward and upward as well as in your own organization.
- Help develop and implement policies and strategies that are aligned with your organization's vision.
- Involve your employees in developing strategies to achieve the vision.

- Give your employees a clear sense of direction, but empower them to determine the best way to achieve your organization's vision.
- Challenge team and individual objectives that do not support the company's vision.

HOW TO DO IT

- Align specific policies, strategies, objectives, and procedures in your organization with the vision.
- Make sure that employees clearly understand the vision and objectives. Clarify any confusion regarding the vision.
- When developing the team vision, encourage employees to consider the larger company vision.
- Encourage employees of all levels to contribute their ideas in developing strategies to achieve the vision.
- Genuinely and actively listen to others' ideas.
- Discuss the team objectives and company vision with your manager and get his or her input.
- Encourage employees to read the company's annual report and the business section of the newspapers.
- Interview managers with whom you most frequently interact to learn more of their departments' objectives and business plans.
- Ask managers who excel at strategy development for advice.

HOW TO USE THIS SKILL FURTHER

- Coach a Little League team or some other group activity.
- Volunteer to participate in projects, teams, or task forces in which senior managers will be actively participating. Use the experience as an opportunity to gain insight into longer, broader-range organizational issues.

RESULTS YOU CAN EXPECT

- Your employees may be less confused and more productive.
- You may be asked to serve on planning teams or implementation task forces.
- You may be asked to serve as an advisor outside your own organization.

READINGS

- *Good to Great: Why Some Companies Make the Leap...And Others Don't.* James C. Collins. 2001. HarperCollins, New York, ISBN 66620996.
- *Leadership and Self-Deception: Getting Out of the Box.* The Arbinger Institute. 2000. Berrett-Koehler: San Francisco, ISBN 1576750949.

- *Seize Tomorrow, Start Today: Renew Your Vision, Revitalize Your Organization, and Stay Ahead of the Future*. James A. Belasco & Jerre L. Stead. 2000. Warner Books: New York, ISBN 446676047.
- *The 3 Keys to Empowerment: Release the Power Within People for Astonishing Results*. Kenneth H. Blanchard, John P. Carlos, & Alan Randolph. 1999. Berrett-Koehler: San Francisco, ISBN1576750604.
- *The 21 Indispensable Qualities of a Leader: Becoming the Person Others Will Want to Follow*. John C. Maxwell. 1999. Thomas Nelson: Nashville, TN, ISBN 0785274405.
- *The One Page Business Plan: Start With a Vision, Build a Company!* James T. Horan, Jr., & Rebecca S. Shaw. 1998. One Page Business Plan Co.: El Sobrante, CA, ISBN 1891315072.

ITEM 28: Clearly Identifies Priorities

WHAT TO DO

- Understand the importance of setting priorities.
- Ensure that you and your work group understand the company's priorities and develop goals and strategies accordingly.
- Actively solicit, listen to, and respond to any concerns from your coworkers regarding priority issues.
- Clearly understand the rationale behind the priorities.
- Ensure that your daily work aligns with your major responsibilities.
- Don't confuse *urgent* matters with truly *vital* ones.

HOW TO DO IT

- Put the organizational priorities in writing, send it to your work group, and ask for feedback.
- Ask follow-up questions to confirm that the priorities are clearly understood.
- Organize your tasks according to importance and how much time they should receive. Start with the high-priority items first. Skim or eliminate low-priority items.
- Adjust you and your work group's schedule and workload as necessary to ensure that the amount of time and energy people spend is aligned with the organizational goals and priorities.
- When prioritizing your tasks, ask yourself
  - Which of these tasks will bring most benefit to my organization?
  - Which tasks do my manager and workgroup consider most important?
  - What are the consequences of not completing these tasks in a specific timeframe?
  - Which tasks are most vital?

- Take time every day to plan and organize.
- Take a course in time management or priority management.
- Get coaching from experts.
- Seek regular feedback from your manager or team about the effectiveness of your priority-setting skills.
- Observe others who are good at identifying priorities, and follow their examples.

HOW TO USE THIS SKILL FURTHER

- Share with others your belief that excellence begins with knowing what the priorities are.
- Volunteer to lead a team or group activity in which identifying and communicating goals and priorities is essential.

RESULTS YOU CAN EXPECT

- Higher quality and productivity may be measurable over time.
- Your internal and external customers may be more satisfied by your products or services.
- You may win a reputation of being highly efficient.

READINGS

- *Eat That Frog!: 21 Great Ways to Stop Procrastinating and Get More Done in Less Time.* Brian Tracy. 2001. Berrett-Koehler: San Francisco, ISBN. 1583762027.
- *Getting Out from Under: Redefining Your Priorities in an Overwhelming World.* Stephanie Winston. 1999. Perseus: Reading, MA, ISBN 0738203246.
- *Getting Things Done: The Art of Stress-Free Productivity.* David Allen. 2001. Viking: New York, ISBN 670899240.
- *How to Get Control of Your Time and Your Life.* Alan Lakein & P. H. Wyden. 1996. New American Library: New York, ISBN 0451167724.
- *Managing Multiple Bosses: How to Juggle Priorities, Personalities & Projects, and Make It Look Easy.* Pat Nickerson. 1998. AMACOM: New York, ISBN 0814470254.
- *Managing Your Priorities from Start to Success.* William J. Bond. 1996. McGraw-Hill:New York, ISBN 0786303875.

ENDNOTES

1. Reprinted with the permission of Simon & Schuster Adult Publishing Group from *Global Literacies: The New Language for Business Leaders* by Robert H. Rosen, Ph.D. with Carl Phillips, Marshall Singer, and Patricia Digh. Copyright © 2000 by RHR Enterprises.

2. Products and services, United States, 29.

3. Telecommunications, United States, 35.

4. Healthcare, France, 52.

5. Products and services, United States, 35.

6. Technology, United States, 33.

7. Information and quotes from interview with Paul Curlander conducted by Cathy Greenberg. April 2002.

8 DEVELOPING PEOPLE

S tirred by pessimistic news reports, global politics, and personal concern, many high-potential leaders are debating the changing nature of work. Discussion has centered on the perceived decline in job security (the lifelong career at a benevolent company is a fading memory) and on the erosion of corporate loyalty.

> It is so difficult to keep people, especially as the organizations are flattening.... If they don't see any opportunities in the short, medium, even the long term, they are going to move.[1]

We tend to focus, understandably, on the profound impact these and other workplace changes are having on the lives of individuals. But, too often, leaders overlook the equally profound impact these changes are having on their organizations. The fact is, the "new work contract"—employees taking responsibility for their own careers and corporations providing them with career-enhancing but impermanent opportunities—can be as difficult for organizations to manage as for individuals. Many global leaders still understand little of the mechanics of developing and retaining people in turbulent times, but *are under great pressure to create opportunities to retain talents.*[2]

The task of retaining high-impact performers is complicated by four less widely acknowledged trends:[3]

1. *The reduced status of working for a Fortune 500 corporation.* John Kotter notes that from 1974 through 1994 Harvard Business School graduates who worked for smaller corporations tended to make more money and have higher job satisfaction than their counterparts in large corporations.[4] In addition, *many of these younger workers have seen their parents laid off by large companies. As a result, they have no loyalty to companies.*[5] A growing number of the top, young MBAs and technical specialists in America now avoid working for Fortune 500 corporations.

2. *The frequent lack of connection between pay and contribution.* A recent survey involving more than 2,000 managers from a wide variety of major organizations included the question, "What is the typical difference in contribution between a top performer and a below-average performer at the same pay-grade level?" The average answer was "over 100 percent." When asked, "What is the typical pay difference?" the average answer was "between 5 and 10 percent." Many managers cited cases of younger employees who were contributing more to the company than older employees but making less money.

3. *The decline in the number of titled positions in the hierarchy.* Restructuring has led to fewer layers of management in many corporations that now use a project-team approach rather than a hierarchical executive approach. A company that uses the project-team approach will have teams in areas such as provider services, marketing, and communications. Within each area there will be a team leader, a project manager, and subject matter experts (SMEs); however, because each position requires different expertise, a team leader of marketing will not necessarily have the skills to become a team leader in communications, and vice versa. Although there is a decline in executive positions when using the project-team approach, there is not a lack of opportunities. The difference is that promotions are based on projects rather than executive hierarchy, which is virtually eliminated as those team leaders with certain skill sets and competencies are progressively promoted into more challenging and complex projects. In addition, compensation is project-based rather than based on individual tenure. This focuses team leaders on working with teams across the organization to handle projects, issues, and people with industry and leadership expertise. (See Figure 8.1.)

4. *The rise in the influence of the "knowledge worker."* Peter Drucker has noted the dramatically increased importance of the knowledge worker in modern organizations. Yet, we are often still unsure what that means for how we should lead. Microsoft chairman Bill Gates recently remarked that Microsoft would do "whatever it takes" to attract and retain the brightest software developers in the world. In tomorrow's world the "intellectual capital" brought in by high-knowledge employees will be a major, if not the primary, competitive advantage for many corporations. As the perceived value of key knowledge workers increases, the competition to hire these workers will intensify. While the economic shift in the early 2000s will make it easier to retain mid-level talent, it may become even more difficult to retain the top knowledge workers.

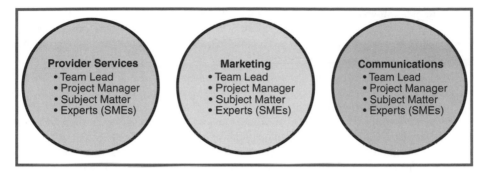

Figure 8.1
Project-team approach.

A Strategy for Developing and Retaining High-Impact Performers

The effective global leader can no longer afford to let the vagaries of the job market determine who leaves and who stays with the organization. These leaders must learn to manage human assets with the same rigor that they devote to financial assets. In our study, we involved the highest potential future leaders. Each of these employees could find another job with a pay raise with very little effort. We asked them to describe the key behaviors that leaders needed to demonstrate to keep people like them involved. The following steps, discussed in the remainder of the chapter, can help organizations keep the great leaders of the future:

1. Show respect and dignity.
2. Create a thriving environment.
3. Provide training.
4. Be a coach.
5. Provide feedback.
6. Reward and recognize others' achievements.

Show Respect and Dignity

Effective global leaders treat those around them the same way that they would like to be treated: with kindness, respect, and dignity. It is this ability to preserve the dignity of individuals and to respect their contributions that will elicit the continued loyalty of employees to both the leader and the organization.

This has implications for how leaders communicate, give feedback and instructions, and set up reward systems and incentives. Although it is possible to succeed in leading people toward a particular goal through fear and intimidation, such a leadership style will not retain or develop people.

Recently at a research and development pharmaceutical company, an executive attending a meeting became so angry that he threw an orange juice container at one of his colleagues. His inappropriate and unacceptable behavior was written up in nearly every business journal that learned of the story. Most of us read this example and know that this type of behavior is totally unacceptable. But why is it? One reason is because in today's business climate, where most decisions and projects are team-based, blaming and pointing the finger at specific individuals for problems is unacceptable.

Reserving the respect of each individual on the team is crucial if the team is to continue working together. Part of showing dignity and respect for employees also requires a leader to protect the quality of those employees.[6] For example, if one or two people on a team aren't pulling their weight or if they speak negatively about their teammates or the company, these people should be publicly reprimanded. Although this doesn't mean they should be humiliated or demeaned, it does mean that for the sake of the team, they should be called out as a separate entity because they are not contributing or they are pulling down the team. In doing so, leaders show respect to other team members who are carrying the weight of those poorer individuals. This raises morale and self-esteem, and elicits loyalty by getting rid of dead wood and maintaining a level of quality and performance within a team that is consistent with achieving the vision and the mission.

This is different than treating people with the same respect leaders would want to be shown themselves, although that may be part of it; it's about calling into action the ability to recognize when a team is stressed and weeding out those people who are pulling the team down.

CREATE A THRIVING ENVIRONMENT

In recent years many organizations have focused on those people they should get rid of rather than on those they should keep. Many downsizing "packages" give all employees with similar levels of experience the same incentive to leave. Unfortunately—for the organizations—the employees who decide to leave are often the high-impact performers who can find other work quickly.

Each employee within the company is required to have a different set of skills and knowledge if he or she is to fulfill the position satisfactorily. Each individual also has unique talents and personal career goals. Through inquiry and dialogue, effective global leaders maintain a connection with the people in their organizations and fulfill their employees' desire to grow. By asking his or her employees what training, technology, and knowledge they need to maintain and improve productivity, and what knowledge and skill sets they need to fulfill their career goals, the leader creates an environment that allows each individual to thrive.

One challenge is to retain the talent. Another challenge is to meet their personal needs. Leaders must identify the high potential people and individually coach them for their career development. Also, leaders must improve their skill set by providing the right environment to develop their talent.

In addition, leaders must attract the best talent possible and understand people's skills in order to match them with the company's needs.[7]

It is important to create an environment in which people can lead balanced lives. As organizations continue to become more and more "virtual," accommodating employees' needs and requirements both inside and outside of work life and on the job will require flexibility and empathy on the part of the global leader.

In terms of the changing workforce, there is a change in our interpretation of the "work day." There is a more flexible work structure. We need to be able to build a network to work at home.[8]

PROVIDE TRAINING

In today's rapidly changing world, training and ongoing education are necessary for the continued success of any organization. Effective global leaders put the personal development and training of their employees (and themselves) high on their priority list.

It is very important that an organization does not constrain the potential individual in his or her growth by bureaucratic rules and regulations. The organization must create and stimulate learning opportunities.[9]

By promoting and encouraging ongoing training and development, these leaders prepare people not only to do their jobs properly, but to improve upon existing and/or outdated systems. In turn, this long-term focus leads to increased shareholder value and more motivated employees. Even though the technological advancements of the 21st century will have a profound effect on the way organizations will function, the true core of any organization will remain the employees (more complex than any electronic tool).

A global leader can best prepare a person to succeed by giving him or her experience and training in the different aspects of the company as well as in his or her specific job. Cross-training helps individuals understand the value that they bring to the company (how others rely on the role they provide) and gives opportunities for cross-fertilization of ideas between departments and across regions and countries.

Bringing individuals together to share ideas and goals is one method of cross-fertilization. In the mid-1990s, a large global pharmaceutical organization brought 200 employees and leaders from its companies around the world to corporate headquarters to be part of the development of the organization's strategic plan. Because many people did not speak English, groupware was installed with which each person communicated his or her ideas and answered specific questions about the plan. The information was aggregated at the end of each day, and a large joint meeting was held in which the answers to each question were perused and analyzed. In doing so, the team was able to eliminate strategic plan items that weren't working for the entire organization but were appropriate for a certain region, functional group, or product, thus narrowing them down to a set of 10 guiding principles upon which they agreed and committed to using to operate the implementation of the mission and vision on each regional level. This style of cooperation and sharing ideas helped make the company a global leader in its industry.

In the late 1990s a global financial institution used the MSPS (motivational needs profiling system) process with the company's CFOs to establish a strategic plan for finance. Over a six-month period, the CFOs met frequently to establish a series of strategic items for the company. The behavior profiles helped the controller (the SVP of CFOs) to understand what motivated each individual, what his or her talents were, and how he or she would best participate, so that when the group was brought together as a collective whole, he was able to leverage the diverse talents of these nearly 20 leaders from countries such as Latin America, Europe, Asia, the United Kingdom, and the United States. In this way, it was possible to bring together the best ideas and leverage the talents of this worldwide group. The end result was a huge reduction in the budget based on the elimination of functional redundancies. Each CFO became the lead of certain projects across the four continents, rather than individual CFOs having responsibility for every project in their country of residence. In this way, the company leveraged the bottom-line effectiveness of doing the same thing in each country, because there's no sense in having four people do the same thing four times!

Many organizations offer leadership training and ongoing educational and training programs. It is the job of the global leader to see that his or her employees are given the opportunity to take advantage of these growth programs.

> I have had an opportunity with this company to get an executive MBA. Also, this organization has offered leadership training including a Masters Degree program in organizational psychology. This company has ongoing educational programs.[10]

Effective global leaders provide opportunities for development and involvement. One of the world's largest consulting/accounting firms recently embarked on an original program to identify and cultivate high-potential leaders. As part of the process, young leaders engage in an "action-learning" project in which they work on real-life problems facing the firm. This gives young global leaders a fantastic developmental opportunity and gives the firm valuable input on solving real problems. It also enhances the young leaders' commitment to stay with the firm. The firm's leaders say that such a process would not have been tried just a few years ago, for fear of alienating other partners, but that today the firm has no choice but to identify, develop, and retain high-impact partners.

Action learning, which originated from Columbia University, brings executives and teams together to focus on operational issues and to diagnose the issues through a series of process decompositions and reengineering and quality techniques. The action-learning model is called *action-learning reflection*. For instance, instead of institutionalizing one solution set, three or four solutions are institutionalized across three or four teams, each trying to solve the problem in different ways. At the end of the test period, the turnaround time (based on the ROI) is determined, and each team delivers its action learning, which is stated in this format: "We had this problem. Our solution set involved A, B, and C. As a result, it cost us D, E, and F. We were able to produce G. In reflection, we should have done H, I, and J."

Action learning has been used for many years in quality circles, but until recently it has not been used outside production and factory manufacturing. However, it can be used for any number of concepts, including boardroom simulations. This works in the following way: An artificial company is set up. Each person is given a role in the company. A problem that needs resolution across the leadership team is set up, and each person is asked to contribute a component of the solution. Many companies have automated these simulations and use a virtual network to track the problem, the solution, and each leader's performance. After trying solutions to problems, action-learning development programs are a great way for teams to reflect on the outcomes of those solutions.

Many companies use action-learning retrospectives to analyze projects after they have been completed. This retrospective or post-mortem analysis includes cross-comparisons of both successful and failed projects, and the goal is to incorporate what works and what doesn't work into a learning program that will teach individuals what they should do and what they should avoid. This process enables people to participate in an artificial environment to learn how the process works before they do it.

Accenture has created ABC classes, which are used at its St. Charles Learning Center. Individuals in these classes participate in simulations of companies that have had problems that Accenture solved. Each class consists of four components:

1. strategy and development
2. IT planning
3. technology implementation
4. human performance component

Using these four components, how the behavior of people will be measured and how a different culture will be institutionalized is discovered. Participants from around the world gather at Accenture's learning centers in the United States, Spain, and Asia to work together in crossfunctional teams to solve client challenges and to develop creative solution sets.

Many companies now have action-reflection programs. For instance, JP Morgan developed such a program to improve its e-commerce strategy. The company set up a separate organization (or think tank) on a floor of the organization in New York, which had an e-commerce strategy team that developed and executed service offerings and products. To maximize learning and to prevent burnout, executives were rotated every three months through the intense, 24-hour-a-day, 7-day-a-week program. This program brought the best thinking in the company into one place and also stressed a global, 24/7 working environment.

BE A COACH

As organizations move from the factory model to the service model, from hierarchies and command-and-control organizations to flatter organizations, there is a major social shift that is moving power from a small number of large organizations to many individual people. One of the big challenges in organizational change over the last decades has been that people were left to their own devices to figure out where they fit in change. By working at the individual level, effective global leaders tap the potency and the power of the coaching approach to organizational change.

They will need to step out of "command-and-control leadership" to become more of a facilitator, coach, and mentor to the people who are involved in an organization that is continually changing.[11]

Coaching gives individuals roles: It gives them a framework for dialogue (an agenda) that is directed toward the development of the individual and the results of the business. In doing so, it humanizes the organization.

You need to establish ground rules that will be the guidelines for effective and constructive disagreement. You need to coach others to appreciate the other's perspective in a team environment.[12]

Coaching can be the key to developing healthy working relationships, because central to coaching is the idea of surfacing and addressing issues and solving problems, which in turn will remove the obstacles to getting business results.

Coaching helps people align their behavior with the values and vision of the organization. By helping people understand how they are perceived as being out of alignment, and then putting these individuals back in alignment, one person at a time, coaching has more impact than organizational data that simply states the problem.

One recent successful example happened when a new sales representative came to our region from the home office. Since he had performed well in his previous job, he was not given any training in his new job in our region. We identified that this was a problem, and we found out what his needs were.

Then we provided coaching and mentoring to help him overcome his weaknesses and grow in his self-esteem. Two managers worked together to develop this person and achieve success.

An example of a failure happened with a management team I led in another area. One non-achiever had not received adequate training. The management team failed to provide coaching and goal-setting. By the time I stepped in, it was too late and we lost this employee after one year.[13]

By becoming effective coaches, global leaders become more credible and thus can be more active as agents of change. As coaches, global leaders help people develop an essential habit for personal or organizational success—follow through. By measuring others on the behaviors and attributes that are valued in the company, the leader cements the bonds of leadership with his or her constituents.

Provide feedback

As leadership and other functions change and combine within organizations at all levels, role management and career/life management grow in importance. Through periodic developmental feedback, the global leader can help individuals actively manage their careers and their personal lives.

At most companies, the norm is to give each employee an annual review, during which time the individual is given feedback against the goals set at the previous annual feedback session. However, global leaders of the future will provide more than once-a-year, professional-level feedback. New generation leaders will also provide feedback and coaching on a personal level. For instance, an individual may want assistance in a certain area, such as developing networks, being a mentor or protégé, or handling life/family balance; leaders will provide opportunities for these types of help as well. In this way, "providing feedback" is not simply annual or even semiannual performance-measure feedback—it becomes a continual process that will come in the forms of mentoring relationships, support groups, action groups, and/or individual mentoring.

Leaders of the future will understand not only the need for periodic developmental feedback, but also the importance of creating infrastructures to support the growth of individuals on a personal level, which is instrumental in retaining talent and creating employee loyalty.

Effective global leaders regularly monitor individuals' progress, listen to their feedback and ideas, and then give timely and constructive feedback in both formal and informal ways.

Many times a leader may have great technical skills, but because there is no personal relationship, the employee will leave the company. Leaders often look at the bottom line and do not develop the person.[14]

In today's fast-changing and complex global environment, global leaders should also work to develop and maintain a competent, well-staffed human resources department to train, monitor, and support individuals and teams at all levels within the organization.

Younger workers are hungry to succeed, and they job hunt a lot because of a lack of a career path. There is a big cost for losing employees, so companies need to provide a career path for them.[15]

Individuals within the company can grow and develop with the help of both personnel managers within the human resources department for their tactical and administrative needs and professional coaches and senior mentors—including direct supervisors—for their strategic, long-term needs.

They must be able to provide a solid career path for people who show promise. If you can't do that, then you will get good talented workers who will be frustrated because they can't move up within your organization.[16]

REWARD AND RECOGNIZE OTHERS' ACHIEVEMENTS

Although compensation is an important factor for retaining high-impact performers, several studies indicate that it is currently not the most important factor. Typically, the chief reasons great people leave major organizations are lack of recognition, lack of involvement, and poor management. The CEO of a leading telecommunications company recently embarked on an innovative approach. Division-level executives provide a quarterly report on high-impact performers who should be recognized. The CEO calls these individuals personally, thanks them for their contributions, and asks for their input on how the corporation can increase effectiveness. The CEO believes this process not only helps retain key talent, but also generates great ideas for continuous improvement.

There must be motivation through nontraditional means, because people are no longer tied to a company and are much more willing to leave for a better opportunity. Nontraditional means include intellectual stimulation, ownership of projects, making the work environment pleasurable, minimizing bureaucracy and "Dilbert" problems, and rewarding and recognizing people. Some of these may not be nontraditional, but they are not promotion and not money.[17]

Amazing as it may seem, many high-impact performers who are asked why they've left an organization report, "No one ever asked me to stay!" Many organizations have deliberately not told high-impact performers that they were special in any way for fear of alienating others. In the future it will become increasingly easy to retain "average" performers and increasingly difficult to retain high-impact performers.

> Most of my colleagues are males, and they are not interested in the emotions or feelings of others. However, I value it. I think it is important to understand how to relate to people. But the people I report to don't do this. My bosses don't care how I feel. Nevertheless, I believe it is important to make sure that employees are getting the recognition and visibility they need.[18]

Effective global leaders will challenge the compensation plan, because organizations unwilling to make performance rather than mere seniority the key driver of pay will face an increasing challenge in keeping top talent, especially young talent. One Fortune 500 industrial company recently refused to implement a variable, performance-based compensation plan because half the employees felt uncomfortable with the concept. However, the corporation neglected to measure *which* half felt uncomfortable "with more differentiated pay." High-impact performers of the future will be able to demand and receive substantially more pay than their lower performing peers. A "socialistic" compensation plan combined with lowered potential for promotion leads to an "average" workforce.

> The great challenge is for an organization to allow its high-potential people to advance quickly in terms of scope of responsibility and/or earnings, *or* get into the game of bringing the free agents in at the appropriate time.... Right now, performance is based on compensation plans—not based on competency.[19]

In addition, as each individual's skill sets, talents, and personal and professional goals differ, so does his or her need for recognition. Effective global leaders strive to understand and appreciate the different personalities, needs, and goals of the individuals on their teams, as well as how they would like to be rewarded and recognized for their efforts. Money and benefits are important, but there are many other ways to reward people, such as more challenging projects, flexible schedules, and travel opportunities. Not everyone wants to be spotlighted as a star and given an award in front of the rest of the company. Not everyone wants a quiet commendation from the senior executive team. Not everyone wants to be singled out; some people would rather their team be highlighted as having achieved a goal. Some people want to be known as an expert. In cross-cultural organizations, there are as many differences as there are people, so it's important for leaders to have a general idea with whom they are dealing in order to reward and recognize them appropriately. Putting in place a reward system that singularizes everyone into one mold will create problems and may possibly cause people to leave the company because they feel uncomfortable or poorly treated.

For example, in Asian companies followers find leaders. People do not follow just because they are told they have a new leader; the position of leadership with willing followers must be earned. In countries that have a degree of Communism, like the emerging markets of the Czech Republic, Hungary, and Poland, individuals are often not comfortable with small teams of collaborators and/or contributors. People associated with a small select group or an elite team are likely to be associated with malevolent leaders of the Communist era.

From these examples, it is evident that leaders must understand how to reward people appropriately and must learn to determine the attention and visibility that each team or individual requires. This can be difficult to evaluate, especially across global organizations. In such instances, if people can contribute ideas on how best to reward people in each local market, leaders will have a far better foundation upon which to base reward and recognition systems across the organization.

CONCLUSION

Every successful global leader understands that highly committed, highly competent people create financial rewards. An organization's investment in its people creates this commitment and competence. Developing individuals both personally and professionally helps companies retain their high-impact people, and it has been established that an intricate and powerful relationship exists between customer satisfaction, customer loyalty, and employee development. Developing people is a strategic process that adds value both to the employees and to the bottom line of the organization.

In the past when a high-impact performer in a major corporation was offered a position at another company, the employee was likely to say no. Most managerial and professional jobs offered good pay, job security, promotion potential, and status. Today the high-impact employee is much more likely to say yes. To retain such talent in the future, organizations must take decisive actions toward developing their people, because only those organizations able to create a dynamic new human resource model will retain the high-knowledge talent needed to succeed in tomorrow's globally competitive environment.

DEVELOPING PEOPLE

ITEM 29: Consistently Treats People with Respect and Dignity

WHAT TO DO

- Demonstrate that you respect people as individuals.
- Establish an organizational climate that is respectful and fair, and that values diversity.
- Create a supportive environment towards people.
- Interact with others in a supportive manner that sustains their dignity.
- Learn more about how others wish to be treated, communicate one-on-one often, and use other means to develop rapport.
- *Express* positive feelings, ideas, or comments to people.
- Ensure that communication with people is respectful, appropriate, and timed appropriately.
- Listen and respond with empathy.
- Never treat someone in a way that you would not want to be treated.
- Manage people, not personalities.
- Respect different opinions.
- Never critique people—critique ideas.

HOW TO DO IT

- Make a list of key ways to treat others respectfully, and use it to guide your behavior.
- On a weekly basis, check your behavior towards others against your list of key ways to treat others respectfully; note any gaps and make changes.
- Help yourself focus by asking, How do I wish to be treated?
- In conversation, listen attentively, make good eye contact, use positive body language, and use the person's name.
- Avoid directing hostile feelings, comments, or actions toward people.
- Listen and respond empathetically. Watch for others' nonverbal behavior that may indicate their feelings.

- Never participate in negative labeling or name-calling of people or groups; do not engage in back-stabbing.
- In conflict situations, strive to remain neutral, use a moderate voice, and avoid being hostile.
- Tell a peer you want to improve in this area and ask for his or her support and suggestions.
- Implement the "$2 rule" with your work group for badmouthing others (people, departments, or groups).
- Ask your manager and employees for constructive feedback.

HOW TO USE THIS SKILL FURTHER

- Ask your spouse or significant other for feedback on what you could be doing better.
- View management videos about how to treat people respectfully.
- Read a self-help book on this topic, and take action on what you read.

RESULTS YOU CAN EXPECT

- Fewer people problems may come up.
- Others in the organization may request to work with you and your group.
- You may earn a reputation for being a good people manager.

READINGS

- *Catching Success: Fishing, Leadership, and Relationships*. Dewey E. Johnson. 2001. Catching Success Press: Fresno, CA, ISBN 970519265.
- *Executive EQ: Emotional Intelligence and Leadership in Organizations*. Robert C. Cooper & Ayman Sawaf. 1997. Grosset-Putnam: New York, ISBN 0399142940.
- *How to Win Friends & Influence People*. Dale Carnegie, Dorothy Carnegie, & Arthur R. Pell. 1998. Pocket Books: New York, ISBN 0671027034.
- *Love 'Em or Lose 'Em: Getting Good People to Stay*. Beverly L. Kaye & Sharon Jordan-Evans. 1999. Berrett-Koehler: San Francisco, ISBN 1576750736.
- *Nuts!: Southwest Airlines' Crazy Recipe for Business and Personal Success*. Kevin Freiberg, Jackie Freiberg, & Tom Peters. 1998. Bantam Doubleday Dell: New York, ISBN 767901843.
- *Say Please, Say Thank You: The Respect We Owe One Another*. Donald W. McCullough. 1999. Perigee: New York, ISBN 0399525386.
- *Working With Emotional Intelligence*. Daniel P. Goleman. 2000. Bantam Doubleday Dell: New York, ISBN 553378589 .

ITEM 30: Asks People What They Need to Do Their Work Better

WHAT TO DO

- Ensure that you are accessible to your people, and invite them to share their work needs.
- Have patience; probe on familiar or "safe" topics to get reticent people to open up on underlying needs.
- Make time and take time to ask questions; stop doing other things, and *listen*!
- Be empathetic, supportive, and helpful when people share their needs with you.
- Have confidence; just ask!
- Follow up on any commitments you make to people about what you have discussed.
- Beware of your preconceived ideas about what others' needs are.
- Create an atmosphere that encourages people's questions and contrasting ideas.

HOW TO DO IT

- Questions about employees' work needs should begin with who, what, where, or when. Use open-ended questions to gain maximum information.
- Ask people, "What would it look like, how would you work better, if you had these needs met?" Listen carefully and make notes on what you hear.
- Regularly review associates' projects with them, and make notes of issues that they have asked you for help.
- Act on items you said you would act on to build credibility and encourage people to come to you with their needs.
- Avoid making any commitments that you can't keep.
- If someone's needs concern you or your management style, refrain from "building your defense." Focus on what he or she is asking about or for.
- To guard against preconceptions, remind yourself that your own needs cannot be second guessed; so do not tell people their needs before you hear them out.
- To ensure understanding of people's needs, summarize the conversation and stay open to input.
- Hold regular follow-up sessions with people to provide status or answers regarding the needs they identified when you asked.
- Observe peers and senior managers who are approached by others who share their concerns; make note of how they behave, and decide how you will adopt some of those behaviors.
- Promote the idea of "white space," where people can have some time to strategize, think, or plan, and do not have to attend meetings or work on "today's deadline." White space is often when the best ideas arise.

HOW TO USE THIS SKILL FURTHER

- With family or close friends, make a list of your assessment of their needs on some familiar topics, share it with them, and ask for their feedback.
- Practice with your spouse or significant others.

RESULTS YOU CAN EXPECT

- People may come to you more often and tell you what their needs are in order to do their best work.
- People may comment on or express appreciation for the way you listen and understand their needs.
- Projects and jobs may get done more effectively and on a more timely basis!

READINGS

- *A Practical Guide to Needs Assessment*. Kavita Gupta. 1998. Pfeiffer & Co.: New York, ISBN 0787939889.
- *Coaching for Improved Work Performance*. Ferdinand F. Fournies,. 1999. McGraw-Hill: New York, ISBN 0071352937.
- *Employee Surveys That Make a Difference: Using Customized Feedback Tools to Transform Your Organization*. Joe Folkman & Jack Zenger. 1999. Executive Excellence: Provo, UT, ISBN 1890009431.
- *First, Break All the Rules: What the World's Greatest Managers Do Differently*. Marcus Buckingham & Curt Coffman. 1999. Simon & Schuster: London, ISBN 684852861.
- *Listening and Helping in the Workplace: A Guide for Managers, Supervisors and Colleagues Who Need to Use Counseling Skills*. Frank Parkinson. 1995. Souvenir Press: London, ISBN 0285632426.
- *On Becoming a Servant-Leader*. Robert K. Greenleaf, Don T. Frick, & Larry C. Spears. 1996. Jossey-Bass: San Francisco, ISBN 0787902306.
- *The Gains of Listening: Perspectives on Counseling at Work*. Colin Feltham. 1997. Taylor & Francis: London, ISBN 0335192815.
- *The Handbook of Coaching: A Comprehensive Resource Guide for Managers, Executives, Consultants, and HR*. Frederic M. Hudson. 1999. Jossey-Bass: San Francisco, ISBN 787947954.
- *The Intelligent Organization: Engaging the Talent & Initiative of Everyone in the Workplace*. Gifford Pinchot & Elizabeth Pinchot. 1996. Berrett-Koehler: San Francisco, ISBN 1881052982.

ITEM 31: Ensures that People Receive the Training They Need to Succeed

WHAT TO DO

- Realize that the best development opportunities often occur on the job.
- Be sure that employees have the skills needed to do their best work. If not, provide them with the necessary training.
- Ask employees if they need additional training to accomplish the assigned project.
- Provide adequate orientation to new employees. Conduct an orientation training program for them that takes minimum time to administer, yet effectively integrates them into your organization.
- Identify and clearly communicate the purpose, goals, and expected results of the training for your employees.
- Involve your employees in deciding their training needs, and identify possible programs or seminars for them.

HOW TO DO IT

- If you are not always available, assign a mentor within your organization to assist new employees. Make sure the experienced employees understand their responsibility.
- Ask the mentors for feedback on the new employees in order for you to determine the additional training needs.
- Encourage employees to ask questions and express their concerns.
- Discuss specific training needs and programs with your employees to increase their interest and willingness to participate and learn.
- Ask your employees to make a presentation to their peers about what they learned from the training.
- Give developmental feedback to your employees on how they apply the new skills on the job.
- Study existing training materials at your organization to determine what you could use for your people.
- Discuss techniques with managers who excel at training and developing people.

HOW TO USE THIS SKILL FURTHER

- Assign people to leading-edge projects.
- View videotapes or read books about effective quality management.
- Practice with your spouse or significant others.

RESULTS YOU CAN EXPECT

- The productivity of your organization may increase.
- Employees may comment on or express appreciation for the way you listen and provide support on their developmental needs.

READINGS

- *Building Leaders: How Successful Companies Develop the Next Generation*. Jay Alden Conger & Beth Benjamin. 1999. Jossey-Bass: San Francisco, ISBN 787944696.
- *Coaching for Leadership: How the World's Greatest Coaches Help Leaders Learn*. Marshall Goldsmith, Laurence Lyons, & Alyssa Freas. 2000. Jossey-Bass: San Francisco, ISBN 787955175.
- *Distance Training: How Innovative Organizations Are Using Technology to Maximize Learning and Meet Business Objectives*. Deborah A. Schreiber & Zane L. Berge. 1998. Jossey-Bass: San Francisco, ISBN 0787943134.
- *Effective Training Strategies: A Comprehensive Guide to Maximizing Learning in Organizations*. James R. Davis & Adelaide B. Davis. 1998. Berrett-Koehler: San Francisco, ISBN 157675037X.
- *Executive Development and Organizational Learning for Global Business*. J. Bernard Keys & Robert M. Fulmer. 1998. Haworth: Binghamton, NY, ISBN 0789004798.
- *Living Strategy: Putting People at the Heart of Corporate Purpose*. Lynda Gratton. 2000. Financial Times Prentice Hall: New York. ISBN: 0273650157.
- *Personal Coaching for Results: How to Mentor and Inspire Others to Amazing Growth*. Louis E. Tice & Joyce Quick. 1997. Thomas Nelson: Nashville, TN, ISBN 785273557.
- *Structured On-The-Job Training*. Ronald L. Jacobs & Michael J. Jones. 1995. Berrett-Koehler: San Francisco, ISBN 1881052206.
- *The Leadership Investment: How the World's Best Organizations Gain Strategic Advantage Through Leadership Development*. Robert M. Fulmer & Marshall Goldsmith. 2000. AMACOM, New York, ISBN 814405584.

ITEM 32: Provides Effective Coaching

WHAT TO DO

- Recognize that coaching and guidance are communication skills aimed at motivating members of your work group to put forth their best effort to achieve results.
- Recognize that effective coaching requires the leader to understand before he or she tries to be understood.

- Expect the best of people.
- Review performance of subordinates on a regular basis to determine the need for coaching support.
- Recognize that a good coach is a good listener, learner, and teacher.
- Provide support whenever needed, and monitor progress routinely to ensure that everything is going smoothly.
- Use encouragement and motivation techniques rather than punishment and threats.
- Let employees know that you have a personal stake in their success and well-being.
- Recognize that even a winning team needs to be coached.
- Be aware of the overall team picture, and be sensitive to diversity in your work group that can affect communication.
- Develop your skills in supporting others, creating choices, setting commitment, and encouraging openness.
- Achieve a balance between being supportive and being firm about what is expected.
- Focus on behavior that requires change, not on the person.
- Agree on a plan and follow up with performance feedback.
- Establish clear expectations for performance.

HOW TO DO IT

- Practice your skills in observing performance in order to spot opportunities for performance improvement.
- Set up a coaching session to discuss one or two issues at a time. Schedule the meeting at a time and place convenient for the individual or team.
- Assess the situation by asking questions rather than by making statements.
- Present your comments with warmth, optimism, and open-mindedness.
- Get input for an action plan and timeline from the team or person you are coaching.
- Agree on a plan that includes follow-up steps for each of you.
- Praise improvements. Celebrate successes one-on-one or in groups.
- Provide more coaching if the desired results are not produced.
- Give performance feedback in a supportive manner.
- Take the initiative with your manager or a peer and ask her or him to coach you on a problem you are experiencing.
- Analyze the coaching session, and ask yourself what went well and what could have been improved.
- Ask your manager or coach to give you regular developmental performance feedback.

HOW TO USE THIS SKILL FURTHER

- Expand your use of coaching skills "up and out" (beyond your own work group) when opportunities arise.

- Think of a time when someone tried to help you improve a skill. Were you successful? Did the coaching you received make a difference? If not, what do you think was missing? What would have helped?
- Observe an associate or a friend to spot an opportunity for improvement. Tell the person you would like to practice your coaching skills, and ask for feedback during the meeting. (Agree on identifying a problem, discuss possible solutions, and reach agreement on an action plan.)
- Help yourself become an effective coach by asking, How do I prefer performance feedback to be given?"

RESULTS YOU CAN EXPECT

- People in your group may be more enthusiastic about your leadership and express this by initiating contact with you to get coaching and guidance.
- People in your work group may feel more supported, and you may be able to measure positive results in quality and productivity.
- Employees may be more interested in skill development and taking on new assignments.
- Employees may compliment you on how you help them with their performance issues.
- There may be an absence of surprises or "rude awakenings" when employees receive corrective performance feedback.
- Employees' performance may noticeably improve, because they have the information they need, when they need it, in order to make changes in their performance.

READINGS

- *Coaching for Leadership: How the World's Greatest Coaches Help Leaders Learn.* Marshall Goldsmith, Laurence Lyons & Alyssa Freas. 2000. Jossey-Bass: San Francisco, ISBN 787955175.
- *Personal Coaching for Results: How to Mentor and Inspire Others to Amazing Growth.* Louis E. Tice & Joyce Quick. 1997. Thomas Nelson: Nashville, TN, ISBN 785273557.
- *Structured On-The-Job Training.* Ronald L. Jacobs & Michael J. Jones. 1995. Berrett-Koehler: San Francisco, ISBN 1881052206.
- *The Handbook of Coaching: A Comprehensive Resource Guide for Managers, Executives, Consultants, and HR.* Frederic M. Hudson. 1999. Jossey-Bass: San Francisco, ISBN 787947954.
- *The Heart of Coaching: Using Transformational Coaching to Create a High-Performance Culture.* Thomas G. Crane. 1998. F T A Press: San Diego, CA, ISBN 966087402.
- *Up Is Not the Only Way: A Guide to Developing Workforce Talent.* Beverly L. Kaye. 1997. Consulting Psychologists Press: Palo Alto, CA, ISBN 891060995.

ITEM 33: Provides Developmental Feedback in a Timely Manner

WHAT TO DO

- Create a developmental climate.
- Demonstrate your belief that employees can do their best.
- Acknowledge employees' accomplishments or performance improvements as well as existing strengths.
- Learn about the different types of feedback, assess which types individual employees prefer, and apply the corresponding techniques.
- Anticipate the consequences of withholding performance feedback.
- Determine the best time to give performance feedback.
- Ensure that feedback is accurate and balanced as well as timely.
- Focus on behavior that requires change, not on the person.
- Avoid mixing emotional responses or personality observations with developmental performance feedback.
- Establish clear expectations for performance. At the time work is assigned, let people know what results you expect as they complete the work.
- Dispense recognition for outstanding performance immediately after the performance.
- Celebrate successes one-on-one or in groups.

HOW TO DO IT

- When assigning work to employees, agree on a plan and follow up with performance feedback.
- Observe employee's performance in order to spot opportunities for performance improvement.
- Make time in your schedule to give performance feedback. Make sure you and the employee have time to listen and focus during feedback.
- Give performance feedback in a supportive manner.
- Conduct regular sessions for performance feedback.
- Anchor your feedback by referring to previously established, clear performance standards.
- Hold regular debriefing sessions after key tasks or projects are completed. Ask employees what went well and what they would do differently next time.
- Create a development climate by rewarding and recognizing those who take on developmental tasks or projects.
- Practice a supportive feedback approach by criticizing in private, recognizing in public, using techniques that maintain the person's self-esteem, and planning sufficient time for feedback and discussion.

- Get employees to take stock of their performance by reflecting on how they are performing, explaining how you believe they are succeeding, and identifying what they will commit to do to improving.
- Ask associates to assess their own strengths and development needs. Have them write a plan to work on the areas of development. Take time to discuss the plan with them.
- Take the time to describe what was done well and why it was important.
- Ask employees how they would like to get feedback. Make notes and retain for reference.
- Take a course to learn about the different motivators of people and how to use them to manage performance.
- Encourage people to ask for help and feedback.
- Ask your manager to give you regular performance feedback.
- Make providing feedback, both positive and negative, part of your daily "To Do" list.

HOW TO USE THIS SKILL FURTHER

- Help yourself focus by asking, How do I prefer performance feedback to be given?
- Practice giving feedback with your children and family and ask them how you are doing.

RESULTS YOU CAN EXPECT

- There may be an absence of surprises or "rude awakenings" when employees receive corrective performance feedback.
- Employees' performance may noticeably improve, because they have the information they need, when they need it, in order to make changes in their performance.

READINGS

- *360 Degree Feedback: The Powerful New Model for Employee Assessment & Performance Improvement*. Mark R. Edwards & Ann J. Ewen. 1996. AMACOM: New York, ISBN 814403263.
- *Difficult Conversations: How to Discuss What Matters Most*. Douglas Stone, Bruce Patton, Sheila Heen, & Roger Fisher. 2000. Penguin USA: New York, ISBN 014028852X.
- *Encouraging the Heart: A Leader's Guide to Rewarding and Recognizing Others*. James M. Kouzes & Barry Z. Posner. 1999. Jossey-Bass: San Francisco, ISBN 787941840.
- *Make Success Measurable!: A Mindbook-Workbook for Setting Goals and Taking Action*. Douglas K. Smith. 1999. John Wiley & Sons: New York, ISBN 471295590.

- *Management of Organizational Behavior: Leading Human Resources.* Paul Hersey, Kenneth H. Blanchard, & Dewey E. Johnson. 2000. Prentice Hall: Upper Saddle River, NJ, ISBN 130175986.
- *Structured On-The-Job Training.* Ronald L. Jacobs & Michael J. Jones. 1995. Berrett-Koehler: San Francisco, ISBN 1881052206.
- *Turning Feedback into Change: 31 Principles for Managing Personal Development Through Feedback.* Joe Folkman & Gene Dalton. 1996. Executive Excellence: Provo, UT, ISBN 963491725.

ITEM 34: Provides Effective Recognition for Others' Achievements

WHAT TO DO

- Communicate clear performance standards and expectations.
- Find out the values and motivators of each employee, and reward accordingly.
- Provide timely positive feedback. Be specific.
- Reward individual and team achievements.
- Celebrate success with your work group.
- Make it your priority to recognize employees' performance regularly.
- Catch someone doing something right.

HOW TO DO IT

- Interview your workers and ask questions regarding values and motivators toward goal-directed behavior.
- Tell workers what was done well and why it was important.
- Give positive feedback and relate it specifically to the action or behavior at target points of task completion.
- Be cheerful and enthusiastic about the success of others.
- Use one-on-one communication, staff meetings, performance appraisals, and merit increase recommendations as tools to recognize achievement of quality and productivity goals.
- Promote high performers.
- Make sure responsibility and accountability are clearly assigned and communicated.
- Review progress with teams or individuals on a regular basis.
- Discuss techniques with managers who excel at rewarding and recognizing people.
- When you have identified individuals who are high performers, sit in on their meetings or meet one-on-one to listen to their ideas and get their input.
- Delegate more responsibility to high performers.

HOW TO USE THIS SKILL FURTHER

• Gather ideas for ways to provide recognition by thinking about your own most successful accomplishment. What made it feel good to you? What kind of recognition did you get?
• Ask people whom you respect these same questions.

RESULTS YOU CAN EXPECT

• More top priority items may be completed on time.
• Your workers may be less frustrated.
• You may notice more energy, productivity gains, and higher quality performance in your organization.
• Your organization may be known as a "good place to work."

READINGS

• *Encouraging the Heart: A Leader's Guide to Rewarding and Recognizing Others.* James M. Kouzes & Barry Z. Posner. 1999. Jossey-Bass: San Francisco, ISBN 787941840.
• *First, Break All the Rules: What the World's Greatest Managers Do Differently.* Marcus Buckingham & Curt Coffman. 1999. Simon & Schuster: London, ISBN 684852861.
• *Leader to Leader.* Frances Hesselbein & Paul M. Cohen. 1999, Jossey-Bass: San Francisco, ISBN 0787947261.
• *Love 'Em or Lose 'Em: Getting Good People to Stay.* Beverly L. Kaye & Sharon Jordan-Evans. 1999. Berrett-Koehler: San Francisco, ISBN 1576750736.
• *Managing with Carrots: Using Recognition to Attract and Retain the Best People.* Chester Elton & Adrian Robert Gostick. 2001. Gibbs Smith Publisher: Layton, UT, ISBN 1586850776.
• *Why We Do What We Do: Understanding Self-Motivation.* Edward L. Deci & Richard Flaste. 1996. Penguin USA: New York, ISBN 0140255265.
• *You Made My Day: Creating Coworker Recognition and Relationships.* Janis Allen & Michael McCarthy. 2000. Lebhar-Friedman Books: New York, ISBN 0867307870.

ENDNOTES

1. Healthcare, Philippines, 36.
2. Investments, United States, 27.

3. Information adapted from "Retaining High Impact Performers" by Marshall Goldsmith. *Leader to Leader,* No. 1, Summer 1996. Published jointly by the Drucker Foundation and Jossey-Bass.

4. Kotter, J. *The New Rules: Eight Business Breakthroughs to Career Success in the 21st Century.* Free Press: New York. 1997.

5. Telecommunications, United States, 35.

6. Larson, Carl E., & Frank M. J. LaFasto. *TeamWork: What Must Go Right/What Can Go Wrong.* Newbury Park, CA: Sage Publications, 1989.

7. Technology, Japan, 41.

8. Government, Canada, 34.

9. Technology, Taiwan, 23.

10. Products and services, United States, 42.

11. Products and services, United States, 35.

12. Technology, United States, 34.

13. Products and services, United States, 41.

14. Products and services, United States, 41.

15. Technology, United States, 28.

16. Telecommunications, United States, 32.

17. Technology, United States, 32.

18. Healthcare, United States, 33.

19. Technology, United States, 45.

9 EMPOWERING PEOPLE

W hile the previous chapter focused on the importance of developing people, this chapter focuses on the need to empower people after they are ready to assume responsibility. Today's workers want influence on decisions that affect the way their expertise is used. They want to be treated as "partners" rather than as employees, with information and opinion flowing up as well as down. In addition, leadership expectations for employees have increased significantly. At a minimum, every person is expected to lead herself or himself; most employees at some point are also expected to lead formal and informal teams and organization units.

Because we are working in a business environment with less and less hierarchy, leaders are "thought" leaders who must use knowledge to lead their teams. Global leaders must be willing to give leadership to the person with the most knowledge about the particular challenge or issue at hand. There must be an open environment to communicate and share information, which will stimulate creativity, increase knowledge, and create a team environment. Global leaders of the future must let go of control that is not necessary. The CEO of one of the world's largest global companies received feedback that he was too stubborn and opinionated. He learned that he needed to do a better job of empowering others to make decisions and to focus less on "being right" himself. For one year, he practiced a simple technique. He would take a breath before speaking and ask himself a question: "Is it worth it?" He learned that 50 percent of the time, his comments may have been correct, but they weren't worth it. He began to focus more on empowering others and letting them take ownership and commitment for decisions, and less upon his own need to add value.

BUILDS PEOPLE'S CONFIDENCE

After training employees to understand their tasks, roles, and functions within the company, empowering these individuals requires the leader to first give people opportunities and then let go of the process in which the job gets done.

> Give people the space and opportunity to grow…. Trust your people and give them opportunities.[1]

However, a crucial point may be missed if the following concept is not grasped: It is not possible for a leader to "empower" someone to be accountable and make good decisions. People must empower themselves. The effective global leader can facilitate empowerment only by encouraging and supporting a decision-making environment in which people feel comfortable making decisions and by giving people the tools and knowledge they need to take action upon those decisions. In our work in executive coaching, we have done extensive "before and after" studies on the impact of coaching on the long-term behavioral change of the person being coached. The key variable in increased leadership effectiveness is the *leader,* not the *coach.* In the same way, managers must ensure that their teams are composed of individuals who are willing to take personal responsibility for the organization's success, and they must *provide a favorable environment in which people are encouraged to grow.*[2]

In other words, the leader must build confidence within the organization. By creating an environment within which employees feel they can make decisions and act upon their own initiative, the leader has helped them reach an empowered state. However, the leader didn't empower the person; he or she created an environment in which the employee feels strong enough to adopt the behavior of an empowered employee.

> Create an environment where they get the chance to surprise themselves.[3]

Going about the process of empowering by building confidence in the organization takes longer, but it is effective. For instance, if a company has a history of shutting down or letting go of initiators, a leader can't just tell employees that they are empowered to make decisions. The global leader must first create a safe environment by encouraging constructive dialogue, asking for input, and sharing knowledge. However, it is counterproductive for executives to "announce" that employees are empowered. Employees will only *believe* they are empowered when they are left alone to accomplish results over a period of time.

> Sometimes, leaders may need to restore confidence, and leaders should always maintain the positive and cut down on the negative.[4]

Part of this concept of building an empowering environment is highly dependent on the leader's ability to run interference on behalf of his or her team. *They will need to let people know that they are safe at their job.*[5] An ongoing discussion of needs, opportunities, tasks, obstacles, projects, what's working, and what's not working is crucial to the development and maintenance of a safe working environment. Therefore, the empowering global leader is likely to spend much of his or her time in dialogue with other leaders, employees, team members, and peers.

Encourage people to have their own dream, to think big—and support them.[6]

TAKING RISKS; GIVING FREEDOM

As the role of the global leader evolves into a new form in which the central task is developing other leaders committed to the company vision and actively helping followers reach their own potential, leaders must lose the mindset that they have the monopoly on good ideas within the organization.

Today there is too much hierarchy. We must work with the people and use their talents and potential.[7]

The fact is that in most cases the global leader of the future won't *know* enough to tell people what to do, and the leader who tries to know it all and to tell everyone what to do is doomed to failure. An example is the old AT&T system, where one executive joked, "We have procedures on how to do everything but go to the bathroom, and we have a taskforce assigned to study that." In today's new world of telecommunications, change occurs far too rapidly for leaders to depend upon top-down structure and direction. However, the leader who *lets the staff have more chances to make decisions*[8] strengthens the organization by (1) developing each individual's decision-making capabilities; (2) energizing people with responsibility and accountability; and (3) creating a team of competent individuals who can handle company and industry challenges more quickly and with greater success.

Leaders must be good at managing teams. They must foster learning; increase their knowledge base; be flexible and help the group to be flexible; empower people to make decisions; and give their workers information to make good decisions.[9]

DEVELOPING EACH INDIVIDUAL'S DECISION-MAKING CAPABILITIES

As the need for creative and innovative experts—knowledge workers—increases in the organization, so does the need to allow each of these valuable individuals to lead when a challenge in his or her field of expertise is at hand. In order to do so, the traditional decision-making process that entails many layers of hierarchy must be devolved. Gifford Pinchot, co-author of *Intrapreneuring in Action: A Handbook for Business Innovation,* has helped many organizations move from a hierarchical model toward an *intrapreneurial* model to help them achieve new levels of innovations.

> Our company is a highly decentralized model. But, it pays to have some sort of semblance of a centralized structure. This lends itself to the leveraging our strengths, ideas, information, etc. We will maintain high decentralization, especially in terms of local decision-making.[10]

The effective global leader will replace traditional hierarchical leadership with more subtle methods of leadership, including dialogue, influence, accountability, and responsibility, to create a team of people who work for the common good of the organization.

> Leaders can be successful when they give power and credibility to those working under them. It is important for leaders to empower their employees and build expertise and trust in them. This way, there is not such a hierarchy. For example, at my company, we have a team of six groups who are currently working on a class-action lawsuit. I trust the leaders of these groups to work on their own without my constant supervision. I can coordinate activities between the groups and oversee the entire process without having to be involved in each group's actions every day. There is clear communication and reciprocal trust so that the goals are met.[11]

ENERGIZING PEOPLE WITH OPPORTUNITY, RESPONSIBILITY, AND ACCOUNTABILITY

Knowledge workers have enormous (often untapped) ingenuity, intelligence, and talent that lays dormant if they do not also have a challenge, responsibility, and accountability.

> Leaders must be able to disseminate information so that they can trust their subordinates to be more responsible and accountable. They must instill the

corporate vision and execution approach in their employees. Communication is a big factor. We must send a clear message. They must be able to trust and empower their frontline people and hold them accountable.[12]

The effective global leader of the future will hire talented employees, teach them the core values and mission of the company, clearly identify goals and priorities, impart responsibilities and accountability, and then let go.

Effective executives are open to different ideas and don't manage how the job is done, which is style. Leaders should allow freedom for people to get the job done, as long as there isn't a negative effect on the company; results will be reached with people expressing their own style.[13]

Knowledge workers should have responsibility for their own contribution. Individuals should help decide accountability in terms of quality and quantity in respect to time and in respect to cost.

I want more freedom to do my thing. I have my way of achieving the goal, so don't tell me how to do it. I want to be involved in the decision-making process. I want leaders to take my input. I want to make my voice heard and be a more empowered part of the organization.[14]

Lastly, if people see opportunities for ownership and personal development, they are much more likely to stay with the organization. For example, companies can *provide intrapreneurial opportunities.* Gifford Pinchot (who coined the term *intrapreneur*) has shown how major corporations can provide opportunities for semiautonomous enterprises to operate within the larger corporate structure. By allowing high-potential leaders to "run a business" inside a larger business, corporations can gain commitment while simultaneously developing people.

CREATING A TEAM OF COMPETENT INDIVIDUALS WHO CAN HANDLE COMPANY AND INDUSTRY CHALLENGES MORE QUICKLY AND WITH GREATER SUCCESS

Competency comes with experience. Leaders develop the capabilities of their people by pushing decision-making down to those who are closest to the customer or activity. In doing so, it's important to allow people to make mistakes and then to help them recover quickly.

Companies are going to be flatter. They will be getting decisions made at the lowest possible level in the organization. The less interference you have, the better.[15]

Because quick, informed decision making is imperative if a company is to compete in today's global and fast-paced marketplace, it is well worth risking a blunder or two. The effective global leader will put safety checks in place to guard from certain disasters and will maintain an open-door policy with employees to discuss current projects and challenges. McKinsey and Company is a benchmark organization for encouraging challenge inside the work team and simultaneously building support for the final team decision.

I think organizations will move to flatter structures which empower employees to make decisions as long as there are certain checkpoints. You have to limit risk to a certain degree.[16]

HOARDING POWER VERSUS ENCOURAGING ACHIEVEMENT

The foundation of empowering relationships between global leaders and their employees is trust.

They [global leaders] must have the "trust factor." We must trust that people are doing their jobs.[17]

Leaders who do not trust will micromanage the process in which people do their work, and they will probably keep many projects for themselves because they don't trust anyone else to do them right.

They must let go of details, but they still need to make sure that the organization is going in the right direction. Instead of the leaders giving out orders of how things should be done, they must now serve the organization under them.[18]

This not only stifles creative thinking, but it undermines workers' confidence. Any sense of autonomy is destroyed, and the leader is left with the bulk of the burden because employees will only do what they are told; they will not strive to improve. Frances

Hesselbein, former CEO of the Girl Scouts of the United States, was a role model for encouraging achievement and not hoarding power. She created an environment in which the person in the mailroom defined himself as the heart of the organization who was responsible for communications in and out as opposed to defining himself as a person who took orders and did mundane work.

WHAT DRIVES YOU?

Effective global leaders should be able to paint a picture of where the company is headed, what roles people will play, and what goals must be accomplished, and also able to inspire and motivate others to work toward that point in a way that embodies excellence. In a rapidly changing future, executives will need to learn not only to let go but they will need to learn to let go quickly. One executive who was listed as an excellent future leader consistently told his people, "Get back to me when you need or want help; otherwise, I'm going to assume that you are getting the job done."

By looking closely at personalities and experiences, one can evaluate how a given individual can lead best and in what context that leadership will likely be successful. A crucial factor in such an evaluation is the individual's motivation: As an example, an interesting comparison is between personalities who are more achievement-motivated and those who are more power-motivated.

> These executives are able to identify who the leaders are. Then they can empower those leaders. They find "the best to help the rest." They understand different styles and know when to accept the difference. These leaders can identify someone's strengths and weaknesses and find workers who complement each other.[19]

Achievement-motivated people are logical and organized; they complete assigned tasks well; they raise standards. High achievers want predictability, order, improvement, and they are diligent about technique and process. They are skilled at showing others what needs to be done and how it should be done to meet different goals successfully. However, they are uncomfortable with the lack of control they feel when they hand projects off; therefore, they are not as likely to be successful high-level leaders.

The concept of *power* often gets a bad reputation, but it is actually the process of influencing and having impact on whole constituencies of people. Power-motivated people inspire others to do tasks well; they create coalitions for change; they have the capacity to see the big picture and link individuals and constituencies with it. However, in many cases their capacity to carry out detailed work themselves may be limited; they prefer instead to influence others to carry out these detailed tasks, but now with more confidence that they will be in service of the "greater good" rather than of a largely individual agenda.

Every individual has a different mixture of achievement, affiliation, power, and autonomy drivers. Successful leaders recognize how these particular drivers can be deployed for best effect; they also recognize the accompanying limitations of the motivational "jigsaw" and accordingly plan for the partnering of executives with complementary strengths. Gaining insight into these motivators can be an extremely useful tool in determining what style of leadership a person will have and if he or she will be an effective leader within a specific business context.

CONCLUSION

Trusted, responsible, knowledgeable—*empowered*—workers are the foundation upon which successful companies are based. However, only if employees feel that their abilities and contributions are fully valued will they share their ideas and expertise. Company bureaucracy, excessive meetings, and micromanaging leaders undermine workers' sense of autonomy and professionalism. A more effective leader will define roles, goals, schedules, and requirements, and then delegate specific projects to teams of individuals.

The role of the global leader is to create an environment within which people feel confident making decisions, taking responsibility, and sharing ideas and knowledge, and then give them the space and freedom they need to do their jobs well. This is especially important in today's environment, in which the workforce is often so physically scattered that leaders can't be operationally involved in each task. As such, they must let go of the details and put their efforts into guiding the course of the organization.

JUMPING IN WITH BOTH FEET[20]

Every person has talents; you just have to cast them properly.

As president of Anthem Blue Cross and Blue Shield East, Marjorie Dorr is responsible for a $4 billion business, which includes operations in the Northeast, encompassing Connecticut, Maine, and New Hampshire. Her responsibilities include the company's customer business units, which focus on sales and service. In addition, she is responsible for actuarial services, provider relations/contracts, medical management, quality management, marketing, communications, and support services.

Taking Chances

Highly recognized for her positive and enthusiastic spirit, Marjorie is not afraid to jump in with both feet. She is also not against throwing her people into the deep end. "A lot of companies fail because they try a 'cookie-cutter' approach," says Marjorie. "We work in a highly regulated business, so it is easy to get paralyzed by the system. We counter this by getting ideas from lots of different sources and often doing things that are totally unheard of in this system." Marjorie is proud that she has been able to give people the same breaks that she was given. "I have hundreds of people whose [careers have] totally blossomed. I have been disappointed maybe five times out of a hundred."

Pulling the Wires Together

The key to success, says Marjorie, is "lots of communication and giving opportunities." Through her direct and open style of communication, Marjorie develops the trust and confidence that enables her to rely heavily on her people. Marjorie gives her people permission to do things "outside the box" and rewards the highly innovative people whose ideas help keep Anthem moving and growing.

With strong communication channels and a clear vision established, Marjorie has been able to capitalize on the strengths and characteristics of her diverse team and the positive elements of the company's history. She calls it "pulling the wires together," and it's definitely working. In February 2002, *Fortune* named Anthem one of the 10 most admired healthcare companies in America for the second consecutive year.[21]

EMPOWERING PEOPLE

ITEM 35: Builds People's Confidence

WHAT TO DO

- Recognize small improvements in performance.
- Recognize desired behavior that leads to expected performance.
- Criticize constructively and in private. Let people know you have confidence that they can make the needed changes in their performance.
- Delegate assignments and *let go*! Empower people to pursue the assignment their way, within set parameters and deadlines.
- Cultivate a work climate that allows people to learn from their mistakes.

HOW TO DO IT

- Praise when it is justified, and be specific about what you are praising.
- Have people represent you at meetings or prepare documents for your signature.
- Understand the current performance levels of your employees, and recognize what is beyond that level. Coach your employees to maximize their potential.
- Tell people what they did right, and then illustrate how they can use that experience to build on improving in the area they did not do well.
- Explain to people that you intend to "let go" and allow them to complete assignments on their own. Let them know it is okay to ask for assistance when they need it.
- Encourage people to ask you open-ended questions about what they should do or say on your behalf in meetings or in documents for your signature.
- Demonstrate that it is okay to make mistakes by not punishing people.
- Reward high performers with more responsibilities and promotional opportunity.

MORE HOW TOs

- Discuss techniques with managers who excel at building people's confidence.
- Encourage people to come up with different ideas and perspectives to solve problems and spot opportunities.
- Create a favorable environment in which people are encouraged to grow their skills.

HOW TO USE THIS SKILL FURTHER

- Help yourself focus by asking, "What was done for me to make me feel like a winner?"
- Practice this skill with your spouse, significant other, and your children.

RESULTS YOU CAN EXPECT

- Employees may say they enjoy working for you.
- Employees' performance may improve because they have greater self-confidence.

READINGS

- *21 Irrefutable Laws Of Leadership*. John C. Maxwell. 1998. Thomas Nelson: Nashville, TN, ISBN 785274316.
- *Encouraging the Heart: A Leader's Guide to Rewarding and Recognizing Others*. James M. Kouzes & Barry Z. Posner. 1999. Jossey-Bass: San Francisco, ISBN 787941840.
- *Learning Journeys: Top Management Experts Share Hard-Earned Lessons on Becoming Great Mentors and Leaders*. Marshall Goldsmith, Beverly L. Kaye, & Ken Shelton. 2000. Davies-Black Publishing: Palo Alto, CA, ISBN 891061479.
- *Management 21C: Someday We'll All Manage This Way*. Subir Chowdhury. 1999. Financial Times-Prentice Hall: Upper Saddle River, NJ, ISBN 273639633.
- *Managers As Mentors: Building Partnerships for Learning*. Chip R. Bell. 1998. Berrett-Koehler: San Francisco, ISBN 1576750345.
- *Personal Coaching for Results: How to Mentor and Inspire Others to Amazing Growth*. Louis E. Tice & Joyce Quick. 1997. Thomas Nelson: Nashville, TN, ISBN 785273557.
- *Self Esteem at Work*. Nathaniel Branden & Warren G. Bennis. 1998. Jossey-Bass: San Francisco, ISBN 787940011.
- *Work and Motivation*. Victor H. Vroom. 1995. Jossey-Bass: San Francisco, ISBN 0787900303.

ITEM 36: Takes Risks in Letting Others Make Decisions

WHAT TO DO

- Risk taking plays a part in nearly every decision. Understanding the risks and the potential benefits of each decision is essential to the success of all managers.
- Involve people in more problem solving and decision making.
- Encourage associates to solve their own problems rather than coming to you.

- Provide others with sufficient information and support to empower them to make informed decisions .
- Don't take unnecessary risks. Try to eliminate those risks that are in your power.
- Give assignments describing the outcome desired (clear performance goals), but let the employee use the means he or she thinks best.
- Encourage and reward problem solvers and decision makers.
- Don't second guess others' decisions.
- Review and discuss all risks (the probability of failure and its consequences) before agreeing on a decision or trying out a new idea.
- Be clear about boundaries. Let people know what is and what is not open for negotiation.
- Make sure the impact of the decision on other operations and other work units is fully explored and resolved before a decision is finalized.
- Give people room for some errors.
- Promote a feeling of employee ownership with their projects.
- Make people aware that they are accountable for their decisions.

HOW TO DO IT

- Ask employees which projects or duties they would like full responsibility for.
- Help someone else assess the risks and benefits of a decision or approach they want to try out. Determine the consequences of failure and the benefits of success.
- Hold regular meetings with others (managers, peers, workers) to share information and data, and identify possible pitfalls for their decisions.
- Give people discretion and autonomy over their tasks and resources.
- Respect the talents of the team or person. Let them design a plan of action in the way they know how.
- Maintain objectivity when reviewing others' decisions.
- Set appropriate follow-up meetings to review progress and take corrective action if necessary.
- Supply the resources and information others need to make decisions.
- Determine the "area of freedom" for new ideas, where ideas can be tried out without violating any contractual, safety, or other nonnegotiable requirements.
- Model the behavior of making sound decisions and taking appropriate risks.
- Identify projects or assignments that could be delegated for developmental purposes. Discuss those opportunities with subordinates to gain their commitment.

HOW TO USE THIS SKILL FURTHER

- Ask people in positions similar to yours what sorts of tasks they commonly delegate. Plan to delegate similar tasks when appropriate.
- Remind yourself how you learned by doing as well as by being directed.

RESULTS YOU CAN EXPECT

- People may feel more responsible for their decisions and generate more ideas for solving problems.
- Your group may make more mistakes than before, but may experience more successes.
- You may spend less time directing other's projects and have more time for strategic planning.

READINGS

- *In Praise of Good Business: How Optimizing Risk Rewards Both Your Bottom Line and Your People*. Judith M. Bardwick. 1998. John Wiley & Sons: New York, ISBN 047125407X.
- *Knowledge and Decisions*. Thomas Sowell. 1996. Basic Books: New York, ISBN 0465037380.
- *Smart Choices: A Practical Guide to Making Better Decisions*. John Hammond, Ralph Keeney, & Howard Raiffa. 1998. Harvard Business School Press: Boston, ISBN 0875848575.
- *Sources of Power: How People Make Decisions*. Gary Klein. 1998. MIT Press: Cambridge, MA, ISBN 0262112272.
- *The Knowing Organization: How Organizations Use Information to Construct Meaning, Create Knowledge, and Make Decisions*. Chun Wei Choo. 1997. Oxford University Press: Oxford, ISBN 0195110129.
- *Working Knowledge*. Thomas Davenport & Laurence Prusak. 2000. Harvard Business School Press: Boston, ISBN 1578513014.

ITEM 37: Gives People the Freedom They Need to Do Their Job Well

WHAT TO DO

- Give power away to strengthen others.
- Define the limits of decision-making power.
- Encourage associates to solve their own problems rather than coming to you.
- Ask your staff if your involvement or direction in the assignment is at the appropriate level.
- Have an efficient updating process that gives you enough information to allow the team or individual the ability to work independently.
- Give visibility to others and provide recognition for their efforts.
- Don't second guess decisions.

- Give assignments describing the outcome desired (clear performance goals), but let the employee use the means he or she thinks best.
- Encourage and reward problem solvers and decision makers.
- Ask for employee input and take time to listen.
- Reward performers with responsibility.
- Involve people in more problem solving and decision making.
- Give people room for some errors.
- Cultivate a climate in which people feel free to take initiative on assignments.
- Promote a feeling of employee ownership with their projects.

HOW TO DO IT

- Give people discretion and autonomy over their tasks and resources.
- Respect the talents of the team or person. Let them design a plan of action in the way they know how.
- Monitor your own involvement with the project. Consider whether your past actions have been beneficial to the project as a whole. Let the individual or team do their jobs.
- When discussing the responsibility to be delegated, work with the associate to determine decision-making parameters and how to overcome other issues or concerns.
- Consider yourself a resource rather than the manager.
- Let associates speak for themselves to higher management rather than go through you.
- Set appropriate follow-up meetings to review progress and take corrective action if necessary.
- Discuss with your staff ways to give them greater freedom to do their job.
- State approval of employee approaches by saying such things as, "I can see you have a lot of good ideas."
- Ask employees which projects and duties they would like full responsibility for.
- Take time to think of areas in which more power might be shared. List the pros and cons of giving people greater work freedom.
- Lead a task force that requires a lot of delegating, and request a member or an observer give you feedback on how well you are doing.
- Ask people in positions similar to yours what sorts of tasks they commonly delegate. Plan to delegate similar tasks when appropriate.
- Identify projects or assignments that could be delegated for developmental purposes. Discuss those opportunities with subordinates to gain their commitment. Follow through with the delegation.

HOW TO USE THIS SKILL FURTHER

- Delegate more to your people.
- Remind yourself how you learned by doing as well as by being directed.

RESULTS YOU CAN EXPECT

- More of your delegations may be carried out meeting deadlines and quality standards.
- You may spend less time directing others' projects and have more time for management planning.
- You may develop a sense of accomplishment from the accomplishments of your people rather than from your own efforts.
- People may say they feel they are more like partners.
- Your associates may be more satisfied with their work.

READINGS

- *A Company of Leaders: Five Disciplines for Unleashing the Power in Your Workforce*. Gretchen M. Spreitzer & Robert E. Quinn. 2001. John Wiley & Sons: New York, ISBN 0787955833.
- *Empowering Employees*, Kenneth L. Murrell, Mimi Meredith, 2000, McGraw-Hill Professional Publishing, NY, ISBN 0071356169.
- *Essential Managers: How To Delegate*. Robert Heller & Tim Hindle. 1999. DK Publisher: London, ISBN 0789428903.
- *Intrinsic Motivation at Work: Building Energy & Commitment*. Kenneth W. Thomas. 2000. Berrett-Koehler: San Francisco, ISBN 1576750876.
- *The 3 Keys to Empowerment: Release the Power Within People for Astonishing Results*. Ken Blanchard, John C. Carlos, & Alan Randolph. 1999. Berrett-Koehler: San Francisco, ISBN 1576750604.
- *The Self-Managing Organization: How Leading Companies Are Transforming the Work of Teams for Real Impact*. Ronald Purser & Steven Cabana. 1998. Free Press: London, ISBN 068483734X.

ITEM 38: Trusts People Enough to Let Go (Avoids Micromanagement)

WHAT TO DO

- Give power away to those who have demonstrated the capacity to handle the extra responsibility.
- Define the limits of decision-making power.
- Encourage associates to solve their own problems rather than coming to you.
- Ask your staff if your involvement or direction in the assignment is at the appropriate level.
- Have an efficient updating process that gives you enough information to allow the team or individual the ability to work independently.

- Don't second guess others' decisions.
- Give assignments describing the outcome desired (clear performance goals), but let the employee use the means he or she thinks best.
- Encourage and reward problem solvers and decision makers.
- Reward performers with responsibility.
- Involve people in more problem solving and decision making.
- Give people room for some errors.
- Cultivate a climate in which people feel free to take initiative on assignments.
- Promote a feeling of employee ownership with their projects.

HOW TO DO IT

- Give people discretion and autonomy over their tasks and resources.
- Respect the talents of the team or person. Let them design a plan of action in the way they know how.
- Monitor your own involvement with the project. Consider whether your past actions have been beneficial to the project as a whole. Let the individual or team do their jobs.
- When discussing the responsibility to be delegated, work with the associate to determine decision-making parameters and how to overcome other issues or concerns.
- Consider yourself a resource rather than the manager.
- Let associates speak for themselves to higher management rather than through you.
- Set appropriate follow-up meetings to review progress and take corrective action if necessary.
- Discuss with your staff ways to give them greater freedom to do their jobs.
- State approval of employee approaches by saying such things as, "I can see you have a lot of good ideas."
- Ask employees which projects and duties they would like full responsibility for.
- Take time to think of areas in which more power might be shared. List the pros and cons of giving people greater work freedom.

HOW TO USE THIS SKILL FURTHER

- Lead a task force that requires a lot of delegating, and request a member or an observer to give you feedback on how well you are doing.
- Ask people in positions similar to yours what sorts of tasks they commonly delegate. Plan to delegate similar tasks when appropriate.
- Remind yourself how you learned by doing as well as by being directed.

RESULTS YOU CAN EXPECT

- More of your delegations may be carried out meeting deadlines and quality standards.

- You may spend less time directing others' projects.
- You may develop a sense of accomplishment from the accomplishments of your people rather than from your own efforts.
- People may say they feel they are more like partners.
- Your associates may be more satisfied with their work.

READINGS

- *30 Days to a Happy Employee: How a Simple Program of Acknowledgment Can Build Trust and Loyalty at Work.* Dottie Bruce Gandy. 2001. Fireside: Columbus, OH, ISBN 068487329X.
- *Building Trust at the Speed of Change: The Power of the Relationship-Based Corporation.* Edward M. Marshall. 1999. AMACOM: New York, ISBN 0814404782.
- *Driving Fear Out of the Workplace: Creating the High-Trust, High-Performance Organization.* Kathleen Ryan & Daniel K. Oestreich. 1998. Jossey-Bass: San Francisco: ISBN 0787939684.
- *Hidden Value: How Great Companies Achieve Extraordinary Results with Ordinary People.* Charles A. O'Reilly & Jeffrey Pfeffer. 2000. Harvard Business School Press: Boston, ISBN 875848982.
- *Living Strategy: Putting People at the Heart of Corporate Purpose.* Lynda Gratton. 2000. Financial Times Prentice Hall: New York. ISBN: 0273650157.
- *Trust and Betrayal in the Workplace.* Dennis S. Reina & Michelle L. Reina. 1999 Berrett-Koehler: San Francisco, ISBN 1576750701.

ENDNOTES

1. Healthcare, Australia, 34.
2. Technology, South Korea, 36.
3. Products and services, Switzerland, 45.
4. Transportation, Canada, 47.
5. Healthcare, Taiwan, 41.
6. Technology, Taiwan, 32.
7. Products and services, Brazil, 49.
8. Technology, Taiwan, 32.
9. Products and services, Brazil, 34.
10. Healthcare, Philippines, 36.
11. Investments, United States, 27.
12. Products and services, United States, 33.

13. Transportation, United States, 40.

14. Products and services, United States, 27.

15. Products and services, Switzerland, 45.

16. Pharmaceutical, United States, 31.

17. Government, Canada, 34.

18. Investments, United States, 27.

19. Telecommunications, United States, 35.

20. Information and quotes from interview with Marjorie Dorr conducted by Cathy Greenberg. April 2001.

21. *http://www.anthem.com/jsp/maroon/frameset.jsp.*

10

ACHIEVING
PERSONAL MASTERY

The traditional view of the leader—unemotional, supremely rational, and essentially mechanistic—is based on the vertically integrated, hierarchical Industrial Age organization. In a less structured, more dynamic global organization, however, the leader can no longer act as supreme puppeteer, simply pulling the strings to make things happen. That is, good leadership, and consequently organization sustainability, will be less about what the leader does and more about who the leader is—and in particular, about two key traits: *personal mastery* and *flexibility* (which is discussed in Chapter 13, "Leading Change").

SELF-AWARENESS: THE MARK
OF A GREAT LEADER

Leaders have always worked to understand others, but in the future, they must devote the same kind of effort to understanding themselves—that is, to personal mastery. Personal mastery essentially means having a heightened self-awareness—a deep understanding of one's own behavior, motivators, and competencies—and having "emotional intelligence" that allows one to monitor and manage—rather than control or suppress—one's emotional state.

Leaders need to balance their emotions. They should not overreact to situations, but they should not be totally cold, either. Positive emotions can have a positive impact to drive others.[1]

As well as demonstrating effective emotional responses in a variety of situations, he or she will demonstrate self-confidence and integrity as a leader, thus inspiring and influencing others to follow his or her vision. For instance, during a media interview, Bob Nardelli, CEO of Home Depot, was confronted about a very negative article written and published by a dissatisfied female customer.[2] In the article, the woman described her bad experience getting help at Home Depot and told how the competition had been much more helpful. Home Depot, which had found its niche in providing great customer service and assistance, had failed this customer. Bob Nardelli, rather than taking offense to what was written in the article, told the interviewer that he apologized to the public for the service breakdown and that Home Depot was doing and would continue to do everything possible to rectify the situation. Most importantly, Bob explained that companies, especially large companies like Home Depot, are going to have hiccups. He explained that Home Depot has used the situation as a learning experience to create new opportunities and to grow. Through his even-tempered, positive approach, Bob inspired and influenced others to take responsibility and to learn from mistakes.

Global leaders must take it upon themselves to be deeply aware of their personal values and match them to the stakeholders of their organizations. In other words, global leaders' personal values must be reflected in the stakeholders of the organization and their communities. The senior executive team of a global food corporation, focused on company strategy and leadership alignment, acknowledged a connection between the alignment of individual values and principles and company performance. With the help of a consulting firm, the team developed a model whereby the values and principles of individuals were factored in as part of their recruitment practice. The team found that individuals who prospered through training and education would find great opportunities to develop careers at the company; however, individuals who went through training and were unable to grasp the company's philosophy, although given time to work at it, most often weren't successful. The team quickly realized that if there was a mismatch between the values and principles of an individual and the organization, it didn't matter how much training or experience the individual was given, the individual would not be successful at the company.

The leader of the future will willingly admit to personal shortcomings and strive to improve by making a significant investment in ongoing personal development. The CEO of a large mid-Atlantic financial organization realized that he had a lack of understanding for different perspectives, cultures, and lifestyles. As a white male and an economist, he had always been surrounded with people like himself. He decided to make an effort to improve this shortcoming. First, he communicated his challenge to others within the company. Next, he diversified his leadership team to include, as the head of HR, an innovative African American woman. She started a mentoring program that partnered people with very different perspectives together. In fact, she (a gay, female artist-type as she describes herself) paired herself with the CEO. Through this relationship, he discovered that his personal shortcomings around understanding cultural diversity and differing viewpoints was having a real impact on the bottom line of the company, especially given that 70 percent of his core corporate administration and support were African American women. From his partner, he learned that people evaluate information and emotions, and make decisions in a manner different from his. He learned to consider others' values, principles, and decision-making criteria. The mentoring partnership helped him integrate and understand the different value sets and principles of those with whom he worked, so that in the long run he turned his "personal shortcoming" into an admired leadership attribute.

He or she will endeavor to deeply understand his or her own strengths and weaknesses, and will not only *have a good consulting team to help bridge the information gap,*[3] but will involve others who have strengths that the leader does not possess. *These leaders will appreciate others being able to do what they are not able to do.*[4] There are many reasons that a leader may not be able to complete a specific task or accomplish a certain goal. For instance, perhaps he or she does not have the expertise to solve a problem or does not have the time to focus on it. However, unlike micromanagers, successful leaders will recognize that the outcome will be much greater if they put in place a team of people who have the skills and capabilities needed to handle these challenges more effectively and with deeper focus.

Successful CEOs will know how to divest themselves of the day-to-day solutions and problem-solving activities of the company in order to maximize strategic and relationship building efforts, which contribute to the overall forward momentum of the company. They will recognize the difference between what they need to do versus what they should pass along to their teams. A CEO or chairman should be involved in the minutia of a solution only if everybody else has been unsuccessful or if it's a regulatory or personal relationship that requires a CEO-to-CEO conversation. However, this doesn't always work. For instance, the CEO of a large, global insurance company has become a bottleneck at her company, because nearly every problem and decision goes through her. A people pleaser, the CEO retains power through her relationships, which has become a serious hindrance to the success of the company. The CEO involves herself in nearly every problem that comes through the operations area, because of her personal relationships with the individuals and companies involved. This has slowed the progress of the company down to nearly a standstill.

Leaders' commitment to personal mastery is integral to the financial success and sustainability of an organization. Leaders who find a balance between self mastery, relationship building and the bottom line of the company will be more successful and will avoid "bottlenecking" due to people-pleasing and "cooking the books" to improve stock prices, as in the cases of Enron and Worldcom.

INSIDE-OUT LEADERSHIP

Traditionally, leadership development programs have sought to instill particular capabilities in their subjects. This is considered "outside-in" leadership, because it asks the leader to look at his or her own personal profile and motivations first and then adapt accordingly. A new school of thought is emerging, however, which claims that leaders must

LEADERSHIP AND ORGANIZATIONAL SUSTAINABILITY

The link between leadership and organizational sustainability is a concept that has long been discussed. For instance, in their book *Corporate Culture and Performance*, John Kotter and John Heskett offer a comprehensive analysis of the powerful influence of an organization's culture on performance. The authors' assertion is that effective leadership is crucial in making unhealthy cultures more adaptive.[5] In his "Academy of Management" report, based on his doctoral dissertation conducted at Case Western Reserve University, Dr. Eric Harter provides the research that supports this theory.[6]

A Little About the Study

Nearly 150 chief executive officers and senior executive subordinates representing 35 firms participated in the study, which used "The Leadership Profile" (TLP), a validated 360-degree leadership assessment questionnaire, to measure leadership. After developing a financial database focused on specific organizational financial measures, 272 of the 900 healthcare organizations contained in the initial sample were selected for further study. The 35 firms in the final sample were divided into three groups: sustainable, weakly sustainable, and least sustainable.

Observations

Harter found significant differences between the leadership scores of leaders in the sustainable and the least sustainable organizations. Those leaders who scored significantly higher on the TLP were the leaders of financially sustainable organizations. These leaders were more transformational. However, the most noteworthy finding was the consistent differences between self and others' ratings for leaders of the least sustainable organizations. This was contrasted with the invariable agreement between others' ratings and self ratings of leaders of sustainable organizations. A key indicator of self-awareness is the degree to which self-other agreement coincides. This is also an indicator of "emotional intelligence." The results of Harter's research indicate that leaders of the least financially sustainable organizations were much less self-aware when compared to leaders of organizations judged sustainable.

first understand themselves: their motivations, preferences, and risk tolerances. Leadership development must always begin with the careful recognition of core individual values. Through this "inside-out" approach, leaders will be able to respond to or modify their environment to align with their unique, personal leadership capabilities.

There is not a singular model that describes an effective leader for all companies in all industries at all times. Leaders must understand what is required and evaluate their own capabilities and respond accordingly, either by focusing on their strengths, developing new skills, or teaming with others who have the skills that they lack. The leaders of Electronik Inc., COO Johanna Hambrose and CEO Harold Hambrose, separate responsibilities, because they realize that each person has strengths that the other does not. Johanna is more adept at developing marketing strategies, whereas Harold is more capable at design. As such, they lead different teams. Johanna leads the organization's sales force and business development group, and Harold leads the design team.

According to Manfred Kets de Vries, executives have a notoriously underdeveloped capacity for self-reflection, in part because the myopic, action-oriented environment in which many executives operate does not encourage this kind of self-examination.[7] Despite this inherent difficulty, the changing work environment is making self-awareness all the more important.

In order to influence others, it is vital that the leader first understand his or her strengths and limitations. As in many facets of leadership, understanding oneself is the first step toward developing an effective style for influencing others.

CHANGING THE LEADERSHIP TRADITION

As part of this personal mastery and self-awareness, effective leaders will be proficient at what John O'Neil calls "ego management"—at listening to other viewpoints rather than simply defending their own—and at not having to "win" whenever there is a difference of opinion. They will also cultivate the quality of *empathy,* which is the ability to read emotions in others and to see oneself through the eyes of others.

Empathy will be important in communicating across cultures; in understanding and motivating knowledge workers who tend to respond to mutual respect and open communication; and in being able to tap into the ideas and abilities of other people and foster collaboration.

This can be a difficult challenge for global leaders, as people around the world express and communicate feelings differently. For instance, a global financial institution hired a Chinese American male, who had been raised in China by his Chinese mother, as SVP of International Banking. According to his coworkers in the United States, he did not show his emotions. In fact, they complained that because he had no affect, they could not read his responses, and so he was very difficult to work with. As a result of these difficulties in communicating, a consulting firm was brought in to help the international team work together. During an interview, the SVP revealed the difference he had found between how people from the two cultures express emotions. When communicating with people from the United States, he looked at their eyes and facial expression to garner their responses. However, in China, it is inappropriate to show such facial expressions—for instance, a wide smile—after a certain age, so he would read the mouth and chin. He would notice if the mouth were inverted or pursed, or the chin puckered. In doing so, he would know if a person was happy, sad, upset, or tense. This was second nature to him, but before it was explained, it was very confusing to his coworkers.

Open communication regarding body language, empathy, motivational style, and so on is crucial across cultures if we are to understand each other and work together. Certain gestures, such as maintaining eye contact and not showing facial expressions, appreciated in one culture, may be a sign of disrespect in another. As such, to foster collaboration and engender cultural empathy, global leaders must put cultural biases aside and directly communicate with each other in order to learn how to relate to different people in different ways.

> It is important to talk openly when going through a conflict. We should talk about emotion, because that will build a solid team. I believe it's the only way you really get to the core of having a solid team that is working together with great trust in one another. There must be some vulnerability and we must get to know the whole person, not just how bright [the person is] or how well [he or she] thinks through things. We need to know what [he or she] feels and how it impacts us. Also, we need to know ourselves well and allow people to be open with us.[8]

This focus on the emotional side is a far cry from the traditional leadership ideal and so strikes some executives as "not real." However, there are solid business reasons for the leader to develop self-awareness. With strong self-awareness, the leader

- Has a clear sense of his or her capacity for and comfort with risk, stress, and change.

- Has a solid "center" that helps in dealing with multiple cultures, ambiguity, change, and uncertainty.

- Is better able to collaborate as opposed to control.

- Is better able to understand and relate to diverse groups of business partners, employees, and customers.

- Knows his or her strengths and weaknesses, and the areas where the complementary skills and strengths of others can be best brought to bear.

- Can find balance in his or her life, know when and how to recharge physically, mentally, and emotionally, and be more resilient in the face of pressure and stress.

> I am a lot less hot-headed, now, than I used to be. You learn to see it coming. You learn to not do damage.[9]

Ultimately, self-awareness will be central to effective leadership because it can have a powerful impact on the perceptions of those in the organization and their willingness to follow the leader—and help build the sense of trust needed to hold distributed, networked organizations together. Effective leaders must understand the impact they have on others, and then they can more effectively manage their emotional responses and reactions.

THE POWER OF CONGRUENCY

The global leaders of the future must continually practice personal mastery; that is, they need a high degree of self-awareness to monitor their own behavior and leverage their personal strengths, as well as to fill gaps in competencies. In building a holistic leadership team, a leader, such as CEO of Home Depot Bob Nardelli, whose background and expertise is engineering, should not hire just like-minded people to be on his leadership team. In some industries—especially those that have engineering at their core, such as utilities and telecommunications—leaders have typically surrounded themselves with people who have the same competencies that they do. For this reason, the leadership teams and thus the company become mired in too much analysis and detail. They do not focus on the market or research design, and as a result there are shortcomings in the distribution and/or execution of the product or service.

At a utilities company, the HR team investigated why it seemed that everyone in the company was analytical and driven by data. After inventorying the cultural profile of the entire company, including the HR team itself, the team found a highly disproportionate number of people with the same cultural profile. Nearly everyone tested out as an ISTJ (introverted, sensing, thinking, judger). This meant that the company had a huge gap in its competencies and would likely not do well at growth or extending its opportunity base.

Leaders must be trustworthy and driven by core personal and often spiritual values, possessing in high degree a good balance of emotional, intellectual, and business intelligence. During an interview, Michael Eskew, chairman and CEO of UPS, was asked about his work ethic as compared to a person who works at a 24/7 pace. He revealed that while he has a strong work ethic, work-life balance is a crucial, core, personal value to him. Thus, he finds ways to balance his work time with other areas of focus, such as himself and his family.[10]

The ability of leaders to create a shared vision and inspire others to achieve that vision will be greatly enhanced if their personal values and goals are congruent with what they are being asked to do to lead the business. When these two aspects are working together, the leader will be energetic, passionate, inspirational, and enthusiastic. The following diagram illustrates the importance of congruency between the leader's goals, values, and motivations and the vision and environment of the organization. (See Figure 10.1.)

The circle at the top of the diamond represents the business context within which the leader operates. It is important for the leader to understand what the business context is or is becoming so that the environment within which he or she is required to lead is clear from a business perspective.

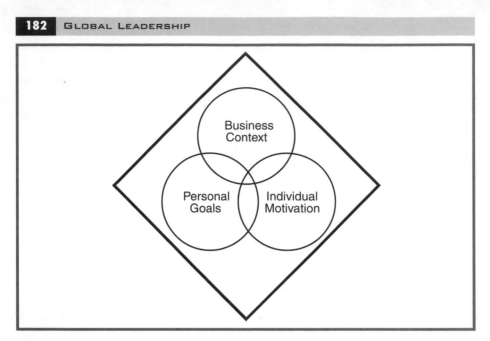

Figure 10.1
Personal and organizational congruency exercise.

Ask yourself these questions:

What is the business context within which you are currently working?

_____
_____
_____

What is it becoming?

_____
_____
_____

What is the environment within which you are required to lead?

_____
_____
_____

The circle at the bottom left of the diamond represents the leader's personal goals and life journey—what he or she wants from life, how he or she attains balance, how he or she defines success, and what he or she wants to accomplish.

Ask yourself these questions:

What are your personal goals?

_____

_____

_____

What is your life journey?

_____

_____

_____

What do you want from life?

_____

_____

_____

How do you define success?

_____

_____

_____

What do you want to accomplish?

_____

_____

_____

The last circle represents the motivation of the individual: his or her passion, motivators, desires, triggers, what causes him or her to behave in certain ways in order to have an impact on whatever it is he or she want to change.

Ask yourself these questions:

What are you passionate about?

_____

_____

_____

What motivates you?

_____

_____

_____

What makes you want to impact changes?

_____

_____

_____

How do you accomplish change?

_____

_____

_____

Where the three circles are congruent, the situation will exist that psychologists call "flow"; in other words, the organization's goals, the individual's personal goals, and the individual's motivation set are all in synch. In such a situation, high performance, high productivity, and personal satisfaction are all likely to result.

When the three circles are largely or completely separate, it is equally likely that the individual will underperform as a leader in the given business context and will probably be unhappy at the same time. In this instance, the individual would be well advised to seek an alternative business context within which to lead.

The other relevant point to note about this construct is that in moving from one business context to another, any individual needs to reassess the "fit" with personal goals and motivation. Leading successfully in context A does not necessarily guarantee similar success in context B, which is why, in our view, it is not possible to have an "always true" list of what defines the perfect leader in any context.

CONCLUSION

Global leaders who continually strive to achieve personal mastery are essential to business growth and survival. Many leadership traits can be taught, coached, developed, and internalized, and corporations are constantly searching for new ways to develop them, whether through challenging job assignments, classroom learning, or personal coaching and mentoring. However, the most valuable leadership quality is self-awareness, so that the strengths, weaknesses, and preferences of the organization and its leaders can be understood and counterbalanced. Combining that knowledge with the business strategy creates the best environment for delivering business results.

Developing leaders in the organization requires identifying the individuals with competencies that make them influential and who are capable of navigating through a network of relationships. Thus, self-assessment is needed at both the personal and corporate levels. Executives need to determine their strengths and weaknesses, likes and dislikes, risk tolerances, and developmental needs. They must do the same for the human capital of the whole organization. Comparing the results with the attributes needed to realize the company vision will reveal the gaps between where the leadership is and where it needs to be.

Shifting values to suit the business of the future can be accomplished if future leaders are aware of the current mismatch and their own strengths and weaknesses. In practice, few current and future leaders are properly prepared in terms of balance, alertness, self-knowledge, resilience, respect for others, and collaboration, not domination. Shifting values requires work that must begin with a consistently applied set of initiatives with wholehearted participation by the leaders. There are no easy methods or shortcuts.

Value changes are embedded in deep personal change. Many leaders need to increase their emotional maturity: their ability to make creative connections and to empathize deeply with others. They also need to manage ego and pride, and to have an insatiable appetite for new learning.

Many current and future leaders are unprepared for these changing values. Often, little attention is paid to mismatches among cultures, generations, and professions. Yet, *awareness of cultural differences, etiquette, relationship management, self-awareness, and awareness of others are skills that a global leader must have in order to manage networked alliances.*[11]

Present leaders must either change, share, or even relinquish their leadership role. For those near retirement, this may not be an issue. For middle-aged leaders who lack the new skills, this may be difficult. They will have to understand what they need to learn and be shown how they can practice it, and the organization's performance measurement and reward system will need to be changed to promote the desired personal mastery competencies.

LEARNING TO APPLY PERSONAL MASTERY[12]

In 1891, Anthony J. Drexel created the Drexel Institute of Art, Science and Industry. This unique university stressed "not just knowledge, but also its application, preparing young men and women for the opportunities of a new industrial economy."[13] With such a distinctive mission, it is no wonder that engineer and educator Dr. Constantine Papadakis (Taki) has found his way to becoming its leader.

Achieving Personal Mastery

As a young boy in his native Greece, Taki determined to work hard to achieve his goals. Realizing that there were many children who were just as smart and talented as he, if not more so, he concluded that having knowledge was good but having the tenacity, strength, and discipline to apply the knowledge would lead to success.

At age 13 Taki put his theory to work. After making a lousy grade in gym class, he picked up athletics with a passion. Not a natural athlete, he had to train for hours a day with persistence and focus. At 16, Taki became one of the best shot-putters and discus throwers on the national, teenage Greek track and field team!

Know Yourself

Today, at Drexel University, Taki has surrounded himself with team members who "like to do the things he doesn't like to do." Taki realizes that if he enjoys a task, he will do it well. He knows that his strengths lie in engineering (analyzing, synthesizing, and problem solving). When he arrived at Drexel, a technological school, engineers were at the helm to the exclusion of those from other fields. Although the faculty wanted him to hire another engineer as chief academic officer, one of the first things Taki did in his role as president was hire into this position an English major. This new addition had no strength in budgeting, complicated problem solving, or finances, yet did have the caliber to identify excellence in learning and to be engaged in academic enterprise. The result? The two leaders complement each other without overlaps; they are able to handle many constituents with varying approaches; and it creates *constructive conflict*, which, within the framework of friendship and collaboration, challenges them to create solutions from a dual standpoint rather than a one-dimensional point of view.

With confidence and optimism (and he would tell you "good luck"), Taki has managed a successful group effort to turn around the fate of Drexel University. By maintaining high-quality education and focusing on its unique assets, as compared to the competition, Drexel's student body has doubled in less than five years. It is Taki's simple philosophy to work hard, to know his strengths and weaknesses, to involve people whose strengths are his weaknesses, and to focus on the goal that has helped to turn this organization around.

THROUGH THE YEARS

In the early 1980s, Paul Wieand was the youngest CEO of one of the most successful financial institutions in the United States. He didn't come to this position easily. As a youth, Paul had a learning disability that made it difficult for him to integrate information. Although he had a phenomenal way of gathering facts, he found it difficult to catalogue and combine knowledge into a coherent message. Upon entering college, his roommate and mentor, a philosophy major, helped him to address and work with this disability. With work and dedication Paul was finally able to put many facts, figures, and thoughts together and he soon found success in the financial industry.

As CEO, Paul's greatest talent was strategizing and creating a vision. He surrounded himself with individuals who were exceptional at effectively implementing and executing his vision. However, his idea of principles and values about success and those of the people around him were quite different. He realized this when he lost the support of the board of directors, which in large part was the cause of his downfall. He found himself ineffective in dealing with their emotional demands, and he lost his job. Paul learned that his inability to understand emotional capacity and emotional intelligence was the straw that broke the camel's back.

In a significant state of depression, Paul ventured into psychotherapy in pursuit of his own "emotional barriers to performance." He has come to understand that there was a two-stage process that cost him his job: (1) People had followed him because he performed; and (2) there were so many opportunities because of the massive period of consolidation that was going on at the time that it was hard not to be successful.

In his personal search for self-knowledge, Paul discovered some things about being a leader that he believes are crucial to an individual's success:

- Know values: Leaders who know their values will surround themselves with committed individuals who are dedicated to similar value systems. These individuals will likely support the leader even during times of industry downtown and economic decline. If performance is more highly regarded than personal values, then individuals will likely "jump ship."

- Develop emotional maturity: Leaders with emotional maturity will find it far easier to recognize value discrepancies between themselves and their teams. This may not help leaders avoid the failure altogether, but it will help leaders to be better prepared.

- Understand abilities and limitations: Great leaders have balance in their lives. If a leader is in the wrong leadership role, he or she will be pulled in directions that are likely to be uncomfortable. To counterbalance this discomfort, the leader may self medicate with alcohol, drugs, unethical behavior, overwork, and so on.

- Have humility: Leaders are often high achievers and may feel superior because of their success and position. However, it's important to recognize that everyone has weaknesses that can be either ignored or acknowledged. Leaders who acknowledge personal weaknesses and/or challenges and then either improve or share leadership with others whose strengths are in those areas will be more likely to succeed in the long term.

- Consistency of personality: Leaders with consistently good or even bad personalities (to a point) build trust with their peers, coworkers, and employees. People know what to expect and can handle themselves accordingly. Leaders who waver and have extreme highs and lows are far more difficult for people to gauge and thus trust.

In 1993, after much soul searching and earning a doctorate in clinical psychology, Paul founded the Center for Advanced Emotional Intelligence. He now joins with other psychotherapists who specialize in helping executives and entrepreneurs overcome these emotional barriers to performance.

Achieving Personal Mastery

ITEM 39: Deeply Understands Her or His Own Strengths and Weaknesses

WHAT TO DO

- Constantly monitor your own performance, and make notes on those areas you excel in, you need improvement in, and processes you might help streamline or improve. Communicate these experiences to your team to help improve their effectiveness.
- Think and act positively when mistakes occur.
- Realize that failures and mistakes are just one step on the road to success.
- Recognize that *being aware* of the impact that your behavior has on other people is a critical managerial skill.
- The capacity to encourage and stay open to feedback is essential to the improvement of your managerial skills.
- The feedback you ask for is generally of a higher quality and easier to receive than if unsolicited—so ask often!
- When criticism is difficult to accept, there is probably some truth to it.
- Recognize that providing feedback is difficult for both the giver and the receiver.
- Don't take criticism personally; it is an opportunity for growth.

HOW TO DO IT

- Learn to give yourself and others credit for improving.
- Adopt a "can-do" attitude, take a break from the problem, and come back later with a fresh perspective.
- Don't hesitate to ask for help or advice.
- Ask coworkers for feedback about how you are doing in this area.
- Ask for small amounts of feedback on a regular basis, so that it doesn't pile up.
- When there is a problem you need to address, use active listening skills to check your understanding and let the person know that you heard him or her accurately.

- Thank the person who has given you feedback or bad news.
- Be aware of defensiveness, and avoid arguing, defending, or rationalizing your behavior.

HOW TO DO IT

- Ask an effective leader to role-play interactive situations with you. Ask him or her to provide you with specific behavioral feedback and to suggest alternative behavior that might enhance your ability to lead.
- Solicit feedback on your personal leadership as part of your subordinates' performance appraisal and coaching sessions by asking questions such as, "What am I doing to hinder your goal accomplishment?" and "What would you suggest I do differently?"

HOW TO USE THIS SKILL FURTHER

- Read self-help books written to help you understand yourself.
- Practice this skill with your family and close friends.

RESULTS YOU CAN EXPECT

- You may better understand yourself, your actions, and those around you.
- You may be involved in fewer conflicts as a result of your deeper understanding.
- People may comment on or express appreciation for the way you share your experiences and knowledge with others.

READINGS

- *Buy, Lie, and Sell High: How Investors Lost Out on Enron and the Internet Bubble.* D. Quinn Mills. 2002. Financial Times Prentice Hall: New York. ISBN: 0130091138.
- *Do What You Are: Discover the Perfect Career for You Through the Secrets of Personality Type.* Paul D. Tieger & Barbara Barron-Tieger. 2001. Little, Brown & Company: New York, ISBN 0316880655.
- *Life Launch: A Passionate Guide to the Rest of Your Life.* Frederic M. Hudson, Pamela D. McLean. 2000. Hudson Press: Santa Barbara, CA, ISBN 1884433847.
- *Maximum Achievement: Strategies and Skills That Will Unlock Your Hidden Powers to Succeed.* Brian Tracy. 1995. Fireside: Columbus, OH, ISBN 684803313.
- *The Art of Living Consciously: The Power of Awareness to Transform Everyday Life.* Nathaniel Branden. 1999. Fireside: Columbus, OH, ISBN 684838494.
- *The Leader of the Future: New Visions, Strategies, and Practices for the Next Era.* Frances Hesselbein, Marshall Goldsmith, Richard Beckhard, & Peter Ferdinand Drucker. 1997. Jossey-Bass: San Francisco, ISBN 787909351.
- *The Other 90%: How to Unlock Your Vast Untapped Potential for Leadership and Life.* Robert K. Cooper. 2001. Crown: Victoria, BC, ISBN 812932870.

- *Understanding the Enneagram: The Practical Guide to Personality Types*. Don Richard Riso & Russ Hudson. 2000. Houghton Mifflin: Boston, ISBN 0618004157.
- *What Color Is Your Parachute? 2001*. Richard Nelson Bolles. 2000. Ten Speed Press: Berkeley, CA, ISBN 1580082424.
- *Why We Do What We Do: Understanding Self-Motivation*. Edward L. Deci & Richard Flaste. 1996. Penguin USA: New York, ISBN 0140255265.
- *Working With Emotional Intelligence*. Daniel P. Goleman. 2000. Bantam Doubleday Dell: New York, ISBN 553378589.

ITEM 40: Invests in Ongoing Personal Development

WHAT TO DO

- Decide on clear, long-term goals for yourself, then establish what you need to do and what attitudes you need in order to achieve them.
- Keep a list of the knowledge and skills that you want to learn in the next 5, 10, and 20 years.
- Commit to being a lifelong learner. Approach every situation by asking yourself, What can I learn from this?
- View mistakes as a necessary learning tool.
- Request project assignments in other areas of the company.
- Develop additional skills as a hobby, and keep your manager informed of your progress.

HOW TO DO IT

- Spend five minutes daily to visualize yourself attaining your goals.
- Identify what skills are required for success, and ask your manager to give you assignments in those areas.
- Perform other tasks or contribute ideas even if not requested, then show your work to your manager and others. Even if not used, they will see that you are capable of doing other jobs.
- Make public speeches and presentations in your area of expertise.
- Attend seminars and training sessions on management and leadership skills.
- Request an assignment that requires management skills rather than technical skills.
- Take classes at local colleges and universities. Attend inhouse and outside training seminars and workshops.
- Observe and learn from managers who are skilled or savvy in the areas you are attempting to develop. Ask them how they developed a particular skill.
- Discuss techniques with managers who excel at continuous self-improvement.

- Get involved in a task force to develop your crossfunctional knowledge.
- Volunteer for tasks that require you to learn new information and skills.
- Ask for feedback from your peers, managers, and workgroup.

HOW TO USE THIS SKILL FURTHER

- Take on more assignments, particularly challenging ones.
- Assist others who are experiencing leadership problems.
- Make your learning style more visible so you can serve as a model for others.

RESULTS YOU CAN EXPECT

- You may be recognized for your efforts to improve your leadership skills.
- Others may ask you for advice on personal development.

READINGS

- *Be Your Own Mentor: Strategies from Top Women on the Secrets of Success*. Sheila W. Wellington & Betty Spence. 2001. Random House: New York, ISBN 037550060X.
- *Business 2010: Positioning Your Company and Yourself in a Rapidly Changing World*. Frederick G. Harmon. 2001. Kiplinger Books: Washington, DC, ISBN 938721844.
- *Control Your Destiny or Someone Else Will: Lessons in Mastering Change-From the Principles Jack Welch Is Using to Revolutionize GE*. Noel M. Tichy & Stratford Sherman. 1999. HarperBusiness: New York, ISBN 887306705.
- *Creating You & Co: Learn to Think Like the CEO of Your Own Career*. William Bridges. 1998. Perseus: Reading, MA, ISBN 738200328.
- *Leadership and Self-Deception: Getting Out of the Box: Doing Versus Saying the Right Thing*. The Arbinger Institute. 2000. Berrett-Koehler: San Francisco, CA, ISBN 1576750949.
- *Leadership from the Inside Out*. Kevin Cashman. 1999. Executive Excellence: Provo, UT, ISBN 1890009318.
- *Learning Journeys: Top Management Experts Share Hard-Earned Lessons on Becoming Great Mentors and Leaders*. Marshall Goldsmith, Beverly L. Kaye, & Ken Shelton. 2000. Davies-Black Publishing: Palo Alto, CA, ISBN 891061479.
- *The Other 90%: How to Unlock Your Vast Untapped Potential for Leadership and Life*. Robert K. Cooper. 2001. Crown: Victoria, BC, ISBN 812932870.
- *The Power of Purpose: Creating Meaning in Your Life and Work*. Richard J. Leider. 1997. Berrett-Koehler: San Francisco, ISBN 1576750213.
- *Who's Running Your Career?: Creating Stable Work in Unstable Times*. Caela Farren. 1997. Bard Press: Marietta, GA, ISBN 1885167172.

ITEM 41: Involves People Who Have Strengths that He or She Does Not Possess

WHAT TO DO

- Understand your own strengths and weaknesses.
- Determine how your strengths benefit the organization.
- Surround yourself with those whose strengths not only are different from your own, but that complement your weaker areas.
- Recognize that every organization is a "human" organization. Get to know people and establish a rapport with them.
- Consider those who possess different strengths and talents than you as potential collaborators.
- Develop a team made up of people with complementary strengths. Understanding the strengths and weaknesses of other people in your organization can help you build a high performing, competitive team.
- Get individuals on your team to see how their jobs or tasks and responsibilities are interdependent.
- Identify the advantages that come from teaming with diverse talents in the organization
- Meet with each of your team members to identify what you can do to help them develop to their full potential.

HOW TO DO IT

- List your strengths and weaknesses.
- Ask others for feedback on your areas of strength and weakness.
- Analyze the individuals on your team. Identify possible missing skills, expertise, or perspectives.
- Develop and train your staff to meet those needs that are not being met by either you or your team.
- Hire people who will add to the whole team or organization, not just people who can do a specific job.
- Push yourself to spend the time and effort to actively seek people with different skills, opinions, and expertise.
- Define each individual on your team in terms of his or her strengths and weaknesses. List knowledge, skills, and capabilities, and identify gaps that may need to be filled.
- Comprise a strategic plan that includes future challenges for your team or organization.

- List the necessary requirements for each job and role on your team in terms of both specific skills and overall perspectives.
- Hire employees who possess skills sets, experience, and work styles that differ from yours.

HOW TO USE THIS SKILL FURTHER

- Make your work style more visible to the members of your team so that you serve as a role model.
- Practice team-building techniques with a group outside of work.
- Ask your family and friends what they believe are your strengths and weaknesses. Add these descriptions to your own list.

RESULTS YOU CAN EXPECT

- You may discover other talents in your employees to further increase the productivity of your work unit.
- The productivity of your organization may increase.
- People may comment on or express appreciation for the way you value people's strengths and effectively utilize them.

READINGS

- *Dance Lessons: Six Steps to Great Partnerships in Business & Life*. Chip R. Bell & Heather Shea. 1998. Berrett-Koehler: San Francisco, ISBN 1576750434.
- *Encouraging the Heart: A Leader's Guide to Rewarding and Recognizing Others*. James M. Kouzes & Barry Z. Posner. 1999. Jossey-Bass: San Francisco, ISBN 787941840.
- *High Five! The Magic of Working Together*. Ken Blanchard, Sheldon M. Bowles, Don Carew, & E. Parisi-Carew. 2000. William Morrow & Co: New York, ISBN 688170366.
- *The Intelligent Organization: Engaging the Talent & Initiative of Everyone in the Workplace*. Gifford Pinchot & Elizabeth Pinchot. 1996. Berrett-Koehler: San Francisco, ISBN 1881052982.
- *Love 'Em or Lose 'Em: Getting Good People to Stay*. Beverly L. Kaye & Sharon Jordan-Evans. 1999. Berrett-Koehler: San Francisco, ISBN 1576750736.
- *Management 21C: Someday We'll All Manage This Way*. Subir Chowdhury. 1999. Financial Times-Prentice Hall: Upper Saddle River, NJ, ISBN 273639633.
- *Organizing Genius: The Secrets of Creative Collaboration*. Patricia Ward Biederman & Warren G. Bennis. 1998. Perseus: Reading, MA, ISBN 201339897.
- *The 17 Indisputable Laws of Teamwork: Embrace Them and Empower Your Team*. John C. Maxwell. 2001. Thomas Nelson: New York, ISBN 0785274340.

- *The Boundaryless Organization: Breaking the Chains of Organizational Structure*. Ron Ashkenas, Dave Ulrich, Todd Jick, & Steve Kerr. 1998. Jossey-Bass: San Francisco, ISBN 787940003.

ITEM 42: Demonstrates Effective Emotional Responses in a Variety of Situations

WHAT TO DO

- When under stressful situations, don't overreact. Calmly think about how to handle the situation and then proceed to do so.
- Evaluate your reactions to negative situations; formulate plans on how to handle them more effectively if they should recur.
- Handle sensitive matters with discretion.
- Take responsibilities for your actions.
- Use objective, performance-based data in managing others' performance or administering discipline.

HOW TO DO IT

- Use calm, clear, objective language when communicating your ideas or position.
- Openly admit your mistakes and take responsibility for your actions when things don't go as planned.
- Stand up for what you believe is important. Be gracious whether your ideas are accepted or rejected.
- Treat personal matters in confidence.
- Resolve interpersonal difficulties directly with the other person.
- Exercise discretion in communicating information of a sensitive nature (e.g., choose the right time, setting, audience).

HOW TO USE THIS SKILL FURTHER

- Ask trusted colleagues, family, and friends to tell you when they observe you doing anything that might appear to show a lack of emotional maturity.

RESULTS YOU CAN EXPECT

- People may tell you they have noticed a positive change in how you handle yourself.
- Employees may seek your advice in dealing with problem issues.
- Fewer complaints may be made regarding your attitudes or behaviors.

READINGS

- *Credibility: How Leaders Gain and Lose It, Why People Demand It.* James S. Kouzes, Barry Z. Posner, & Tom Peters. 1995. Jossey-Bass: San Francisco, ISBN 787900567.
- *Control Yourself!* M. K. Gupta & Linda Scura. 1997. Indus Publishing: New Delhi, India ISBN 1890838012.
- *Emotional Intelligence at Work.* Hendrie Weisinger. 2000. Jossey-Bass: San Francisco, ISBN 0787951986.
- *Love 'Em or Lose 'Em: Getting Good People to Stay.* Beverly L. Kaye & Sharon Jordan-Evans. 1999. Berrett-Koehler: San Francisco, ISBN 1576750736.
- *The Power of Ethical Management.* Ken Blanchard & Norman Vincent Peale. 1996. Ballantine Books: New York, ISBN 0449919757.
- *Working With Emotional Intelligence.* Daniel P. Goleman. 2000. Bantam Doubleday Dell: New York, ISBN 553378589.

ITEM 43: Demonstrates Self-Confidence as a Leader

WHAT TO DO

- Identify your most deeply held values and principles, and use them to guide your leadership.
- Have the courage to say no.
- Take calculated risks.
- Realize that being a leader is not a popularity contest.
- Show the courage to let your people learn from their mistakes.
- Believe that you can make a difference.
- Admit your mistakes and take responsibilities for the consequences.
- Take the initiative to correct problems before being asked.
- Give recognition to people for their achievements.
- Keep your manager and coworkers informed of your progress on their requests or suggestions.
- Demonstrate shared leadership. Include others in decision making.
- Remain open to alternatives and new ideas.

HOW TO DO IT

- Be willing to say no clearly and explain why.
- Use simple, clear, objective language when communicating your ideas or position.
- Acknowledge both your successes and your failures with equal candor.

- Stand up for what you believe is important. Be gracious whether your ideas are accepted or rejected.
- Prepare plans in advance for handling possible emergencies and crises.
- Encourage and reward people who help solve problems and make effective decisions.
- Schedule your actions and write plans if necessary. Respond quickly and in the style most preferred by your manager, peers, and work group.
- Listen to all alternatives before deciding on one alternative.
- Observe and learn from managers who demonstrate self-confidence.
- Get your coworkers' feedback on how you are doing in this area.

HOW TO USE THIS SKILL FURTHER

- Ask for expanded responsibilities.
- Develop new skills and set challenging goals for yourself.

RESULTS YOU CAN EXPECT

- You may be respected and viewed by others in the organization as a confident, strong leader.
- Your manager may delegate more responsibilities to you.

READINGS

- *Emotional Intelligence.* Daniel Goleman. 1997. Bantam Books: New York, ISBN 0553375067.
- *In Praise of Good Business: How Optimizing Risk Rewards Both Your Bottom Line and Your People.* Judith M. Bardwick. 1998. John Wiley & Sons: New York, ISBN 047125407X.
- *Intrapreneuring in Action: A Handbook for Business Innovation.* Gifford Pinchot & Ron Pellman. 1999. Berrett-Koehler: San Francisco, ISBN 1576750612.
- *Leading Change.* John P. Kotter. 1996. Harvard Business School Press: Boston, ISBN 875847471.
- *Leading People: The 8 Proven Principles for Success in Business.* Robert H. Rosen & Paul B. Brown. 1997. Penguin USA: New York, ISBN 140242724.
- *The 21 Indispensable Qualities of a Leader: Becoming the Person that People Want to Follow.* John C. Maxwell. 1999. Thomas Nelson: New York, ISBN 785274405.
- *The Hungry Spirit: Beyond Capitalism: A Quest for Purpose in the Modern World.* Charles Handy. 1999. Broadway Books: New York, ISBN 767901886.
- *The Leadership Moment: Nine True Stories of Triumph and Disaster and Their Lessons for Us All.* Michael Useem & Warren G. Bennis. 1999. Times Books: New York, ISBN 812932307.

- *The Power of Purpose: Creating Meaning in Your Life and Work.* Richard J. Leider. 1997. Berrett-Koehler: San Francisco, ISBN 1576750213.

ENDNOTES

1. Pharmaceuticals, United Kingdom, 30.

2. *PBS CEO Exchange Series.* Hosted by Jeff Greenfield, October 2002.

3. Research and development, United States, 47.

4. Technology, United States, 34,

5. J. Heskett & J. Kotter. *Corporate Culture and Performance.* Free Press: ISBN 0029184673., April 1992.

6. E. S. Harter & M. Sashkin. "The Relationship Between Leadership and Organizational Sustainability." This report is based on the doctoral dissertation research of Eric Harter, conducted at Case Western Reserve University.

7. Kets De Vries. *M. F. R. Leaders, Fools, and Impostors: Essays on the Psychology of Management.* Jossey-Bass: San Francisco, 1993.

8. Products and services, United States, 42.

9. Pharmaceutical, United States, 41.

10. *PBS CEO Exchange Series.* Hosted by Jeff Greenfield, October 2002.

11. Technology, United States, 32.

12. Information and quotes from interview with Constantine Papadakis conducted by Cathy Greenberg. February 2002.

13. Taken from Drexel University: A University with a Difference: The Unique Vision of Anthony J. Drexel, 2001 Newcomem Publication Number 1565.

11

ENCOURAGING
CONSTRUCTIVE
DIALOGUE

Leaders have always been encouraged to engage in frequent and widespread communication in support of their role of defining and moving towards the future. Some have become public spokespersons for their company, as is the case at Ford; others speak in the company's annual report; while still others direct their corporations from within, from mission statement to memos. However, it is not unusual for these same well-intentioned leaders to fall into the trap of having their communication be largely going one way; in other words, they are mostly in "transmit" mode, and only rarely in "receive."

Sometimes they rationalize this as a consequence of shortage of time, the need for speed, and the rapid coalescing of a workforce around a new sense of direction. What they forget, however, is that there is rarely a "coming together" of a workforce in a truly committed sense without some involvement in the definition of that direction, input into the jigsaw puzzle that will emerge as the picture of the future business.

This involvement is not meant to be permission seeking or some business version of democracy. What it should be is a means by which people at many levels can input ideas, voice reactions, and share opportunities, fears, and questions. If this occurs, leaders will find their organizations ultimately much more committed, feeling less as if they have been simply directed and more as if they have genuinely been part of a dialog in forging a path to the future.

LEARNING TO ASK

Peter Drucker defined the crucial difference between the traditional leaders of yesterday's organizations and the leaders of the future when said, "The leader of the past was a person who knew how to *tell*. The leader of the future will be a person who knows how to *ask*."[1]

The traditional hierarchical model of leadership will not work effectively for major organizations in tomorrow's changing world. The organization of the future is based on the "team approach," in which shared leadership, building alliances, and empowering people are essential to the success of the company. A leader will no longer be the sole decision maker. In the future, and in many companies right now, before global goals and objectives are fully adopted and incorporated into both short-term and long-term projects, the global leader will get input and buy-in from all levels. This process takes time, but it is time well spent and should be treated as a priority.

> The tendency right now is to flatten the corporation. The long chain of command is no longer effective. Our company has [fewer] people with bigger jobs....Flatter companies will be more flexible, have more effective communication, and have the freedom to react and respond to business needs.[2]

The effective global leader of the future will need to consistently ask for feedback and to solicit new ideas. A variety of key stakeholders, such as present and potential customers, suppliers, team members, cross-divisional peers, direct reports, managers, other organizational members, researchers, and thought leaders, will be vital sources of information. Leadership inventories, satisfaction surveys, phone calls, voice mail, email, the Internet, satellite hook-ups, and in-person dialogue are some of the many ways a leader ask for feedback.

The trend toward asking is already clear. Twenty years ago top executives rarely asked for feedback. Today the majority of leaders in the most highly respected organizations in the world regularly ask for feedback. The global leader must rely heavily on his or her ability to ask questions that will enhance the exchange of personal and organizational knowledge. Asking the right questions will bring to surface any underlying issues and may help the executive reconsider a behavior, a decision, or a possible course of action.

By asking the right questions, the beliefs, behaviors, and actions of the leader will be either supported or confronted, and his or her current course will be either validated or challenged. Whether positive or negative, this feedback gives the leader insight into his or her personal leadership style and also helps keep business risks in check. For instance, James Despain, while acting as a corporate leader in turning around the globally active Caterpiller corporation, encouraged several levels of information exchange, going far beyond just a suggestion box.

Aside from the obvious benefit of gaining new ideas and insights, asking by top global leaders has a secondary benefit that may be even more important. The leader who asks is providing a role model. Sincere asking demonstrates a willingness to listen and learn, a desire to serve, and a humility that can be an inspiration for the entire organization. Despain, for example, was showing, not telling, his colleagues—all the way to night sweeper (a position, by the way, at which he first started with the company)—that he could hear them and wanted to hear from them.

Asking and listening create the basis of mutual trust and true dialog that are fundamental to the networking of ideas. In today's rapidly fluctuating marketplace, this is critical to good decision making and the formation of a robust, resilient workforce.

LISTENING WITH AN OPEN MIND

At the heart of encouraging constructive dialogue is the ability to listen: Who will continue to speak to someone who hasn't the ability to listen? Open-minded listening leads to a two-way dialogue between the leader and the other person; thus it is a necessary skill for true communication in any arena. Effective global leaders have the ability to two-way communicate, which means they can listen as well as give feedback. The leader does not necessarily have to agree with the opinions and feedback he or she receives. However, by listening to and understanding the information, the global leader builds valuable resources upon which to draw when attempting to understand and solve employee and organizational challenges.

> One person who comes to mind listens a lot more than he speaks. He makes sure that what he says is thoughtful. He is supportive of others and empathetic to their situations. 'You have two ears and one mouth, use your ears, hear twice as much.'[3]

Each leader will possess many skills and attributes, but no leader will possess them all. However, many of these skills can be learned and many mistakes can be avoided if the leader has the ability and patience to listen to others, especially to those who possess the skills, knowledge, and attributes that the leader does not possess. On the other hand, the leader will not learn or expand his or her knowledge without possessing this attribute.

The value and benefits of listening are great. In fact, listening is possibly the one absolutely necessary skill for a global leader to be successful, because listening leads to learning—learning about self, others, the organization, and the industry.

ACCEPTING CONSTRUCTIVE FEEDBACK

Effective global leaders create an atmosphere that welcomes constructive feedback by avoiding defensive reactions, such as responding to feedback with negative and destructive comments about the other person, speaking over the person giving the feedback, and defending and justifying actions and behaviors rather than listening to and accepting the feedback as valuable. These unproductive reactions to feedback create an atmosphere of cynicism and apathy, undermining any possibility of change.

Global leaders will need to provide recognition and support for people who have the courage to tell the hard truth before issues become disasters. Asking for input, and then "shooting the messenger" who delivers the bad news is worse than not asking at all.

Effective global leaders are not defensive when receiving feedback, because they value what is being said. They focus on the value of other people's opinions, fight the urge to prove them wrong, and simply accept their opinions as their perceptions of reality. The effective global leader of the future understands that being defensive bars him or her from hearing and understanding new ideas and suggestions, which will most likely lead to missed opportunities for change.

> Effective leaders are able to listen to others without making judgments too quickly. They can listen to one side of the story completely without a reaction (good or bad), until the whole situation is presented. Then, once they understand all of the perspectives, they can formulate the best response.[4]

Leaders who can listen to, accept, process, and learn from feedback will have a tremendous competitive advantage, because they will make fewer mistakes and miss fewer opportunities than those leaders who do not value others' opinions.

PUTTING YOURSELF IN SOMEONE ELSE'S SHOES

Perhaps one of the greatest challenges of the global leader of the future is the ability to interact effectively with people on all different levels throughout an organization. Leaders must be able to discuss company issues with top management, middle management, and those employees at the lower levels in a way that each group can understand. One of the great leaders who is a role model for this behavior is Alan Mulally, who runs Boeing Commercial Aircraft. Alan makes a regular practice of conducting "town hall meetings" that may involve customers, suppliers, and employees at all levels in his organization. He not only has a clear focus on communicating important messages to people across the organization, he also reaches out on a consistent basis to ask for their input and hear what they have to say.

Possibly even more challenging than the ability to interact with people throughout the organization is looking at and understanding different situations from another person's point of view. However, the global leader of the future will make a conscious effort to understand his or her colleagues' and workers' perspectives and expectations. They will seek to understand by asking questions and by remaining open to different ideas.

Another technique Alan Mulally uses is to ask team members at the end of every discussion, "Are there any ideas that we may have left out? Are there any people we may have left out?" This technique has helped Alan do an even better job of encouraging constructive dialogue.

> Effective leaders can put themselves in someone else's shoes and understand their expectations. They must lead this way in order to move and motivate people. Money is not always what motivates people.[5]

Part of understanding another person's frame of reference means listening to the content of what he or she says as opposed to just responding to the way in which it is said.

Different people communicate differently, and effective leaders will be able to get around this boundary. They will be capable of empathizing to the extent of understanding the other person's perspective, without necessarily agreeing with what is being said. By putting themselves in others' shoes, by understanding others' motivations, values, and ambitions, the global leader can determine their best qualities and attributes, and be confident that he or she is putting individuals into positions in which they will be most beneficial to the company and most happy in their jobs.

WELCOMING NEW IDEAS

The global leader of the future will be surrounded by people with diverse views and opinions, and needs to be able to take advantage of these valuable perspectives. A leader in one of the world's largest human resources services firms recently rolled out a global initiative. Before any formal communication occurred, he enlisted the support of a representative global team to ensure that communications would be understood and well received around the world. Not only does this leader have the ability to listen and understand different points of view, he welcomes new ideas.

> Executives who are able to openly listen to and consider a broad range of viewpoints, make the tough decisions, and yet leave people understanding that their input was carefully considered, can then forge a common purpose.[6]

This person is intrigued, not threatened, by different perspectives. He or she encourages people to challenge the status quo by asking questions to clarify and understand different positions. Obstacles and barriers that interfere with innovation are removed, and the climate is such that people feel they have a voice in company decisions.

CONCLUSION

Besides face-to-face dialogue, there are many methods that a global leader can use to encourage constructive dialogue, including 360-degree feedback surveys, mini-surveys, and questionnaires. As long as there are not too many questions, feedback can be gathered from a myriad of sources, such as the leader's manager, team members, customers, and colleagues. Such feedback may be taken on a regular (biyearly or even quarterly) basis and after significant milestones, depending on the type of work executed by the leader. Each local manager should evaluate the global leader, and questionnaires may be used to garner whether or not people from different backgrounds accept someone as a global leader.

The global leader will need to keep tabs on his or her ability to accept, listen to, and respect feedback from many different sources, because the global success of his or her company may be highly dependent on the leader's ability to encourage constructive dialogue, listen without judgment or defensiveness, and appreciate and understand the many different viewpoints and perspectives of his or her own culture as well as the many cultures around the world.

ENCOURAGING CONSTRUCTIVE DIALOGUE

ITEM 44: Asks People What He or She Can Do to Improve

WHAT TO DO

- Recognize that success in your career requires continued development of skills and knowledge.
- Recognize that the capacity to encourage and stay open to feedback is essential to the improvement of your managerial skills.
- Recognize that feedback you ask for is generally of a higher quality and easier to receive than if unsolicited.
- Learn from your mistakes.

HOW TO DO IT

- When soliciting feedback from others, use open-ended questions, such as what? how? and why?
- Actively ask your managers for feedback on a continuing basis. Ask for specific comments and suggestions in the areas that you want to improve.
- Encourage your employees and coworkers to provide ongoing feedback. Ask them, "What can I do to be more effective?" and "What can I do to help you be more effective in your job?"
- When someone gives you vague feedback, ask for more specific information and examples.
- Thank the person who has given you feedback.
- Be aware of defensiveness and avoid arguing, denying, or rationalizing your behavior.
- After receiving feedback, think about it, decide if you want to change your behavior or approach, and act on it immediately.
- Select one to three areas that you want to improve based on the feedback you received, and develop an action plan.

- Follow up with your direct reports and coworkers every two to three months to see how you are doing.
- Schedule regular feedback sessions with your peers, employees, and coworkers. Former managers and coworkers may be good resources as well.
- Determine who is especially good at asking and accepting feedback, and get his or her advice.

HOW TO USE THIS SKILL FURTHER

- Practice by asking family and friends for feedback.
- Become a member in team or group activities where giving and receiving feedback is highly valued.
- Ask for feedback on how well you ask for feedback.
- Keep a record of the feedback you get, including frequency, topics, and what your response was.

RESULTS YOU CAN EXPECT

- You may expect others to be more willing to give you feedback.
- You may gain insight into yourself that will improve your life both at work and at home.
- You may improve your skills through continuous learning.

READINGS

- *360 Degree Feedback: The Powerful New Model for Employee Assessment & Performance Improvement.* Mark R. Edwards & Ann J. Ewen. 1996. AMACOM: New York, ISBN 0-8144-0326-3.
- *Coaching for Leadership: How the World's Greatest Coaches Help Leaders Learn.* Marshall Goldsmith, Laurence Lyons, & Alyssa Freas. 2000. Jossey-Bass: San Francisco, ISBN 787955175.
- *Making Feedback Work: Turning Feedback from Employee Surveys into Change.* Joe Folkman. 1998. Executive Excellence: Provo, UT, ISBN 1890009423.
- *The Leader of the Future: New Visions, Strategies, and Practices for the Next Era.* Frances Hesselbein, Marshall Goldsmith, & Richard Beckhard. 1996. Jossey-Bass: San Francisco, ISBN 0787901806.
- *Wisdom Circles: A Guide to Self-Discovery and Community Building in Small Groups.* Charles Garfield, Cindy Spring, & Sedonia Cahill. 1999. Hyperion: New York, ISBN 786883634.

ITEM 45: Genuinely Listens to Others

WHAT TO DO

- Recognize that you gain ideas from others through listening.
- Expect others to have good ideas.
- Create time for listening.
- Express an interest in what is being said.
- Suspend judgment while you concentrate on understanding an idea.
- Check your understanding and let others know you have heard them accurately.
- Follow through; let the speaker know about any results.
- Be an active listener.
- Focus your attention on ideas.
- Keep an open mind.
- Become aware of feelings of the other person; watch nonverbal behavior and note voice characteristics.
- Analyze what is being said nonverbally.

HOW TO DO IT

- Avoid being sidetracked by your reactions to the speaker's status, sex, method of delivery, or cultural differences.
- Put aside any negative feelings about past experiences with the speaker.
- Include time for listening in your daily schedule.
- Work to reduce distraction by having phone calls held and other interruptions prevented when you are meeting with someone.
- Encourage the speaker to continue by smiling, nodding, and saying "Yes, I see, please go on."
- Allow pauses to make sure the speaker has the time he or she needs to communicate.
- Use open-ended questions such as "Explain, describe, say more..." to encourage the speaker.
- Be sensitive to the feelings of the other person. Ask yourself, Why did he or she say that? and What was meant?
- Frequently clarify, paraphrase, and/or summarize to make sure you understand both content and feelings.
- Don't react until you are sure you have fully understood the other person.
- Have more one-on-one meetings to establish rapport and to learn others' viewpoints.

- Use open-ended questions that invite more than one-word answers.
- Listen for central ideas. Pick out the ideas as they are stated, sorting the facts from assumptions, evidence from opinion.
- Instead of judging what the person says as wrong, clarify meaning by restating in your own words what you thought was said.
- Observe people who are good listeners, and ask them for tips.
- Tell others you want to improve your listening skills.
- Ask others to tell you when they feel you are not listening to them

HOW TO USE THIS SKILL FURTHER

- Practice active listening with family and friends, and observe how these relationships improve.
- Use active listening in various social situations, and watch your popularity grow.
- Assume a facilitator role in group discussions.
- Ask your work unit, associates, and managers for feedback on how well you listen to them.
- Track the number of ideas your work group suggests.

RESULTS YOU CAN EXPECT

- You may have better rapport with coworkers.
- Communication with others may improve.
- The number of ideas developed through others may increase.

READINGS

- *Effective Listening Skills*. Dennis M. Kratz & Abby Robinson Kratz. 1995. McGraw-Hill: New York, ISBN 0786301228.
- *Listening: The Forgotten Skill*. Madelyn Burley-Allen. 1995. John Wiley & Sons: New York, ISBN 0471015873.
- *The Good Listener*. James E. Sullivan. 2000. Ave Maria Press: Notre Dame, IN, ISBN 0877939438.
- *The Leader of the Future: New Visions, Strategies, and Practices for the Next Era*. Frances Hesselbein, Marshall Goldsmith, & Richard Beckhard. 1996. Jossey-Bass: San Francisco, ISBN 0787901806.
- *The Zen of Listening: Mindful Communication In The Age Of Distraction*. Rebecca Z. Shafir. 2000. Quest Books: Wheaton, IL, ISBN 0835607909.

ITEM 46: Accepts Constructive Feedback in a Positive Manner (Avoids Defensiveness)

WHAT TO DO

- Recognize that being aware of the impact your behavior has on other people is a critical managerial skill.
- Recognize that feedback you ask for is generally of a higher quality and easier to receive than if unsolicited—so ask often!
- Encourage and stay open to constructive feedback from your coworkers.
- When criticism is difficult to accept, there is probably some truth to it.
- Recognize that providing feedback is difficult for both the giver and the receiver.
- Don't "shoot the messenger" of bad news.
- Don't take criticism personally. It is an opportunity for growth.
- Learn not to take yourself too seriously.

HOW TO DO IT

- Schedule feedback sessions with your manager and members of your work group frequently.
- Ask for small amounts of feedback on a regular basis so that it doesn't pile up.
- Be specific about the skills or behaviors you want feedback on.
- Think about ways that make it easier for you to respond to criticism
- When there is a problem you need to address, use active listening skills to check your understanding and let the person know you heard him or her accurately.
- Ask for behavioral examples when criticism is not clear.
- Think about ways to make it easier for others to give you feedback. For example, you could tell the person ahead of time what you want to talk about and why.
- Thank the person who has given you constructive feedback.
- Obtain feedback from a variety of sources to get a more complete picture.
- Use open-ended questions such as "Explain, describe, say more..." to encourage the speaker.
- Be aware of defensiveness, and avoid arguing, denying, or rationalizing your behavior.
- Take time to evaluate the feedback received and determine whether more feedback is needed and what, if any, action or behavioral change is necessary.
- Ask for suggestions on your developmental areas.
- Determine who is especially good at dealing with criticism and get his or her advice. List possible questions and names of people you could ask. Don't forget to consider former managers, customers, family members, and peers.

- Solicit feedback on your personal leadership as part of your subordinates' perform-ance appraisals and coaching sessions by asking questions such as, "What am I doing to hinder your goal accomplishment? and "What would you suggest I do differently?"
- Ask an effective leader to role-play interactive situations with you. Ask him or her to provide you with specific behavioral feedback and to suggest alternative behav-ior that could enhance your ability to lead.

HOW TO USE THIS SKILL FURTHER

- Practice by asking family and friends for feedback.
- Become a participant in team or group activities where giving and receiving feedback is highly valued.
- Ask for feedback on how well you accept constructive criticism.
- Keep a record of the feedback you get, including frequency, nature, and what your response was.
- Look for positive feedback on the improvements you have made and for additional input on further improvements you might make.

RESULTS YOU CAN EXPECT

- You may expect others to be more willing to give you feedback.
- You may improve your skills effectively through continuous learning.

READINGS

- *Choosing 360: A Guide to Evaluation Multi-Rater Feedback Instruments for Management Development*. Ellen Van Velsor, Jean Brittain Leslie, John W. Fleenor. 1997. Center for Creative Leadership: Greensboro, NC, ISBN 1882197305.
- *Designing Feedback: Performance Measures for Continuous Improvement*. Carl G. Thor. 1998. Crisp Publications: Menlo Park, CA, ISBN 1560524685.
- *Employee Surveys That Make a Difference: Using Customized Feedback Tools to Transform Your Organization*. Joe Folkman & Jack Zenger. 1999. Executive Excellence: Provo, UT, ISBN 1890009431.
- *Feedback to Managers: A Review and Comparison of Multi-Rater Instruments for Management Development*. Jean Brittain Leslie & John W. Fleenor. 1998. Center for Creative Leadership: Greensboro, NC, ISBN 1882197356.
- *Job Feedback: Giving, Seeking, and Using Feedback for Performance Improvement*. Manuel London. 1997. Lawrence Erlbaum: Mahwah, NJ, ISBN 0805824758.
- *Maximizing the Value of 360-Degree Feedback: A Process for Successful Individual and Organizational Development*. Walter W. Tornow. 1998. Jossey-Bass: San Francisco, ISBN 0787909580.

- *The Leader of the Future: New Visions, Strategies, and Practices for the Next Era.* Frances Hesselbein, Marshall Goldsmith, & Richard Beckhard. 1996. Jossey-Bass: San Francisco, ISBN 0787901806.
- *The Official Criticism Manual.* Deborah Bright. 1997. Bright Enterprises: New York, ISBN 0963578308.

ITEM 47: Strives to Understand the Other Person's Frame of Reference

WHAT TO DO

- Realize that differences in race, culture, and background are advantages, not deficits, for effective teamwork and problem solving.
- Recognize the value of having a diverse workforce by utilizing the full potential of all employees and building on complementary skills, backgrounds, and cultural knowledge.
- Assess and appreciate the different styles and approaches in people.
- Realize that understanding others' thinking may enhance your own ideas and make you appear less stubborn.
- Recognize that you gain ideas from others through listening and understanding.
- Expect others to have good ideas.
- Express an interest in what is being said.
- Suspend judgment while you concentrate on understanding others' frames of reference.
- Check your understanding, and let others know you have heard them accurately.
- Keep an open mind.

HOW TO DO IT

- Encourage people to come up with different ideas and perspectives to solve problems and spot opportunities.
- Involve a wide variety of people in your professional and personal life. Take the time to get to know them.
- Put yourself in the other person's shoes. Look at the situation from the other person's point of view before defending your own.
- Don't argue about why you are right. Simply state your point of view.
- Put aside any negative feelings about past experiences with the speaker.
- Include time for listening in your daily schedule.

- Don't react until you are sure you have fully understood the other person.
- Have more one-on-one meetings to establish rapport and to learn others' viewpoints.
- Instead of judging what the person says as wrong, examine your assumptions and clarify understanding by restating in your own words what you think was said.
- Use open-ended questions that invite more than one-word answers to further understand others' frames of reference.
- Ask others for their opinion before you state yours. When stating your opinions, preface your statements with words such as, "In my opinion…" or "I think…."
- Ask your manager, associates, and employees to give you feedback on how you are doing in this area. Solicit suggestions that could develop your skill.
- Observe people who are flexible and open minded, and ask them for tips.

HOW TO USE THIS SKILL FURTHER

- Learn to appreciate people from diverse backgrounds through travel, books, and films, and by attending local cultural events.
- Become friends with individuals whose backgrounds and experiences are different from your own.
- Practice listening with family and friends, and observe how these relationships improve.
- Assume a facilitator role in group discussions.

RESULTS YOU CAN EXPECT

- Work groups may be more open to ideas from all members.
- You may have better rapport with coworkers.
- The number of ideas developed through others may increase.

READINGS

- *Building a House for Diversity: A Fable About a Giraffe & an Elephant Offers New Strategies for Today's Workforce.* Marjorie I. Woodruff & R. Roosevelt Thomas, Jr. 1999. AMACOM: New York, ISBN 814404634.
- *Human Dynamics: A New Framework for Understanding People and Realizing the Potential in Our Organizations.* Sandra Seagal & David Horne. 2000. Pegasus Communications: Williston, VT, ISBN 1883823072.
- *Mentoring and Diversity.* Belle Rose Ragins, David Clutterbuck, & Lisa Matthewman. 2001. Butterworth-Heinemann: Woburn, MA, ISBN 750648368.
- *Redefining Diversity.* R. Roosevelt Thomas. 1996. AMACOM: New York, ISBN 814402283.

- *Riding The Waves of Culture: Understanding Diversity in Global Business*. Alfons Trompenaars & Charles Hampden-Turner. 1997. McGraw-Hill: New York, ISBN 786311258.
- *Workforce 2020: Work and Workers in the 21st Century*. Richard Judy & Carol D'Amico. 1997. Hudson Institute: Santa Barbara, ISBN 1558130616.

ITEM 48: Encourages People to Challenge the Status Quo

WHAT TO DO

- Encourage others to be less conservative and more willing to take risks when making decisions.
- Remove obstacles or barriers in your organization that interfere with initiatives to achieve innovation.
- Try to understand why others resist changes or are against innovation.
- Encourage people to stand up for what they believe in, even under pressure.
- Help others develop a positive attitude when facing objections.
- View the objections or obstacles as opportunities to find innovative solutions.
- Set a climate in which people feel free to air their opinions.
- Ask people to tell you their concerns.
- Be receptive to questions.
- Listen when others disagree. Don't discourage others when this type of discussion occurs.
- Work to gain support and cooperation from the key individuals in your organization.

HOW TO DO IT

- When considering new and innovative ideas, ask yourself and others "why not?" instead of "why?"
- Communicate new ideas with confidence and enthusiasm, and convey a can-do attitude.
- When presenting a new idea, provide as much background information as possible to your work group.
- Be open and friendly. Let people know they can question and disagree.
- When you are questioned, respond in a nondefensive manner; this gives people permission to question.
- Remain nondefensive; actively listen to their reasons.
- Indicate approval by saying such things as, "I can see how this type of thing could cause a problem...."

- Take the time to listen and respond to people's questions, opinions, and concerns.
- Don't punish people for speaking up or for delivering bad news.
- Identify one or two people in your organization who can help you make the change a reality.

HOW TO USE THIS SKILL FURTHER

- Increase your interaction with employees and colleagues.
- Learn from colleagues who excel at challenging the status quo.
- Ask your manager and coworkers for specific feedback on how you are doing in this area.
- Practice open communication with your spouse and children.

RESULTS YOU CAN EXPECT

- You may be seen by others as assertive and cooperative.
- You may have a better understanding of how others around you feel.
- Respect from your work group may increase.
- You may solve problems or overcome obstacles much more quickly.

READINGS

- *10 Lessons From the Future: A Personal Seminar on Tomorrow*. Wolfgang Grulke. 2000. Financial Times–Prentice Hall: Upper Saddle River, NJ, ISBN 273653296.
- *Age of Unreason, Charles Handy*. Warren G. Bennis. 1998. Harvard Business School Press: Boston, ISBN 875843018.
- *Beyond Reengineering: How the Process-Centered Organization is Changing Our Work and Our Lives*. Michael Hammer. 1997. HarperCollins: New York, ISBN 887308805.
- *Business Climate Shifts: Profiles of Change Makers*. W. Warner Burke, Richard Koonce, & William Trahant. 1999. Butterworth-Heinemann: Woburn, MA, ISBN 750671866.
- *Evolve!: Succeeding in the Digital Culture of Tomorrow*. Rosabeth Moss Kanter. 2001. Harvard Business School Press: Boston, ISBN 1578514398.
- *First, Break All the Rules: What the World's Greatest Managers Do Differently*. Marcus Buckingham & Curt Coffman. 1999. Simon & Schuster: London, ISBN 684852861.
- *Management 21C: Someday We'll All Manage This Way*. Subir Chowdhury. 1999. Financial Times–Prentice Hall: Upper Saddle River, NJ, ISBN 273639633.

ENDNOTES

1. Peter Drucker made this comment in a meeting of the Drucker Foundation Advisory Board in 1993.

2. Products and services, Mexico, 46.

3. Technology, United States, 32.

4. Products and services, United States, 29.

5. Products and services, Mexico, 46.

6. Products and services, United States/England/Norway, 49.

12 DEMONSTRATING INTEGRITY

E thical behavior is a key characteristic of the global leader of the future. Young leaders place great value on ethics, think they are sorely lacking in current leaders, and feel that ethical behavior will become the most important characteristic of future leaders.[1] This is not surprising in a time when shredding documents, creative accounting, and ruthless tactics come to light in the media on a fairly regular basis.

In this new atmosphere global leaders must draw on more than status in the hierarchy to motivate those in their spheres of influence and to produce results. They will depend on their ability to build trust and respect within the organization if they are to motivate and lead people who are beyond their direct authority. Recent events in the United States involving companies such as Enron and Worldcom have illustrated how integrity lapses can lead even "benchmark companies" into bankruptcy.

PERSONAL VALUES

A global leader must demonstrate honest, ethical behavior, because without doing so, trust cannot be achieved. People need to trust that a leader is bringing them to a place where they want to be and that they will be treated well in the process. People will not follow a leader whom they do not trust.

People expect high levels of integrity from global leaders in all interactions, including those with their colleagues, the public, the government, and the media. Leaders must be able not only to say the right things, but also to implement the right things. The disasters at Enron and Worldcom illustrate the connection between encouraging constructive dialogue (Chapter 11) and demonstrating integrity. In both cases, employees who had ethical concerns either felt unable to express their concerns or felt their constructive criticism was not heard.

In order to meet these high expectations, leaders must be clear about their values as well as whether they are naturally *self-directed* (with a solid core of direction, or what Stephen Covey calls a "compass") or *other-directed* (which George West references in his work with leaders who appear to be more driven by the wants and needs of others). They must be able to distinguish between what is right and what is wrong for themselves, their companies, and their teams; and they must expect their decisions and actions to be scrutinized by those around them. In the negative examples of Enron and Worldcom, key executives consistently tried to shield themselves from the feedback and scrutiny of important stakeholders to the ultimate detriment of the corporation.

ORGANIZATIONAL VALUES

Part of a global leader's role is to ensure that the highest standards for ethical behavior are practiced throughout the organization. In other words, does the organization really "walk its talk"? The global leader should partake in regular and consistent two-way feedback and evaluation loops to make certain that the company's mission, vision, and values are understood and practiced by peers, subordinates, and leaders. For instance, many of the world's leading companies, such as American Express, General Electric, and UBS Financial Services Group, have developed leadership profiles that are designed to give managers feedback on the match between their observed leadership behavior and the stated values of the company.

> The role of the global leader includes [managing] an organization that is far more diversely located while maintaining a coherent culture and set of work disciplines.[2]

As companies globalize and the sphere of influence of the global leader grows, this becomes more difficult. In order to fulfill this role effectively, the leader's values should be compatible with the organization's values, or the leader may become frustrated and unable to produce satisfactory results. In developing corporate values, it is important for future leaders to be sensitive to cultural differences and not confuse *integrity* with *cultural preference*.

AVOIDS POLITICAL OR SELF-SERVING BEHAVIOR

In today's changing atmosphere, global leaders are expected to share leadership, to build partnerships within and outside of the company, and to complete successful mergers and alliances. More than ever before, leaders not only must make decisions for the good of all involved, they must include others in the decision-making process.

> The failures result when there is not complete involvement, because people are looking solely for personal gains—when someone's personal agenda is opposite of the team agenda.[3]

Success is dependent on group effort. A self-serving individual can easily upset any group effort, making it nearly impossible to achieve company goals. A global leader makes decisions based on what will benefit the entire company rather than trying to force his or her personal agenda on others.

> When there is failure in collaborative leadership it is due to a lack of integrity, lack of trust, and the presence of a political agenda.[4]

STAND UP, SPEAK UP

To build trust, leaders must integrate their personal values into their business practices. People will not follow a leader who does not stand by his or her values or who does not have the courage to speak his or her convictions. Johnson & Johnson (J&J) is one of the world's most valuable companies (at the time of this writing it was ranked sixth in the world). It is also one of the world's most ethical corporations. J&J's key executives make a point of traveling around the world to discuss integrity and corporate values with their global management team. They want to ensure that managers not only understand the corporate values, but also know how to execute decisions in a way that demonstrates those corporate values.

Global leaders should be clear about their personal values and beliefs. They must be seen as consistent in their choices and actions, not as chameleons that change all the time. If they are not clear about their convictions, they are much more likely to change their position with any change in trends or with the latest opinion poll, which will cause others to distrust what they say and do. This lack of clarity can be combated with training and vision. For instance, at Merck & Co., a leading research-driven pharmaceutical products and services company, leaders are trained *never* to sacrifice long-term patient care in order to make a profit for the corporation.

Global leaders need discipline and conviction. They must be able to stick to the plan and have enough discipline to make tough decisions. They must be committed to what they are doing.[5]

LIVES THE VALUES

People expect global leaders to adhere to the highest levels of integrity and ethics in the operation of their organizations. Leading by example, they establish the ethical standards for their companies.

The leader must "walk the talk" and live the mission and vision of the company—not just put the statements on the wall. The leader needs to speak with conviction and drive people to follow him [or] her. [6]

Character matters, and the best leaders live the principles they promote. In this way, they are simple and easy for people to understand.

The leader must "model" behavior, not just talk about what people should do.[7]

People will trust a leader who acts in line with the values he or she espouses. A leader who plays games of manipulation or who acts duplicitously will not have the respect and trust of those with whom they work or do business. Such a leader will not be able to do what is necessary to get the job done in today's world. For instance, after ex-President Bill Clinton was caught lying about his sexual relations with an intern, he nearly lost his job, and he lost the respect and support of many of even the most avid of democrats.

CONCLUSION

Integrity rests partly on courage, partly on honesty, and greatly on integrating one's beliefs with one's actions. It will not be enough to simply espouse values. To be successful, the global leader of the future will have the added responsibility of influencing others through personal example. In order to establish trusting relationships with workers, peers, competitors, and customers, the global leader will have to demonstrate integrity in both personal values and business values. The unfortunate negative public examples of integrity violations have clearly made the "business case" for including integrity as a key quality for the leader of the future.

DEMONSTRATING INTEGRITY

ITEM 49: Demonstrates Honest, Ethical Behavior in All Interactions

WHAT TO DO

- Understand and communicate company and professional standards to others when appropriate to do so.
- Recognize that you are a model for those whom you lead.
- Demonstrate a commitment to high ethical standards in all business transactions.
- Be consistent and clear about your ethical standards.
- Look at the possible consequences of your behavior; good intentions are not enough.
- Handle sensitive matters with discretion.
- Provide facts, not smokescreens.
- Value the truth and speak up even when it may be risky to do so.
- Make realistic promises and keep them.
- Deal ethically with confidential information.
- Challenge any system that encourages dishonesty or rewards unethical behavior.

HOW TO DO IT

- Periodically discuss your company's code of ethics with managers and your work group.
- Include stakeholders in decision making to ensure that ethical standards are clear and are applied to both processes and results.
- Encourage people to express concerns about questionable practices; don't shoot the messenger.
- Talk to those you respect about a question of ethics or fairness as soon as it comes up.
- Review concerns with managers and team members.
- Identify your ethical standards. Use your standards to guide your leadership.
- If in doubt, don't do it.

- Offer open, candid feedback to management and coworkers.
- Treat personal matters in confidence.
- Don't ask anyone to do something you wouldn't do.
- Don't do anything you would not want others to do.
- Keep your commitments; do what you say you're going to do.
- Resolve interpersonal difficulties directly with the other person; don't play games.
- Seek feedback from peers and subordinates on your level of commitment to high ethical standards.

HOW TO USE THIS SKILL FURTHER

- Write down your principles, and communicate them at staff meetings.
- Ask people to tell you if your actions don't match your intentions.
- Keep all commitments, large and small, with friends and family.
- Think of someone you admire at work because of his or her integrity. What does that person do that you respect? Apply what you learn from this example.

RESULTS YOU CAN EXPECT

- Peers and subordinates may want to discuss their concerns about ethics with you and ask you for advice.
- Customers and suppliers may let you know they trust and respect you.
- Members of your work group may follow the example you have set for them.

READINGS

- *Credibility: How Leaders Gain and Lose It, Why People Demand It*. James S. Kouzes, Barry Z. Posner, & Tom Peters. 1995. Jossey-Bass: San Francisco, ISBN 787900567.
- *On Becoming a Leader*. Warren G. Bennis. 1994. Perseus: Reading, MA, ISBN 201409291.
- *Playing for Keeps*. Frederick G. Harmon. 1996. John Wiley & Sons: New York, ISBN 047159847X.
- *The Leader of the Future*. Frances Hesselbein, Marshall Goldsmith, & Richard Beckhard. 1996. Jossey-Bass: San Francisco, ISBN 0787901806.
- *The Soul of the Firm*. C. William Pollard & Carlos H. Cantu. 2000. Zondervan Publishing House: Grand Rapids, MI, ISBN 310234875.
- *Working With Emotional Intelligence*. Daniel P. Goleman. 2000. Bantam Doubleday Dell: New York, ISBN 553378589.

ITEM 50: Ensures that the Highest Standards for Ethical Behavior Are Practiced Throughout the Organization

WHAT TO DO

- Recognize that honesty and fairness in all relations with others is important.
- Recognize that you are a role model for those whom you lead.
- Challenge any system or procedure that encourages dishonesty or rewards unethical behavior.
- Demonstrate a commitment to high ethical standards in business transactions, and encourage others to do the same.
- Be consistent and clear about ethical standards and expectations.
- Use objective, performance-based data in managing other's performance and administering discipline.

HOW TO DO IT

- Include employees in the decision-making process to ensure that ethical standards are clear and are applied to both processes and results.
- Encourage people to express concerns about questionable practices; don't shoot the messenger.
- Talk to those you respect about a question of ethics or fairness as soon as it comes up.
- Review ethical concerns with your staff and management.
- If in doubt, don't do anything you feel is unethical.
- Take time to ask others how they see situations regarding integrity; listen to and recognize their ideas.
- Offer open, candid feedback to management and coworkers.
- Make sure you are aware of what's going on; manage by walking around your organization.
- Openly admit your mistakes and take responsibility for your role when things don't go as planned.
- Exercise discretion in communicating information of a sensitive nature (e.g., choose the right time, setting, and audience).
- Avoid "bending the truth" with others, and encourage them to be candid with you.
- Don't ask anyone to do something you wouldn't do.
- Don't do anything you would not want others to do.

HOW TO USE THIS SKILL FURTHER

- Write down your principles, and communicate them at staff meetings.
- Think of someone you admire at work because of his or her integrity. What does that person do that you respect? Apply what you learn.
- Ask trusted colleagues and employees to tell you when they observe you doing anything that even appears to show a lack of integrity.

RESULTS YOU CAN EXPECT

- Your coworkers may want to discuss their concerns about ethical standards with you and ask you for advice.
- Customers and suppliers may tell you that they trust and respect you and your staff.
- Members of your work group may follow the example you have set for them.
- You may find that no complaints are made regarding your department's ethics.

READINGS

- A Better Way to Think about Business: How Personal Integrity Leads to Corporate Success. Robert C. Solomon. 1999. Oxford University Press: Oxford, ISBN 0195112385.
- *Integrity at Work*. Ken Shelton. 1999. Executive Excellence: Provo, UT, ISBN 1890009326.
- *Integrity Management: A Guide to Managing Legal and Ethical Issues in the Workplace*. Debbie Thorne Leclair, D. C. Ferrell, & John P. Fraedvich. 1997. University of Tampa Press: Tampa, FL, ISBN 1879852551.
- *Thank God It's Monday!: 14 Values We Need to Humanize the Way We Work*. Ken Cloke, Joan Goldsmith, & Warren G. Bennis. 1997. McGraw-Hill: New York, ISBN 786310960.
- Trust in the Balance: Building Successful Organizations on Results, Integrity, and Concern. Robert Bruce Shaw. 1997. Jossey-Bass: San Francisco, ISBN 0787902861.

ITEM 51: Avoids Political and Self-Serving Behavior

WHAT TO DO

- Understand that being competent in your job is still the most effective method of achieving career success.
- Foster an environment that utilizes constant communication, clarity of ideas, and performance plans that will encourage open communication.

- Realize that organizational politics take many forms. List the tactics of organizational politics of which you are aware.
- Combat job politics through objective measurements of performance, providing an atmosphere of trust and setting good examples that demonstrate that political behavior is not desired.
- Have strong communication pathways that keep everyone informed. Secretive behavior and actions might be seen as politically motivated.
- Let people know exactly what they need to do to be promoted; this way there is less need for political maneuvering.
- Practice ethical and sensible organizational politics.
- Be sensitive to verbal and nonverbal communication that promote the "selfish" intentions rather than the company's and its people's needs first.

HOW TO DO IT

- Make time to ask questions, stop doing other things, and *listen*; when appropriate, be empathetic.
- Create an atmosphere that encourages people's questions and contrasting ideas.
- Do not accept undue credit—share in recognition.
- Be a team player.
- Treat people with respect and dignity.
- Use discretion in socializing with individuals in your work group.
- Avoid abrasive behaviors. This includes self-centeredness, isolation from others, contempt for others, and a tendency to attack people.
- Listen and respond empathetically. Watch for others' nonverbal behavior that may indicate they feel they are not being treated respectfully.
- Never participate in negative labeling or name-calling of people or groups; do not engage in back-stabbing.
- Have employees discuss the similarities between government and organizational politics.

HOW TO USE THIS SKILL FURTHER

- Ask your coworkers for feedback on how you are doing in this area.
- Volunteer to preview management videotapes about how to treat people respectfully.
- Read a self-help book on this topic and take action on what you read.

RESULTS YOU CAN EXPECT

- You may build trust between yourself and employees and peers.
- You may have more loyal employees.

READINGS

- *Don't Sabotage Your Success! Make Office Politics Work*. Karen Ginsburg Wood. 2000. Bookmasters: Mansfield, OH, ISBN 0970214308.
- *Enlightened Office Politics*. Michael S. Dobson & Deborah S. Dobson. 2001. AMACOM: New York, ISBN 0814470653.
- *Managing With Power: Politics and Influence in Organizations*. Jeffrey Pfeffer. 1996. Harvard Business School Press: Boston, ISBN 875844405.
- *Positive Politics: Overcome Office Politics & Fast-Track Your Career*. Mark Holden & Robert S. Muscat. 1999. Verlag Business & Professional Publishing: New York, ISBN 1875680381.
- *The Female Advantage: Women's Ways of Leadership*. Sally Helgesen. 1995. Currency/Doubleday: New York, ISBN 385419112.
- *The New Machiavelli: The Art of Politics in Business*. Alistair McAlpine. 1999. John Wiley & Sons: New York, ISBN 0471350958.
- *The Secret Handshake: Mastering the Politics of the Business Inner Circle*. Kathleen Kelly Reardon. 2000. Doubleday: New York, ISBN 0385495277.

ITEM 52: Courageously Stands Up for What She or He Believes In

WHAT TO DO

- Risk taking plays a part in nearly every decision made. Understanding the risks and the potential benefits is part of the game and is essential to the success of all managers.
- Be willing to stand up for what you believe in, even under pressure or when the opinion is unpopular.
- Be willing to take risks to achieve excellence and stay competitive.
- Value the truth and speak up even when it may be risky to do so.
- Encourage and support others to speak up and voice their viewpoints.
- Develop a positive attitude when facing objections.
- View the objections or obstacles as opportunities to find innovative solutions.
- Try to understand when others don't see eye to eye with your decisions or opinions.
- Remove obstacles or barriers in your organization that interfere with your initiatives to achieve excellence.

HOW TO DO IT

- Strive for a win-win solution—one that meets the needs of both sides as much as possible.
- When taking an unpopular stand, ask yourself and others "Why not?" instead of "Why?"

- Communicate your idea or vision with confidence, and convey a can-do attitude.
- When presenting a new idea or different perspective, provide as much background information as possible to your audience.
- Identify one or two people in your organization who will support your decision making.
- Work to gain support and cooperation from the key individuals in your organization.
- Don't hesitate to ask for advice or help.
- Talk with colleagues who excel at taking a stand on unpopular decisions.

HOW TO USE THIS SKILL FURTHER

- Ask people you work with for specific feedback on how you are doing in this area.
- Read the works of visionary writers to develop a sense of how to deal with ambiguity, map the environment, and open your mind to new ways to seeing.
- Volunteer to lead projects involving innovation and creativity.

RESULTS YOU CAN EXPECT

- You may be seen by others as assertive and cooperative.
- You may feel more in control and less like a victim.
- Respect from your work group may increase.
- You may succeed in changing or eliminating policies or procedures identified as roadblocks.

READINGS

- *A Better Way to Think about Business: How Personal Integrity Leads to Corporate Success.* Robert C. Solomon. 1999. Oxford University Press: Oxford, ISBN 0195112385.
- *Aiming Higher: 25 Stories of How Companies Prosper by Combining Sound Management and Social Vision. David Bollier.* 2000. AMACOM: New York, ASIN: 0814403190.
- *Business by the Book: The Complete Guide of Biblical Principles for the Workplace.* Larry Burkett. 2000. Thomas Nelson: Nashville, TN, ISBN 0785271414.
- *Counting What Counts: Turning Corporate Accountability to Competitive Advantage.* Marc J. Epstein & Bill Birchard. 2000. Perseus: Reading, MA, ISBN 0738201065.
- *Defining Moments: When Managers Must Choose Between Right and Right.* Joseph L. Badaracco, Jr. 1997. Harvard Business School Press: Boston, ISBN 0875848036.
- *How Good People Make Tough Choices: Resolving the Dilemmas of Ethical Living.* Rushworth M. Kidder. 1996. Fireside: Columbus, OH, ISBN 0684818388.

ITEM 53: Is a Role Model for Living Our Organization's Values (Leads by Example)

WHAT TO DO

- Think as if you were the owner of the company.
- Walk the talk. Be an example of what you want your employees to be.
- Be sure your performance reflects the best standards.
- Be open to new ideas and alternatives; demonstrate that you are a good listener.
- Acknowledge the unique knowledge and talents of others.
- Consider ways to share power in the interest of achieving overall organizational goals.
- Set challenging yet realistic goals for yourself and your group.
- Strive to achieve results within budget and on time.
- Manage by "wandering around."
- Set your priorities with a proper sense of importance or urgency.
- Use your time efficiently.
- Demonstrate your pride in your company.
- Coach employees to follow your example of performing to high standards.

HOW TO DO IT

- Write a list of standards by which to manage. Live by it on a day-to-day basis.
- Practice listening to peoples' ideas and opinions without bias, and respond with tact.
- Take a course in managing diversity, and take action to let people know you appreciate their unique perspective and talents.
- Assess where and when it can be more advantageous or productive to share power; take action and clearly explain the level of authority people have.
- Include others in decision making whenever possible.
- Get involved in projects with your workers, and demonstrate your leadership on specific skills you wish them to model.
- Check regularly with employees, customers, and suppliers so you maintain an accurate picture of what is urgent and important; coach others in setting priorities.
- Ask your employees for their input to goals.
- Based on realistic goals, build check points and contingency plans into implementation; monitor progress toward deadlines and budgets.
- Assess your time wasters and learn to eliminate them; strive to avoid wasting others' time.

- Take time to explain to employees, customers, and suppliers the positive contributions that your organization makes to the community and the society.
- Attend a course in coaching, and learn to specify what skill or behavior you expect from employees and how you expect them to achieve the change in performance.

HOW TO USE THIS SKILL FURTHER

- Discuss techniques with managers who excel at leading by example.
- Be assigned to work with groups that need more teamwork and leadership.
- Delegate more to your people.

RESULTS YOU CAN EXPECT

- Turnover may drop.
- Morale and commitment may increase.

READINGS

- *Accountability: Establishing Shared Ownership*. Debbe Kennedy. 2000. Berrett-Koehler: San Francisco, ISBN 1583760539.
- *Hesselbein on Leadership*. Frances Hesselbein. 2002. Jossey-Bass: San Francisco. ISBN: 0787963925
- *Leadership and Self-Deception: Getting Out of the Box*. The Arbinger Institute. 2000. Berrett-Koehler: San Francisco, ISBN 1576750949.
- *Leadership from the Inside Out*. Kevin Cashman. 1999. Executive Excellence: Provo, UT, ISBN 1890009318.
- *Nuts!: Southwest Airlines' Crazy Recipe for Business and Personal Success*. Kevin Freiberg, Jackie Freiberg, & Tom Peters. 1998. Bantam Doubleday Dell: New York, ISBN 767901843.
- *The New Global Leaders: Richard Branson, Percy Barnevik, and David Simon and the Remaking of International Business*. Manfred F. R. Kets De Vries & Elizabeth Florent-Treacy. 1999. Jossey-Bass: San Francisco, ISBN 787946575.

ENDNOTES

1. In partnership with the Accenture Institute for Strategic Change, Alliance for Strategic Leadership (A4SL) investigated the attitudes and opinions of the next U.S. generation of leaders. A student at the University of Pennsylvania, Lauren Wagner, was commissioned by A4SL to interview 100 student leaders of the top undergraduate business programs across the United States (as determined by *US News & World Report,* September 18, 1997).

2. Investments, Taiwan, 32.

3. Technology, Spain, 39.

4. Products and services, United States, 42.

5. Technology, Poland, 39.

6. Healthcare, Indonesia/Malaysia, 46.

7. Products and services, United States, 42.

13 LEADING CHANGE

The global leader of the future will be faced with new business challenges for which there is no established model of leadership. Although executive management models of the past provide some guidance for the leadership models of the future, in today's complex and ever-changing worldwide business environment, no specific, established model will fit the broad range of situations that global leaders will encounter.

Throughout this book you have considered traits that the global leader must have to some degree. Future leaders must excel in each of these areas, or they must be able to draw upon the collective expertise of those around them if they are to be successful in the future global marketplace. Some of these attributes, such as anticipating opportunities, creating a shared vision, and maintaining competitive advantage, are based on management models of the past. Those qualities that are becoming increasingly important are in the areas of building partnerships, encouraging constructive dialogue, sharing leadership, empowering people, thinking globally, appreciating diversity, and developing technologically savvy. It is in these arenas that global leaders will be looked upon to direct and guide their organizations through uncharted and often unanticipated global shifts, to bring value to their investors, employees, partners, and customers.

CHANGE IS AN OPPORTUNITY

Throughout most of corporate history, executives have derived power largely from their position and authority in the organization. Power was, and in many cases still is, vested in the job and formalized in an organization chart. Individuals have authority over those below them in the pyramid. This design works well as long as companies need workers to perform narrowly defined jobs under close supervision.

> We are very specialized today. There are leaders who have people skills, leaders who have management skills, leaders who have financial skills, et cetera. The future leader will need to be a well-rounded leader and master all of these skills.[1]

As the business environment changes, the complexity, speed, and scale demanded by global business make it more difficult for companies to go it alone with the traditional, vertically integrated structure. As a result, alliances, partnerships, virtual companies, joint ventures, strategic sourcing, and outsourcing are all growing fast as companies strive for access to the full range of skills, capabilities, and resources they need.

> Global leaders of the future don't fear change. They cope with change and view it as a positive.[2]

This new environment demands greater speed and dynamism. Next-generation companies derive the necessary fluidity and flexibility from organizations that are less structured and with fewer established lines of authority. Traditional functional boundaries are dissolving with the advent of process-oriented management operating in networks rather than hierarchies. Information flows in all directions, and people work in teams that form and reform with considerable autonomy.

> The working environment will change. There will be tremendous growth in our company that we've never gone through before. I will not be able to ask older leaders for help, because they have not experienced what we will be experiencing. I will have to lead in the growth and rely on innovation.[3]

The greatest constraint in creating a networked organization of specialized yet interdependent units is the shortage of executives with experience, skills, knowledge, and finesse to operate in a more tightly linked but less classically hierarchical global network, and herein lies a great opportunity for the global leader of the future.

The leader of the international division of an international hotel chain struggled to create such a network in order to build an American hotel name outside of the United States. His challenge was not due to a lack of talented leaders on whom to rely; his challenge came from his personal leadership style. This controlling leader had a great history of success in managing the franchise network and building relationships; however, he wanted to handle nearly every situation personally. The pace was too much, and the leader was forced to let go of some of his duties. Although it was a struggle, the leader has slowly changed his leadership style from telling to coordinating, from hierarchical to devolved leadership. He has hired local leaders whom he is comfortable with to make and implement decisions, rather than taking these decisions on as part of his own workload, and he has found leaders around the world whom he trusts to be part of his interdependent leadership network.

LEADERSHIP VERSUS MANAGEMENT: CHALLENGING THE STATUS QUO

As the pace and scale of change increases, the difference in the real world between a manager and a global leader becomes clearer. A manager is an organizer and problem solver. While this is an important business function, the reactionary skill sets of the traditional manager cannot be expected to solve the challenges brought about by such forces as technology and globalization.

> The stereotype of the corporate leader as a middle-aged white male with a secretary and high blood pressure is obviously changing.[4]

Traditionally, managers have been rewarded for being "on time and on budget" and for always having the answer. A national service entity in Canada takes this notion to the extreme. Each morning the top 30 executives of the 250,000-person company meet for one to two hours to discuss any problems of a consumer nature that may have arisen in the previous 24 hours and to answer questions posed regarding problems in each executive's area. Executives enter the meeting fully apprised and able to explain the "reasons why" there may have been a problem; not to do so would mean personal embarrassment in this goldfish bowl environment. Although the attention top management pays to customer satisfaction is laudable, the way in which issues are addressed is questionable. With modern technology, companies have the ability to record, analyze, categorize, and trend-analyze customer problem instances on a daily basis. The information can then be reviewed by employees in lower level positions. There does not need to be such high involvement by the senior management team. The cultural style driving the company, which is based on leaders' attention to the smallest of details, perpetuates leadership in which the manager is a reactionary organizer and the problem solver rather than an empowering and entrusting leader of change and anticipator of trends.

On the other hand, the proactive qualities of a global leader, such as sharing leadership, anticipating opportunities, and building partnerships, are absolutely critical to success in the future.

> The future global leaders will need to be much more creative. They will have to take risks and use new models for success. They will not always be able to do what past role models have done in order to be successful.[5]

Warren Bennis, one of the authorities on leadership, acknowledged in the second edition of his book, *On Becoming a Leader*,[6] "I didn't put as much emphasis [in the first edition] on the distinction between 'leading' and 'managing' as I should have, because I did not fully anticipate the seismic shakes and quakes that would unhinge our world. Staying with the status quo is no longer acceptable," he says, so "followers need from people three basic qualities: they want direction; they want trust; and they want hope. That's what leaders must provide, whether we're talking about General Motors, a nation-state, or a nonprofit organization."

Tomorrow's global leaders are *part of a new generation. We will be breaking free from stereotypes and from the traditional way of doing work.*[7] Strategic opportunities will undoubtedly arise unexpectedly and often amidst seeming failure brought about by adherence to the status quo, and the global leaders of the future will *view failure [their own and that of others] as an opportunity for change.*[8]

This can be quite a difficult philosophy for leaders to incorporate into their leadership styles. For instance, even an R&D team, whose professional focus is change, risk, and experimentation, is likely to find it difficult to move away from the traditional management style of "always having the answer," as the authors found in their recent work with a pharmaceutical company. The R&D team of this company, while very comfortable with change and risk taking of an intra-human nature, such as experimentation to produce change of a drug-development nature, was very uncomfortable with change of an inter-human nature, such as changing relationships with each other as scientists or between the functional areas of the R&D system. Leaders need to be able to experiment and make mistakes; however, even groups that experiment and make mistakes as a profession will likely find it difficult to incorporate the value of failure into their leadership style.

Global leaders will be ready to quickly shift gears to pursue new goals. In such a turbulent and unexplored environment, *there needs to be plenty of growing room so that global leaders can experiment and make mistakes and learn from them.*[9] IBM is a benchmark organization that has demonstrated the ability to successfully shift gears and enter a very different type of business. The IBM move into services can be a role model for other organizations with maturing technology.

As discussed earlier, developing and operating efficiently under new, complex, and shifting social architectures means that tomorrow's leaders will function inside of alliances, partnerships, and ventures like never before. Leadership in the future will require teams of collaborative leaders, each possessing many of those skills required for effective global leadership. As such, a bias toward the status quo is an unaffordable luxury. *Global leaders of the future cannot stick to the old way of doing things.*[10] They will need to be less controlling, more emotionally astute, culturally attuned, and most important, willing to share authority and decision making. Extensive research on leadership effectiveness by the Alliance for Strategic Leadership has shown that leaders who are willing to change and are open to employee input will be consistently viewed as more effective than those who are not.[11]

FLEXIBILITY

The global leader of the future will have to have a lot of flexibility and be very self-confident in order to create a 'win-win' solution.[12] Flexibility is an admittedly broad term, but in the context of tomorrow's leadership, it has two distinct meanings:

1. the flexibility to work across cultures and around the world, and
2. the flexibility to deal with uncertainty, ambiguity, and change.

In terms of cultural flexibility, leaders will have to transcend cultural boundaries and embrace the wide variety of business approaches and social customs that are inherent to conducting business globally. They will have to understand that no single style of leadership will work in all cultures. As such, global leaders will have to modify their behaviors to suit their audience. For instance, Yo Miyoshi of the HB Fuller Company in Tokyo relayed that when he discusses an issue with leaders of the U.S. office, he tries to be "Western." However, when he deals with people at the Japanese office, he is Japanese. In other words, he alters his personal leadership style to handle the two cultures.[13] Being different things to different people so that people can understand where the leader is coming from is a behavior that must be learned, by educating its leaders to understand and deal with a great diversity of people, is imparting to them just this lesson.

In some countries, the forging of personal relationships will be critical, while in others the ability to create contractual relationships will be of key importance; in some countries, fast action will be respected, while in others, deliberation and consensus-building will be needed.

For instance, in Latin America relationships are very important. Thus, the ability to make deals and negotiate terms is heavily predicated on an individual's ability to build trust with others, often very quickly, through paying attention to developing the relationship. This is counterpointed with the cultural styles of Germany and the UK, wherein relationships fall secondary to the high emphasis on getting to the facts. An important point to note is that in these more fact-oriented cultures, the greatest leaders are those who recognize what others need in a relationship sense. These leaders are very much aware of which relationship buttons they might press to influence others. This ability to influence better as a result of assessing and reacting to individual relationships and communication needs is called "self-monitoring." In other words, the leader orchestrates his or her own behavior in order to have the maximum influence on another individual.

For instance, in *Churchill: A Biography,* Roy Jenkins discusses Winston Churchill's lack of academic success but avid interest in the sensitivities, hot buttons, and personalities of others. Jenkins relays that Churchill, as a student of people, learned to be what he needed to be in order to establish the relationships necessary for "success" and in order to influence other leaders, such as George Patton, Franklin D. Roosevelt, and Josef Stalin.[14]

In terms of being flexible in the face of change, global leaders will have to adopt a different mindset toward planning. Instead of planning and executing in successive steps, the global leader will have to be prepared to plan and then adjust the plan as it is executed—or even to plan and execute simultaneously. In order to be successful, *leaders will have to adapt quickly to changes in the environment—faster than the competition.*[15] An unfortunate example of rigid adherence to plan involved the space shuttle Challenger, which ultimately exploded after takeoff on January 28, 1986. Rather than being open to new ideas and willing to change, leaders let adherence to plan override ability to listen to new input and respond. The result was a devastating tragedy and the loss of seven lives.

In today's rapid-paced business world, the global leader will not always have sufficient time to analyze and strategize. Decisions will have to be made sometimes without benefit of the supporting facts and analysis that make the leader feel absolutely comfortable. However, decisions have to be made—and made quickly. For this reason, *the global leader of the future should be change-oriented, move quicker, and more flexible.*[16]

By being flexible about plans—and new ideas from new quarters—leaders are less likely to become complacent based on past success and are more likely to learn from and take advantage of the changes taking place in the world today.

This is especially difficult for leaders of family-run businesses, who often have the most difficulty creating change and avoiding complacency, because family pride is associated with company success. For instance, leaders of a Latin American business and a major hotel chain, both family owned, experienced difficulty making changes and getting past family politics and relationships. The leadership teams of both companies spent considerable time discussing the key business and leadership elements of their cultures. First, they explored what had made the companies successful, and a conscious effort was made to ensure that the companies kept the exceptional qualities they had demonstrated up to this point. Second, the teams looked at what might be added to these core elements to help deal with new market situations and to move forward into a successful future. Thus, both leadership teams demonstrated that while they had much pride in their successes to date, they were flexible enough to grow into the future.

It's important for companies not only to plan for future success, but also to take time to consider past successes. For example, if a company is highly successful, changing the core structure or modus operandi of the company is probably not going to work, and it will waste time and energy. Instead, the team leaders may choose to keep the operational foundation of the company as it is, because this is the basis upon which the company's success has been built and the reason for which the company has a presence in the industry. But, rather than be complacent in the company's success, the team leaders may opt to add onto, rather than reengineer, that structure in order to further the organization.

ENCOURAGING CREATIVITY

The global leader of the future who maintains the status quo will be easily defeated by competitors who are willing to try new ideas, to seek out new opportunities, and who are ready for change—within both the corporation and the industry. McDonald's has shown that even unquestioned industry leaders can lose market share to innovative, creative competitors who are willing to give consumers new products that meet changing needs. Creativity and innovation are key to the continued success of any organization, and using this key depends on global leaders who *encourage and embrace the innovation and creativity of others.*[17]

> Successful leaders will be known by how well we get people energized to do the job, ...how quickly change is coming, and how quickly we adjust to it.[18]

Andy Grove, former chairman of Intel, once revealed that the company's most significant strategic decision was made by those managers on the frontlines who were actively involved in the corporation's marketing and investment activities rather than as a result of the corporate vision. To Harvard Business School's Christopher Bartlett and Sumantra Ghoshal, who quoted Grove approvingly, he is typical of the more successful, progressive leaders they have encountered who are striving to articulate a clear vision and letting individuals creatively interpret the company's objectives.

That may be a trifle idealized, but studies of such leaders' schedules show that they spend up to 90 percent of their time in face-to-face discussions with colleagues, contacts, and members of their teams. They are picking up the vital implicit knowledge, impressions, and ideas that no reporting system can reveal, but they also are winning support for their vision and purpose, which their followers will interpret and implement.

> Global leaders need to be flexible enough to allow lots of different "how's" to get to the same "what." These leaders need to let go of the more superficial trappings of organizations, such as dress codes and office codes, and focus more on the outcomes.[19]

Global leaders need to structure their companies so that they facilitate creativity from the lower ranks. The restructuring of many organizations reflects this need. As the traditional hierarchical pyramid, with layer upon layer of carefully delineated management to turn the central strategy into detailed action plans, gives way to flatter, broader shapes based on processes rather than functions, it becomes apparent that the trend is to *streamline companies in order for individuals to make an impact in their organizations.*[20] Karen Garrison, a key executive at Pitney Bowes has created an environment where every level of employee knows they have an open invitation to express their opinions to her. This leadership style leads to both commitment and personal ownership on the part of all employees.

However, although it is widely believed that *global companies should decrease the layers between the CEO and entry-level workers, because entry-level workers are the frontline employees who directly affect the business,*[21] the vertical dimension is still significant, but with expansion and with internal organizations now resembling networks more than chains of command, the qualities of empowerment, encouragement, and understanding are at a premium. In short, networked leadership is required at an all-time high. For instance, in the healthcare industry, drugs are no longer developed by scientists working with other scientists in laboratories. They are developed by comprehensive teams of scientists and business leaders who represent the entire spectrum of the corporation.

TRANSLATING IDEAS INTO RESULTS

There is little doubt that the networked, outsourced, allied company is the pattern of the future. However large the leading oil and motor corporations, or the pharmaceutical, software, finance, and telecommunications groups may become, their internal structures and external links make the task of leadership different in kind than in the past. The Northrop Grumman Corporation, in recognition of the key role of network relationships with suppliers, has made commitment to suppliers one of its key corporate values.

> The future leaders need to have a scope of vision that is broad enough to see what's available to them. They must take on risks.[22]

CONCLUSION

As the international business network expands, it incorporates many different national cultures, meaning that attitudes to authority differ and assumptions and ambitions vary. Leaders must adapt to these differences, and they must also cope with the ambiguities of an unavoidably complex international structure. The challenge for global leaders today is to guide and direct their organizations and employees in this era of unprecedented complexity and fast-paced world change. This chapter has illustrated that in order to effectively lead change, the global leader must have a proactive and positive mindset. Global leaders must be open-minded, prepared, flexible, and farsighted if they are to effectively guide their organizations to achieving desired results.

NEVER SET THE BAR

Eric Greenberg—founder, chairman, and CEO of Acumen Sciences, LLC, and president and CEO of Innovation Investments, LLC—wants to change the world.[23] Widely regarded as a pioneer in Internet, intranet, and security-related technologies, Eric is a self-described "obsessive maniac" who "loves to create something completely new out of nothing." A short list of Eric's creations includes Twelve Entrepreneuring, a technology operating company; Scient, a consulting firm focused on e-business and emerging technology; and Viant, an Internet systems integrator.

Eric believes that there is no formula for success. His philosophy of leadership is to "be a student of life and know what you're good at." Analyzing his own success in the technology industry, he credits it to two things: (1) his ability to look ahead and "connect the dots" to the future; and (2) his talent for recruiting, building, and mobilizing teams. We'll add one more: Eric isn't afraid to take risks.

Connecting the Dots

Following the advice of Peter Drucker, Eric often takes time out to think. Every so often, he shuts his office door for an hour or two and just thinks. "Thinking is an individual act," he says. "Every invention came out of one person's brain; it's modified and put forth by a team, but the initial idea came from one person." Once he comes up with an idea, often in the middle of the night, Eric calls three or four people together, tells them the idea, and listens to them talk about it. In this way, he watches the idea grow into something tangible.

Great Teams

"To be somebody that matters and to change the world, you have to do it with and through people." With such an attitude, it's no wonder that one of Eric's talents is building great teams. He has the ability to place people so that they are doing what they want to do, which is very often what they are good at as well. He accomplishes this by figuring out each individual's frame of reference so that he or she can shape his or her own progress. "A leader is someone who helps others to understand what makes them tick," says Eric. "People have to have the incentive measurement and reward systems that keep them with the company, but what they want at the end of the day is to learn, to do exciting work and feel like their career is progressing [toward] have an increasingly better life or opportunity."[24]

Taking Risks

Eric views business as the same old, same old as destructive and ideas as adventures to be taken. He believes that this is what makes him a leader. "If you want to change the world, you have to make things happen, you have to take risks. This scares people," says Eric. "Not everyone is a leader, because not everyone can take risks." Eric is different: His core belief is, "If you can conceive the dream, you can achieve it." This is the stuff of which great entrepreneurs and successful leaders are made.

LEADING CHANGE

ITEM 54: Sees Change as an Opportunity, Not a Problem

WHAT TO DO

- Realize that to effectively manage change, it's important to understand your own reactions to change.
- Realize that change is an ongoing process for improvement.
- Convey a positive attitude toward change.
- Anticipate the possible consequences of the change.
- Develop a plan to implement the change.
- Involve people who will be affected by change in the planning and execution process.
- Share as much information as you can with people during the process of organizational change.
- Identify the opportunities for change, and tell people what you think the change will mean for them.
- Expect people's resistance to change.
- Be open to listen to people's reactions to the proposed change.
- Develop strategies to deal with the resistance to change.
- Realize that it takes time to work through the resistance to change.

HOW TO DO IT

- Think about past changes that have created opportunities in your job and in your personal life. Recall how you felt and reacted during these changes.
- Analyze the causes of your reactions to change, and evaluate what you did to successfully manage the change. Use those successful strategies to manage future changes.
- Be honest and straightforward in explaining the change.
- Convince key individuals in the organization to view change as opportunity, and gain support and commitments from them.
- Discuss the proposed change with key individuals. Solicit their input regarding the rationale for change, the potential benefits, and the execution plan.

- Encourage people to openly express their feelings about the change.
- Carefully listen to people's concerns about change, understand the reasons for resistance, and deal with the problems in a timely manner.
- Study books or take courses to learn how people change and how to better manage change.
- Develop formal communication channels such as emails, frequently asked questions databases, and other electronic forms of communication or a departmental bulletin board to keep people informed on the change.
- Talk with managers who have implemented change successfully. Learn the steps they have taken to solve problems, and seek specific advice for your own situation.

HOW TO USE THIS SKILL FURTHER

- Volunteer to work on a task force at your company that deals with organizational change.
- Volunteer to help a nonprofit organization manage change.

RESULTS YOU CAN EXPECT

- The transition process may be smoother.
- People may ask you for advice to deal with change.

READINGS

- *Business Climate Shifts: Profiles of Change Makers.* W. Warner Burke, Richard Koonce, & William Trahant. 1999. Butterworth-Heinemann: Woburn, MA, ISBN 750671866.
- *Control Your Destiny or Someone Else Will: Lessons in Mastering Change—From the Principles Jack Welch Is Using to Revolutionize GE.* Noel Tichy & Stratford Sherman. 1999. HarperBusiness: New York, ISBN 887306705.
- *Gung Ho! Turn On the People in Any Organization.* Ken Blanchard & Sheldon Bowles. 1997. William Morrow: New York, ISBN 068815428X.
- *Hidden Value: How Great Companies Achieve Extraordinary Results with Ordinary People.* Charles O'Reilly & Jeffrey Pfeffer. 2000. Harvard Business School Press: Boston, ISBN 875848982.
- *In The Face of Uncertainty.* Editor Martha I. Finney. Contributor John Alexander. 2002. AMACOM: New York. ISBN: 0814471617
- *Leading Change.* John Kotter. 1996. Harvard Business School Press: Boston, ISBN 875847471.
- *Managers As Mentors: Building Partnerships for Learning*: Chip R. Bell: 1998: Berrett-Koehler: San Francisco, ISBN 1576750345.
- *Organizing Genius: The Secrets of Creative Collaboration.* Patricia Ward Biederman & Warren G. Bennis. 1998. Perseus: New York, ISBN 201339897.

- *Playing For Keeps: How the World's Most Aggressive and Admired Companies Use Core Values to Manage, Energize, and Organize Their People, and Promote, Advance, and Achieve Their Corporate Missions.* Frederick Harmon. 1996. John Wiley & Sons: New York, ISBN 047159847X.
- *Taking Charge of Change: 10 Principles for Managing People and Performance.* Douglas Smith. 1997. Perseus: Reading, MA, ISBN 201916045.
- *The Dance of Change: The Challenges to Sustaining Momentum in Learning Organizations.* Peter Senge, Art Kleiner, Charlotte Roberts, George Roth, Rick Ross, & Bryan Smith. 1999. Doubleday: New York, ISBN 385493223.

ITEM 55: Challenges the System When Change Is Needed

WHAT TO DO

- Recognize that innovation and change are vital to continuous improvement efforts.
- In order to stay competitive, managers need to let go of the status quo in favor of strategies that can increase benefits. Challenge yourself and challenge others to do the same.
- Provide others with sufficient information to permit them to develop creative yet workable ideas.
- Find and leverage trusted peers to communicate among constituents—peers who deliver messages about issues will have a better adoption rate by their cohorts (constituents).
- View past practices as a place to start rather than as "the way we always do it."
- When making decisions, try to be less conservative and more willing to take risks.
- Remove obstacles or barriers in your organization that interfere with new initiatives to make needed changes.
- Try to understand why others are against innovation or resist changes.
- Be willing to stand up for what you believe in, even under pressure.
- Be aware of those who are afraid of change or are always happy with the status quo. Find other ways that they can be productive without standing in your way.
- Develop a positive attitude when facing objections.
- View the objections or obstacles as opportunities to find innovative solutions.
- Identify areas in which changes are needed; encourage and support others to seek improvements in those areas.
- Develop action plans and set deadlines to implement the change.

HOW TO DO IT

- When considering making changes, ask yourself and others "Why not?" instead of "Why?"
- Communicate the change with confidence, and convey a can-do attitude.

- When presenting a new initiative, provide as much background information as possible to your work group.
- Interview others who have been successful outside or inside your industry, or use consultants to help you find those who are willing to share.
- Identify one or two people in your organization who can help you make the change a reality.
- Work to gain support and cooperation from the key individuals in your organization.
- Don't hesitate to ask for advice or help.
- Use benchmark data from associations in which you have access to it.
- Hold regular meetings with others (managers, peers, and employees) to share information and data, and identify possible areas for improvement.
- Make sure that others have a clear understanding of their customers' needs and requirements. Provide a communication link between them.
- Read the works of visionary writers to develop a sense of how to deal with ambiguity, map the environment, and open your mind to new ways of seeing and thinking.
- Identify an innovative company and think about the differences between its management's involvement and yours. Talk to managers and employees to identify all the differences you can. Work with others to identify and make appropriate changes in your own organization.
- Model the behavior of making sound decisions and taking appropriate risks; act on new ideas without delay.

HOW TO USE THIS SKILL FURTHER

- Try making changes in your personal life by focusing on problems you have been trying to solve.
- Help someone else act on a new idea or approach they want to try out.
- Volunteer to lead projects involving change management.
- Strive for a win-win solution—one that meets the needs of both sides as much as possible.

RESULTS YOU CAN EXPECT

- Customer expectations may continue to be met or exceeded using new and better ways of working.
- You may be seen by others as a change agent.
- You may feel more in control and less like a victim.
- Others may come to you for support.

READINGS

- *Beyond Certainty: The Changing Worlds of Organizations.* Charles Handy. 1998. Harvard Business School Press: Boston, ISBN 875847633.

- *Business 2010: Positioning Your Company and Yourself in a Rapidly Changing World*. Frederick Harmon. 2001. Kiplinger Books: Washington, DC, ISBN 938721844.
- *Evolve!: Succeeding in the Digital Culture of Tomorrow*. Rosabeth Moss Kanter. 2001. Harvard Business School Press: Boston, ISBN 1578514398.
- *Fumbling the Future: How Xerox Invented, Then Ignored, the First Personal Computer*. Douglas Smith & Robert Alexander. 1999. iUniverse.com: Silicon Valley, CA, ISBN 1583482660.
- *Imagination Engineering: Your Toolkit for Business Creativity*. Paul Birch & Brian Clegg. 2000. Financial Times–Prentice Hall: Upper Saddle River, NJ, ISBN 0273649299.
- *Intrapreneuring in Action: A Handbook for Business Innovation*. Gifford Pinchot & Ron Pellman. 1999. Berrett-Koehler: San Francisco, ISBN 1576750612.
- *Linkage Inc.'s Best Practices in Leadership Development Handbook : Case Studies, Instruments, Training*. 2000. Editors Louis Carter, David Giber, Marshall Goldsmith. With Warren G. Bennis. Jossey-Bass: San Francisco. ISBN: 0787952370
- *Reengineering the Corporation: A Manifesto for Business Revolution*. Michael Hammer & James Champy. 2001. HarperBusiness: New York, ISBN 66621127.
- *Seize Tomorrow, Start Today: Renew Your Vision, Revitalize Your Organization, and Stay Ahead of the Future*. James A. Belasco & Jerre L. Stead. 2000. Warner Books: New York, ISBN 446676047.

ITEM 56: Thrives in Ambiguous Situations (Demonstrates Flexibility When Needed)

WHAT TO DO

- Maintain a positive attitude toward ambiguous situations.
- Be willing to listen and stay open when dealing with ambiguity.
- Realize that understanding others' thinking may enhance your own ideas and help you make the right decision.
- Keep your sense of humor.
- Analyze and prepare for the possible consequences of an ambiguous situation.

HOW TO DO IT

- Analyze your own reaction to ambiguity, and learn to see ambiguity as a challenge, not a threat.
- Think about past changes (both positive and negative) that you have encountered on your job and in your personal life. Recall how you felt and reacted during these uncertain situations.

- Analyze the causes of your reactions to ambiguity, and evaluate what you did to successfully manage the situation. Use those successful strategies to manage future changes.
- When dealing with ambiguous situations, have more one-on-one meetings with key stakeholders to share information, establish rapport, and learn others' viewpoints.
- Schedule listening time with key members of your team, leaders in the organization, or external constituents.
- Observe people who are flexible and open minded; ask them for tips.
- Tell others you want to improve your listening skills.
- Ask for feedback on your openness to new or different ideas. Solicit suggestions that could develop your skill.
- Study books or take courses to learn how people deal with change and how to better manage ambiguity.
- Talk with managers who have demonstrated flexibility in ambiguous situations and handled change positively. Learn from them.
- Analyze "what if" situations and prepare several approaches to deal with problems that may occur.

HOW TO USE THIS SKILL FURTHER

- Volunteer to work on a task force at your company that deals with organizational change.
- Volunteer to help a nonprofit organization manage change.
- Serve as an alternate channel for complaints and questions for other manager's associates.

RESULTS YOU CAN EXPECT

- The process for change may be smoother.
- People may ask you for advice in dealing with ambiguity.

READINGS

- *Age of Unreason*. Charles Handy & Warren Bennis. 1998. Harvard Business School Press: Boston, ISBN 875843018.
- *In The Face of Uncertainty. Editor Martha I. Finney.* Contributor John Alexander. 2002. AMACOM: New York. ISBN: 0814471617
- *Leading Change*. John P. Kotter. 1996. Harvard Business School Press: Boston, ISBN 875847471.
- *Reengineering the Corporation: A Manifesto for Business Revolution*. Michael Hammer & James Champy. 2001. HarperBusiness: New York, ISBN 66621127.
- *Relax, It's Only Uncertainty: Lead the Way When the Way Is Changing*. Randall P. White & Philip Hodgson. 2001. Financial Times–Prentice Hall: Upper Saddle River, NJ, ISBN 0273652419.

- *Surfing the Edge of Chaos: The Laws of Nature and the New Laws of Business.* Richard Tanner Pascale, Mark Milleman, & Linda Gioja. 2000. Crown: Victoria, BC, ISBN 0812933168.
- *Taking Charge of Change: 10 Principles for Managing People and Performance.* Douglas K. Smith. 1997. Perseus: Reading, MA, ISBN 201916045.
- *Thriving in 24/7: Six Strategies for Taming the New World of Work.* Sally Helgesen. 2001. Free Press: London, ISBN 684873036.
- *Who's Running Your Career?: Creating Stable Work in Unstable Times.* Caela Farren. 1997. Bard Press: Marietta, GA, ISBN 1885167172.

ITEM 57: Encourages Creativity and Innovation in Others

WHAT TO DO

- Create an atmosphere that encourages people's creativity and contrasting ideas.
- Value those who can think outside the box. Maintain an atmosphere in which these people feel safe to innovate, and provide the support they need.
- Value the input of others. Don't hesitate to change your strategies if someone else comes up with a better idea. Consider all your options, and don't be afraid to take one step back if it will lead you two steps ahead.
- Show interest in gathering and developing ideas of others.
- Identify and reward those who are self-starters and can "go with the flow."
- Identify areas in which creativity and innovation are appropriate; encourage and support others to seek improvements in those areas.
- Establish an objective, consistent way of gathering and evaluating ideas.
- Let others know they can question and disagree.
- Concentrate on ideas, not on personalities.
- Ask probing question when others seem reticent.
- Be open to the risks and possible mistakes that new ways of working can create.

HOW TO DO IT

- Keep your innovators sharp by having them attend workshops, seminars, and other opportunities to network and exchange ideas. Encourage their involvement with customers, various committees, and brainstorming sessions.
- Get associates together for brainstorming sessions to generate creative ideas.
- Collect ideas from people who normally don't deal with the problem.
- Include subject matter experts where appropriate (academics and consultants).

- When others disagree with you, respond in a nondefensive manner; this gives people permission to question and come up with alternative solutions.
- Ask open questions that require more than a yes or no response.
- Get support from customers, peers, and subordinates for new ways of doing work by discussing change ideas with them and getting their input.
- Investigate and practice various techniques for generating new ideas.
- Promote the idea of "white space" in which people can have some time to strategize, think, or plan without having to attend meetings or work on "today's deadline."

HOW TO USE THIS SKILL FURTHER

- Volunteer to plan and participate in brainstorming sessions.
- Ask for assignments that require creativity.
- Take a class on developing creativity.

RESULTS YOU CAN EXPECT

- You may implement more innovative approaches.
- You may be asked to join new projects or task forces.
- Productivity of your group may increase.

READINGS

- *Corporate Creativity: How Innovation and Improvement Actually Happen.* Alan G. Robinson & Sam Stern. 1998. Berrett-Koehler: San Francisco, ISBN 1576750493.
- *Imagination Engineering: Your Toolkit for Business Creativity.* Paul Birch & Brian Clegg. 2000. Financial Times–Prentice Hall: Upper Saddle River, NJ, ISBN 0273649299.
- *Intrapreneuring in Action: A Handbook for Business Innovation.* Gifford Pinchot & Ron Pellman. 1999. Berrett-Koehler: San Francisco, ISBN 1576750612.
- *Managing for Excellence: The Guide to Developing High Performance in Contemporary Organizations.* David L. Bradford & Allan R. Cohen. 1997. John Wiley & Sons: New York, ISBN 0471127248.
- *Positive Turbulence: Developing Climates for Creativity, Innovation, and Renewal.* Stanley Gryskiewicz. 1999. Jossey-Bass: San Francisco, ISBN 0787910082.
- *The Age of Innovation: Making Business Creativity a Competence, Not a Coincidence.* Felix Janszen. 2000. Financial Times–Prentice Hall: Upper Saddle River, NJ, ISBN 0273638750.

ITEM 58: Effectively Translates Creative Ideas Into Business Results

WHAT TO DO

- Recognize that innovation and change are vital to value-generating efforts.
- Provide others with sufficient information to permit them to develop creative yet workable ideas.
- Identify areas in which creativity and innovation are appropriate; encourage and support others to seek improvements in those areas.
- Review and discuss all risks (the probability of failure and the consequences of failure) before implementing a new idea.
- Make sure the impact of new approaches on other operations and other work units is fully explored and resolved before a new idea is implemented.
- Make people aware that they are accountable for their decisions.
- Develop action plans and set deadlines to implement new ideas.

HOW TO DO IT

- Use benchmark data from associations in which you have access to it.
- Hold regular meetings with others (managers, peers, and employees) to generate and share creative ideas for improving business results, and develop business plans to implement the ideas.
- Work with your group to develop specific action plans, assign responsibilities within the team, and set a realistic timeline to complete the task.
- Supply the resources and information others need to implement creative ideas and deliver business results.
- Follow up regularly to ensure the ideas are implemented as planned.
- Make sure that others have a clear understanding of their customers' needs and requirements. Provide a communication link between them.
- Maintain objectivity when reviewing new ideas and decisions.
- Determine the "area of freedom" for new ideas—where ideas can be tried out without violating any contractual, safety, or other nonnegotiable requirement.
- Identify an innovative company and think about the differences between its management's involvement and yours. Talk to managers and employees to identify all the differences you can. Work with others to identify and make appropriate changes in your own organization.
- Model the behavior of making sound decisions and taking appropriate risks; act on ideas without delay.
- Keep a file entitled "New Ideas." Each time you hear or see something related to your job, write it down and file it. Periodically review the file.

- Devise alternative, more effective, and efficient methods for handling your routine job responsibilities.

HOW TO USE THIS SKILL FURTHER

- Try out some of your own creative ideas on problems that you have been trying to solve.
- Help someone else act on a new idea or approach they want to try out.

RESULTS YOU CAN EXPECT

- Your work group may generate and implement more creative ideas to improve business results.
- Customer expectations may continue to be met using new and better ways of working.
- Your group may make more mistakes than before, but may experience more successes.

READINGS

- *Corning and the Craft of Innovation*. Margaret B. W. Graham & Alec T. Shuldiner. 2001. Oxford University Press: Oxford, England, ISBN 195140974.
- *Freedom and Accountability at Work: Applying Philosophical Insight to the Real World*. Peter Koestenbaum & Peter Block. 2001. Pfeiffer & Co.: New York, ISBN 787955949.
- *In Praise of Good Business: How Optimizing Risk Rewards Both Your Bottom Line and Your People*. Judith M. Bardwick. 1998. John Wiley & Sons: New York, 047125407X.
- *Innovation: Breakthrough Thinking at 3M, DuPont, GE, Pfizer, and Rubbermaid*. Rosabeth Moss Kanter, Fred Wiersema, John J. Kao, & Tom Peters. 1997. HarperBusiness: New York, ISBN 088730771X.
- *Leading on the Creative Edge: Gaining Competitive Advantage Through the Power of Creative Problem Solving*. Roger Firestein. 1996. Pinon Press: Colorado Springs, ISBN #0891099751.
- *Make Success Measurable!: A Mindbook-Workbook for Setting Goals and Taking Action*. Douglas K. Smith. 1999. John Wiley & Sons: New York, ISBN 471295590.
- *Organizing Genius: The Secrets of Creative Collaboration*. Patricia Ward Biederman & Warren G. Bennis. 1998. Perseus: Reading, MA, ISBN 201339897.
- *The Creative Priority: Putting Innovation to Work in Your Business*. Jerry Hirshberg. 1999. HarperBusiness: New York, ISBN 0887309607.

ENDNOTES

1. Products and services, United States, 41.

2. Technology, Poland, 39.

3. Healthcare, United States, 33.

4. Products and services, Brazil/United States, 29.

5. Investments, United States, 27.

6. Warren Bennis. *On Becoming a Leader.* Perseus: New York. Copyright © 1989, 1994.

7. Government, Canada, 34.

8. Research and development, United States, 56.

9. Non-profit, United States, 24.

10. Products and services, United States, 32.

11. See "The Impact of Direct Report Feedback and Follow-up on Leadership Effectiveness," a study by A4SL, which involved more than 8,000 respondents.

12. Products and services, Brazil, 49.

13. R. T. Moran. "Handling Two Swords at the Same Time." *International Management.* July 1986.

14. R. Jenkins. *Churchill: A Biography.* Plume/Penguin Putnam Inc.: NY 2002.

15. Products and services, Switzerland, 45.

16. Telecommunications, United States, 34.

17. Technology, South Korea, 43.

18. Products and services, 45, Switzerland.

19. Pharmaceuticals, United States, 41.

20. Technology, United States, 34.

21. Pharmaceuticals, United Kingdom, 30.

22. Transportation, Canada, 47.

23. Information and quotes taken from interview with Eric Greenberg conducted by Cathy Greenberg. May 2002.

24. Interview with Eric Greenberg, chairman and founder of Scient, January 11, 2000. *http://leadership.wharton.upenn.edu/ecommerce/interviews/greenberg.shtml.* The Wharton School at the University of Pennsylvania.

14 ANTICIPATING OPPORTUNITIES

The global leader of the future will have the ability to create a clear and compelling vision for his or her organization and a great capacity for communicating the vision in such a way as to inspire and stretch people beyond expectations. First, though, in order to create this vision and to lead others to a destination, the leader must anticipate the opportunities (and also the roadblocks) ahead. The leader must know which direction and which opportunities will take the company where he or she wants it to go.

The critical difference between management and leadership is reflected in the root meanings of the two words—the difference between what it means to handle things and what it means to go places. The unique role of leaders is to take us to places we've never been before.[1]

In order to "take us places we've never been before," global leaders will spend a good deal of their time focusing on the following four aspects of leadership:

1. Investigating future trends,
2. Anticipating future opportunities,
3. Inspiring people to focus on future opportunities (not just present objectives), and
4. Developing ideas to meet the needs of the new environment.

The rest of this chapter focuses on these four areas.

INVESTIGATING FUTURE TRENDS

Global leaders must pursue information, research future trends, and educate themselves if they are to effectively anticipate opportunities. This relentless pursuit of knowledge gives the leader a particular advantage to perceive and determine the most likely future trends of the industries within which he or she is involved.

> Leaders need to be proactive in thinking about the future, and this imperative increases with one's hope and level of responsibility.[2]

Customers demand better value, better services, and better products; employees (especially knowledge workers) demand more responsibility, more freedom, and more flexibility. The effective leader of the future must research and project future trends in customer and client relations, products and services, and employee retention while balancing "speed to value" in order to stay competitive in the global marketplace. For instance, Sun Microsystems has been a consistent leader in anticipating future customer needs and developing products that meet these needs before the products were considered a requirement. With the next generations of processors expected to integrate several hundred million transistors, just simulating the operations of new designs requires trillions of calculations over a typical two- to five-year design project life cycle. Thus, to be successful, Sun must anticipate future customer needs years before the customer has even gotten used to the current product. It's this innovative anticipation that has helped make Sun a leader in its field.

Also, it is important for the global leader to encourage feedback, input, and communication from customers, clients, and workers, because it is within these arenas that the leader will find the vital sources of information upon which he or she will be able to project the future trends of the industry, the company, and the workplace. One innovative and successful executive consistently challenged her sales force to ask employees to "tell us what our customers are going to need in the future, not just what they need today." This forward thinking on the part of both the employees and the customers, as well as the executive, gave the company insight into what customers wanted from the company in the future.

> To be successful, a company must perceive the market's need and deliver it. Companies fail when they ignore the market and push their technology to the market without listening to what the customers are saying. Three key things create success:
>
> 1. Ability to listen,
> 2. Ability to deliver, and
> 3. Ability to prioritize.[3]

As Fred Harmon (respected author, Peter Drucker Foundation Thought Leader, and founder of Synthesis Consulting) notes, in determining future trends, leaders must focus on the big picture, especially the forces that are reshaping organizations: technology, freedom, education, demographics, and globalization.[4] By analyzing the impact of these five forces, the global leader will be far better equipped to anticipate changes and trends within the company and its industry. For instance, as technology rapidly links people and companies around the world, it allows for the crosspollination of ideas, which leads to growth, new products, and different ways of accomplishing goals. As closed societies open their doors and organizations network around the world, the freedom to choose between different products and services affects once-dominating providers. Skill sets and information spread rapidly with education. New generations of leaders, customers, and employees are changing marketing strategies, and with the advent of globalization, new markets, previously closed or unreachable, are opening.

Rather than focusing on a short-term perspective, the global leader must look at the impact of the five forces discussed by Harmon and project trends for the long term. However, it is important to note that in many industries, *leaders will need to get used to thinking that long term is only a few years and that change is very rapid. The concept of long-term shareholder value is going to undergo a radical change. The concept of building things 10 to 20 years ahead is going to diminish because of the repetitive changes. It will be increasingly difficult to predict the changes.*[5]

ANTICIPATING FUTURE OPPORTUNITIES

A global leader's capacity to lead a company toward success and longevity is in large part dependent on his or her recognition of future opportunities. In order to anticipate these opportunities, the global leader must be a strategic thinker capable of visualizing, identifying, and following through.

This planning will include the systematic collection and analysis of information, issues, and factors that relate to the organization, its industry, and the global marketplace, and will make the leader far more capable of effectively anticipating future opportunities. *In order to prepare for global leadership, the leader will have to learn from experience, plan and position the company, and take advantage of opportunities.*[6] 3M, a $16 billion diversified technology company with leading positions in healthcare, safety, electronics, telecommunications, industrial, consumer and office, and other markets, has historically been an excellent example of a company that has matched new product innovation with anticipated customer needs. In 2002, in the electronics manufacturing field alone, 3M designed and released new products, such as protective shipping products and a new high-performance touch computer, every month.

In order to identify key strategic opportunities, *the global leader of the future must have the ability for visioning—be able to anticipate new strategies and possibilities long- and short-term.*[7] The effective leader will participate in a regular examination of organizational strengths and weaknesses and possible opportunities and roadblocks that might affect the company's goals, strategies, or position in the global marketplace. In one case, an executive at a large technology firm encouraged employees at every level to analyze how the existing strengths of the corporation matched the anticipated needs of its customers. This led to an ongoing flow of new ideas and served as excellent "preventative medicine" to help stop future problems.

A global leader's capacity to effectively anticipate future opportunities is in part dependent upon being aware of industry trends and developments as well as customer needs and wants, and *they must be able to consider alternatives*.[8]

This ability to see opportunities is also very much reliant upon how clearly the global leader understands the vision and pursues the goals of the company. *These leaders must have a long-term perspective and approach and not just work to satisfy Wall Street*.[9] Unfortunate examples, including Qwest and WorldCom, illustrate how the short-term desire to satisfy Wall Street can lead to long-term disaster.

LOOKING TO THE FUTURE

Successful leaders must inspire people to focus on these future opportunities and not just on present objectives. They must be able to direct energy and mobilize resources toward initiatives that will pay off in the future.

For example, Jack Welch, the almost legendary ex-head of GE, saw the company's income double and its stock price triple in the 1990s. The transformation process was not painless—it involved cutting more than 100,000 jobs and much unnecessary work from the group's varied operations, from capital services to light bulbs. But one of the arts of good leaders is the ability to convince staff that their vision is sufficiently attractive to justify the sacrifice and to give them the confidence that their extra efforts will turn it into a reality. In that, GE succeeded triumphantly. One thing that GE did consistently well was transfer people, knowledge, and capital efficiently across organizational boundaries. Employees were able to participate in a process of letting the organization know where they had expertise and where they needed help. A simple system of "teachers" and "learners" evolved so that future opportunities were understood and acted upon quickly across the organization.

It is up to the global leader to ensure that each individual in the company understands how his or her daily activities, priorities, and decisions help move the company towards its strategic goals. Leaders must hire entrepreneurial people and empower them to focus on those priorities that will impact the future success of the organization, and they must help their teams anticipate future opportunities and challenges.

DEVELOPS IDEAS TO MEET THE NEEDS OF THE NEW ENVIRONMENT

In order to make quality decisions and to guide the company into future success, the leader must be capable of developing ideas that will meet the needs of the customers, employees, and the company in the future. For example, several companies have effectively implemented a "balanced scorecard" approach that evaluates leaders on their ability to meet the needs of multiple stakeholders.

A measurement of the successful global leader is, [Does he or she] build and maintain business opportunities?[10]

In the face of an uncertain future, we depend more than ever on our global leaders to guide and direct us. We put faith in our leaders that they will help us find opportunities, generate new ideas, modify obsolete approaches, and bring diverse viewpoints and perspectives together during difficult times.

The world is constantly changing. At the time that this book was being written, the world had just seen the devastation of the World Trade Centers in New York City. In that instant, on September 11, 2001, the world changed. Much of the world became involved to some extent in something new: the war on terrorism. Due to these events, the global leader has had to switch gears and do so in a manner that supports and maintains trust and calm. The way we gauge leaders' success has changed. During the aftermath of the attacks, the measure the public has used to evaluate leaders is authentic leadership. President George W. Bush; former Mayor of New York Rudolph Guiliani; the New York Police Department; and the New York Fire Department gained recognition and some measure of new respect as a result of their style of authentic empathy and passion for new forms of antiterrorist actions in the wake of their compassion for others' losses.

CONCLUSION

Leaders are initiators. Leaders bring people together and guide them in a common direction. First, though, leaders must know in which direction they will head. Microsoft is an example of a corporation whose leaders saw the changing direction of the new world and not only anticipated the change, but also developed products and services designed to fulfill future customer needs.

In today's radically changed world, this may perhaps be the most important chapter for the global leader of the future to read. This chapter has focused on research, anticipation, and development of future trends and opportunities—all of which are absolutely imperative if a leader is to develop new ideas to successfully meet the needs of the changing global environment.

MOTHERS WORK: OPPORTUNITY IN NECESSITY

Twenty years ago, Rebecca Matthias started a business from her home. Today, her company, Mothers Work, Inc., consists of Mimi Maternity, Motherhood, iMaternity, and A Pea in the Pod. It is a multimillion-dollar maternity clothing empire.[11]

Anticipating the Opportunity

Near the time of her first pregnancy, Rebecca, a mother of three, found it difficult to find suitable maternity clothes for the office. She wasn't alone. Rebecca saw this shift towards more and more women staying in the workforce throughout their pregnancies as an opportunity, a new market. With a small budget of $10,000, she launched a mail-order business selling maternity clothes, and after a great initial response, Rebecca was on her way.

One of Rebecca's rules to succeeding in business is to "think big." She says, "If you see the future, you'll know where you're going. Then it's just a matter of finding your way." Rebecca turned to her own life, her own biggest problem, and solved her dilemma by starting a business to suit her needs. Her biggest problem? As a pregnant vice president of administration, her biggest challenge was "getting dressed in the morning once my zipper wouldn't go up anymore" and "finding the time to shop." After spending an afternoon scouring the maternity stores for a suit that she could wear to work, and finding nothing that would do, Rebecca had an idea for a business: maternity clothes for professional women. She would start selling the clothes through a mail-order catalog as soon as her first baby was born.

Leading the Change

Although the catalogue start-up failed, Rebecca wasn't finished. She took in venture capital to make the investments she needed, and by franchising her stores across the country, her hopes and vision took flight. Over the years, Rebecca has bought back all the franchises and now owns them. Her organization has 5,000 employees and today, 20 years later, it is the largest maternity clothing company in the country.

ANTICIPATING OPPORTUNITIES

ITEM 59: Invests in Learning About Future Trends

WHAT TO DO

- Develop a thorough understanding of the market forces and trends that impact your organization and your competitors, and regularly communicate this information to your employees.
- Constantly research and obtain knowledge of the competition's products, costs, strategies, and philosophies.
- Frequently discuss and share information about new products, strategies, and philosophies that are being developed and implemented within your industry.
- Establish an objective, effective way of learning about your competitors and critical market forces.
- Establish a strategic planning taskforce and change the players every 9 to 12 months.
- Encourage people to raise questions and concerns about the ongoing trends in the industry.
- Recognize and reward people for learning and sharing information about future trends and competitors.

HOW TO DO IT

- Ask your customers for their evaluation of how your company measures up to the competition. Share their input with your work group.
- Ask your company for its evaluation of how it measures up to the competition using both blind studies and focus groups.
- Study competitors' marketing and promotional materials to learn more about their products or services.
- Communicate the latest development about market forces and competitors' business and product at staff meetings.
- Schedule time in staff meetings for sharing market research information.

- Ask employees to consider the changing competitive realities and think strategically.
- Volunteer to serve on a strategic planning committee or task force.
- Get associates together for market trend analysis and discussion.
- Invite people from the sales department to share information about the competitors' products, costs, and strategies.
- Encourage employees to join professional associations or attend conferences so that they can network with people in the industry and acquire up-to-date information about the market trends.
- Network with people from other geographical areas. They may be more willing to share information if they don't see you as a direct competitor.
- Discuss techniques with managers who excel in this area.

HOW TO USE THIS SKILL FURTHER

- Learn from managers and peers who are knowledgeable about the industry, environment, and competition.
- Read publications such as *Business Week, Fortune,* and *The Wall Street Journal,* and identify business trends and development; assess their implications for your company.
- Create a file of newspaper clippings, trade and business journals, annual reports, and marketing research on your customers and competitors to stay in touch with the external business world.

RESULTS YOU CAN EXPECT

- Your employees may be more motivated to improve products and services.
- The department, division, and company may obtain bigger market share, become financially stronger, and revenues may increase.

READINGS

- *10 Lessons From the Future: A Personal Seminar on Tomorrow.* Wolfgang Grulke. 2000. Financial Times–Prentice Hall: Upper Saddle River, NJ, ISBN 273653296.
- *Beyond Certainty: The Changing Worlds of Organizations.* Charles Handy. 1998. Harvard Business School Press: Boston, ISBN 875847633.
- *Building Leaders: How Successful Companies Develop the Next Generation.* Jay Alden Conger& Beth Benjamin. 1999. Jossey-Bass: San Francisco, ISBN 787944696.
- *Evolve!: Succeeding in the Digital Culture of Tomorrow.* Rosabeth Moss Kanter. 2001. Harvard Business School Press: Boston, ISBN 1578514398.
- *Fumbling the Future: How Xerox Invented, Then Ignored, the First Personal Computer.* Douglas K. Smith & Robert C. Alexander. 1999. iUniverse.com: Silicon Valley, CA, ISBN 1583482660.

- *Strategy and Leadership*. MCB University Press: West Yorkshire England, New York.
- *The Agenda: What Every Business Must Do to Dominate the Decade*. Michael Hammer. 2001. Crown: Victoria, BC, ISBN 609609661.
- "The Financial Review: The Boss." *AFR Magazine*. Sydney, Australia. boss@mail.fair-fax.com.au.
- *The Future of Capitalism: How Today's Economic Forces Shape Tomorrow's World*. Lester C. Thurow. 1997. Penguin USA: New York, ISBN 140263284.
- *The Future of Leadership: Today's Top Leadership Thinkers Speak to Tomorrow's Leaders*. Warren G. Bennis, Gretchen M. Spreitzer, & Thomas B. F. Cummins (Eds.). 2001. John Wiley & Sons: New York, ISBN 787955671.

ITEM 60: Effectively Anticipates Future Opportunities

WHAT TO DO

- Stay abreast of market trends and movements.
- Study professional journals regularly to learn the industry trends and anticipated future development.
- Analyze the market forces that affect your organization. This will help you anticipate any barriers to success.
- Learn from individuals who think strategically and are knowledgeable about the market movement.
- Send liaisons to conferences and compare notes and lessons taught to a larger audience.
- Listen to feedback and input from team members and customers to help you foresee opportunities.
- Develop strong analytical skills.
- Identify "critical success factors" for your organization.
- Communicate these areas of focus to employees.
- Make these critical success factors well known to employees through staff meetings, newsletters, bulletin boards, and so on.

HOW TO DO IT

- Make a list of strategic factors in order of degree of criticality to financial or nonfinancial return.
- Get employees to think strategically when developing business plans; interrelate the effects of new plans and ideas on those core success factors.
- Involve your employees in identifying the strategic factors for your organization.

- Work with your employees to create an action plan based on these factors to bring them to life.
- Hold meetings that explain and focus solely on these particular strategic factors for future success.
- Create a business plan that concentrates on promoting these areas further.
- Attend meetings in which the company's past performance and future goals and action strategies are presented and discussed.
- Read publications such as *Business Week, Fortune,* and *The Wall Street Journal,* and identify business trends and developments; assess their implications for your company.
- Create a file of newspaper clippings, trade and business journals, annual reports, and marketing research on your customers and competitors to stay in touch with the external business world.

RESULTS YOU CAN EXPECT

- The department, division, and company may become financially stronger, and revenues may increase.
- People may seek your input and opinions about the future direction of the company.

READINGS

- *10 Lessons From the Future: A Personal Seminar on Tomorrow.* Wolfgang Grulke. 2000. Financial Times–Prentice Hall: Upper Saddle River, NJ, ISBN 273653296.
- *Built to Last.* James C. Collins & Jerry I. Porras. 1997. HarperBusiness: New York, ISBN 887307396.
- *Business 2010: Positioning Your Company and Yourself in a Rapidly Changing World.* Frederick G. Harmon. 2001. Kiplinger Books: Washington, DC, ISBN 938721844.
- *Business Climate Shifts: Profiles of Change Makers.* W. Warner Burke, Richard Koonce, & William Trahant. 1999. Butterworth-Heinemann: Woburn, MA, ISBN 750671866.
- *Competing for the Future.* Gary Hamel & C. K. Prahalad. 1996. Harvard Business School Press: Boston, ISBN 875847161.
- *Focus: The Future of Your Company Depends on It.* Al Ries. 1997. HarperBusiness. New York, ISBN 887308635.
- *Free Market Fusion.* Glenn R. Jones. 1999. Cyber Publishing Group: Englewood, NJ, ISBN 1885400683.
- *The Attention Economy: Understanding the New Currency of Business.* Thomas H. Davenport & John C. Beck. 2001. Harvard Business School Press: Boston, ISBN 157851441X.

ITEM 61: Inspires People to Focus on Future Opportunities (Not Just Present Objectives)

WHAT TO DO

- Recognize that innovation and change are vital to the success of your business.
- See change as an opportunity, not a problem.
- Stay abreast of market trends and movements.
- Encourage and support others to seek new opportunities to benefit the organization.
- Frequently communicate with your team to update them on new developments on strategies and directions.
- Make sure that team members have a clear understanding of the big picture.
- Review and discuss all risks (the probability of failure and the consequences of failure) before agreeing on a decision or acting on a new idea.
- Work with employees to develop action plans and set deadlines to capture future business opportunities.
- Value those who can think outside the box. Maintain an atmosphere in which these people feel safe to innovate, and provide all the support they need.

HOW TO DO IT

- Use benchmark data from associations in which you have access to it.
- Hold regular meetings with your managers, peers, and employees to share information and data, and identify potential business opportunities.
- Work with your employees to evaluate the business opportunity, analyze pros and cons, and get input from others who have expertise in that area.
- Follow up regularly to ensure the opportunities are being worked on as planned.
- Make sure that you and your employees have a clear understanding of your customers' needs and requirements. Provide a communication link between them.
- Maintain objectivity when reviewing new ideas and business situations.
- Supply the resources and information others need to focus on future opportunities.
- Determine the "area of freedom" for new ideas, where ideas can be tried out without violating any contractual, safety, or other nonnegotiable requirement.
- Identify a successful company in your industry and think about how it stays ahead of the game. Work with others to identify the success factors of such organizations, and make appropriate changes in your own organization.
- Model the behavior of making sound decisions, taking appropriate risks, and acting on ideas without delay.

- Keep a file entitled "New Ideas." Each time you hear or see something related to your job, write it down and file it. Periodically review the file.
- Keep some of your budget available for the implementation of new ideas or innovations.
- Keep your employees sharp by having them attend workshops, seminars, and other gatherings to network and exchange ideas. Encourage their involvement with customers, various committees, and brainstorming sessions.

HOW TO USE THIS SKILL FURTHER

- Get employees to think strategically when discussing business plans; interrelate the effects of new plans and ideas on those core success factors.
- Discuss techniques with managers who excel at helping employees see future opportunities.

RESULTS YOU CAN EXPECT

- The department, division, and company may become financially stronger, and revenues will increase.
- Your employees may be more motivated to improve products and services.
- Your team may become a role model for the company.

READINGS

- *Coaching for Action: A Report on Long-Term Advising in a Program Context*. Victoria A. Guthrie. 1999. Center for Creative Leadership: Greensboro, NC, ISBN 188219750X.
- *Coaching for Leadership: How the World's Greatest Coaches Help Leaders Learn*. Marshall Goldsmith, Laurence Lyons, & Alyssa Freas. 2000. Jossey-Bass: New York, ISBN 787955175.
- *Innovation: Breakthrough Thinking at 3M, DuPont, GE, Pfizer, and Rubbermaid*. Rosabeth Moss Kanter, Fred Wiersema, John J. Kao, & Tom Peters. 1997. HarperBusiness: New York, ISBN 088730771X.
- *Personal Coaching for Results: How to Mentor and Inspire Others to Amazing Growth*. Louis E. Tice & Joyce Quick. 1997. Thomas Nelson: New York, ISBN 785273557.
- *Pioneering Organizations: The Convergence of Individualism, Teamwork, and Leadership*. Larry N. Davis & Chip R. Bell. 2000. Executive Excellence: Provo, UT, ISBN 1890009849.

ITEM 62: Develops Ideas to Meet the Needs of the New Environment

WHAT TO DO

- Recognize that innovation and change are vital to the success of your organization.
- Stay abreast of market trends and movements.
- Prepare detailed plans with resources required for change.
- Recognize that innovation and change are vital to continuous improvement efforts.
- Provide others with sufficient information to permit them to develop creative yet workable ideas.
- View past practices as a place to start rather than as the "way we always do it."
- Encourage and support others to seek new opportunities to benefit the organization.
- Review and discuss all risks (the probability of failure and the consequences of failure) before agreeing on a decision or acting on a new idea.
- Make sure the impact of new approaches on other operations and other work units is fully explored and resolved before a new idea is implemented.
- Develop action plans and set deadlines to implement new ideas.
- Value those who can think outside the box. Maintain an atmosphere where these people feel safe to innovate, and provide all the support they need.

HOW TO DO IT

- Use benchmark data from associations in which you have access to it.
- Hold regular meetings with others (managers, peers, workers) to share information and data, and identify possible areas for improvement.
- Make sure that others have a clear understanding of their customers' needs and requirements. Provide a communication link between them.
- Maintain objectivity when reviewing new ideas and decisions.
- Supply the resources and information others need to develop ideas.
- Determine the "area of freedom" for new ideas, where ideas can be tried out without violating any contractual, safety, or other nonnegotiable requirement.
- Work with your group to develop specific action plans, assign responsibilities within the team, and set a realistic timeline to complete the task.
- Follow up regularly to ensure the ideas are implemented as planned.
- Identify an innovative company and think about the differences between its management's involvement and yours. Talk to managers and employees to identify all the differences you can. Work with others to identify and make appropriate changes in your own organization.

- Model the behavior of making sound decisions, taking appropriate risks, and act on ideas without delay.
- Keep a file entitled "New Ideas." Each time you hear or see something related to your job, write it down and file it. Periodically review the file.
- Keep some part of your budget available for new ideas or innovations.
- Keep your innovators sharp by having them attend workshops, seminars, and other gatherings to network and exchange ideas. Encourage their involvement with customers, various committees, and brainstorming sessions.

HOW TO USE THIS SKILL FURTHER

- Try out some of your own creative ideas on problems you have been trying to solve.
- Help someone else act on a new opportunity or approach they want to try out.

RESULTS YOU CAN EXPECT

- You may gain a reputation for being a "change agent."
- Your group may make more mistakes than before, but may experience more successes.
- Customer expectations will continue to be met using new and better ways of working.

READINGS

- *Competing for the Future*. Gary Hamel & C. K. Prahalad. 1996. Harvard Business School Press: Boston, ISBN 875847161.
- *Corning and the Craft of Innovation*. Margaret B. W. Graham & Alec T. Shuldiner. 2001. Oxford University Press: Oxford, England, ISBN 195140974.
- *Innovation: Breakthrough Thinking at 3M, DuPont, GE, Pfizer, and Rubbermaid*. Rosabeth Moss Kanter, Fred Wiersema, John J. Kao, & Tom Peters. 1997. HarperBusiness: New York, ISBN 088730771X.
- *Intrapreneuring in Action: A Handbook for Business Innovation*. Gifford Pinchot & Ron Pellman. 1999. Berrett-Koehler: San Francisco, ISBN 1576750612.
- *Jumping the Curve: Innovation and Strategic Choice in an Age of Transition*. Nicholas Imparato & Oren Harari. 1996. Jossey-Bass: San Francisco, ISBN 787901830.
- *The Intelligent Organization: Engaging the Talent & Initiative of Everyone in the Workplace*. Gifford Pinchot & Elizabeth Pinchot. 1996. Berrett-Koehler: San Francisco, ISBN 1881052982.

ENDNOTES

1. James M. Kouzes & Barry Posner. *The Leadership Challenge,* p. 36.

2. James M. Kouzes & Barry Posner. *The Leadership Challenge,* p. 100.

3. Technology, Poland, 39.

4. Fred Harmon. *Business 2010.* The Kiplinger Washington Editors: Washington, DC. 2001. p. 5–7.

5. Healthcare, France, 44.

6. Research and development, United States, 46.

7. Technology, Spain, 39.

8. Financial Services, Germany, 42.

9. Products and services, United States, 27.

10. Products and services, United States, 44.

11. Information and quotes from interview with Rebecca Matthias conducted by Cathy Greenberg, November 2001. Also, see *Mothers Work: How a Young Mother Started a Business on a Shoestring and Built It Into a Million-dollar Company.* Rebecca Matthias. Doubleday: New York, 1999.

15 ENSURING CUSTOMER SATISFACTION

Customer satisfaction is undoubtedly one of the top strategic issues for every company. A major topic of discussion in boardrooms, chat rooms, and lunchrooms, the exact formula for ensuring customer satisfaction is still unknown. One thing is clear: *The customer function is the "fluid" throughout the whole organization. All departments must work collaboratively with each other as a team in order to serve the customer and fulfill the customer's requirements.*[1]

Given that customer satisfaction is positively related to loyalty, which in turn leads to increased profitability, market share, and growth, the importance of understanding how to achieve and ensure customer satisfaction is critical to the success of any leader.

The following sections discuss the skills, traits, and concentration that those surveyed in our research thought to be most valuable in ensuring customer satisfaction. These include inspiring people to achieve high levels of customer satisfaction, viewing business processes from the ultimate customer perspective, regularly soliciting input from customers, consistently delivering on commitments to customers, and understanding the competitive options available to customers.

RAISING THE BAR

Successful global leaders are unwilling to settle for mediocrity. As exhibited throughout this book, they inspire people by, among other things, genuinely listening to others, creating a shared vision, providing effective recognition, empowering others, and appreciating diversity. These leaders cultivate a desire to get ahead. By setting bold, challenging, yet attainable, goals they bring the best out in their people and create an environment in which high levels of customer satisfaction are achieved. 3M Worldwide, a $16 billion diversified technology company with leading positions in healthcare, safety, electronics, telecommunications, industrial, consumer and office, and other markets, is an example of a rapidly changing organization. Its success is in large part due to the fact that its leaders know that yesterday's success is only a floor for the greater achievement that will be expected tomorrow. 3M's CEO since January 2002, James McNerney, Jr., is "leading by example" and teaching employees how they can create an environment to ensure ongoing increases in performance.

The bottom line is that the global leader will do what it takes to help employees *improve service to the customers,* [2] because if employees are happy, customer service will improve, which will make customers happy. If customers are happy, the organization as a whole will benefit, thus completing the cycle of success from leader to employee to customer to the organization and back again.[3] Many leaders understand this formula for success. As a result, there are numerous methods for ensuring customer satisfaction, such as asking for customer feedback regarding products and services, gathering employee input on service, products, leadership, and equipment, and so on.

We are now running the business on a profit/loss basis. We are being held more accountable for financial results at a smaller level. Now that we are competing for customers, we must keep the employees, shareholders, *and* customers happy.[4]

With fewer layers of middle management and a shorter distance between the CEO and the customer, companies are delegating more responsibility and autonomy to frontline workers, who are often the interface with the customer. For example, as part of its marketing campaign, a large hotel franchise has put into action a strategy in which any employee can compensate dissatisfied customers with a complimentary service, bonus travel points, a free meal, or even a free night at the hotel. This does two things: It relieves the customer of the inconvenience of complaining to more than one party (first the employee and then the manager); it delegates responsibility of the customer and his or her satisfaction and compensation to the frontline employee.

The organization will be less formal, highly networked, customer-driven, and flatter.[5]

These workers are expected to make decisions and to contribute ideas to the company based on their understanding of customer needs, thereby improving customer service and increasing company profits. In many companies, individuals are encouraged to submit their ideas. For instance, at a large governmental agency, managers gathered employees' input each month. At the end-of-the month meeting, those employees whose ideas had been implemented and had benefited the company, either in cost-saving measures or employee satisfaction strategies, were rewarded with prizes.

CHANGING WITH THE CUSTOMER[6]

Over the past decade, a major shift in customer behavior has reshaped the nature of many markets, which has led to profound changes in how companies attempt to serve those markets. For example, more and more business customers have stopped buying standalone products and have started buying integrated solutions. This trend means that leaders of successful organizations need to develop different organizational structures, systems, and skills. Many companies are merging and forming alliances and partnerships with organizations that offer complementary products and services, such as Hewlett-Packard's purchase of Compaq. The nature of Compaq was to provide customers with services related to computers. HP, which was more a products than a services company, bought Compaq so as to be able offer its customers more of an integrated computer products and services solution, and thus be more competitive in the industry. EDS is another example of an organization that provides integrated solutions. An organization can hire EDS to manage its entire computer network, from equipment to IT support. This relieves the EDS customer of the IT burden so that the customer can focus on other areas.

Several factors have helped accelerate the move to integrated solutions. Many technologies—computers, copiers, fax machines, and other office equipment—are converging. The Handspring Treo is just one such example: This relatively new gadget combines phone, organizer, email, and Web into one small electronic device. Sprint PCS Vision combines digital camera, instant messaging center, and Web capabilities into a cell phone.

Companies in these industries are responding in surprising ways. A large percentage of IBM's business, for example, now involves customized solutions incorporating non-IBM products and services. For instance, in an attempt to enhance and expand its consulting services, IBM acquired PriceWaterhouse Coopers.

While the idea of IBM selling non-IBM products was almost unheard of in the past, it is now commonplace—to the benefit of customers and, in the long run, IBM itself. Likewise, leading telecommunications and other equipment providers are competing effectively by offering "network solutions" involving many products formerly sold separately.

As the world becomes more complex, customers' need to "keep it simple" increases. Many customers would rather go to a large, one-stop retail store, such as Wal-Mart or Target, that sells a wide range of products and services, from electronic products to gift wrap to home improvement supplies, rather than go to several specialty shops. However, making things simple for customers may not be simple for providers. Integrating processes from autonomous units (or even separate companies) poses political and organizational challenges often greater than the technical challenges. The global leader will need to not only *seek out consumer preferences in different cultures and people,*[7] but he or she *will also have a global awareness of business practices and customer requirements.*[8] Marriott International has been quite successful in integrating its services with those of other products and service providers frequented by its customers. The organization has ceased to be a call center for receiving hotel reservations. Customers are offered assistance in booking rentals cars, entertainment, and meals. This helps keep travel simple for the customer but makes customer service complicated for representatives of the hotel, who must be far more aware of customer needs and requirements than in the past.

Tough competition for customers is requiring firms to innovate more and more to differentiate from one another. With access to the Internet and technology so readily available, today's consumers can learn more about a company's products and services than ever. MySimon.com, a comparison shopping Web site, helps people make more informed decisions by providing them with product and pricing information across the Web. Travelers can quickly compare airline fares between various destinations by going to travel sites such as Orbitz.com or Travelocity.com. Empowered consumers are using such Web sites to compare companies, prices, and product information and to make informed decisions about their purchases. *Consumers will be more demanding and request more information and more involvement.*[9] Quality—of both products and services—provides the company with a huge opportunity to distinguish itself from the competition. As consumers become smarter and more informed, they demand more value for their money, and they expect the companies from which they make their purchases to be responsible and accountable to them—or they will most likely find another place to shop.

CUSTOMER INPUT

An organization's survival depends upon the customers whom it serves. If customers buy the organization's product or service, the company is successful. In order to ensure customer satisfaction, companies must solicit input from their customers to determine whether or not they are satisfied and what it will take to make or keep them satisfied. Statistics show that only a small percentage of dissatisfied customers (1 out of 26) complain of their own accord; therefore, companies need to make it extremely easy for customers to give feedback.[10]

The effective global leader understands that it is more costly to gain new customers than it is to retain existing customers, and statistics show that the longer a company keeps a customer, the more money it will make. In fact, it can cost five times more to buy new customers than to retain existing ones, and reducing customer defections can boost profits by 25 percent to 85 percent.[11]

Good service and quality products are the foundation upon which successful companies build a satisfied and loyal customer base. For this reason, many companies have set up toll-free customer service numbers that customers can call if they have a complaint about products or services. Companies that offer online services often follow up with an email to the customer that asks for feedback. Many restaurants, motels, and hotels have feedback forms at the dining tables or in the guest rooms. These are all methods by which companies build a strong customer base of loyal and satisfied customers.

Although first-time consumers may spend slowly, repeated good experiences with the company, its people, and its services or products lead to increased spending and more prompt bill paying—and thus more profits for the company. A 1 percent cut in customer service problems could generate an extra £16 million or $25 million in profits for a medium-sized company over five years.[12] A survey of 3,000 businessmen by PriceWaterhouse Coopers and the University of Bradford showed the benefits of customer service. The study revealed that where there was high customer satisfaction, bills were paid on average at least 14 days earlier than where there was poor customer satisfaction.[13]

Firms perceived as having better customer service can charge more for their products and services, and still have higher market shares and returns on sales than their competitors.[14] An example is the success of the major car rental agency, Hertz. Although Hertz tends to be more expensive, its superior customer service has helped it to expand across the world and make it the world's leading vehicle renting organization.

More and more, cost becomes an issue. So, we have to have an interdependent partnership within the organization as well as an external partnership with customers. One of the success factors has been our ability to work with customers to develop mutual objectives that will support the organization.[15]

The best way to determine customer satisfaction is to ask the customer. Whether the goal is to launch a new product or to improve an existing service, customer feedback is the best source of information. Author of *Moments of Truth* and former chairman of Scandinavian Airlines Systems (SAS) Jan Carlson improved SAS with the philosophy that every customer contact, whether by phone, in person, or via email, is a "moment of truth." In the early 1980s, Jan drove the program of customer service at SAS with his notion that moments of truth drive customer retention and satisfaction, and thus lead to organizational success. The company, which was losing $20 million a year when Jan came on board, increased its earnings by $80 million in the first year alone by focusing on the customer. By opening the lines of communication with consumers, the global leader clears the path to launch products more quickly, make changes to existing products, and allocate resources appropriately.

Direct input from consumers can redirect focus to "what really matters" and safeguard against poor business decisions. In return, customers become more committed to the business, because they are satisfied. British Airways found that 69 percent of its unhappy customers do not report their dissatisfaction to anyone at the airline. They estimated that this cost them 423 million pounds of potential lost revenue.[16]

The global leader understands that follow-up to customer feedback is imperative. Therefore, the company should encourage customers' ongoing participation in feedback processes not only by showing appreciation, but even more importantly, by communicating to the customers what changes have taken place as a result of their input. For this reason, a customer service email to Amazon.com is automatically acknowledged and subsequently followed up by an email from a customer service representative, who responds to the particular issue in his or her own name.

KEEPING COMMITMENTS

Commitment is an industry buzzword meant to attract customers. Nearly every company in existence professes some type of commitment, whether it is to quality, excellence, customers, or all of the above. However, not every company follows through on its promises. A large international product company gave points to consumers each time they bought one of the company's products. After the consumers collected so many points, they sent them in to get a free prize. One particular prize was so popular that the company's supply ran out before it had filled all the orders. The company told customers that they were out of luck. Compare this response to that of another company in a similar situation. After it ran out of stock, the second company sent a check to its customers for what the prize would have cost at a retail store so that they could go and buy it. As the consumer becomes more and more educated about different companies, products, and services, *there will be a different expectation.*[17] The educated and informed consumer will quickly drop companies that do not follow through on their promises.

What is commitment? It is the single most important factor to success, and it begins with a sound set of beliefs and then faithful adherence to those beliefs with action. Many successful people, hailed as visionary leaders, are actually just individuals who follow through on a simple set of commitments. It is the strength of these commitments that leads to business success.

Customer feedback is one method for the global leader of the future to gain insight into how well the organization is keeping its products, services, customer service, and leadership commitments. Another method is to review returns and allowances. If either is high, then customers are sending a strong message of dissatisfaction with the company's products or services. A third indicator is internal reject or yield rates. If rejects are high or yields are low, it is almost certain that a bad product is getting out to the customer.

UNDERSTANDING THE COMPETITION

As part of their function in the organization, global leaders will have the responsibility to truly understand their competition. To appreciate the strengths and weaknesses of the competition's products and services, leaders will have to ensure that organizational members spend sufficient time on the continuous learning needed to keep up with rapidly changing customer environments, and rather than learn just the basic skills required to sell and support a product, employees will need to develop the ability to solve complex problems and maintain diverse relationships both domestically and globally.

In all interactions, the global leader keeps in mind that a competitor one day may be a customer the next. AT&T and BellSouth, Netscape and Oracle, Johnson & Johnson and Merck are all examples of companies that deal with one another at various times as customers, competitors, and partners. In a world where today's competitors become tomorrow's partners or customers, simply "beating the other guy" is not always the answer, as this may destroy any chance for a relationship that may be beneficial in the future. For this reason, global leaders will need to ensure that even competitors view the organization as tough but fair and as a good potential partner. Leaders must not underestimate the value of diplomacy, reputation, and goodwill in today's interconnected world.

CONCLUSION

Ensuring customer satisfaction means ensuring global business success, for without a customer, there can be no business. The global leader understands that this simple formula for success entails excellent customer service, inspired employees, quality products and services, customer feedback, commitment, and understanding the competition. Leaders who can master the skills called for in this new environment stand to reap tremendous advantages for their organizations; those who cling instead to what has worked in the past do so at their own peril.

HARRAH'S: SURVEY SAYS!

William Harrah arrived in Reno, Nevada, in May 1937. Just 26 years old at the time, he opened a bingo parlor in the gambling heart of the city.[18] By 1946, Harrah's, a glass-fronted, plushly carpeted casino, was in full swing, with black jack, roulette, and liquor. In 1959, Harrah relocated the casino to create the world's largest single structure devoted to gambling. The new casino had a 10-acre parking lot and an 850-seat theater-restaurant that drew star entertainers. By 1973, Harrah had constructed the highest building in Reno, a 24-story hotel, near his casino, as well as an 18-story hotel in Lake Tahoe. By 2000, Harrah's Entertainment was well known in the gaming industry and operated casinos in 17 different cities, including Las Vegas, Lake Tahoe, Laughlin, Reno, and Atlantic City.

The growth and success of Harrah's is attributed in large part to customer satisfaction and loyalty, which has always been a focus at Harrah's. However, prior to hiring Gary Loveman as chief operating officer in 1998, Harrah's method for acquiring guest opinions on service was limited to comment cards in the guest rooms.

One of Loveman's early goals was to introduce the idea throughout the organization that loyalty could drive profitability. He implemented a more comprehensive guest sampling procedure, where 800 surveys were mailed to Harrah's customers each month. Over the next three years, the survey effort became significantly more widespread and sophisticated.

By 2001, each casino mailed to recent customers enough surveys to receive back at least 2,400 responses per quarter. In addition to the actual questionnaire,

HARRAH'S: SURVEY SAYS! (CONT.)

survey recipients received a promotional offer that was tied to the timely completion of the survey. (Timely completion was critical so that Harrah's could quickly react to issues brought to light.)

John Bruns, corporate director of customer satisfaction assurance, and Gary Loveman felt strongly about the need to communicate information gathered from the extensive customer surveys to every level of the organization to both identify weaknesses in processes and improve customer service levels. Of equal concern was determining which aspects of the survey results to emphasize to employees. Subsequently, employee and manager attention was focused on two survey measurements within each customer service area: customer perception of employee friendliness and helpfulness, and customer perception of waiting time in lines.

Largely as a result of such intensive customer satisfaction survey methods and the attention given to following through on customer feedback, in 2002, Harrah's boasted a quantity and geographical diversity of properties unlike that of any of its competitors.

ENSURING CUSTOMER SATISFACTION

ITEM 63: Inspires People to Achieve High Levels of Customer Satisfaction

WHAT TO DO

- Constantly remind employees that high quality and good customer service result in business success.
- Involve employees in decisions that affect customer service.
- Identify your internal and external customers.
- Determine customer requirements.
- Work with your group to get their ideas about what customer satisfaction means.
- Find ways to measure customer satisfaction.
- Develop a clear vision and strategy tuned to customers' specific needs and business situations.
- Keep lines of communication open to your customers.
- Treat your customers as individuals, and let them know that you are open to their ideas and suggestions.
- Reinforce the value of customer satisfaction in your work group.
- Reward employees, coworkers, and colleagues who demonstrate commitment to meeting all client needs.

HOW TO DO IT

- Share your views with your group about customer satisfaction as a priority. Ask members for ideas about how to gather information on customers' current and future needs.
- Ask your customers what your group did that served them well and what areas need improvement.
- Avoid talk or behavior that devalues or deprioritizes customer's needs.
- Present customer responses to your work groups. Help members think about ways to deal with customer concerns; support changes that make use of their ideas.

- Provide training for all employees on client service. Explain how their work affects clients; share tips on how to handle difficult clients and how to implement service-related company policies and strategies.
- Meet with your customers on a regular basis. Make it clear that their phone calls are welcome and that you and your employees are prepared to *listen* and *respond* to their concerns.
- Examine everything you do, asking yourself, "Does this task contribute to meeting customer needs?"
- Get a better feel for the type of service your work unit provides. Attempt to look at your work unit from the customer's point of view. What is your first impression? How easy is it to get service? What is the tone or atmosphere? What interferes with good service? How good is your service follow-through? Make note of barriers and develop a plan for implementation.
- Work with your group to set up a tracking procedure to log customer concerns, follow-through actions taken, and response time.
- Look for improvements in response time and reliability (i.e., delivering what was promised dependably and accurately).
- Provide management-level information (e.g., customer survey results from corporate marketing) to your work group on a regular basis.
- Keep your work group advised about customer-related issues that are being worked on in your organization.
- Reward people for receiving positive customer feedback.

HOW TO USE THIS SKILL FURTHER

- Think about your own experience as a customer. What company comes to mind as "outstanding" in providing products or services that you have used? What makes the company so outstanding?
- Ask your employees the same two questions.
- Brainstorm with them about ways to use "benchmark companies" as examples to improve customer satisfaction in your work group.

RESULTS YOU CAN EXPECT

- You may receive positive feedback and fewer complaints from customers.
- As your employees gain skill in handling customer concerns more effectively, the number of complaints that you have to handle personally may decline.
- You may have more repeat customers.

READINGS

- *Customer Satisfaction Is Worthless, Customer Loyalty Is Priceless: How to Make Customers Love You, Keep Them Coming Back and Tell Everyone They Know.* Jeffrey Gitomer. 1998. Bard Press: Marietta, GA, ISBN 188516730X.

- *Customer Winback: How to Recapture Lost Customers—And Keep Them Loyal.* Jill Griffin, Michael W. Lowenstein, Don Peppers, & Martha Rogers. 2001. Jossey-Bass: San Francisco, ISBN 787946672.
- *E-Customer: Customers Just Got Faster and Smarter—Catch Up.* Max McKeown. 2000. Financial Times–Prentice Hall: Upper Saddle River, NJ, ISBN 273650203.
- *Free, Perfect, and Now: Connecting to the Three Insatiable Customer Demands: A CEO's True Story.* Curtis Hartman & Robert Rodin. 1999. Simon & Schuster: New York, ISBN 0684850222.
- *Leapfrogging the Competition: Five Giant Steps to Becoming a Market Leader.* Oren Harari. 1999. Prima Publishing: Roseville, CA, ISBN 761519734.
- *Nuts!: Southwest Airlines' Crazy Recipe for Business and Personal Success.* Kevin Freiberg, Jackie Freiberg, & Tom Peters. 1998. Bantam Doubleday Dell: New York, ISBN 767901843.
- *The 100 Absolutely Unbreakable Laws of Business Success.* Brian Tracy. 2000. Berrett-Koehler: San Francisco, ISBN 1576751074.
- *The Agenda: What Every Business Must Do to Dominate the Decade.* Michael Hammer. 2001. Crown: Victoria, BC, ISBN 609609661.
- *The Attention Economy: Understanding the New Currency of Business.* Thomas H. Davenport & John C. Beck. 2001. Harvard Business School Press: Boston, ISBN 157851441X.
- *The Customer Comes Second: Put Your People First and Watch 'Em Kick Butt.* Hal F. Rosenbluth & Diane McFerrin. 2002. HarperBusiness: New York, ISBN 0060526564.
- *The Ultimate CRM Handbook: Strategies and Concepts for Building Enduring Customer Loyalty and Profitability.* John G. Freeland (Ed.). 2002. McGraw-Hill: New York, ISBN 0071409351.

ITEM 64: Views Business Processes from the Ultimate Customer Perspective (Has an "End-to-End" Perspective)

WHAT TO DO

- Talk to your clients often. Ask them questions that ensure you obtain specific information about your ability to satisfy.
- Constantly remind employees that high quality and good customer service result in business success.
- Explain to employees the importance of balancing the needs of internal and external customers.
- Ask employees to put themselves in customers' shoes and strive to understand customers' perspectives.
- Continually monitor client satisfaction and look for ways to improve.

- Reward employees, coworkers, and colleagues who demonstrate commitment to meeting all client needs.
- Think of external and internal customers as part of your team.
- Involve employees in decisions that affect customer service.
- Learn to recognize which decisions about clients' needs can be made alone and which involve others.

HOW TO DO IT

- Develop and publicize a mission statement for your company that includes a commitment to building long-term relationships with customers..
- Meet and communicate with customers often.
- Let your customers know what actions you are taking as a result of their input.
- In meetings and conversation, use the term *client* or *customer* for any recipient of your services; frame questions, department objectives, and meeting agendas in terms of meeting customer needs and how to accomplish that.
- Cultivate knowledge about your clients; get to know "their language" and "their business."
- To develop a client orientation, define your success as "meeting customers' needs." Get into the habit of often asking your customers, "How else can I be of help?"
- As appropriate, express empathy for customer's input.
- Avoid talk or behavior that devalues or deprioritizes customer's needs.
- Meet with your employees to discuss how you can be more helpful and supportive of their efforts to satisfy clients.
- Recognize the importance of clients who rely on you for their success. Create a list of ideas that would improve the service that you provide to them, and encourage feedback from clients on your proposals.
- Provide training for all employees on client service. Explain how their work affects clients; share tips on how to handle difficult clients and how to implement service-related company policies and strategies.

HOW TO USE THIS SKILL FURTHER

- Remind yourself daily who your customers are, and check to see if your work group can do anything today to show your commitment to building effective relationships with customers.
- Discuss this topic with coworkers who demonstrate an end-to-end perspective, and ask for feedback.

RESULTS YOU CAN EXPECT

- People may comment on your demonstrated commitment to customer satisfaction.

- Employees may model your behavior, and you may notice its favorable impact on their work.
- Customers may notice your commitment and express appreciation.

READINGS

- *301 Great Customer Service Ideas: From America's Most Innovative Small Companies*. Nancy Artz & Harvey Mackay. 1998. Thomson Learning: Stamford, CT, ISBN 1880394332.
- *Achieving Customer Delight in Your Organization: Positioning Your Organization to Stand Out, Field Book*: John J. Paul & Sheryl T. Paul. 1999. Association Works: Dallas, TX, ISBN 1893827003.
- *Achieving Excellence Through Customer Service*. John Tschohl. 1996. Best Sellers: Bloomington, MN, ISBN 0963626841.
- *Best Practices in Customer Service*. Ron Zemke & John A. Woods. 1999. AMACOM: New York, ISBN 0814470289.
- *From the Ground Up: Six Principles for Building the New Logic Corporation*. Edward E. Lawler III. 1996. Jossey-Bass: San Francisco, ISBN 0787902411.
- *Supply Chain Management: Strategy, Planning and Operations*. Sunil Chopra & Peter Meindl. 2000. Prentice Hall: Upper Saddle River, NJ, ISBN 0130264652.
- *The Service Profit Chain: How Leading Companies Link Profit and Growth to Loyalty, Satisfaction, and Value*. James L. Heskett, W. Earl Sasser, Jr., Leonard A. Schlesinger. 1997. Free Press: London, ISBN 0684832569.
- *The Ultimate CRM Handbook: Strategies and Concepts for Building Enduring Customer Loyalty and Profitability*. John G. Freeland (Ed.). 2002. McGraw-Hill: ISBN 0071409351.

ITEM 65: Regularly Solicits Input from Customers

WHAT TO DO

- Recognize that the capacity to encourage and stay open to customer feedback is essential to excellent customer service.
- Recognize that the feedback and input you ask for is generally of a higher quality and easier to receive than if unsolicited—so ask your customers often!
- Recognize that when criticism is difficult to accept, there is probably some truth to it.
- Based on customer feedback, present specific and measurable goals and solutions to meet their needs.
- Don't shoot the messenger of bad news.
- Revise goals and approaches based on customer's input.

HOW TO DO IT

- Invite clients and customer service staff to important company meetings and activities. Ask them for input on specific topics to improve customer service.
- Identify which customers and employees you want to invite to important meetings, and send out invitations and reminders in advance.
- Summarize in writing what you think the customer's feedback is, and ask your customer to verify or correct what you have written.
- Schedule meetings with your manager and members of your work group frequently to share customer input.
- Ask for small amounts of feedback on a regular basis so that it doesn't pile up.
- Thank the customer who gave you input.
- Keep a record of the customer input you get, including frequency, nature, and your response.
- Let your customers know what actions you are taking as a result of their input.
- Obtain feedback from a variety of sources to get a more complete picture.
- Use open-ended questions that begin with "Explain…" "Describe…," and "Say more…" to encourage customers for more input.
- Take time to evaluate the input received. Determine whether more information is needed and what, if any, action should be taken.

HOW TO USE THIS SKILL FURTHER

- Practice by asking family and friends for input on various issues.
- Become a participant in team or group activities in which giving and receiving input is highly valued.
- Ask others for feedback on how well you accept constructive criticism and input.
- Look for positive feedback on the improvements you have made.

RESULTS YOU CAN EXPECT

- Customers may volunteer feedback more often.
- You may become known as a manager who knows how to effectively get input from clients.
- You may improve your skills effectively through continuous learning.

READINGS

- *Best Practices in Customer Service*. Ron Zemke & John A. Woods. 1999. AMACOM: New York, ISBN 0814470289.
- *Customer Satisfaction Is Worthless, Customer Loyalty Is Priceless: How to Make Customers Love You, Keep Them Coming Back and Tell Everyone They Know*. Jeffrey Gitomer. 1998. Bard Press: Marietta, GA, ISBN 188516730X.

- *Customer Winback: How to Recapture Lost Customers—And Keep Them Loyal.* Jill Griffin, Michael W. Lowenstein, Don Peppers, & Martha Rogers. 2001. Jossey-Bass: San Francisco, ISBN 787946672.
- *Fabled Service.* Betsy Sanders. 1995. Pfeiffer & Company: San Diego, CA, ISBN 0893842702.
- *High Performance Sales Organizations.* Kevin Corcoran, Laura Petersen, Daniel Baitch, & Mark F. Barrett. 1995. Irwin Professional Publishing: Burr Ridge, IL, ISBN 0786303522.
- *The Discipline of Market Leaders: Choose Your Customers, Narrow Your Focus, Dominate Your Market.* Michael Treacy & Fred Wiersema. 1997. Perseus: Reading, MA, ISBN 201407191.
- *The Ultimate CRM Handbook: Strategies and Concepts for Building Enduring Customer Loyalty and Profitability.* John G. Freeland (Ed.). 2002. McGraw-Hill: New York, ISBN 0071409351.

ITEM 66: Consistently Delivers on Commitments to Customers

WHAT TO DO

- Recognize that keeping commitments to customers is doable and desirable.
- Keep customer commitments in front of you daily.
- Create and use a tickler file to serve as a reminder.
- Return calls promptly or when you say you will.
- Be responsive to customers' requests.
- Seek to complete work on schedule. Do not sacrifice the long term by slipping short-term schedules.
- Put commitments to customers in writing.
- Ensure that others involved with meeting commitments understand and agree with those commitments.
- Build contingency plans into goals.
- Before and during projects, ask those with experience to point out potential problems.
- Ask the customer for feedback regularly; schedule periodic meetings.
- Communicate any meaningful changes to those working on meeting customer commitments.
- If deadlines slip, inform customers as soon as you know about it.
- Establish a tracking system to measure your performance in meeting customer commitments.
- Avoid overcommitment.
- Provide the necessary support and resources for customer service staff.

HOW TO DO IT

- Use open-ended questions with the customer to ensure that you and the customer understand the commitments made and to get clarification.
- Create a priority list that helps you track and accomplish customer commitments. Keep the list within sight on your desk
- Review your activities and progress against commitments to keep on track. Stop doing tasks that do not help meet customer requirements.
- Use an outline to capture commitments and to brief others involved with the task.
- Break commitments into small elements; start elements in phases; track progress at each phase; implement recovery plans at the earliest time problems are noticed.
- Use guidelines and progress milestones to help monitor progress and obtain feedback on work in progress.
- Always deliver by or before the agreed-upon date. Follow up if you are unable to make the deadline.
- Give your employees latitude and flexibility to meet each customer's needs in a timely manner.
- Keep a tracking system to determine turnaround time and to identify the obstacles that delay the process. Find effective ways to overcome the roadblocks.
- Ask your support staff to help you keep a tickler file.
- In discussion with the customer, repeat what you have heard to ensure that you are clear about what the commitment is with the customer.

HOW TO USE THIS SKILL FURTHER

- Keep your commitments with family and friends; be open to feedback.
- Keep a log of one week's worth of commitment-keeping activity; analyze the data and eliminate the most frequently occurring cause of broken commitments.

RESULTS YOU CAN EXPECT

- You and your department may gain a reputation for meeting commitments and being responsive to customers' needs.
- Customers may request that you handle their needs.
- Productivity may rise measurably.

READINGS

- *Achieving Customer Delight in Your Organization: Positioning Your Organization to Stand Out, Field Book*. John J. Paul & Sheryl T. Paul. 1999. Association Works: Dallas, TX, ISBN 1893827003.
- *Best Practices in Customer Service*. Ron Zemke & John A. Woods. 1999. AMACOM: New York, ISBN 0814470289.

- *Customer Equity: Building and Managing Relationships As Valuable Assets.* Robert C. Blattberg, Gary Getz, & Jacquelyn S. Thomas. 2001. Harvard Business School Press: Boston, ISBN 0875847641.

- *Customer Satisfaction Is Worthless, Customer Loyalty Is Priceless: How to Make Customers Love You, Keep Them Coming Back and Tell Everyone They Know.* Jeffrey Gitomer. 1998. Bard Press: Marietta, GA, ISBN 188516730X.

- *Customer Winback: How to Recapture Lost Customers—And Keep Them Loyal.* Jill Griffin, Michael W. Lowenstein, Don Peppers, & Martha Rogers. 2001. Jossey-Bass: San Francisco, ISBN 787946672.

- *Fabled Service.* Betsy Sanders. 1995. Pfeiffer & Company: San Diego, CA, ISBN 0893842702.

- *The Ultimate CRM Handbook: Strategies and Concepts for Building Enduring Customer Loyalty and Profitability.* John G. Freeland (Ed.). 2002. McGraw-Hill: New York, ISBN 0071409351.

ITEM 67: Understands the Competitive Options Available to Her or His Customers

WHAT TO DO

- Develop a thorough understanding of the strengths and weaknesses of other successful competitors in the market.
- Research and obtain comprehensive knowledge of your competitors' products, costs, strategies, and philosophies.
- Frequently discuss and share information about competitors' products, strategies, and philosophies with your work group.

HOW TO DO IT

- Ask your customers for their evaluation of how your company measures up to their expectations and the competition. Share their input with your work group.
- Study other leaders' leadership style, management philosophy, strengths, and weaknesses. Use that information to benchmark against your own style.
- Develop an action plan, including specific milestones, to improve your work group's performance.
- Share your action plan with your manager and coworkers, and ask for their feedback.
- Involve your manager and employees in understanding competitive realities and setting strategic goals for your organization.
- Review your competitors' marketing and promotional materials to learn more about their products or services.

- Communicate the latest development about competitors' business and product at staff meetings.
- Develop a detailed profile of each competitor; include the following factors: (1) quality and price of the products or services, (2) market share, (3) marketing strategies, (4) research and development, (5) recent business development, (6) top leaders and their philosophies, and (7) strengths and weaknesses.
- Request and study the analysts' reports on your competitors.
- Remind yourself to consider the changing competitive realities and think strategically when developing, implementing, and evaluating a business plan.

HOW TO USE THIS SKILL FURTHER

- Learn from managers who excel at this area.
- Volunteer to serve on a planning committee or task force that deals with problems relevant to your company's competitors.

RESULTS YOU CAN EXPECT

- Your department, division, and company may obtain a bigger market share, become financially stronger, and revenue may increase.
- People may want to discuss with you about competitors and ask you for advice.

READINGS

- *E-Customer: Customers Just Got Faster and Smarter—Catch Up*. Max McKeown. 2000. Financial Times–Prentice Hall: Upper Saddle River, NJ, ISBN 273650203.
- *Leapfrogging the Competition: Five Giant Steps to Becoming a Market Leader*. Oren Harari. 1999. Prima Publishing: Roseville, CA, ISBN 761519734.
- *Marketing Management and Strategy*. Peter Doyle. 1998. Prentice Hall: Upper Saddle River, NJ, ISBN 132622394.
- *Marketing Strategy: Planning and Implementation*. Orville C. Walker Jr., Harper W. Boyd Jr., & Jean-Claude Larreche. 1996. Richard D Irwin: Burr Ridge, IL, ISBN 256222460.
- *Marketing Warfare*. Al Ries & Jack Trout. 1997. McGraw-Hill: New York, ISBN 70527261.
- *Nuts!: Southwest Airlines' Crazy Recipe for Business and Personal Success*. Kevin Freiberg, Jackie Freiberg, & Tom Peters. 1998. Bantam Doubleday Dell: New York, ISBN 767901843.
- *The Agenda: What Every Business Must Do to Dominate the Decade*. Michael Hammer. 2001. Crown: Victoria, BC, ISBN 609609661.
- *The Attention Economy: Understanding the New Currency of Business*. Thomas H. Davenport & John C. Beck. 2001. Harvard Business School Press: Boston, ISBN 157851441X.

- *The Discipline of Market Leaders: Choose Your Customers, Narrow Your Focus, Dominate Your Market.* Michael Treacy & Fred Wiersema. 1997. Perseus: Reading, MA, ISBN 201407191.

- *The Ultimate CRM Handbook: Strategies and Concepts for Building Enduring Customer Loyalty and Profitability.* 2002. John G. Freeland (Ed.). McGraw-Hill: New York, ISBN 0071409351.

ENDNOTES

1. Products and Services, Brazil, 49.

2. Pharmaceutical, United Kingdom, 30.

3. H. F. Rosenbluth & D. McFerrin. HarperBusiness: August 2002.

4. Telecommunications, United States, 34.

5. Telecommunications United States, 36.

6. Much of this section is taken from "On a Consumer Watershed" by Marshall Goldsmith. Article published in *Leader to Leader*, No. 5, Summer 1997. Published by The Drucker Foundation and Jossey-Bass. This material is used by permission of John Wiley & Sons, Inc.

7. Products and services, United States, 36.

8. Technology, United States, 33.

9. Pharmaceuticals, United States, 31.

10. "Consumer Complaint Handling in America: An Update Study." The United States Office of Consumer Affairs. 1986.

11. "Fast Guide: The Business Case for Customer Excellence" Customer Service Network. *www.customernet.com.* 2002.

12. Ibid.

13. "Fast Guide: The Business Case for Customer Excellence" Customer Service Network. *www.customernet.com.* 2002.

14. The Profit Impact of Market Strategy (PIMS) database (see the Strategic Planning Institute).

15. Healthcare, Australia, 36.

16. W. Earl Sasser Jr., & Norman Klein. "British Airways: Using Information Systems to Better Serve the Customer." Harvard Business School Case Study. *Harvard Business Review.* October 21, 1994. Rev. November 28, 1994.

17. Healthcare, France, 52.

18. Information taken from Alastair Robertson's interview with Gary Loveman as well as the Harrah's Entertainment "Customer Service Satisfaction Assurance Program." © 2002. Harrah's.

16 MAINTAINING A COMPETITIVE ADVANTAGE

G ood leadership can have dramatic effects on corporate performance at all levels. Well-led teams produce significantly greater output than do poorly led teams, and they suffer fewer conflicts and less stress. Therefore, effective leadership is crucial to maintaining a competitive advantage in the global marketplace.

To maintain a competitive advantage, the global leader must guide the organization to produce better results faster; share knowledge; train and empower others to improve existing systems, products, and services; streamline the company; eliminate waste and unneeded cost; provide high-quality, unique products; and achieve results that will add long-term value to the shareholder.

PERFORMANCE: FASTER, BETTER

In the modern marketplace, global or local, no company can hope to achieve world-class performance in everything it does, yet, increasingly, that is what is needed to stay competitive against all kinds of rivals. For instance, a large healthcare organization has a formal program in place in which monthly customer satisfaction surveys are used to measure how effectively its strategies are being executed. Those hospitals that measure 85 percent satisfaction are considered four-star hospitals; those that rate 90 percent satisfaction are five-star hospitals. The organization's goal is to have every hospital in its system at 100 percent.

One thing driving the changes in my leadership role is the stress to constantly perform from quarter to quarter—faster and faster.[1]

For many companies, the solution is to decide on what its corporate core competencies are (or should be), and rely on partners for the rest

It is important to protect the values of the company, but at the same time, embrace the vision and move forward faster than any of the competitors. Constant awareness of the market changes and reacting quickly are important in order to move ahead.[2]

A new technology, a new territory, or a new channel of distribution may not be a realistic prospect except through an alliance; the superior performance required from data systems may be accessible only if they are outsourced to a specialist. A company might form an alliance to outsource the manufacturing of a component of a product to another organization. For example, Intel builds the processors used in many PCs. Companies might also outsource a transaction that is part of an entire process. *Business process outsourcing* (BPO) refers to the transaction component of the data that flows through the system. Because so many organizations are on overload and finding it impossible to do everything from sales to marketing, transaction processing to customer service, and human resources, companies that fill specific niche operations are forming. For instance, in the healthcare industry a larger organization might hire a niche company to handle its customer service, claims recovery, or billing. In this way, the company offloads those transactional processes to a specialist while retaining its core competency.

In such cases, leaders have to work with partners and inspire management teams over which they may have little or no direct control. For instance, Accenture temporarily outsourced one of its leaders to assist a large Australian financial services firm during a period of significant change. The leader was made resident at the firm and given the high-ranking title of CIO. The CIO was expected to run the firm's technology organization during the company's projected six-month to one-year transition from a privately held to a publicly held company; however, because of his inspiring leadership style and the value that he brought to the firm, he held this position for an unexpected four years.

Team leaders, conversely, need the skill to satisfy two or more masters whose underlying objectives and expectations may be at variance, while enthusing their own staff with a coherent and compelling vision. Recently, Accenture was asked by a large international insurance company to overlay its management style and culture on the company's leadership team. As a result, the client's peer review procedure was changed. Employees were reviewed not only by their department manager, but also by team leaders from Accenture. In this way, employees were reviewed on the basis of how they were using Accenture methodologies and project management skills, and also on the basis of how they were living the values of the client company. If this type of leadership is to work, both companies must openly collaborate, sharing information, methodologies, and performance management tools with each other.

INTELLECTUAL CAPITAL

Former leadership styles rested not just on personal dominance—they tacitly assumed that the leader, like the captain of a ship, had all the information at his or her command to enable him or her to plot the right course and make the right decisions. However, the concept of intellectual capital—ranging from the patents and technical know-how through corporate systems and databases to customer goodwill and individual skills and experience—implies that the assumption that the leader has all the answers at his or her fingertips is no longer valid (if it ever was). For example, in 1999 Hershey Foods Corporation launched an SAP AG system to automate shipments of candies in time for Halloween. When the supply chain component malfunctioned, Hershey didn't know which orders to fill or which orders had been filled, and they didn't have an inventory. The company ended up losing $150 million in candy sales. Rather than becoming adversarial, the management teams of SAP and Hershey worked together, using their experience, know-how, and intellectual capital to correct the problem.[3]

Intellectual capital is distributed throughout the organization through human and computer networks, and success depends on the speed and effectiveness with which this capital is deployed. Thus, an organization's *real competitive advantage is the people of the company, because everything can be copied so quickly that you can be first to market something, but three months later you are no longer first. A level of continuous innovation needs to be reached through people.*[4] Barnes and Noble gained the advantage on its competition, Borders Group, by actively putting its employees to work on making the company successful on the World Wide Web. Barnes and Noble increased sales and thus the value of its stock through its innovative use of the Web. Borders dragged behind Barnes and Noble in making the speed-to-value judgment on the Web, and as a result it has been less successful in recent years.

Technology can marshal information, process it, analyze it, and focus it in new and ever more powerful ways. The use of e-commerce to distribute information to consumers has become incredibly pervasive. For instance, people are now learning about their health conditions through information found on the Web. In addition, consumers are now more actively participating in their healthcare management; for example, by investigating treatments and medications, consumers can have informed input in determining their care.

Intranets make information available instantly around the globe. As a result of this global accessibility of information, governments are rapidly creating, instituting, and changing regulations, safeguards, and assurances in order to ensure that the information distributed on the Web is correct. For instance, senior executives, such as the CFO and CEO, now must sign financial statements confirming that the information included in the statement is valid and accurate.

But the quantity and complexity of global challenges mean that leaders can no longer claim to know everything, whether in operations or strategy. The speed of change requires people on the frontlines to be not only empowered to make decisions, but accountable for those decisions on the basis of their own bank of knowledge and experience.

ELIMINATE WASTE AND UNNECESSARY COST

As technology and global competition incite ever-shortening deadlines, global leaders must do more in less time with fewer resources.

> *The driver for change will be that leaders will have to be increasingly more efficient with less.*[5]

Eliminating waste and unnecessary cost is an important aspect of the global leader's role. It can lead to increased profitability and a stronger, better equipped, and more adaptable organization. As can be seen in the following quotes, the organizational structure of the company is, for many, the place to begin making changes.

1. Eliminate bureaucracy: *Leaders will need to train and empower people to leverage their knowledge and make decisions on the frontlines without having to go through layers and layers of bureaucracy.*[6]

2. Eliminate structure: *Companies will require a lean structure in the future, because it makes decision making faster and it makes it easier to respond to the rapidly changing marketplace.*[7]

3. Eliminate layers: *The organizational structure will be flatter because multilevel companies have more overhead and are less flexible.*[8]

4. Eliminate highly specialized jobs: *The future companies will have more individuals who are multidisciplinary.*[9] This change can be seen in many industries. For example, in the past, many consulting companies set up specialized industry areas, such as telecommunications, high-tech, healthcare, human resources, and financial services. In addition, consultants were valued for competencies in area specialties, such as strategy, human performance, and process. Now, as industry boundaries shift and overlap, we are starting to see that competence and understanding across disciplines and incorporating a wide range of perspectives into the solution set is critical to problem solving and solution creation.

The operating models (how people get into roles, get rewarded for roles, get assigned to different parts of the organization, how they go after customers, etc.) within organizations will be required to shift with the changing business climate: Strategies by which organizations have operated in the past will have to change. This must be done with great care and forethought, for although each of the above proposals has its merits, and some are indeed realistic trends for the future, there is a strong possibility that some of these proposals can, if not managed carefully, damage the viability of the organization. For example, eliminating organizational bureaucracy, structure, and layers, while speeding up the decision-making process and moving the company forward, can have serious consequences if those at the top are not aware of the decisions made by those at lower levels in the company. Recently, the upper-level management of a large hospital franchise, which had quickly gained billions in revenue, found that 50 percent of its revenue had come at the expense of the government. When the government community came after the franchise, the chairman was caught unawares, because the management team that had created the financial model had not told him about the cost-saving strategy. In this case, eliminating bureaucracy, layers, and structure may prove to be quite detrimental to the company.

Negative methods for reducing costs are well known and include downsizing and/or restructuring without knowing the impact on the company's operations; reducing customer service, which can cause many customers to discontinue relations with the company; and cutting corners in production methods, which can cause repair and modification costs to go up.[10]

For instance, as a result of the high financial cost of the talent wars of recent years, many organizations are faced with reducing recruiting and lowering the quality of the recruits hired. As a result, many companies are not able to keep up with services, orders, or a need for talent. This is negatively impacting companies' relationships with their customers and suppliers, as well as the global market.

An effective way to reduce costs is to keep workers up to date through training and development. Realizing that informed workers can make better decisions and are likely to make fewer blunders, many companies, including General Electric, Johnson & Johnson, and Hewlett-Packard, have established education and training programs for employees. Another effective way to reduce costs, customer dissatisfaction, and returns is to ensure that suppliers deliver high-quality products and services.[11]

Some simple things to do to cut costs are

1. Travel awareness: Is the trip really necessary? What technology or communication medium can get the job done without requiring a physical meeting?

2. Procurement: Is the company getting the best rates on products and services? Can it strategically join a buying consortium? Can it use software to help manage costs?

3. Look beyond today's needs: Is a new piece of expensive equipment really a sensible purchase when the technology may be out of date in the next year or two?

4. Space: Is there a way to reuse or lease unused office space? Is it possible to electronically archive paper files and thus gain more space?

Another area in which companies might save costs and/or eliminate waste is in the use of paper products. According to a *Worldwatch News Release,*[12]

> Global paper use has grown more than six-fold since 1950.... Computers, fax machines, and high-speed printers and copiers make it possible to churn out vast quantities of paper. In the United States, the average office worker uses some 12,000 sheets of paper per year. Of the major grades of paper, printing

and writing paper is both the most polluting and the fastest growing world-wide.... Bank of America, the largest bank in the country, reduced its paper consumption by 25 percent in just two years with online reports and forms, e-mail, double-sided copying, and lighter-weight papers. It also recycles 61 percent of its paper, saving about half a million dollars a year in waste hauling fees. Companies that use the Internet instead of paper for purchase orders, invoices, etc., can save $1 to $5 per page by eliminating paper and reducing labor costs and time.

Solutions to waste, such as the paper waste illustrated in the news release above, include *e-books, which may replace print magazines, and our company does all it's job advertising on the Web.*[13] By utilizing the technological advances that make sense for the company, global leaders can eliminate waste, cut costs, and thereby maintain a competitive advantage.

PROVIDE GREAT PRODUCTS AND SERVICES

Competition is a part of every business, whether it is a sales business or not. Maintaining the advantage becomes a primary goal of any global leader.

Highly effective global leaders know that maintaining a competitive advantage is, to a great extent, dependent upon customer satisfaction.[14] They look at the company in terms of how high customers and potential customers rank its products and services. A large hospital franchise makes every effort to satisfy its customers. However, customers are determined to be not only the patients of the hospital, but also the employees, administrators, and doctors who work at the hospital. The hospital gives monthly customer satisfaction surveys to determine what type of care its patients are receiving, if the doctors are happy with how their patients are being treated, and if the medical and administrative staff is satisfied with their positions. The management team at the hospital has found that by making every attempt to keep all "customers" satisfied, the patient experience has improved greatly. Understanding that it is the customer who determines the most important attributes of a product, service, or organization, the global leader works to maintain and expand these desired attributes.

Once aware of the attributes that are most valued by customers and potential customers—whether cost, customer service, quality, speed of service, or convenience—the global leader takes the necessary steps to ensure that the company and its people perform exceptionally well in these areas, thus achieving and maintaining competitive advantage. For instance, the leaders at a large technological services company had their performance management tied to people performance issues and to ensuring that their people were doing everything possible to support the company's competitive advantage. This link was key to the success of not only the workers in the company, but also of its leaders.

ACHIEVING LONG-TERM SHAREHOLDER VALUE

Companies are expected to provide returns to their shareholders. One expectation is to have shorter-term profits, which require a different kind of management. *There are pressures that come from outside as well as within the company, and it is necessary to find the right balance between those.*[15]

The model of success that is being perpetuated in the current economy ensures that many employees have the opportunity to be owner-operators in stock purchase plans. When using this model, care must be taken to balance the concept of owner-operators and stock purchase plans with rewarding companies, in their stock value, for retaining talent and intellectual capital. Because so many global leaders are being recognized with stock options, it is perpetuating the use of financial gain in the value of stock as a motivational factor for their work. As such, we may be heading towards an economy in which leaders are rewarded simply for the valuation of the company's stock and not for the retention of intellectual capital. This is a serious shortcoming.

In addition, the ready availability and mobility of intellectual capital via the World Wide Web can mean that the stock valuation of companies that are quick to jump on a fleeting advantage might be mislabeled or miscalculated based on the momentary competitive advantage. As a result, there would be companies that were overvalued based on intellectual capital and talent that couldn't be retained. In this context, there needs to be a balance of focus on economic security. In order to achieve such results for the shareholder, *effective global leaders need a good grasp of finance and knowledge of their own company's long-term liability.*[16]

The global leader will not only have to effectively manage people and satisfy customers, but he or she must also have the ability to meet financial requirements and to achieve visible results for the shareholder.

CONCLUSION

The global leaders of the future will be required to have not only the professional knowledge to lead, but also the innovative and strategic mindset to maintain a competitive advantage in the industry. The pressure to continually deliver more, better, and faster results will require the global leader to rely on the intellectual capital within the organization and perhaps even outside of it. As the world rapidly changes and the marketplace becomes increasingly global, the competition within each industry becomes ever tougher. To keep costs down and profits up, the global leader is required to determine what is waste and what costs are unnecessary, and to provide the best possible product and/or service to the customer. The final goal in maintaining competitive advantage is to achieve results that lead to long-term shareholder value.

MAINTAINING A COMPETITIVE ADVANTAGE[17]

James M. Klingensmith, Sc.D. (group executive vice president of health insurance operations at Highmark Blue Cross Blue Shield) believes that leadership is a function of two primary elements: (1) understanding the economics of the particular business within which the leader is involved, and (2) aligning the organization around those fundamentals. Here is how he has put his beliefs to work to gain and maintain competitive advantage for Highmark.

Assessing Reality

Jim provides executive leadership and the strategic direction for Highmark's Health Insurance Group, which includes information services, marketing, sales, operations, and health services, and he still vividly remembers June 10, 1997—the day he received the financials for his first month at the company. The financials showed the company losing $1 million a day! Every product was a loser.

Jim believed that if Highmark, now one of the ten largest insurers in the nation, was to be competitive, and if he was to be a leader, he was going to have to figure out where to lead. He took the financials apart piece by piece, going all the way to the genetic code of the business, and then assimilated it back together. From this assessment, he decided to start a program designed to change those metrics.

Finding the Advantage

Here is an example of part of that program. In early 1999, a task force with the goal of identifying ways to gain competitive advantage in the retail insurance industry was formed at Highmark. The task force saw opportunity for great cost savings and improved customer satisfaction in the effective use of the Internet.

As a result, Highmark became "the first in the nation to offer a completely paperless system for evaluating, selecting, and enrolling in insurance plans that fit members' unique needs.... In addition to attracting key clients, this new product firmly established Highmark as a technological leader in the Blue Cross Blue Shield family."[18]

Says Jim, "Our CHM Web initiatives have firmly established Highmark's position of Internet technology leadership in the insurance industry. Our success validates that we had the right strategy and made the right choices...."[19]

The results from this and other ventures are quite impressive. In 2000, Highmark *earned* a million dollars a day rather than lost it.

Maintaining
a Competitive Advantage

ITEM 68: Communicates a Positive, Can-Do Sense of Urgency Toward Getting the Job Done

WHAT TO DO

- Take the initiative to do things beyond what is expected.
- Seek out future avenues. Go on site visits inside and outside your industry to compare practices that you can apply.
- At times when your group is required to make extra effort to get things done, encourage them to do so willingly.
- If you or your group consistently work long hours, keep track of the time and evaluate how each member manages his or her time on each project. You may find that you need to hire more staff, re-prioritize, delegate more, or convince your group to accept the number of extra hours.
- Ensure that each team member understands her or his role and responsibility.
- Stop making excuses. Convey and keep a positive attitude toward achieving results.
- Focus on the results achieved, not the number of hours worked.
- Go the extra mile.
- Create an environment in which people can work hard and have fun.

HOW TO DO IT

- Avoid and discourage destructive comments about working too hard or too long.
- If you or your group cannot work extra hours to complete a project, let your manager or colleagues know, explain the reason, express your concerns, and help find someone who can do it.
- Work with your group to look for productive, constructive ways to get things done, not excuses why it cannot be done.
- Communicate the long-term benefits that working hard will bring.

- Take the initiative to help your team or department get things done without being told or asked to do so.
- Encourage the full participation of team members by ensuring that they have received adequate training in relationship skills, group process, and decision making.
- Solicit input from your people on what you can do to make your organization a fun place to work.
- Actively participate in office social activities to get to know your people better.
- Look for additional challenges, and let people know that you expect them to have increased responsibility and personal growth.
- Ask your manager and coworkers for feedback on how you are doing in this area.
- Ask your superior to identify a person or a team who best demonstrates a can-do attitude, and observe them in action. Ask others who work with them to provide specific examples, and learn from them.
- Ask people for ideas about what you can do to make your organization a fun place to work and to increase their sense of ownership.

HOW TO USE THIS SKILL FURTHER

- Seek ways to further support others. Anticipate their needs and meet them.
- Ask someone you trust to let you know when you are making excuses, procrastinating, or displaying a negative attitude toward getting the job done.
- Implement various team-building activities that people enjoy to motivate your group.

RESULTS YOU CAN EXPECT

- You may earn a reputation of being positive, responsible, and easy to work with.
- Your manager may give you positive feedback about your ability to accomplish tasks on time.
- You may be assigned to more challenging and interesting projects.
- Your work group may be more enthusiastic and productive.

READINGS

- *Get Better Or Get Beaten.* Robert Slater & Jeffrey A. Krames. 2001. McGraw-Hill: New York, ISBN 71373462.
- *Leading People: The 8 Proven Principles for Success in Business.* Robert H. Rosen & Paul B. Brown. 1997. Penguin USA: New York, ISBN 140242724.
- *Peak Performance: Aligning the Hearts and Minds of Your Employees.* Jon R. Katzenbach. 2000. Harvard Business School Press: Boston, ISBN 0875849369.
- *Playing For Keeps: How the World's Most Aggressive and Admired Companies Use Core Values to Manage, Energize, and Organize Their People, and Promote,*

Advance, and Achieve Their Corporate Missions. Frederick G. Harmon. 1996. John Wiley & Sons: New York, ISBN 047159847X.

- *Practice What You Preach: What Managers Must Do to Create a High-Achievement Culture*. David H. Maister. 2001. Free Press: ISBN 743211871.

- *Seize Tomorrow, Start Today: Renew Your Vision, Revitalize Your Organization, and Stay Ahead of the Future*. James A. Belasco & Jerre L. Stead. 2000. Warner Books: New York, ISBN 446676047.

- *The Dance of Change: The Challenges to Sustaining Momentum in Learning Organizations*. Peter M. Senge, Art Kleiner, Charlotte Roberts, George Roth, Rick Ross, & Bryan Smith. 1999. Doubleday: New York, ISBN 0385493223.

- *The Intelligent Organization: Engaging the Talent & Initiative of Everyone in the Workplace*. Gifford Pinchot & Elizabeth Pinchot. 1996. Berrett-Koehler: ISBN 1881052982.

ITEM 69: Holds People Accountable for Their Results

WHAT TO DO

- Make it clear to your employees that they are responsible for their actions.
- Emphasize the importance of delivering results.
- Resist taking responsibility for your people when they fail to deliver results.
- Give constructive and timely feedback to your employees.
- Don't fix the problems for others. Let them keep the "monkey" and find the solution.
- Encourage people to make realistic commitments.
- Ensure that people receive adequate training to do their work.
- Be a role model in taking responsibility for achieving results.

HOW TO DO IT

- Look at your group and ask yourself if you are spending more energy protecting them than holding them accountable.
- If you tend to be more protective, remind yourself that by holding people accountable, you are building their skills and helping them to rely less and less on you.
- Work with employees to determine the reasons why the results weren't produced. Point out the consequences, and ask them to find a solution to fix the problem.
- Ask people what they need in order to produce the results desired.
- Provide coaching and consulting to help your people understand their potential and limits before making a commitment.

- Show an active interest in your employees' progress, but avoid taking charge or getting in the way.
- Ask coworkers and your manager for feedback about how you hold others accountable for achieving results.
- Discuss techniques with managers who excel at this area.

HOW TO USE THIS SKILL FURTHER

- Consider ways of applying responsibility-building practices to the team with which you are now working.

RESULTS YOU CAN EXPECT

- Your group may require less monitoring.
- You may be more effective at delegating.

READINGS

- *A New Vision for Human Resources: Defining the Human Resources Function by Its Results*. Jac Fitz-Enz & Jack J. Phillips. 1999. Crisp Publications: Menlo Park, CA, ISBN 156052488X.
- *Effective Phrases for Performance Appraisals: A Guide to Successful Evaluations*. James E. Neal. 2000. Neal Publications: Perrysburg, OH, ISBN 1882423097.
- *First, Break All the Rules: What the World's Greatest Managers Do Differently*. Marcus Buckingham & Curt Coffman. 1999. Simon & Schuster, New York, ISBN 684852861.
- *Freedom and Accountability at Work: Applying Philosophical Insight to the Real World*. Peter Koestenbaum & Peter Block. 2001. Pfeiffer & Co: New York, ISBN 787955949.
- *Make Success Measurable!: A Mindbook-Workbook for Setting Goals and Taking Action*. Douglas K. Smith. 1999. John Wiley & Sons: New York, ISBN 471295590.
- *Taking Charge of Change: 10 Principles for Managing People and Performance*. Douglas K. Smith. 1997. Perseus Pr, Reading, MA, ISBN 201916045.
- *The Boss's Survival Guide*. Bob Rosner, Allan Halcrow, & Alan S. Levins. 2001. McGraw-Hill: New York, ISBN 71362738.
- *The HR Scorecard: Linking People, Strategy, and Performance*. Brian E. Becker, Mark A. Huselid, & Dave Ulrich. 2001. Harvard Business School Press: Boston, ISBN 1578511364.
- *Tomorrow's HR Management: 48 Thought Leaders Call for Change*. David Ulrich, Michael R. Losey, & Gerry Lake. 1997. John Wiley & Sons: New York, ISBN 0471197149.

ITEM 70: Successfully Eliminates Waste and Unneeded Cost

WHAT TO DO

- Manage the business as if it were your own.
- Realize that a business process that worked well at one time under certain circumstances may no longer be effective or efficient.
- Involve your employees in the process of simplifying business processes and cost reduction.
- Look for new technology that can simplify business processes and increase your department's efficiency.
- Identify the costs and procedures that you currently use to accomplish key tasks in your organization.
- Eliminate unneeded cost without losing production capacity or sacrifice quality.
- Find ways to reduce the duplication of effort in your organization.
- Monitor resources to avoid wasting time or duplicating efforts.
- Create structures to monitor expenses for the duration of each project.
- Use a resource only if it will produce the most cost-effective results.
- Get others you trust to challenge your financial ideas to test their soundness.

HOW TO DO IT

- Talk with other managers about how they develop and implement a strategic plan to maximize productivity and how they identify and eliminate unnecessary expenses.
- Communicate the long-term corporate goals and short-term objectives to your work group. Take the time to invite ideas and input from your employees for maximizing productivity and profit.
- Give recognition and rewards for people with useable suggestions.
- List each step that must occur from the time a task enters your department until it leaves your department. Eliminate unnecessary steps that will detain you from effectively maximizing productivity.
- Explain to your employees how costs and profits are projected and what happens when projections do not match actual goals.
- Train others to spot unnecessary expenses.
- Set coordinated goals and procedures to unite the various business units.
- Look at successful cost-saving programs in other industries or companies.
- Try out new cost prevention or reduction ideas for a test period to allow a complete and fair test without as much liability.

- Conduct brainstorming sessions on cost-saving with coworkers, management, and customers.
- Ask employees and customers for their ideas on cost prevention, eliminating waste, and cost cutting.
- Challenge your work group to identify tasks or procedures that are outdated, overly time-consuming, or difficult to complete.
- Determine whether the processes are necessary and if any can be combined with another step to save time and money.
- Study the business processes and budgets of other departments in your organization to see how their work processes are set up, what works well, what doesn't, and why.

HOW TO USE THIS SKILL FURTHER

- Talk to managers who have effectively streamlined business processes and eliminated waste, and learn their methods and approaches.
- Volunteer to work on a committee or task force whose assignment is to examine and improve your organization's work process and productivity.
- Take on projects with bigger budgets and payoffs.
- Use a budget in your home.
- Handle finance or productivity for a volunteer, social, or recreational group outside of work; ask for feedback on how you are doing.

RESULTS YOU CAN EXPECT

- Morale may improve as others feel they have a stake in deciding how to improve processes.
- Others may ask your advice on improving productivity and eliminating unnecessary expenses.
- You may receive recognition for achieving results or exceeding expectations on time and within budget.

READINGS

- *Essential Drucker: In One Volume the Best of Sixty Years of Peter Drucker's Essential Writings on Management.* Peter Ferdinand Drucker. 2001. HarperBusiness: New York, ISBN 66210879.
- *First, Break All the Rules: What the World's Greatest Managers Do Differently.* Marcus Buckingham & Curt Coffman. 1999. Simon & Schuster: New York, ISBN 684852861.
- *Gemba Kaizen: A Commonsense, Low-Cost Approach to Management.* Masaaki Imai. 1997. McGraw-Hill: New York, ISBN 0070314462.
- *Jack: Straight from the Gut.* Jack Welch. 2001. Warner Books: New York, ISBN 0446528382.

- *Lean Thinking*. James P. Womack & Daniel T. Jones. 1996. Simon & Schuster: New York, ISBN 0684810352 .
- *Lean Transformation: How to Change Your Business into a Lean Enterprise*. Bruce A. Henderson, Jorge L. Larco, & Stephen H. Martin. 1999. Oaklea Press: Richmond, VA, ISBN 0964660121.
- *Robust Engineering: Learn How to Boost Quality While Reducing Costs & Time to Market*. Genichi Taguchi, Subir Chowdhury, & Shin Taguchi. 1999. McGraw-Hill: New York, ISBN 71347828.

ITEM 71: Provides Products and Services That Help Our Company Have a Clear Competitive Advantage

WHAT TO DO

- Instill a commitment to quality and excellence in your organization.
- Understand the budgeting process so that you can contribute ideas for maximizing productivity and profitability.
- Develop a strategic plan that creates increasing economic value for the key stakeholders, and determine how best to use the company's resources.
- Establish high performance standards and promote product and service excellence.
- Define your success as "meeting or exceeding customer requirements."
- Communicate payoffs for your company and your own group that come with improving products and services.
- Ask customers what they want with respect to products and services, then stop and listen.
- Keep your efforts focused on improving the delivery and quality of products and services.
- Strive to meet customer deadlines within costs as promised.
- Define clear expectations for quality of products, services, and processes for your department.

HOW TO DO IT

- Ensure that measurements are in place to assess the quality and cost (as defined by your customer) of the product or service you provide.
- Write and publicize your performance standard for quality as "meeting customer needs, including cost and schedule."
- Analyze your work processes and determine how to apply quality management principles to improve your overall products and services.
- Prepare detailed plans with resources required to achieve quality in products and services at a competitive price.

- At least once a day, check your efforts against the standard, and identify any gaps. Work to bring your efforts into closer alignment with your standard.
- Check with your work group to make sure they are clear about customer and supplier requirements. Get their input on achieving goals, cutting costs, and improving quality.
- When asking customers what they want or what their needs are, also ask if they foresee any problems—listen carefully and make notes for reference.
- To guard against relying on preconceived ideas of what the customer needs, make sure to check for understanding with the customer at the outset and regularly thereafter. Listen carefully, document what is said, and get the customer's agreement.
- When holding follow-up meetings with customers, include key employees who worked on meeting their needs, and ask "What went right?" and "What can we do to meet your needs better?"

HOW TO USE THIS SKILL FURTHER

- Ask managers who are good at this to explain their methods.
- Learn from managers who continuously produce high-quality services and products within budget.
- Read books about effective quality management.

RESULTS YOU CAN EXPECT

- You may be recognized as a model of someone who continuously pursues excellence.
- Your customers may often be satisfied with the way you meet their needs.
- Customers may request your services or that you be assigned to assist them.

READINGS

- *Competitive Advantage: Creating and Sustaining Superior Performance*. Michael E. Porter. 1998. Free Press: London, ISBN 0684841460.
- *General Electric's Six Sigma Revolution: How General Electric and Others Turned Process Into Profits*. George Eckes. 2000. John Wiley & Sons: New York, ISBN 047138822X.
- *Getting Results: Five Absolutes for High Performance*. Clinton O. Longenecker & Jack L. Simonetti. 2001. John Wiley & Sons: New York, ISBN 0787953881.
- *Making Quality Work: A Leadership Guide for the Results-Driven Manager*. George Labovitz, Yu Sang Chang, & Victor Rosansky. 1995. John Wiley & Sons: New York, ISBN 047113211X.
- *The New Market Leaders: Who's Winning and How in the Battle for Customers*. Fred Wiersema. 2001. Free Press: London, ISBN 0743204654.
- *The Power of Six Sigma: An Inspiring Tale of How Six Sigma Is Transforming the Way We Work*. Subir Chowdhury. 2001. Dearborn Trade: Chicago, ISBN 793144345.

- *The Quest for Global Dominance: Transforming Global Presence into Global Competitive Advantage*. Vijay Govindarajan, Anil K. Gupta, & C. K. Prahalad. 2001. Jossey-Bass: San Francisco, ISBN 0787957216.

ITEM 72: Achieves Results That Lead to Long-Term Shareholder Value

WHAT TO DO

- Determine how best to use the company's resources within its competitive environment.
- Actively look for and introduce new ideas.
- Strive to eliminate or minimize unnecessary bureaucracy and politics.
- Develop a strategic plan that creates increasing economic value for the company's shareholders and employees yet also meets the needs of your customers.
- Study your company's long-range plan and consider its implications for your department.
- Identify and convey the long-term corporate goals to employees.
- Involve your employees in the budgeting process so that they can contribute ideas for improving profitability and understand the financial impact of decisions.
- Be sensitive to verbal and nonverbal communication that promotes the "selfish" intentions rather than the company's needs first.

HOW TO DO IT

- Analyze capital markets, related industries, and competition to help you understand the company's long-term vision.
- Examine existing procedures and policies, then streamline them. Focus on efforts that will yield maximum results.
- Review goals and priorities by linking task objectives to the overall organizational goals.
- Identify interrelationships between divisions, departments, and the company as a whole.
- Set coordinated goals and policies to unite the business units.
- Identify and communicate to employees the desired results that lead to long-term shareholder values.
- Conduct quarterly meetings with your employees to communicate organizational goals. Explain how your department's goals support shareholder value. Respond to questions and check for understanding.
- Obtain your staff's input on ways to effectively increase shareholder value.

- Lead by example; be sure your own behavior reflects a commitment to your company's long-term interests.
- Discuss techniques with managers who excel at balancing meeting the need to achieve results with meeting the needs of shareholders.
- Ask your managers to give you feedback on how you are doing in this area.

HOW TO USE THIS SKILL FURTHER

- Make lists that compare short-term results to long-term benefits so that employees can see the differences.
- Volunteer to write strategic plans for major projects within the organization.

RESULTS YOU CAN EXPECT

- You may recognize much greater gains in all aspects of the business.
- Company strategies and goals for the future may be clear from all levels of management.

READINGS

- *Creating Shareholder Value: A Guide for Managers and Investors*. Alfred Rappaport. 1997. Free Press: London, ISBN 0684844109.
- *Developing Business Strategies*. David A. Aaker. 1995. John Wiley & Sons: New York, ISBN 0471118141.
- *Don't Park Your Brain Outside: A Practical Guide to Improving Shareholder Value With Smart Management*. Francis T. Hartman. 2000. Project Management Institute Publications: Newtown Square, PA, ISBN 1880410486.
- *Playing For Keeps: How the World's Most Aggressive and Admired Companies Use Core Values to Manage, Energize, and Organize Their People, and Promote, Advance, and Achieve Their Corporate Missions*. Frederick G. Harmon. 1996. John Wiley & Sons: ISBN 047159847X.
- *The Value Imperative: Managing for Superior Shareholder Returns*. James M. McTaggart, Peter W. Kontes, & Michael Mankins. 1994. Free Press: London, ISBN 0029206707.
- *Value-Based Marketing: Marketing Strategies for Corporate Growth and Shareholder Value*. Peter Doyle. 2000. John Wiley & Sons: ISBN 471877271.

ENDNOTES

1. Pharmaceuticals, United States, 41.
2. Products and services, United States, 36.

3. W. Tanaka. "Software Is a Dandy If It Helps Move the Candy." *The Philadelphia Inquirer,* November 1, 2002.

4. Investments, United States, 48.

5. Products and services, United States, 33.

6. Healthcare, Taiwan, 41.

7. Healthcare Indonesia/Malaysia, 46.

8. Products and services, United States, 35.

9. Products and services, United States, 35.

10. Ron Kurtus, *www.school-for-champions.com.*

11. Ibid.

12. Worldwatch Institute. *Cutting the Costs of Paper: Saving Forests, Water, Energy and Money.* Janet N. Abramovitz & Ashley T. Mattoon. December 11, 1999. Copyright © 2002, *www.worldwatch.org.*

13. Telecommunications, United States, 36

14. Please see Chapter 15, "Ensuring Customer Satisfaction," for more information on this subject.

15. Investments, United States, 36.

16. Healthcare, Philippines, 36.

17. Information from interview with Jim Klingensmith conducted by Cathy Greenberg, December 2001.

18. Sun Microsystems Success Story. ©2001. *http://www.sun.com/servers/success-stories/highmark.html.*

19. Ibid.

CHAPTER TEN

Using this book to Help Develop Yourself as a Leader

Peter Drucker is generally considered the world's greatest authority on management. Peter has said that Frances Hesselbein is the most effective executive that he has ever met. Frances served for thirteen years as the Executive Director of the Girl Scouts of the USA. She has served for ten years as CEO of the Drucker Foundation. Frances is a model for demonstrating the process of receiving feedback, listening carefully to what is learned, and being a role model for self-development. While managing the Girl Scouts, she led the process of determining the profile of the ideal leader of the future. She received feedback about herself and consistently followed up with her people. In doing so, she demonstrated how to "walk the talk" as a leader.

You can use the Global Leader of the Future Inventory in the same way. Ask your key stakeholders how your current leadership behavior compares with this desired profile. Learn from them what you are doing well and what you may need to change. Follow up with them on your progress in selected areas for improvement. You may well see the same positive results as demonstrated by Frances!

Frances consistently points out that leaders focus on what to *be*, not just on what to *do*. Some things have not changed from the past. The leader of the future will have to demonstrate the personal integrity that shows how behavior matches personal beliefs. Leaders who consistently demonstrate this internal congruence best illustrate the concept of "flow." The high-potential participants in our research impressed us as much with their great *commitment* as with their great *ideas*! It was clear that the vision of leadership they describe is not just behavior they want to observe, but behavior they want to demonstrate!

USING THIS BOOK TO HELP DEVELOP YOUR TEAM

Throughout this book, we have focused on 15 key qualities of effective global leaders. While no one leader will necessarily be skilled at all 15, a leadership team can be developed to "cover the bases" necessary for success. It might be a good idea to review each of the 15 qualities with your team to determine how important each quality is for your organization's future and how capable you are as a team. As a leader of the team, you can use the 360-degree feedback tool to measure how *your* behavior matches the desired behavior described in this book. Your team members' perceptions of your behavior may be a better guide than your self-assessment of your behavior. Each of your team members could benefit from the same type of assessment.

The former mayor of New York, Rudy Giuliani, attributes much of his success in managing the 9/11 crises to the *team* of leaders who had supported him over the years. He believes that the breadth and depth of knowledge in his team helped the entire city make it through this difficult period. He believes that the strong foundation of teamwork that occurred before the disaster enabled the team to handle the challenges that arose after the disaster. In the same way, global leaders need to prepare their teams *today* for the upcoming challenges of tomorrow. This book provides a good "crystal ball" to help the reader determine what those challenges might be. The resource guide provides a road map on how to meet these challenges.

GLOBAL LEADERSHIP: THE NEXT GENERATION

We feel privileged to have interviewed over 200 very special people who contributed their insights to *Global Leadership: The Next Generation*. The leaders who participated in this study were seen as the "highest potential" of the high-potential leaders around the world.

As noted in the first chapter, we learned that the global leader of the future will have a challenging job! Not only will the "old qualities" of leadership, such as vision and integrity, be important, but new qualities, such as global thinking, demonstrating technological savvy, and developing cross-cultural awareness, also will need to be added to the leader's skills.

The future leaders that we interviewed believe that new times will require new skills. Unfortunately, many of today's leaders have not been educated in these skills or even encouraged to believe that these skills are important.

To prepare for success in the next millennium, organizations will have to either change the mindset of many leaders or change their leadership status. Leaders will have to understand why the new skills are important. They will have to discern what they need to learn and how they can best learn it. The organization's reward and reinforcement system will need to reflect these new competencies.

Every major change produces a challenge. The bad news is that many of today's leaders do not see the importance of these new competencies. The good news is that most of the high-potential leaders we interviewed do see the need for these competencies.

Historically, existing leaders have been expected to mentor and develop future leaders. While this idea will still be true in the future, there may be a major addition to the process—future leaders may also be expected to help mentor and develop present leaders. If future leaders have the wisdom to learn from the experience of present leaders, and present leaders have the wisdom to learn new competencies from future leaders, both parties can share leadership in a way that can benefit their organization.

A
RESEARCH
METHODOLOGY
FOR THE GLOBAL
LEADER OF THE
FUTURE PROJECT

Cathy Greenberg, Alastair Robertson, Maya Hu-Chan, and Marshall Goldsmith have made an ongoing commitment to building knowledge around the future of executive leadership with a global scope. As part of this commitment, a multiple-method research plan was created that would span two years of knowledge acquisition. The plan used a four-stage process for knowledge development: assess data, generate knowledge, embed knowledge, and transfer knowledge. An overview of each phase is given below.

PHASES OF KNOWLEDGE DEVELOPMENT

PHASE ONE: ASSESS

The first phase of knowledge development about global leadership involved assessing the current state of knowledge. This roughly one-year process began in 1997. The initial research involved bringing together recognized thought leaders and futurists in the realm of global leadership (see Table A–1). This process created a working definition of the desired knowledge and conceptual terms. An initial database and bibliography were created. A wide "net" for secondary research was cast to build upon the knowledge gathered from the initial research. A variety of business and academic sources created a rich set of books, articles, theories, practical stories, and other data that was used in expanding the knowledge base.

TABLE A.1 Phase 1 Thought Leaders and Futurists

- Warren Bennis, University of Southern California—The Leadership Institute
- Jim Bolt, Executive Development Associates
- Jay Conger, University of Southern California—The Leadership Institute
- Ted Forbes, Darden School, University of Virginia
- Marshall Goldsmith, Alliance for Strategic Leadership
- Frances Hesselbein, Drucker Foundation
- Lynn Isabella, Darden School, University of Virginia
- Jennifer James, Futurist
- Bob Johansen, Institute for the Future
- Henry Kissinger, Former Secretary of State
- John Kotter, Harvard Business School
- Carl Larson, University of Denver
- Quinn Mills, Harvard Business School
- John O'Neil, Center for Leadership Renewal
- Lester Thurow, Massachusetts Institute for Technology
- Watts Wacker, First Matter
- George West, Consultants for Management Development
- Abe Zaleznik, Harvard Business School

During this phase, an initial set of data about global leadership was created and a white paper—"CEO of the Future"—was written. Additionally, alliance partnerships were created between CEOs and academics in one-on-one focus sessions with either Warren Bennis, Marshall Goldsmith, or John O'Neil to guide the remaining phases of knowledge acquisition and dissemination.

PHASE TWO: GENERATE

The second phase of the project began in 1998. It drew upon the concepts identified in the first phase to generate ideas and hypotheses around global leadership. These ideas and hypotheses were then refined and validated with the alliance partners. A questionnaire to measure the criticality of various dimensions of global leadership for the past, present, and future was then designed and pilot tested for reliability and validity. Provocative thoughts and findings were identified, and the *Evolving Role of Executive Leadership Report* was created to capture the results of Phases One and Two. This phase completed the research portion of the knowledge generation process.

Phase Three: Embed

The third phase began in 1999. Knowledge generated and synthesized from the prior two phases supported a new level of investigation. Cathy Greenberg, Alastair Robertson, and Marshall Goldsmith identified value propositions and the steps needed for further development. The research team was able to engage future leaders in dialogue about what value they could generate to support their roles in a changing leadership environment. Here is where official support for the research ended and the investigators pushed on independently to grow the research further across projects, academia, and alliances with other research groups and thought leaders to embed their findings into the greater wealth of published information on leadership worldwide. Such publications included *Leading Beyond the Walls* (1999), *Coaching for Leadership* (2000), and *The Leader of the Future* (2001).

Phase Four: Transfer

The fourth and final phase of the project began in 1999 and is ongoing. This phase transfers knowledge from the research and development phases into practical applications. The groups responsible for Phase Three continue to have responsibility for this phase. Cathy Greenberg and Alastair Robertson engaged in the development of approaches, frameworks, methodologies, resources, market planning, and Master Class development to effectively transfer knowledge. This resulted in knowledge creation and transfer through articles, books, and conferences. Recently, a new phase of the research focused on the application of these findings in e-leadership and what it takes to be an e-manager in the world of e-commerce.

Research Plan and Methods

A multiple-method research plan was created to consolidate existing knowledge on global leadership and then to expand upon that knowledge. The initial thought leader and futurist panels were identified on recommendations from partners and the Fortune Global 100. Organizations that participated in subsequent research were chosen from lists of identified global organizations, partner suggestions, and external alliance partner recommendations. The selected organizations represented a wide range of global industries, sizes, geographies, and lifecycle development phases. (See Table A–2 for a list of participating organizations.)

Four major research methods were used as described below.

1. Thought Leader Panels

External thought leaders in the areas of global leadership and futurism were identified. Their published research was reviewed, and they were then invited to participate in a series of thought leader panels. These panels produced new and

TABLE A.2 Participating Organizations

Acer (Taiwan)
African Development Foundation (USA)
Alcoa (Switzerland, USA)
Allianz (Germany)
AMD (USA)
American Friends Service Committee
 (USA)
Ameritech (USA)
Aracruz Cellulose (Brazil)
Avon (Japan)
Banque Agricole W.I. Carr Indosuez
 (Taiwan)
BASF/Knoll Pharmaceutical (USA)
Bechtel (Brazil, Chile)
Bekaert (Belgium)
Bellsouth (USA)
Boise Cascade (USA)
Bombardier Aerospace (Canada)
Canadian Federal Government
 (Canada)
Citibank (Taiwan)
Cox Communications (USA)
Crimson Asia (Taiwan)
Center for International Dialogue (USA)
Cockerill CMI (Belgium)
Diners Club (Brazil, USA)
DHL (South Africa, USA)
Eastman Kodak (India, Malaysia,
 Taiwan, Thailand)
Effem Mexico (Mexico)
Ericsson (Spain)
Ericsson Radio Systems (Sweden)
Friends Committee National Legislation
 (USA)
Fluor (USA)
Ford Motor (USA)
GTE (China, USA)

Honeywell (USA)
International SEMATECH (USA)
IBM (Japan, UK)
John Hancock (USA)
Johnson & Johnson (Indonesia,
 Philippines, Taiwan)
MediaOne Group (Japan, USA)
Merck Sharp Dhome (Brazil)
National Instruments (USA)
Oracle (China, USA)
Primax (Taiwan)
Raytheon (Canada)
ResMed (Australia)
Samsung Global Strategist Group
 (South Korea)
Samsung Semiconductor (USA)
Sandia National Laboratories (USA)
San Ildefonso Pueblo Nation (USA)
SBC Communications (Switzerland,
 USA)
Smithkline Beecham (USA)
Society for Intercultural Education,
 Training and Research
 (The Netherlands)
Solution Bank (Japan)
Square D (USA)
Sun Microsystems (USA)
Texaco (USA)
UM Engineering (Belgium)
United Nations High Commission for
 Refugees (Switzerland)
US Peace Corps (USA)
US West (USA)
Valvoline (USA)
Warner Lambert (France, UK, USA)
Wayne-Dresser (USA)
Weyerhaeuser (Hong Kong, USA)

**(Locations of individual research participants in parenthesis)

provocative insights on the concept of global leadership. This rich, deep data provided insights for the development of the initial hypotheses that guided the subsequent research efforts.

2. FOCUS/DIALOGUE GROUPS

Four types of focus groups were designed and implemented to build upon the emerging knowledge. The first focus groups were the four *CEO of the Future Dinner Series*. Dinners were held in New York, San Francisco, London, Melbourne, and Sydney with a total of 28 CEOs participating. The dinner dialogues were led by the team's co sponsors, managing partner Cathy Greenberg, partner Alastair Robertson, and the three alliance partners: Warren Bennis, Marshall Goldsmith, and John O'Neil.

The second type of focus group was the *Global Leader of the Future Network Forum*. With assistance from alliance partners, current and future global leaders from many global firms were identified. They were invited to participate in a daylong focus group/dialogue forum preceded by a dinner the evening before. These forums were designed to elicit additional insights and to validate initial hypotheses about global leadership. The forums were held in Barcelona; Melbourne; Sydney; New York; San Francisco; Prague, Czech Republic; and Budapest, Hungary (emerging markets) where a total of 75 participants attended. (See Figure A–1.) Forum participants subsequently completed the Global Leader of the Future Survey Questionnaire. (To review the survey, please see Appendix C.)

A third type of focus group followed the same general format as the *Global Leader of the Future Network Forum*. These forums differed in that they were held in conjunction with other conferences, including the World Economic Forum, the Pacific Coast Gas Association Roundtable, the Health Care Industry Conference, Linkage, the Group of 200, and the International Utilities Executives Annual Conference. These groups were led by Cathy Greenberg, Accenture managing partner for the Leadership Theme Team, Institute for Strategic Change. Either the Global Leader of the Future Questionnaire was distributed to these focus group participants or findings were discussed and hypotheses tested.

The fourth type of focus group, a short version of the *Global Leader of the Future Network Forum*, was utilized for the internal Accenture community and led by Cathy Greenberg. A special *Analyst and Consultant Mini Forum* was held with 12 participants. Similar forums were also held at three Women's Mentoring Programs with approximately 120 men and women. These participants also received the Global Leader of the Future Survey Questionnaire.

3. INTERVIEWS

This part of the research phase, which was conducted by Maya Hu-Chan and Jeremy Solomons, began in August 1998 when senior HRD officers at over 200 global organizations were personally asked to participate in the research. A standard set of interview questions and a template for recording data were developed (see Appendix B).

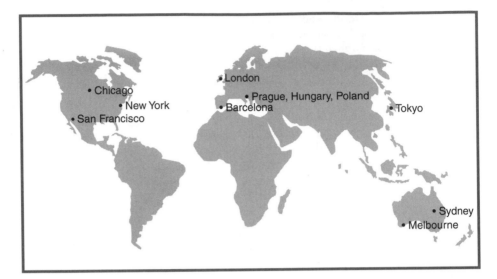

Figure A.1
Locations of research events.

Participants came from six distinct geographic regions—Africa, Asia, Australasia, Europe, North America, and South America—and resided in five of these regions. Seventy-four percent of the participants were male, 26 percent were female.

By extrapolating valid data, over three-fifths of the 202 high-potential leaders who participated in these interviews, were under age 40, and over a third of those were in their 20s.

The participants worked at over 60 for-profit, governmental, multilateral, and non-profit organizations around the world. The most frequently represented industries were telecommunications and media, pharmaceuticals, and high-tech.

Once approval was given, the participants were invited to nominate three (to five) high-potential leaders, who would have ideally been in their 20s, 30s, and 40s respectively. Each nominee was then contacted individually about participating in a structured telephone interview for 20 to 40 minutes and filling out an anonymous 82-question survey.

A good way to begin thinking about the future is by reflecting on the past and present, learning from mistakes, and collecting best practices. With this in mind, research participants were asked to think about real-life examples of effective global leadership from their own perspective and experience.

Some interviewees started by naming people whom they deemed to be effective global leaders. In joint first place were Bill Gates of Microsoft and Mahatma Gandhi of India. Close behind were Winston Churchill of the United Kingdom and Ronald Reagan of the United States.

Some leaders, such as the Pope and Kofi Annan of the United Nations, were mentioned largely because of the global mandates of their jobs. Others, such as Gates and

Churchill, were cited because of the global impact of their work. A third group, topped by Gandhi and Nelson Mandela of South Africa, were named because of the way they led/lead by example through their innate and learned qualities.

Other interviewees began by citing both positive and negative examples of such key elements of effective global leadership as collaborative leadership and managing thought and style differences.

The negative examples were particularly enlightening. They included giving up too soon; hidden, personal agendas; ignoring cultural differences; not taking time to think things through and do things properly; not having clear objectives; and not understanding people.

What emerged was a surprisingly unified list of the key skills and characteristics that effective global leaders—whether high-profile politicians or unsung country managers—have displayed up until now. It is from this list that the final Global Leader of the Future Inventory with its 15 characteristics and 72 items was developed.

QUANTITATIVE SURVEY QUESTIONNAIRE

A questionnaire was developed with leadership from Marshall Goldsmith in combination with Cathy Greenberg and Alastair Robertson to measure perceptions of the criticality and importance of 14 global leadership dimensions for the past, present, and future. Additionally, Cathy Greenberg and John O'Neil combined efforts to interview executives and government officials, including individuals from top companies in Australia and New Zealand, at the World Economic Forum Davos Connection over a two-year period. These participants also received the Global Leader of the Future Survey questionnaire. The 14 dimensions were:

1. Demonstrating Integrity
2. Encouraging Constructive Dialogue
3. Creating a Shared Vision
4. Developing People
5. Building Partnerships
6. Sharing Leadership
7. Empowering People
8. Thinking Globally
9. Appreciating Diversity
10. Developing Technological Savvy
11. Ensuring Customer Satisfaction
12. Maintaining a Competitive Advantage

13. Achieving Personal Mastery

14. Anticipating Opportunities

Eighty-two items were developed to measure the 14 dimensions. (To review the survey, see Appendix C.) It is from this questionnaire that the Global Leader of the Future Inventory, with its added 15th dimension of "Leading Change" and its 72 items was developed.

This questionnaire was piloted and validated by Marshall Goldsmith before application with the various focus group participants. After it was determined that the questionnaire met the standards for quantitative research, it was distributed to more than 200 participants in the aforementioned forums and focus groups. Seventy-three usable questionnaires representing five global regions (Australia, Pacific Rim, North America, Europe, and Emerging Markets) were returned. The respondents encompassed a variety of industries and managerial levels. (Please see Appendix D for a more detailed description of the statistical analysis for the quantitative questionnaire.)

PROFILE OF THE GLOBAL LEADER OF THE FUTURE

The questions currently on the minds of all CEOs and executives are the following:

- What will effective leaders be like in the future?
- What competencies must a leader have to be successful in the changing global marketplace of the future? and
- What is the profile of the Global Leader of the Future?

While it is difficult to provide a complete answer to these questions, analysis of the research data suggests some initial conclusions. Results from the quantitative analysis of the Global Leader of the Future survey questionnaire data were validated by the qualitative data collected from thought leader panels, focus groups, interviews, and observations. Findings show profiles and trends for the global leader of the past, present, and future. These profiles and trends were relatively consistent across global regions.

This section examines the Global Leader profiles, identifies differences for the three time periods, and presents implications for leadership development.

GLOBAL LEADER OF THE FUTURE PROFILE TRENDS

While distinct profiles emerged for each of the time periods, it is the differences between the profiles that are most interesting. Results show a clear trend for all 14 dimensions of global leadership to increase significantly in importance over time.

Participants were able to identify certain competencies as being more important than others for past and present leaders. However, they responded that all of the leadership dimensions are highly critical to the success of future leaders.

Figure A–2 provides the profile of the global leader for the past, present, and future time periods. The level of importance for each dimension by time period is displayed; the higher the importance rating, the more critical the dimension.

Each of the 14 dimensions is shown to be increasing in importance with time. The fourteen leadership dimensions are all seen as extremely important for the Global Leader of the Future. The questionnaire responses indicate that future leaders must excel at all 14 dimensions to be successful in the future global marketplace—at the very least, they must be able to draw upon the collective expertise for all 14 dimensions. This is in agreement with the information from the interviews and focus groups—those participants indicated that either "a Super Leader, who excels in all dimensions or a leadership team that can gather expertise from multiple leaders" will lead the future global organization. Most participants believe that the challenges facing future leaders will be too great for any one individual.

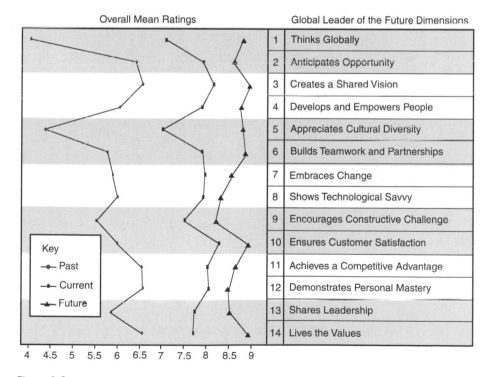

Figure A.2
Global Leadership profiles by time period.

DIFFERENCES BY TIME PERIOD

All leadership dimensions will be critical for future leaders. However, by examining the differences in ratings across both time periods (future vs. past, future vs. present), large differences were found for the following dimensions:

- Thinks Globally
- Develops and Empowers People
- Appreciates Cultural Diversity
- Builds Teamwork and Partnerships

Given the higher future and lower past importance for these dimensions, current and future leaders may need to focus significant development efforts on them.

For the future, large differences between the future and past time periods were also found for:

- Embraces Change
- Shows Technological Savvy
- Encourages Constructive Challenge
- Ensures Customer Satisfaction
- Shares Leadership

The average ratings for each dimension and the largest differences between the future and past profiles, and between the future and present profiles, are indicated in Table A–3.

ITEM ANALYSIS BY TIME

When the 82 specific items that make up the 14 leadership dimensions were analyzed, some commonalities across time periods emerged. The top items (determined by highest mean rating) were identified and compared across time period to identify any significant trends.

Certain items were critical for past, present, and future time periods:

- Creates and communicates a clear organization vision
- Clearly identifies priorities; focuses on a vital few

Several items were common for both present and future:

- Views business from the ultimate customer perspective

- Unites organization into an effective team
- Genuinely listens to others

Items unique to the future top list included the following:

- Builds effective alliances with other organizations
- Makes decisions that reflect global considerations
- Builds effective partnerships across the company
- Consistently treats people with respect and dignity

These results are validated by the qualitative research and are represented by the increased importance of certain dimensions for the global leader of the future: Thinks Globally, Appreciates Cultural Diversity, and Encourages Constructive Challenge.

The top items for each time period are displayed in Table A–3.

TABLE A.3 Top 10 Items by Time Period (1–Important, 10–Extremely Important)

ITEMS	FUTURE	PRESENT	PAST
Builds effective alliances with other organizations	9.19		
Genuinely listens to others	9.13	8.32	
Creates and communicates a clear organization vision	9.1	8.49	7
Is a role model for living the organization's values	9.05		6.89
Unites organization into an effective team	9.03	8.33	
Makes decisions that reflect global considerations	9.01		
Views business from the ultimate customer perspective	8.97	8.42	
Clearly identifies priorities; focuses on a vital few	8.97	8.29	6.89
Builds effective partnerships across the company	8.97		
Consistently treats people with respect and dignity	8.97		
Demonstrates self confidence as a leader		8.97	8.09
Strives to achieve personal excellence		8.42	7.54
Achieves results for long-term shareholder value		8.31	6.72
Inspires people to commit to achieving the vision		8.28	
Ensures customer commitments are met		8.25	
Expects the highest standards of performance			6.94
Demonstrates honest, ethical behavior always			6.87
Develops an effective strategy to achieve the vision			6.8
Inspires others to achieve the highest levels of quality			6.8

B

THE GLOBAL LEADER OF THE FUTURE INTERVIEW QUESTIONS

W e suggest that you use these interview questions as an exercise for yourself and those with whom you work. Ask yourself the questions outlined below. Distribute these questions to your teams, peers, employees, coworkers, and managers. Use these questions to promote discussions of leadership and the qualities of leaders that will lead your organization to success.

PERSONAL LEADERSHIP SKILLS

Demonstrating integrity has been and continues in the future to be one of the most highly rated behaviors for leaders. How does one stand out as a role model for living his or her organization's values? What examples of honest, ethical behavior can you provide to show the usefulness of acting in this fashion?

Genuinely listens to others is an almost timeless behavior of a leader. It is a key ingredient of "encouraging constructive dialogue." What can you tell us about your struggles and successes as a listener?

Confidence as a leader continues to be considered an important characteristic of the next generation leader. It is considered a critical aspect of "achieving personal mastery." What examples might you give us regarding your challenges and how confidence has played a part in your eventual success?

Appreciating diversity is an increasingly important attribute for tomorrow's leaders. In fact, the behavior "effectively motivates people from different cultures and backgrounds" was the second highest gainer in importance of the 82 behaviors rated by next-generation leaders. And, the third highest gainer in importance was "appreciates the value of diversity (avoids discrimination). What follows is a two-part question: (1) What type of diversity is needed in tomorrow's organizations? and (2) How do we demonstrate that we value this diversity?

Consistently treating people with respect and dignity is the second highest rated behavior for the next five years. What advice can you give a leader regarding the process of respect and dignity? What should you not do, and what should you do?

The pace of change seems relentless. How does one best challenge the system when change is needed? How does one effectively translate creative ideas into business results?

TEAM LEADERSHIP SKILLS

Creating a shared vision ties for third place in importance of all leadership behaviors. Can you provide some insight into both the word "vision" and the word "shared?" Vision has often been denigrated as being too ethereal and soft. At the day-to-day level, a useful vision should help people focus on the "vital few," or in other words, to prioritize. How have you seen vision help in the day-to-day running of a business?

One of the top ten behaviors is in the category of building partnerships. This behavior is, "unites his or her organization into an effective team." Assuming a shared vision has been achieved, what else is required for an effective team, and how does leadership shape these requirements?

"Building effective partnerships across the company" and "building effective alliances with other organizations" are the fourth and fifth highest gaining behaviors for the future as seen by next generation leaders. What insight can you provide regarding how to be effective in partnerships and alliances?

Sharing leadership is tricky business. What positive and negative examples do you have with regards to the sharing of leadership? Consider this with business partners and within the organization. From a personal note, where have you utilized people who have strengths that you do not possess?

Developing and empowering people have long been key roles of leadership. In order to leverage the leadership talent in the organization, leaders need to be both developed and afforded the opportunity to lead. What are your thoughts on the right way to develop people? What are your thoughts on the right way to empower those you are developing?

STRATEGIC LEADERSHIP SKILLS

"Understanding the impact of globalization on her or his business" was the number one rated behavior by the next-generation leaders and received the highest overall gain in importance of any of the 82 behaviors. Obviously, this is an immensely important behavior. How do you develop this understanding in the future?

Given that a leader has a workable understanding of the global landscape, what advice can you give regarding anticipating opportunities? How does one extricate oneself out of the present objectives long enough to see future opportunities?

The younger the next-generation leaders were, the more they felt developing technological savvy was important to future success. What are your thoughts on acquiring the technological knowledge needed to affect strategy decisions? How does one manage the use of technology in the organization?

As many leaders are part of organizations that compete, how do you ensure your organization maintains a competitive advantage?

It is only fitting to end with arguably the most important skill set of a leader, the skills that relate to ensuring customer satisfaction. This skill area had the most behaviors rated in the top dozen in terms of importance. These behaviors were "regularly solicits input from customers" (this behavior also was in the top ten in terms of increased importance for the future); "ensures that the organization consistently meets commitments to customers"; and "consistently treats customer satisfaction as a top priority." Additionally, "views business processes from the ultimate customer perspective" made the top dozen in terms of increasing importance for the future.

C

THE GLOBAL LEADER OF THE FUTURE SURVEY

INSTRUCTIONS FOR COMPLETING THE INVENTORY

The Global Leader of the Future Inventory (see Table C–1) has been developed based on research involving future leaders from over 120 of the world's leading organizations. Use this feedback tool to determine which areas of leadership development you will focus on as you read this book. This tool can also be used to evaluate the leadership capabilities of your managers, peers, and employees.

As you consider the listed behaviors, please circle the response that best describes how satisfied you are with your performance or the performance of the person whom you are evaluating. The more honest you are in your responses, the more useful the feedback will be.

While some items may appear to be similar, treat each item separately. No two items are the same. Although you may not have complete information concerning each item, try to provide a rating based on the information you have. If you feel unable to answer a question, use the "No Information" category. Please do not use the "Neither Satisfied nor Dissatisfied" response if you feel unable to respond to an item.

After responding to the questions, turn to the back page of the Inventory. This "Written Comments" section is for you to provide information about areas where you (or the individual you are evaluating) are especially effective and where you might be more effective. Finally, please supply any additional comments, particularly regarding items that may not have been covered in the questionnaire portion.

The Forum Corporation, a pioneer in the use of 360-degree feedback, is pleased to offer the Global Leader of the Future Inventory for use within your company. If you are interested in using the survey, on its own or as part of a larger leadership development program, visit our Web site *(http://www.Forum.com)* or call one of the following Forum offices for assistance:

- In the United States, Canada, and South America: 1-800-FORUM11 (367-8611)
- In Europe and the Middle East: +44-0-20-7010-2600
- In Asia and the Far East: 852-2810-7071

Forum is a global leader in workplace learning with 700 professionals worldwide. As the corporate learning arm of Pearson plc, Forum partners with the world's leading companies to help them implement strategy, solve problems, and perform better. Forum consultants are recognized experts in leadership development, branding the customer experience, building world-class sales teams, and creating blended learning solutions. Whether your business issue is driving growth and profitability, reducing costs, minimizing employee turnover, developing leadership talent, or improving customer loyalty and retention, Forum aligns your people to your business strategy to deliver tangible business results. Forum's clients are predominately FTSE 250 and Fortune 1000 companies.

GLOBAL LEADER OF THE FUTURE INVENTORY: 360-DEGREE FEEDBACK ASSESSMENT

Instructions: As you complete this questionnaire, please note that each item is preceded by the question, *How satisfied are you with the way this person...?* Your response choices are 1: Highly Dissatisfied, 2: Dissatisfied, 3: Neither Satisfied nor Dissatisfied, 4: Satisfied, 5: Highly Satisfied, or NI: No Information. Please indicate your response by circling your choice to the right of each item.

TABLE C.1 Global Leadership Inventory.

Consider your own (or this person's) effectiveness in the following areas.
How satisfied are you with the way you (or they)…

	Highly Dissatisfied	Dissatisfied	Neither Satisfied nor Dissatisfied	Satisfied	Highly Satisfied	No Information
Thinking Globally						
1. Recognizes the impact of globalization on our business	1	2	3	4	5	N
2. Demonstrates the adaptability required to succeed in a global environment	1	2	3	4	5	N
3. Strives to gain the variety of experiences needed to conduct global business	1	2	3	4	5	N
4. Makes decisions that incorporate global considerations	1	2	3	4	5	N
5. Helps others understand the impact of globalization	1	2	3	4	5	N
Appreciating Diversity						
6. Embraces the value of diversity in people (including culture, race, sex or age)	1	2	3	4	5	N
7. Effectively motivates people from different cultures or backgrounds	1	2	3	4	5	N
8. Recognizes the value of diverse views and opinions	1	2	3	4	5	N
9. Helps others appreciate the value of diversity	1	2	3	4	5	N
10. Actively expands her/his knowledge of other cultures (through interactions, language study, travel, etc.)	1	2	3	4	5	N

Consider your own (or this person's) effectiveness in the following areas.
How satisfied are you with the way you (or they)...

	Highly Dissatisfied	Dissatisfied	Neither Satisfied nor Dissatisfied	Satisfied	Highly Satisfied	No Information
Developing Technological Savvy						
11. Strives to acquire the technological knowledge needed to succeed in tomorrow's world	1	2	3	4	5	N
12. Successfully recruits people with needed technological expertise	1	2	3	4	5	N
13. Effectively manages the use of technology to increase productivity	1	2	3	4	5	N
Building Partnerships						
14. Treats co-workers as partners, not competitors	1	2	3	4	5	N
15. Unites his/her organization into an effective team	1	2	3	4	5	N
16. Builds effective partnerships across the company	1	2	3	4	5	N
17. Discourages destructive comments about other people or groups	1	2	3	4	5	N
18. Builds effective alliances with other organizations	1	2	3	4	5	N
19. Creates a network of relationship that help to get things done	1	2	3	4	5	N
Sharing Leadership						
20. Willingly shares leadership with business partners	1	2	3	4	5	N
21. Defers to others when they have more expertise	1	2	3	4	5	N
22. Strives to arrive at an outcome with others (as opposed to *for* others)	1	2	3	4	5	N
23. Creates an environment where people focus on the larger good (avoids sub-optimization or "turfism")	1	2	3	4	5	N

Consider your own (or this person's) effectiveness in the following areas.
How satisfied are you with the way you (or they)...

	Highly Dissatisfied	Dissatisfied	Neither Satisfied nor Dissatisfied	Satisfied	Highly Satisfied	No Information

Creating a Shared Vision

24. Creates and communicates a clear vision for our organization — 1 2 3 4 5 N

25. Effectively involves people in decision-making — 1 2 3 4 5 N

26. Inspires people to commit to achieving the vision — 1 2 3 4 5 N

27. Develops an effective strategy to achieve the vision — 1 2 3 4 5 N

28. Clearly identifies priorities — 1 2 3 4 5 N

Developing People

29. Consistently treats people with respect and dignity — 1 2 3 4 5 N

30. Asks people what they need to do their work better — 1 2 3 4 5 N

31. Ensures that people receive the training they need to succeed — 1 2 3 4 5 N

32. Provides effective coaching — 1 2 3 4 5 N

33. Provides developmental feedback in a timely manner — 1 2 3 4 5 N

34. Provides effective recognition for others' achievements — 1 2 3 4 5 N

Empowering People

35. Builds people's confidence — 1 2 3 4 5 N

36. Takes risks in letting others make decisions — 1 2 3 4 5 N

37. Gives people the freedom they need to do their job well — 1 2 3 4 5 N

38. Trusts people enough to let go (avoids micro-management) — 1 2 3 4 5 N

Consider your own (or this person's) effectiveness in the following areas. *How satisfied are you with the way you (or they)...*

	Highly Dissatisfied	Dissatisfied	Neither Satisfied nor Dissatisfied	Satisfied	Highly Satisfied	No Information
Achieving Personal Mastery						
39. Deeply understands her/his own strengths and weaknesses	1	2	3	4	5	N
40. Invests in ongoing personal development	1	2	3	4	5	N
41. Involves people who have strengths that he/she does not possess	1	2	3	4	5	N
42. Demonstrates effective emotional responses in a variety of situations	1	2	3	4	5	N
43. Demonstrates self-confidence as a leader	1	2	3	4	5	N
Encouraging Constructive Dialogue						
44. Asks people what he/she can do to improve	1	2	3	4	5	N
45. Genuinely listens to others	1	2	3	4	5	N
46. Accepts constructive feedback in a positive manner (avoids defensiveness)	1	2	3	4	5	N
47. Strives to understand the *other person's* frame of reference	1	2	3	4	5	N
48. Encourages people to challenge the status quo	1	2	3	4	5	N
Demonstrates Integrity						
49. Demonstrates honest, ethical behavior in all interactions	1	2	3	4	5	N
50. Ensures that the highest standards for ethical behavior are practiced throughout the organization	1	2	3	4	5	N
51. Avoids political or self-serving behavior	1	2	3	4	5	N
52. Courageously "stands up" for what she/he believes in	1	2	3	4	5	N
53. Is a role model for living our organization's values (leads by example)	1	2	3	4	5	N

Consider your own (or this person's) effectiveness in the following areas.
How satisfied are you with the way you (or they)...

	Highly Dissastisfied	Dissatisfied	Neither Satisfied nor Dissatisfied	Satisfied	Highly Satisfied	No Information
Leading Change						
54. Sees change as an opportunity, not a problem	1	2	3	4	5	N
55. Challenges the system when change is needed	1	2	3	4	5	N
56. Thrives in ambiguous situations (demonstrates flexibility when needed)	1	2	3	4	5	N
57. Encourages creativity and innovation in others	1	2	3	4	5	N
58. Effectively translates creative ideas into business results	1	2	3	4	5	N
Anticipating Opportunities						
59. Invests in learning about future trends	1	2	3	4	5	N
60. Effectively anticipates future opportunities	1	2	3	4	5	N
61. Inspires people to focus on future opportunities (not just present objectives)	1	2	3	4	5	N
62. Develops ideas to meet the needs of the new environment	1	2	3	4	5	N
Ensuring Customer Satisfaction						
63. Inspires people to achieve high levels of customer satisfaction	1	2	3	4	5	N
64. Views business processes from the ultimate customer perspective (has an "end to end" perspective.	1	2	3	4	5	N
65. Regularly solicits input from customers	1	2	3	4	5	N
66. Consistently delivers on commitments to customers	1	2	3	4	5	N
67. Understands the competitive options available to her/his customers						

Consider your own (or this person's) effectiveness in the following areas.
How satisfied are you with the way you (or they)...

	Highly Dissatisfied	Dissatisfied	Neither Satisfied nor Dissatisfied	Satisfied	Highly Satisfied	No Information
Maintaining a Competitive Advantage						
68. Communicates a positive, "can do" sense of urgency toward getting the job done	1	2	3	4	5	N
69. Holds people accountable for their results	1	2	3	4	5	N
70. Successfully eliminates waste and unneeded cost	1	2	3	4	5	N
71. Provides products/services that help our company have a clear competitive advantage	1	2	3	4	5	N
72. Achieves results that lead to long-term shareholder value	1	2	3	4	5	N

Written Comments

What are your strengths? Or if you are evaluating someone, what does this person do that you particularly appreciate? (Please list two or three *specific* items.)

_____

_____

_____

_____

What *specifically* might you do to be more effective? Or if evaluating someone, what suggestions would you have for this person on how she or he could become even more effective? (Please list two or three *specific* items.)

_____

_____

_____

_____

Additional comments:

_____

_____

_____

D

STATISTICAL METHODS

The pilot questionnaires were administered to 100 participants of the focus/dialogue groups. Fifty usable questionnaires were reviewed for clarity, consistency, and face validity. The questionnaire was deemed suitable for further use.

For the research, two questionnaires were used for data collection. The first, an 82-item scale, asked participants to rate the criticality of each item for global leadership in the past, present, and future with a ten-point scale. The second, a 14-item scale, asked participants to force-rank each of the 14 dimensions for criticality for global leadership in the past, present, and future. The 14-item questionnaire was used as a general validity check, but was not used in data analysis due to the general statistical problems with ranked scales.

The questionnaire was distributed to more than 200 participants of Global Leader of the Future Network Forums and conference focus groups. Profile data were analyzed using multiple methods; cases were divided into five geographical regions (Asia, Australia, Europe, North America, and South America); three time periods (past, present, and future); gender; and five age groups for comparison. Methods included basic statistical analyses, reliability analyses, two-tailed T-tests, factor analyses with Varimax rotation and Kaiser normalization, and multiple analyses of variance. The Statistical Package for the Social Sciences (SPSS) was used to analyze the data.

After missing data analyses were conducted, 73 questionnaires were used for analysis. The respondent profile includes participants from Asia, Australia, Europe, North America, and South America. The profile also represents participants from different organizational levels and stages of leadership (executive, middle, potential), and from multiple industries and organization configurations.

Basic statistical analyses produced expected results with no major abnormalities of distributions. Reliability for dimensions ranged from a minimum of .7553 and a maximum of .9736, indicating that items composing a dimension were highly correlated.

SUMMARY

The first two phases of knowledge development—assess and generate—indicated that there are 14 global leadership dimensions that are critical for the future. Quantitative and qualitative data gathered from thought leaders, CEOs, and current and future global leaders indicated consensus for the findings.

BIBLIOGRAPHY

BOOKS

Allen, Thomas, and Michael S. Scott Morton. *Information Technology and the Corporation of the 1990s*. New York: Oxford University Press, 1994.

Badaracco, Jr., Joseph L. *Defining Moments*. Boston: Harvard Business School Press, 1997.

Bennis, Warren, and Joan Goldsmith. *Learning to Lead*. Reading: Addison Wesley, 1997.

Bennis, Warren. *On Becoming a Leader*. Reading: Addison Wesley, 1994.

Bennis, Warren. *Organizing Genius: The Secrets of Creative Collaboration*. Reading: Addison Wesley, 1997.

Bennis, Warren, and Robert J. Thomas. *Geeks and Geezers*. Boston: Harvard Business School Press, 2002.

Benton, D. A. *How to Think Like a CEO—The 22 Vital Traits You Need to be the Person at the Top*. New York: Warner Books, 1996.

Bower, Marvin. *The Will to Lead*. Boston: Harvard Business School Press, 1997.

Bradford, David L., and Allan R. Cohen. *Power Up: Transforming Organizations Through Shared Leadership*.

Brake, Terence. *The Global Leader: Critical Factors for Creating the World Class Organization*. Chicago: Irwin Professional Publishing, 1997.

Brooking, Annie. *Intellectual Capital*. Boston: International Thomason Business Press, 1996.

Brown, John Seely. *Seeing Differently: Insights on Innovation*. Boston: Harvard Business School, 1998.

Carr, Clay. *Choice, Chance, & Organizational Change: Practical Insights: Evolution for Business Leaders and Thinkers*. New York: AMACOM, 1996.

Carr-Ruffino, Norma. *Managing Diversity*. San Francisco: Thomson Executive Press, 1996.

Chang, Richard Y. *Building a Dynamic Team: A Practical Guide to Maximizing Team Performance*.

Chrislip, David D., and Carl E. Larson. *Collaborative Leadership*. San Francisco: Jossey-Bass Publishers, 1994.

Christensen, Clayton M. *The Innovator's Dilemma*. Boston: Harvard Business School Press, 1997.

Conger, Jay A. *The Charismatic Leader*. San Francisco: Jossey-Bass Publishers, 1989.

Dauphinais, G. William. *Straight from the CEO: The World's Top Business Leaders Reveal Ideas that Every Manager Can Use*. Columbus, OH: Fireside, 1999.

Devanna, Mary Anne, and Noel M. Tichy. *The Transformational Leader: The Key to Global Competitiveness*. NY: John Wiley and Sons, 1997.

Drath, Wilfred H., and Charles S. Pahs. *Making Common Sense: Leadership as Meaning-Making in a Community of Practice*. Greensboro: Center for Creative Leadership, 1994.

Dunnigan, James, and Daniel Masterson. *The Way of the Warrior*. New York: St. Martin's Press, 1997.

Early, P. Christopher, and Miriam Erez. *The Transplanted Executive*. New York: Oxford University Press, 1997.

Ernst, David, and Joel Bleeke. *Collaborating to Compete: Using Strategic Alliances And Acquisitions in the Global Marketplace*. NY: John Wiley and Sons, 1993.

Edvinnson, Leif, and Michael Malone. *Intellectual Capital*. New York: HarperCollins, 1997.

Feldman, Mark L and Michael Frederick Spratt. *Five Frogs on a Log: A CEO's Field Guide to Accelerating the Transitions in Mergers, Acquisitions, & Gut-Wrenching Change*. NY: HarperBusiness, 1999.

Finzel, Hans. *Top Ten Mistakes Leaders Make*. Elgin, IL: David C. Cook Publishing Company, 2000.

Fisher, Kimball, and Duncan Fisher Mareen. *The Distributed Mind*. New York: AMACOM, 1998.

Forum Corporation. *Leadership—A Forum Issues Special Report*. Boston: Forum Corp., 1990.

Gardner, John W. *On Leadership*. New York: Free Press, 1990.

Gibson, Rowan. *Rethinking the Future*. London: Nicholas Brealey Publishing, 1997.

Gilderson, Alan J. *Conflicts of Leadership: Good for People or Good for Business?* New York: John Wiley and Sons, 1996.

Gouillart, Francis J., and James N. Kelly. *Transforming the Organization*. New York: McGraw-Hill, 1995.

Handy, Charles. *Beyond Certainty*. Boston: Harvard Business School Press, 1996.

Heifetz, Ronald. *Leadership Without Easy Answers*. Cambridge: Belknap Press/Harvard University Press, 1994.

Hendricks, Gay, and Kate Ludeman. *The Corporate Mystic*. New York: Bantam Books, 1996.

Hesselbein, Frances, Marshall Goldsmith, and Richard Beckhard. *The Leader of the Future*. San Francisco: Jossey-Bass Publishers, 1996.

Hesselbein, Frances, Marshall Goldsmith, and Richard Beckhard. *The Organization of the Future*. San Francisco: Jossey-Bass Publishers, 1997.

Jaffe, Azriela. *Let's Go Into Business Together: Eight Secrets to Successful Business Partnering*. Franklin Lakes, NJ: Career Press, 2001.

Jaworski, Joseph. *Synchronicity: The Inner Path of Leadership*. San Francisco: Berrett Koehler, 1996.

Johansen, Robert, and Rob Swigert. *Upsizing the Individual in the Downsized Organization*. Reading: Addison-Wesley, 1994.

Kaplan, Robert S., and David P. Norton. *The Balanced Scorecard*. Boston: Harvard Business School Press, 1996.

Katzenbach, Jon R. *Teams at the Top: Unleashing the Potential of Both Teams and Individual Leaders*. Boston: Harvard Business School, 1998.

Katzenbach, Jon R., and Douglas K. Smith. *The Wisdom of Teams: Creating the High Performance Organization*. New York: McKinsey & Company, 1993.

Ket de Vries, Manfred F. R. *Life and Death in the Executive Fast Lane*. San Francisco: Jossey-Bass Publications, 1993.

Kostner, Jaclyn. *Virtual Leadership*. New York: Warner Books, 1994.

Kotter, John, and James L. Heskett. *Corporate Culture and Performance*. New York: Free Press, 1992.

Kotter, John. *Leading Change*. Boston: Harvard Business School Press, 1996.

Larson, Carl E., and Frank M. J. LaFasto. *TeamWork*. Newbury Park: Sage Publications, 1989.

Lazega, Emmanuel. *The Micropolitics of Knowledge: Communication and Indirect Control in Workgroups*. New York: Aldine de Gruyter, 1992.

Lipnack, Jessica, and Jeffrey Stamps. *Virtual Teams*. New York: John Wiley and Sons, 1997.

McCall, Morgan W. *High Flyers*. Boston: Harvard Business School Press, 1998.

McLean, J. W., and William Wietzel. *Leadership—Magic, Myth, or Method?* New York: American Management Association, 1990.

Meirelles, Henrique. "Bank Boston, Managing for Value." Bank Boston 1996 Annual Report.

Meyer, Christopher. "Managing the Volunteer Workforce." Excerpted from his book *What Makes Workers Tick*, in *Inc. Magazine*, December 1997.

Monks, Robert A. G., and Nell Minow. *Corporate Governance*. Cambridge: Blackwell Publishers, 1995.

Monks, Robert A. G., and Nell Minow. *Watching the Watchers*. Cambridge: Blackwell Publishers, 1996.

Morton, Michael S. *The Corporation of the 1990s*. New York: Oxford University Press, 1991.

O'Hara-Devereaux, Mary, and Robert Johansen. *Global Work*. San Francisco: Jossey-Bass Publishers, 1994.

O'Neil, John R. *The Paradox of Success.* New York: Tarcher Putnam, 1994.

Pinchot, Gifford, and Elizabeth Pinchot. *The End of Bureaucracy & The Rise of the Intelligent Organization.* San Francisco: Berrett Koehler, 1993.

Rau, John. *Secrets from the Search Firm Files.* New York: McGraw Hill, 1997.

Robbins, Harvey, and Michael Finley. *Why Teams Don't Work: What Went Wrong and How To Make It Right.* Princeton: Peterson's/Pacesetter, 1995.

Rodrik, Dani. *Has Globalization Gone too Far?* Washington, DC: Institute for International Economics, 1997.

Rosen, Robert H., and Paul B. Brown. *Leading People.* New York: Penguin Books, 1996.

Saratoga Institute. *Leadership Development.* New York: American Management Association, 1998.

Scott Morton, Michael S. *The Corporation of the 1990s.* New York: Oxford University Press, 1991.

Sims, Henry P., Jr., and Charles C. Manz. *Company of Heroes.* New York: John Wiley & Sons, 1996.

Schwartz, Andrew E. *Delegating Authority.* Haupaugge, NY: Barrons Educational Series, 1992.

Tapscott, Don. *Growing up Digital.* New York: McGraw Hill, 1998

Thomas, Gordon. *Leaders Effectiveness Training: The No-Lose Way to Release the Productive Potential of People.* NY: Penguin Putnam Inc./Perigee, 2001.

Vilardi, R. Dante. *Innovation-Based Competition: From Conventional Growth to "Opportunity Space."* Innovation Line Institute, 1998.

Weiners, Brad, and David Pescovitz. *Reality Check.* San Francisco: Hard Wired, 1996.

Wellins, Richard S., William C. Byham, and Jeanne M. Wilson . *Empowered Teams.* San Francisco: Jossey-Bass, 1991.

Yukl, Gary. *Leadership in Organizations.* Englewood Cliffs: Prentice Hall, 1994.

Zaleznick, Abraham. *Human Dilemmas of Leadership.* New York: Harper and Row 1966.

JOURNALS AND MAGAZINES

Bartlett, Christopher A., and Sumantra Ghoshal. "What Is a Global Manager?" *Harvard Business Review,* September–October 1992.

Case, John. "A Company of Businesspeople." *Inc. Magazine,* April, 1993.

Charan, Ram. "Two on Top." *Fortune,* May 25, 1998.

Davenport, Thomas. "Putting the Enterprise into the Enterprise System." *Harvard Business Review,* July–August 1998.

"500 Top Private Companies." *Forbes,* December 1, 1997, pp. 180–262.

"Global Leaders for Tomorrow." *World Link,* February 1997, pp. 114–133.

Goldberg, Beverly. "A New Type of Mentoring Takes Root in U.S. Companies." *Bridge News,* April 20, 1998.

Goldsmith, M. "Retaining High-Impact Performers." *Leader to Leader,* Premier Issue, 1996.

Grove, Andrew S. "A High-Tech CEO Updates His Views on Managing and Careers." *Fortune,* September 18, 1995.

Hamm, Steve. "Overcoming the Generation Gap." *PC Week,* March 18, 1996, p. A1(2)

Hill, Linda, and Suzy Wetlaufer. "Leadership When There is No One to Ask: An Interview with ENI's Franco Bernabe." *Harvard Business Review,* July–August 1998.

Kirkpatrick, David. "Gates Wants All Your Business—And He's Starting to Get It." *Fortune,* May 26, 1997, pp. 58–68.

Koselka, Rita, and Carrie Shook. "Born to Rebel? Or Born to Conserve?" *Forbes,* March 10, 1997, pp. 146–153.

Kotter, John P. "Leading Change: Why Transformation Efforts Fail." *Harvard Business Review,* March–April 1995.

Kruger, Pamela, and Katharine Mieszkowski. "Stop the Fight." *Fast Company,* September 1998.

Levinson, Harry. "Criteria for Choosing Chief Executives." *Harvard Business Review,* July–August 1980.

Lyons, Nancy J. "Managing the Volunteer Workforce." *Inc. Magazine,* December 1997.

Mieszkowski, Katharine. "Report From the Future: Opposites Attract." *Fast Company,* December–January 1998.

McCall, Morgan W., Jr. "Executive Development as a Business Strategy." *The Journal of Business Strategy,* Vol. 13, No. 1. January/February 1992.

Monroe, Ann. "Dennis Dammerman. General Electric Company CFO." The Best of 1998 Cover Story. *CFO,* September 1998.

Munk, Nina. "The New Organization Man." *Fortune,* March 16, 1998, pp. 63–74.

Nolan, Richard L. "Connectivity and Control in the Year 2000 and Beyond." *Harvard Business Review,* July–August 1998.

Prahalad C. K., and Kenneth Lieberthal. "The End of Corporate Imperialism." *Harvard Business Review,* July–August 1998.

Roth, Kendall. "Managing International Interdependence: CEO Characteristics in a Resource-Based Framework." *Academy of Management Journal,* February 1995, pp. 200–231

"Target: Chrysler." *Business Week,* April 24, 1995, pp. 34–39.

Taylor, William. "The Logic of Global Business: An interview with ABB's Percy Barnevik." *Harvard Business Review,* March–April 1991.

"The Best and Worst Boards." *Business Week,* December 8, 1997, pp. 90–98.

Tuck, Edward F., and Timothy Earle. "Why C.E.O.'s Succeed (And Why They Fail): Hunters and Gatherers in the Corporate Life." *Strategy, Management, Competition,* Fourth Quarter 1996, Issue 5.

"Unit of One Anniversary Handbook." *Fast Company,* February–March 1997, pp. 98–107.

NEWSPAPERS

Bannon, Lisa. "She Reinvented Barbie; Now, Can Jill Barad Do the Same for Mattel?" *Wall Street Journal,* March 5, 1997, pp. 1–3.

"Chicago's Top 100." *Chicago Tribune,* May 14, 1995, Special Business Section.

Ewell, Miranda. "California Executives Get Coaching in How to Handle Their Jobs." *San Jose Mercury News,* December 29, 1998.

Franklin, Stephen. "Iacocca Retired, but Hungry for Next Challenge." *Chicago Tribune,* pp. 1, 3.

Groves, Martha. "Careers/Leadership; Cream Rises to the Top, but From a Small Group." *Los Angeles Times,* June 8, 1998.

Grube, Lorri. "CEOs At Risk." *Chief Executive,* November 1995, pp. 42–43.

Gruber, William. "Citicorp, Travelers May Spur Trend: One Step Closer to the One-Stop Shopping Goal." *Chicago Tribune*, April 7, 1998.

Heng, Chan Teng. "Managing Thought Leadership." *New Straits Times-Management Times,* June 6, 1998.

Jones, Tim. "Spirited Seagram Hollywood Move." *Chicago Tribune,* pp. 1, 3.

Jones, Tom. "Madigan next CEO at Tribune." *Chicago Tribune,* pp. 1, 3.

Joyce, Amy. "Young Leaders Sidestepping Old Rules of Management; As Ranks Grow, Twentysomethings Find Ways Around Age Gap." *The Washington Post,* July 19, 1998.

Lancaster, Hal. "Learning to Manage in a Global Workplace." *Wall Street Journal,* June 2, 1998, p. B1

Lewis, Diane E. "Generation X's Rapid Rise in Workplace Leaves Elders Feeling Threatened." *Boston Globe,* June 24, 1998.

Lublin, Joann S. "Aging CEOs Stage Big Deals as Career Finales." *Wall Street Journal,* June 4, 1997, p. B1.

Stevenson, Richard W. "World Bank Chief Asks Slimmer Staffs and Better Landing." *The New York Times,* February 21, 1997, D1–D3.

Young, David. "Johnson & Johnson Exec Named CEO at Brunswick." *Chicago Tribune,* pp. 1–3.

Wollenberg, Skip. "Citicorp, Travelers OK Record Merger." *The Detroit News,* April 6, 1998.

Zachary, G. Pascal. "CEOs Are Stars Now, But Why? And Would Alfred Sloan Approve?" *Wall Street Journal,* September 3, 1997.

STUDIES

"The Impact of Direct Report Feedback and Follow-Up on Leadership Effectiveness." A study involving over 8,000 respondents in one of the 100 largest corporations in the United States, by Keilty, Goldsmith, & Company.

"The Role of the CIO and CTO." By G. Raphaelian, Gartner Group.

"Strategic Alliances: Gaining a Competitive Advantage." By Robert McGuckin, The Conference Board.

"Management of Motives Part 1 Selective Adaptations." By Consultants for Management Development.

"Reinventing the CEO." A Joint Study by Korn/Ferry International and Columbia University Graduate School of Business.

WEBSITES

Bell Atlantic Home Page. "Bell Atlantic and GTE Agree to Merge." July 28, 1998. *www.ba.com/nr/1998/Jul/19980728001.html.*

Bell Atlantic Home Page. "Profile: Ivan Seidenberg." *www.ba.com/nr/1998/Jul/19980728001.html.*

Communication World Online. "Ten Steps for Communicators to Boost Organizational Diversity." *www.iabc.com/cw/news/j_f_m97/mar1697.htm.*

"Executives Explain How to Attract Gen Xers to U.S. Work Force." IABC. *www.iabc.com/cw/news/a_m_j97/may1697.htm.*

GTE Home Page. "Profile: Charles R. Lee." *www.gte.com/g/ghlee.html.*

"Intergraph and Bechtel Sign Global Strategic Supplier Agreement." *Business Wire,* September 25, 1998. *www.busineswire.com.*

Jensen Group, Northern Illinois University. "Failure to Integrate Change." *www.simplerwork.com/a/a3.htm.*

Monsanto Home Page. "American Home Products and Monsanto Announce Plan to Combine to Create $96 Billion Life Sciences Company." June 1, 1998. *www.monsanto.com/monsanto/media/current/980601-merger.html.*

NationsBank Home Page. "Remarks at National Press Conference." October 1, 1998. *www.nationsbank.com/newsroom/speeches/hlmday1.htm.*

NationsBank Home Page. "Profile: Hugh L. McColl, Jr." *www.nationsbank.com/newsroom/speeches/hlmday1.htm.*

NationsBank Home Page. "Profile: David Coulter." *www.nationsbank.com/newsroom/speeches/hlmday1.htm.*

NationsBank Home Page. "Profile: James H. Hance." *www.nationsbank.com/newsroom/speeches/hlmday1.htm.*

PR Central Online News and Intelligence. "Perspectives: Seeking a New Global Awareness from Chief Communications Officers." *www.prcentral.com/iprapr15vogl.htm.*

Seimens Nixdorf Home Page. "Inventing the Organizations of the 21st Century." *www.siemens.com/public/uk_sys/future/21cen/21cen_1/21cen_us.htm.*

"SuperStock Broadens Executive Leadership Team Company Restructures to Create New Marketing Division & Appoints Three New Vice Presidents." *Business Wire,* September 25, 1998. *www.busineswire.com.*

"Survey Reveals Top Ways to Retain Executives, Managers & Front-Line Employees." June 3, 1998. *www.busineswire.com.*

Vision-Nest Publishing. "Business as Community." *www.vision-nest.com/btbc/kgarden/issues.shtml#BIO.*

INDEX